D1474804

International Nuclear Trade and Nonproliferation

Published under the auspices of the Center for International and Strategic Affairs, University of California, Los Angeles

A list of other Center publications appears at the back of this book

International Nuclear Trade and Nonproliferation

The Challenge of the Emerging Suppliers

Edited by

William C. Potter
Monterey Institute of International Studies

Lexington Books
D.C. Heath and Company/Lexington, Massachusetts/Toronto

Library of Congress Cataloging-in-Publication Data

International nuclear trade and nonproliferation : the challenge of
  the emerging suppliers / edited by William C. Potter.
        p.   cm.
    "First drafts of most of the book chapters were presented at a
Conference on the Emerging Nuclear Suppliers and Nonproliferation
held at the . . . Rockfeller Foundation Bellagio Study and Conference
Center, Villa Serbelloni, June 22–26, 1987 [and] . . . sponsored by
CISA"—Pref.
    ISBN 0-669-21120-6 (alk. paper)
    1. Nuclear nonproliferation—Congresses. 2. Nuclear weapons
industry—Congresses.   I. Potter, William C. II. Conference on the
Emerging Nuclear Suppliers and Nonproliferation (1987 : Rockefeller
Foundation Bellagio Study and Conference Center) III. University of
California, Los Angeles. Center for International and Strategic
Affairs.
HD9698.A2I64   1990
327.1'74—dc20   89-35601
                                                                              CIP

Published simultaneously in Canada
Printed in the United States of America
Casebound International Standard Book Number: 0-669-21120-6
Library of Congress Catalog Card Number: 89-35601

The paper used in this publication meets the minimum requirements of
American National Standard for Information Sciences—Permanence of
Paper for Printed Library Materials, ANSI Z39.48-1984. ∞ ™

Year and number of this printing:

90 91 92 10 9 8 7 6 5 4 3 2 1

To Alina

Contents

III Management Strategies 379

Preface and Acknowledgments

The purpose of this book, the culmination of one phase of an ongoing international research project on nuclear suppliers and nonproliferation, is to explore the international political and economic dimensions of nuclear trade, especially as they pertain to the behavior of eleven emerging nuclear-supplier states. More specifically, the book sets forth a conceptual framework for analyzing international nuclear trade; details the domestic and external factors that shape the nuclear export policies of Argentina, Brazil, India, Israel, Japan, Pakistan, the People's Republic of China, South Korea, South Africa, Spain and Taiwan; and identifies and assesses alternative strategies for containing the new proliferation risks posed by these emerging suppliers. The book also describes an innovative effort to utilize a computer-based system for tracking international nuclear trade.

The volume is designed to provide in depth and up-to-date accounts of the nuclear export behavior of the emerging suppliers. It is also intended to serve as a reference source for both the area specialist and the student of nuclear nonproliferation.

This book is a product of the Emerging Nuclear Suppliers and Nonproliferation research project initiated in 1986 at the UCLA Center for International and Strategic Affairs (CISA). First drafts of most of the book chapters were presented at a Conference on The Emerging Nuclear Suppliers and Nonproliferation held at the Rockefeller Foundation Bellagio Study and Conference Center, Villa Serbelloni, June 22–26, 1987. The conference was sponsored by CISA and received generous support from the Alfred Sloan Foundation, the Rockefeller Foundation, and the University of California Institute on Global Conflict and Cooperation. Major support for the research project was provided by the Rockefeller Brothers Fund, the William and Flora Hewlett Foundation, the Ploughshares Fund, Lawrence Livermore National Laboratory, CISA, and the University of California Office of International Studies and Overseas Programs.

I am especially grateful to the extraordinary group of students who worked with me on the project at UCLA. Their enthusiasm, energy, and keen analytical skills were indispensable to the project and bode well for the future of the field. The contributions of Maria Alongi, Nancy Carol, Adam Ettinger, Joel Rothblatt, Stephanie Sharron, Blair Smith, Rodney Snyder, Loel Solomon and Peter Vinh merit special mention. The project also profited enormously from the guidance and encouragement of William Domke, Ed Fei, Edward Laurance, Alden Mullins, Hilary Palmer and Randy Rydell.

Finally, I wish to thank Carol Butcher and Karl Arnold for their assistance in preparing this manuscript for publication.

This volume is dedicated to my wife Alina, who provided the incentive to bring this book to conclusion.

I
Conceptual Issues and the Nature of the Problem

1

The Emerging Nuclear Suppliers and Nonproliferation: An Overview

William C. Potter

Themary to states party to the Nuclear Non-Proliferation Treaty he number of states capable of exporting nuclear material, technology, equipment, and services is large and growing. Once confined primary to states party to the Nuclear Non-Proliferation Treaty (NPT), the list of actual and potential nuclear suppliers now includes many countries that do not subscribe to the NPT or to other international nuclear export control agreements.[1] Although international control accords—such as the Nuclear Exporters' (Zangger) Committee and the London Nuclear Suppliers Group (NSG) guidelines—do not prohibit the export of sensitive nuclear materials and equipment, they do reduce the risks of proliferation by imposing international safeguards as a condition for export. It is the concern of many nonproliferation experts that the emergence of new nuclear suppliers that are not bound by existing international controls could erode the system of export restraints and threaten the viability of the nonproliferation regime.

To date, concern regarding the issue of the emerging nuclear suppliers and nonproliferation has not been matched by systematic research on the topic. Indeed, there is little agreement on who the emerging suppliers are, why they have entered the international nuclear market, and the extent to which they have departed from the export practices of the more established or so-called traditional supplier states. The purpose of this book—the culmination of one phase of an ongoing international research project on the emerging nuclear suppliers and nonproliferation—is to remedy, at least in part, this data deficiency.

The Evolution of International Nuclear Commerce

One product of the race between the United States and Nazi Germany to acquire the atomic bomb was wartime nuclear cooperation—in various degrees—among the Western allies. This period also saw the first expression of concern over potential international competition in nuclear commerce. Indeed, although President Roosevelt and his advisors expressed little concern that Great Britain or France would exploit information from wartime collaboration to build their own atomic bombs, they were afraid of postwar commercial nuclear competition.[2]

This competition did not initially materialize, and the United States occupied a dominant position in the global nuclear market during the 1950s and 1960s. Prior to 1963, this market was limited primarily to research reactors, most of which were supplied by the United States, along with training services and enriched uranium to fuel them.[3] Large-scale trade in nuclear power facilities did not begin until after 1963, when General Electric, followed by Westinghouse, made available turnkey light-water reactors (LWRs) at prices that were competitive with fossil-fuel plants.[4] These U.S. vendors soon acquired a dominant international market position for their reactors. United States enrichment services also enjoyed a virtual monopoly in the supply of uranium fuel for the LWRs. "A consequence was that the U.S. economy was assured of a substantial rent from the worldwide expansion of investment in nuclear power."[5]

During the 1960s, U.S. firms engaged in a number of joint ventures and technology licensing agreements with foreign companies. The U.S. nuclear industry also initially found the European Atomic Energy Committee (Euratom) to be a "convenient channel" for European sales.[6] By the mid-1970s, however, some of these foreign firms, through heavy government subsidies, emerged as U.S. rivals.[7] Canada, France, West Germany, and the Soviet Union all supported companies that offered real competition in the international reactor market. The U.S. monopoly in uranium enrichment also was eroded by the start-up of Eurodif (a French joint venture with Belgium, Iran, Italy, and Spain) and Urenco (a British-Dutch-West German consortium) and by Soviet suppliers. European firms in Belgium, Italy, Sweden, and Switzerland also established a niche for themselves as providers of nuclear technology components and services.[8]

The erosion of U.S. dominance in nuclear trade coincided with (and in some instances was linked to) a number of developments that dramatically changed the complexion of international nuclear relations. At the macro or international systemic level, the loss of U.S. nuclear trade hegemony was symptomatic of a more general decline in the economic and geopolitical influence exercised by the United States. This loss of influence was especially apparent in the energy field after the oil crisis of 1973–74.

One consequence of the oil crisis was a sharp rise in the demand for nuclear energy forecasts for the remainder of the century. Opportunities for nuclear exports also appeared to shift from the industrialized world to developing regions, where support for the nonproliferation regime was often problematic. Countries such as France, West Germany, Canada, and the

Soviet Union saw the developing world as an untapped and attractive nuclear market where the U.S. nuclear industry was not yet entrenched.[9] France and West Germany, in particular, were aggressive in their competition for sales in these regions and showed a readiness to supply nuclear technologies that the United States had withheld because of their proliferation implications. Especially contentious were French plans to supply reprocessing facilities to South Korea and Pakistan and the West German "deal of the century" with Brazil, involving the complete nuclear fuel cycle.

International nuclear relations in the mid-1970s also were affected by the Indian nuclear detonation in May 1974. The Indian test demonstrated that even a relatively poor, developing state could, with sufficient political will, circumvent the proliferation barriers imposed by the NPT. What was particulary troubling for nonproliferation proponents was the demonstration effect the Indian explosion might have on the many countries that had initiated or accelerated nuclear power programs in the aftermath of the 1973–74 oil crisis.

Although not directly a response to the Indian test, a decision was reached in July 1974 by ten of the major nuclear supplier states (members of the Zangger Committee) to adopt a "trigger list" of items whose export would require the application of International Atomic Energy Agency (IAEA) safeguards to the facility for which items were supplied.[10] The United States, however, had reservations about the effectiveness of the Zangger Committee action, in part, because of the items not covered, the safeguards required, and the absence of certain partners (most importantly, France) to the accord. Consequently, in late 1974, it moved to organize a new multilateral body for the purpose of regulating international nuclear commerce. This body, which started meeting in London during 1975, was known as the London Suppliers Group (or Club) and initially consisted of Canada, France, West Germany, Japan, the United Kingdom, the United States, and the USSR.[11] In January 1976, these seven states exchanged letters endorsing a uniform code of conduct for international nuclear exports. The major provisions of the code, which is essentially a gentleman's agreement rather than a treaty, require that before sensitive nuclear materials, equipment, or technology are transferred, the recipient state must:

1. Pledge not to use the transferred materials, equipment, or technology in the manufacture of nuclear explosives;

2. Accept, with no provision for termination, international safeguards on all transferred equipment or technology, including any facility that replicates or otherwise employs transferred technology;

3. Provide adequate physical security for transferred nuclear facilities and materials to prevent theft and sabotage; and

4. Agree not to retransfer the materials, equipment, or technology to third countries unless they too accept the constraints on use, replication, security, and transfer, and unless the original supplier concurs in the transactions.[12]

The London Suppliers Group Agreement of 1976, it should be noted, does not ban nuclear transfers to nonparties of the NPT or to states that refuse to accept "full-scope safeguards" (that is, to place all of their facilities under IAEA safeguards). Nor are members of the group legally bound to act according to the trigger list guidelines. The list is simply a multilateral statement of national policy. As such, it seeks to prevent the erosion of safeguards by unregulated competition.[13]

The London Suppliers Group guidelines succeeded in creating a greater consensus among the traditional suppliers. Relatively uniform minimum standards were adopted, and France was brought into the "club."[14] This assertion of authority over nuclear trade by the traditional suppliers in the 1970s, however, was achieved with little regard for the concerns of the importing states. The developing countries, in particular, tended to perceive both the Zangger Committee and the London Suppliers Group as instruments of the industrialized states seeking to establish a nuclear cartel for the purpose of assuring the economic dependency of Third World nations.[15]

Third World discontent with the trade policies of the traditional nuclear suppliers has not changed very much since the 1970s. What has changed dramatically and has muted the criticism is the collapse of both nuclear markets and the forecast of significant nuclear power demand. Concern over energy supply in most countries, therefore, has been reduced, as has the case for nuclear power and the development of indigenous nuclear fuel cycles.[16]

There are few indications that the rate of nuclear plant ordering will rise significantly in the near future. If ordering does occur, it should be low in comparison with the rates of the 1960s and 1970s.[17] One must be careful, however, not to equate the market for power reactors with the nuclear market as a whole. The latter includes a wide range of nuclear-related technology, equipment, and services for which demand will continue as long as existing power and research reactors are in operation. According to one market analyst, "the maintenance, modernization, and refurbishment of the large stocks of operating reactors will provide both the most consistent and possibly the largest market for the power plant producers up to the end of the century."[18]

At the same time that nuclear trade has diminished as an issue for many developing states, the slowdown in energy demand and nuclear investment domestically has generated strong pressures to export for some states with budding nuclear programs. The paradoxical situation thus evolved in the 1980s that at the peak of the depression in the global nuclear market, a new group of states emerged to challenge the traditional suppliers of nuclear material, technology, equipment, and services. These emerging nuclear suppliers include such countries as Argentina, Brazil, India, Israel, Japan, Pakistan, the People's Republic of China (PRC), South Africa, South Korea, Spain, and Taiwan. Although differing widely in their incentives and capabilities to engage in nuclear commerce and in their commitments to the nonproliferation regime, each of these states has the potential to export one or a combination of sensitive fuel cycle technologies or components, power reactors or components, research reactors or components, and technical training and advice.[19]

The combination of a depressed nuclear market and an increase in the number of nuclear suppliers would appear to signal growing competition in what is essentially a buyer's market. Competitive pressures between the emerging and traditional suppliers and within each group, however, could be accompanied by efforts to create cooperative nuclear ventures. Joint ventures among nuclear vendors, for example, might be particularly attractive to the emerging suppliers that have limited technical and financial resources and not much export experience.[20]

The Emerging Nuclear Suppliers and Nonproliferation Project

In order to assess the challenges posed by the emerging suppliers to the nonproliferation regime and to better understand the incentives and disincentives for new states to enter the international nuclear market, a research project, "The Emerging Nuclear Suppliers and Nonproliferation," was initiated at the UCLA Center for International and Strategic Affairs.

The first phase of the project entailed development of a conceptual framework for analyzing the emerging nuclear suppliers. That framework, described in Randy Rydell's chapter (chapter 2), identifies four basic categories of information relevant to understanding the behavior of nuclear suppliers: transactions, structure, capabilities, and norms. Data on these nuclear supplier attributes were then collected and recorded in machine-readable form. That computer-based data system (described in the Appendix) is now in operation and contains thousands of entries from the post-1982 period from dozens of publications worldwide.[21] The second, data-collection phase of the project is an ongoing one in which sources of data and the time period surveyed are continually expanded.

The third phase of the project entailed the preparation of a series of conceptual and comparative case studies of the emerging nuclear suppliers.

These studies, and the management strategies derived from an analysis of them, constitute the following chapters.

Specific Research Questions

In order to sharpen the volume's focus and to enhance the generalizability of the findings, each of the country case study authors was asked to address the same set of research questions. These questions were grouped under the headings "Transactions," "Structure," "Capabilities," and "Norms."[22]

Questions Pertaining to Transactions

1. What motivates emerging suppliers to enter the international nuclear market (for example, hard currency, prestige, political influence, foothold in markets, barter arrangements for coveted items, and so forth)?
2. What are the major disincentives (economic and otherwise) for entering the international nuclear market?
3. What have been the major nuclear transactions involving technology, equipment, materials, and services since 1980?
4. What additional nuclear transactions are planned?
5. Does the country serve as a transshipper (that is, middleman) for nuclear transactions? If so, for which items and for what countries?
6. What safeguards does the country require for export purposes?
7. What revenues have been derived from nuclear exports and what revenues are projected?
8. Have there been instances when the country has been approached for the sale of nuclear-related items or services but declined?
9. What instances, if any, can you discern of illegal blackmarket activity?
10. What is your overall assessment of the states' nuclear export activity (that is, reckless, prudent)?
11. To what extent has the country's export behavior changed over time? If it has changed, why?

Questions Pertaining to Structure

1. What are the relevant export licensing regulations and procedures? What new regulations, if any, are planned?

2. Who are the relevant governmental agency and individual actors in the export licensing process? What is their relative weight?

3. What role is played by the private sector, quasigovernmental actors, political constituencies (e.g., unions), and multinationals in decisions regarding nuclear exports?

4. What are the major firms engaged in nuclear commerce in the country in question?

Questions Pertaining to Norms

1. What are the country's declaratory policies regarding nuclear exports, the NPT and nonproliferation, and (full-scope) safeguards?

2. To what extent does actual export policy depart from declaratory policy?

3. To what extent are prevailing views on nuclear exports shared by different parties and political actors?

4. What explains the norms that are discerned?

5. What are the prevailing public attitudes toward nuclear power domestically, the NPT, and nuclear exports?

6. What changes in attitude regarding nuclear power, safeguards, and exports can one discern over time? What are the sources for the observed changes?

Questions Pertaining to Capabilities

1. What is the present and planned capability of the country to export nuclear material, technology, equipment, and services?

2. What efforts are being made to expand export capabilities?

3. To what extent is export capability an intentional follow-on to or an unintended consequence of the domestic nuclear power program?

Conclusions

In the concluding chapter of the book, an effort is made to compare the responses to these questions across cases. This comparative approach enables us to formulate more general statements about the sources and the product of emerging nuclear supplier state behavior.

Notes

1. For background on these export control agreements, see L. Manning Muntzing, ed., *International Instruments for Nuclear Technology Transfer* (La Grange Park, Ill.: American Nuclear Society, 1978); and David Fischer and Paul Szasz, *Safeguarding the Atom: A Central Appraisal* (London: Taylor and Francis, 1985).

2. See Arnold Kramish, "Four Decades of Living with the Genie: United States Nuclear Export Policy," in Robert Boardman and James F. Keeley, eds., *Nuclear Exports and World Politics* (New York: St. Martin's Press, 1983), p. 18; and Margaret Gowing, *Britain and Atomic Energy, 1939–1945* (London: Macmillan, 1964).

3. William Walker and Mans Lonnroth, *Nuclear Power Struggles: Industrial Competition and Proliferation Control* (Boston: Allen and Unwin, 1983), p. 25.

4. See Irwin Bupp and Jean-Claude Derian, *Light Water: How the Nuclear Dream Desolved* (New York: Basic Books), 1978; and Walker and Lonnroth, *Nuclear Power Struggles*, pp. 25–26.

5. Walker and Lonnroth, *Nuclear Power Struggles*, p. 27. Walker and Lonnroth point out that because most nuclear trade was safeguarded under bilateral agreements with the United States (requiring, for example, U.S. consent before level of U.S. origin could be reprocessed—a condition waived only for Euratom), the United States acquired a powerful influence over the evolution of nuclear commerce. For a discussion of Soviet efforts to compete in nuclear exports during this period, see William C. Potter, "The Soviet Union and Nuclear Proliferation," *Slavic Review* (Fall 1985): 468–71.

6. Walker and Lonnroth, *Nuclear Power Struggles*, pp. 13–14.

7. John Kurt Jacobsen and Claus Hofhansel, "Safeguards and Profits: Civilian Nuclear Exports, Neo-Marxism, and the Statist Approach," *International Studies Quarterly* (June 1984): 204–5.

8. Britain was excluded from world reactor markets because of its choice of a noncompetitive gas-cooled reactor design. Its nuclear trade was primarily in enrichment and reprocessing services. See Walker and Lonnroth, *Nuclear Power Struggles*, p. 29.

9. See Ibid., pp. 34–36.

10. The ten states adopting the trigger list were Australia, Denmark, Canada, Federal Republic of Germany, Finland, the Netherlands, Norway, the United Kingdom, the United States, and the USSR. For a text of the trigger list, see Muntzing, *International Instruments*, pp. 236–43.

11. The group was expanded in 1978 to include Belgium, Czechoslovakia, East Germany, Italy, the Netherlands, Poland, Sweden, and Switzerland.

12. The Office of Technology Assessment, *Nuclear Proliferation and Safeguards* (New York: Praeger, 1977), pp. 220–23.

13. Fischer and Szasz, *Safeguarding the Atom*, p. 103. A number of supplier states went beyond the London guidelines in their national export policy. The United States, for example, under the 1978 Nuclear Nonproliferation Act, required full-scope safeguards on all nuclear exports to nonnuclear-weapons states. Canada also announced the application of full-scope safeguards as a condition for export, and Australia refused to sell uranium to non-NPT parties. See William Walker,

"Nuclear Trade Relations in the Decade to 1995," in John Simpson, ed., *Nuclear Non-Proliferation: An Agenda for the 1990s* (Cambridge: Cambridge University Press, 1987), p. 71.

14. Fischer and Szasz, *Safeguarding the Atom*, p. 103.

15. For a discussion of this point, see Munir A. Khan, "Nuclear Energy and International Cooperation: A Third World Perception of the Erosion of Confidence," Working Paper for the International Consultative Group on Nuclear Energy, Rockefeller Foundation/Royal Institute of International Affairs, September 1979.

16. Walker, "Nuclear Trade Relations," p. 72.

17. Ibid., pp. 65–66. Walker concludes that although electricity demand will probably grow more rapidly in the developing world than in the industrialized world, nuclear power is unlikely to be the preferred energy source in the Third World as a whole.

18. Ibid.

19. See Lewis Dunn, "The Emerging Nuclear Suppliers: Some Discussions of the Problem," in Rodney W. Jones, Cesare Merlini, Joseph F. Pilat, and William C. Potter, eds., *The Nuclear Suppliers and Nonproliferation: International Policy and Choices* (Lexington, Mass.: Lexington Books, 1985), p. 120.

20. Examples of these joint ventures are provided in the country studies in this book (part II).

21. For an earlier account of the database, see William C. Potter, "Creating a Database on International Nuclear Commerce," CISA Working Paper No. 59 (Los Angeles: Center for International and Strategic Affairs, September 1987).

22. For a discussion of the four categories, see the chapter by Randy Rydell in this volume (chapter 2). I am grateful to Bennett Ramberg for his assistance in generating this list of research questions.

2
Studying the Emerging Nuclear Suppliers: A Framework for Analysis

Randy J. Rydell

In April 1984, shortly after signing a nuclear agreement with Pakistan, a Malaysian prime minister declared: "The Western countries who control nuclear technology will not give it to us in a golden plate and, therefore, the developing countries must cooperate in this field to help each other."[1]

In June 1987, a newspaper in Buenos Aires stated: "As part of an offensive to gain entrance into the restricted international nuclear industry exporter club, Argentina has signed a contract for the sale of enriched uranium to Iran, which will use it in an experimental reactor."[2]

In August 1987, the director of India's Bhabha Atomic Research Center said that India will start exporting nuclear reactors and heavy water technology "in a few years."[3]

In August 1987, CEABAN (The Coordinating Committee of Brazilian and Argentine Businessmen in the Nuclear Area) met to discuss future projects in the nuclear field. The group's creation followed recent governmental efforts to promote greater integration of the Argentine and Brazilian nuclear industries.[4]

In October 1987, a nuclear trade journal reported that Argentina "has made a preliminary decision to export heavy water process technology and know-how in the next decade under International Atomic Energy Agency (IAEA) safeguards to some third world countries."[5]

In September 1988, the IAEA approved Iran's request to receive 115.8 kilograms of 20 percent–enriched uranium from Argentina for use at Teheran University's research reactor.[6] This approval followed an Argentine announcement that 80 kilograms of enriched uranium had been authorized for export to Algeria.[7]

In Cairo on 17 November 1988, Argentina and Egypt signed a fifteen-year nuclear cooperation agreement covering research and development in the nuclear fuel cycle, including fuel fabrication and waste disposal.[8]

The views presented herein represent those of the author.

None of these events—nor any of the many others that are cited in the case studies of this book—can be singled out as heralding a revolutionary transformation of the global nuclear marketplace. The cumulative effect of such developments, however, may well be the emergence of a market in the year 2000 that is far less concentrated than today's market for nuclear reactors and fuel cycle technology.

If this gradual structural transformation is accompanied by the entry into the market of new buyers and sellers that do not accept the Nuclear Non-Proliferation Treaty (NPT), safeguards administered by the IAEA, or other international norms directed at preventing the spread of nuclear weapon capabilities, the result may indeed have revolutionary dimensions for the business, diplomacy, and research of nuclear energy. A similar outcome could arise *even if* these norms are widely accepted but are not matched by an increase in the resources available to national governments and key international agencies that implement these norms.

The greater the complexity and stakes of the emerging nuclear market, the greater will be the demands by researchers and policymakers for analytical tools to interpret developments such as those cited here. And herein lies what may be perhaps the most daunting "challenge of the emerging suppliers": the challenge of analysis—a challenge requiring both a continual reexamination of prevailing assumptions about the market and a multidisciplinary search for research methods to render the isolated facts of emerging nuclear supplier activities into intelligible patterns of behavior.

This chapter will identify some of the pitfalls that researchers often encounter in researching the emerging suppliers and will outline some basic ground rules to guide the collection and interpretation of empirical evidence on supplier behavior.

The Treacherous Road of Analysis: Some Observations

The study of the behavior of the emerging nuclear suppliers, much like the analysis of nuclear proliferation generally, is not for the timid. At first glance, the circumstances could scarcely be worse for systematic inquiry on either of these subjects. First, data are often not readily available, difficult to validate, and subject to bias and political manipulation. Many of the raw facts are shrouded by governmental or corporate secrecy. There is also little consensus on an appropriate level of analysis (for example, individual, group, nation, industrial sector, process, or system). And in the absence of articulated frameworks of analysis, rigorous scholarship often gives way to undisciplined case studies, in which facts are presented more because of their ready availability than because of any contribution they may make to scientific knowledge.[9]

Certain significant areas of the international nuclear market remain uncharted. Knowledge on nuclear transactions is growing but still primitive; equipment and materials sales are more often subjects of analysis than technology transfers and services (which might be more interesting). The "nuclear market" remains largely an enigma. Furthermore, research on the export controls of the emerging suppliers has traditionally focused more on official policy statements than on hard facts about the institutions and procedures that are tasked to implement these statements. Moreover, data on specific nuclear supplier companies (such as management, product lines, sales, major customers, research and development, public sector ties, foreign subsidiaries, marketing techniques, and the like) are often available but seldom collected and rarely analyzed.

The process of gathering data to meet these informational needs is indeed treacherous. Data collection and analysis are hindered by language barriers and by the limited availability of relevant information, especially relating to the implementation of nuclear export controls.

Even the mere collection of published export control regulations is no easy matter. For example, when an analyst goes to the trouble to acquire copies of foreign nuclear export control laws (and—this book excepted—few analysts go even that far), the analyst soon learns (1) that the laws are out of date; (2) that the translation is unofficial or unreliable; (3) that there are inaccessible administrative guidelines that further define the official responsibilities; or (4) that there are unwritten, informal rules of thumb that guide the implementation of the laws. Extensive field research is mandatory to alleviate such collection problems. Yet such research is seldom done.

There are other data collection problems: Published national accounting records of nuclear trade data are seldom standardized; units and values vary; the data seldom break down exports by commodity; the data are not timely; verification is next to impossible; and some data (such as "exports" of consulting skills or know-how) are rarely available. Moreover, much of this information is very expensive to acquire: annual subscriptions to the most influential nuclear trade publications in the United States alone cost thousands of dollars. Identifying, subscribing, translating, and interpreting the multitude of domestic and foreign nuclear trade publications are tasks that few individual analysts, either in or out of government, can manage.

There are also more mundane reasons for the paucity of data. Lack of research funds probably explains a great deal about why more empirical studies are not available about the behavior of new nuclear suppliers. Notwithstanding its official support for the goal of nuclear nonproliferation, the United States government allocates relatively small sums for private sector research in this field: of the 219 unclassified arms control and disarmament studies that were commissioned by U.S. agencies in 1987 and 1988, only eight dealt with nuclear nonproliferation.[10]

Foreign travel and personal interviewing are costly enterprises, yet they are necessary to understand the day-to-day operation of the export control process. Because few analysts have conducted field research on such issues, it comes as no surprise that knowledge about specific export control processes in emerging supplier countries is so weak. The authors of the case studies in this book, however, demonstrate that relevant information is indeed available for those who seek it.

Preliminary Steps toward a Framework for Analysis

Understanding the behavior of the emerging suppliers requires a careful accumulation of empirical evidence—a process that makes sense only if the search for data is structured to answer specific analytic questions. A framework for analysis is needed both as a guide for collecting facts and as a device for guiding the process of interpretation.

Rapid improvements are possible in the collection and interpretation of data. Because of the primitive state of existing knowledge about emerging nuclear suppliers, it is premature to develop an overarching framework for analysis that would be appropriate for investigating all aspects of their behavior. Nevertheless, it is indeed possible to outline the *types* of cross-national data needed to construct an empirical foundation for recommendations both on policy and on subsequent research.

A Typology of Relevant Data

Past research on emerging nuclear suppliers suggests that a typology of fundamental empirical knowledge is needed to understand emerging supplier behavior, regardless of the specific research hypotheses to be explored. Such a typology would organize the search for basic descriptive detail on such classic reportorial questions as

Who are the major actors in the marketplace? Who administers national trade controls and trade promotion activities?

What commodities are being offered for sale? What restraints exist on this trade?

Where are these commodities being bought and sold?

When have these transactions occurred?

How were the transactions negotiated? How does the export licensing process work?

Without first creating a country-by-country database on these questions, it becomes impossible to answer such analytic and prescriptive questions as

Why are exports of specific items taking place? Do supply-push or demand-pull explanations apply?

Which transactions are having or have had the greatest impact on the global regime?

What can best be done to stabilize the regime?

All of these reportorial questions can be subsumed within a simple typology of information. Four generic categories are essential for understanding the behavior of nuclear suppliers: transactions, structures, capabilities, and norms.

Transactions

The study of emerging suppliers is, first and foremost, a matter of tracking commodity flows between the emerging suppliers and their worldwide customers. Transactions include not just things but knowledge. Nuclear trade consists of four different types of commodities: technology, equipment, materials, and services. Published national trade statistics offer a clue about the magnitude of this trade; trade journals and company publications offer more specific evidence of what is being sold; and company product catalogues offer excellent descriptions of what is available for sale. On technology transfer, there is much to be gained from a close examination of ownership patterns for patents and foreign licenses of nuclear technology— much of which is in the public domain.

Given the complexity of the international nuclear marketplace, it is important not only to identify the principal buyers and sellers, but also to examine the roles of commodity transshippers and brokers of commercial sales and the method of trade financing. Financing is especially interesting from the standpoint of determining the role of the state in promoting exports. Indeed, at a time when foreign exchange shortages are endemic in international commerce, attractive financing packages (or the lack thereof) may well be among the most important parameters determining a potential supplier's export potential.

Structures

The structures category embraces all data pertaining to the administrative means by which licenses are granted for the import, export, transit, and retransit of nuclear commodities. It also covers the structure of the private nuclear industry and its relationships with the public sector.

Although emerging supplier governments do have institutional means to regulate such transactions, the legal structures, administrative regulations, enforcement mechanisms, and interdepartmental relations remain terra incognita. Past research that has attempted to address these issues has had a tendency of falling back on discussions about how nuclear policy in general is deliberated, a topic on which there are more secondary references available, rather than how specific decisions are made to approve or disapprove nuclear exports, a topic that requires considerable original research. Copies of export laws, commodity control lists, export license application forms, and organization charts of licensing agencies are often available locally but are seldom gathered by proliferation analysts.[11]

It is conceivable that enterprising researchers might be able to obtain aggregate statistics on the raw numbers of export license applications that the supplier government receives over a specific period; it may also be possible to obtain a simple breakdown showing how many cases were approved, deferred, or denied. Likewise, we now know almost nothing about the personnel who are employed in these licensing agencies, in terms of the numbers of such employees, their technical skills, and their relationships between agencies.

Data on the organization and structure of key private nuclear enterprises and their subcontractors are also essential for understanding supplier behavior. It is useful to know, for example, whether there are any interlocking directorates among these firms, whether the firms have foreign subsidiaries, and whether there are any foreign holdings in local nuclear firms. Data on annual sales, product lines, subsidies, profits, and personnel employed also provide an index of the importance of the industry to the national economy.

Capabilities

A considerable volume of data is easily available on indigenous nuclear capabilities in the emerging supplier countries; consequently, it is not surprising that past research has covered this category of information better than the domestic structures and administrative processes. These capabilities are usually broken down into specific stages of the nuclear fuel cycle, especially in sensitive fuel cycle activities such as enrichment, reprocessing, fuel fabrication, heavy-water production, materials production reactors, and uranium conversion.

The domestic possession of a specific nuclear capability, however, does not guarantee the possession of a capability to *export* that capability. Instead, it is a necessary but not sufficient condition for an export to take place. India, for example, has the most robust domestic nuclear industry among the emerging suppliers, though it has not yet established itself as a major nuclear supplier. The variables that link a domestic capability with the capability to export are buyer confidence in the reliability of the product, marketing technique, availability of information about foreign markets, trade promotion by the buyer government, availability of finance, and willingness to provide know-how along with tangible commodities. Useful indices of nuclear export capability can be found in data on research and development activities in the public and private sectors and in empirical observations about marketing practices of specific firms and supplier countries.

Norms

There is a hierarchy of norms that are relevant to supplier behavior, ranging from the most to the least binding upon the exporting government. The most binding norms are domestic laws and ratified international treaties. These, of course, are available to the public and can be readily assembled for analysis. Next to the laws are the myriad administrative regulations that are issued to clarify how the laws are to be implemented; less binding than laws, they nevertheless create an additional set of expectations about the behavior of individual nuclear exporting companies. Declaratory public policies are another means by which governments attempt to establish guidelines to regulate nuclear exports; though notoriously variable, such public policy statements do help establish a normative framework for export regulation. Last, and obviously least binding, is public opinion, as expressed in policy debates in the legislature, papers by noted academics, and stances taken by unions, business associations, and national political parties.

Spanning the categories of structures and norms is the judicial and law enforcement process: How many violations of export controls have been reported in official statistics? What laws were violated? Who and what was involved in these cases? What penalties were issued by the enforcement and/or judicial agencies? Public policy statements, treaty commitments, and formal nuclear export control regulations are worthless indices of supplier behavior if there is no evidence that these norms are guiding the actions of the enforcement community.

Some Specific Hypotheses for Research

Fact gathering, per se, will provide little enlightenment unless the data are sought to address specific analytic questions about the behavior of emerging nuclear suppliers. It would help, for example, to have a preliminary set of working hypotheses concerning this behavior. The phenomenon that needs to be explained is the propensity of certain firms or countries (depending on the level of analysis) to export or transship—outside of international safeguards—nuclear equipment, materials, technology, or services that would facilitate the ability of the importer to develop nuclear explosive devices. The following are some preliminary working hypotheses for explaining such phenomena.

1. Emerging supplier behavior is a product of an interactive bureaucratic process inside the supplier country.

2. Emerging supplier behavior is a manifestation of broader economic and technological trends in the global economy; for example, a "product life cycle" explanation would hold that original manufacturers first transfer products, then technology, to foreign buyers, who, in time, produce and export such products.[12]

3. Emerging supplier behavior is a product of indigenous economic pressures on individual firms. (This is a "supply-push" hypothesis. Exports occur when the domestic market fails to grow at a rate commensurate with domestic production capability.)

4. Emerging supplier behavior is a consequence of specific public policies. (This is a neomercantilist hypothesis. Exports occur because policymakers seek to acquire foreign exchange, redress trade balances, protect an infant industry, and so forth.)

5. Emerging supplier behavior constitutes an economic response to rising foreign demand. (This is the "demand-pull" hypothesis.)

Any analyst who begins with one or more of these working hypotheses about supplier behavior will tend to tailor the search for facts accordingly: Economic determinists may downplay the importance of political variables, whereas bureaucratic politics specialists may consider economic data interesting only insofar as they are used by political actors as a means to exercise power. Working hypotheses provide the intellectual filters through which information is screened for relevance. Unfortunately, in much of past research on nuclear suppliers, these hypotheses were replaced by unstated assumptions about the nature of the supplier problem.

Since "emerging nuclear suppliers" is itself an emerging field of analysis, we have little empirical grounds for concentrating on any one hypothesis over another. Indeed, in such a new and ill-defined field, research should explore a wide variety of possible explanations for the behavior of supplier governments and exporting companies.

Conclusion: From Database to Framework for Analysis

There are grounds for optimism that the study of emerging nuclear suppliers will soon emerge as a systematic field of inquiry. First, there is a guaranteed constituency for this research: The subject matter is intrinsically interesting to both scholar and policymaker. The behavior of these suppliers will have significant effects on the future evolution of the global nuclear nonproliferation regime and, thereby, on the risk of nuclear war. Scholars will see the behavior of these suppliers in the context of a growing trend in international relations toward a more multipolar world on political, economic, and now technological dimensions. And the greater these suppliers penetrate the world market, the greater will be the demand by policymakers for information about suppliers that is both comprehensive and timely.

Second, great progress has already been made in the construction of an empirical database on the emerging nuclear suppliers. As described in the Appendix to this volume, a project to establish a database on emerging nuclear suppliers is now under way at UCLA's Center for International and Strategic Affairs (CISA). The project is a significant effort to address almost all of the data gaps that have been identified in this chapter.

The CISA database begins with the sobering, unspoken premise that we all have a lot to learn about the emerging nuclear suppliers. It proceeds to outline categories of knowledge that will be useful to make sense of the complex patterns of behavior of these new entrants into the nuclear marketplace. By so doing, the project offers an auspicious beginning on the long, treacherous road of research that should lead both to greater understanding of the problems and to practical recommendations for policymakers.

The analytic merit of the CISA Nuclear Suppliers Database lies in its potential to permit the exploration of diverse hypotheses about supplier behavior. It offers the data that are needed to investigate the relative merits, for example, of the supply-push versus the demand-pull models of the nuclear marketplace. It is a value-neutral tool that can be used by students from virtually any professional background or ideological orientation. If it is constantly maintained and expanded, it will promote the development of more precise frameworks for analysis, which should finally move the field beyond description into the more complicated areas of analysis and prescription.

It may well be that the nuclear nonproliferation regime can be saved simply by the day-to-day process of "muddling through"—the process that has produced current U.S. policy responses to the new challenges from the emerging nuclear suppliers. In an age of nuclear proliferation and high-tech terrorism, however, it is not certain how long improvization can remain the primary basis for policy. Although the emerging suppliers are only just beginning to make their presence known in the world market, their rise will unquestionably have global effects. In Robert Gilpin's words:

> The rise of the newly industrializing countries is already having an important impact on the international balance of economic power and the political economy, an impact that could prove to be as significant as the emergence of Western civilization as the dominant force in international economics.[13]

The country case studies presented in this volume offer a major step forward in meeting the twin challenges of analysis and policy that are presented by the emerging nuclear suppliers.

Notes

1. Mahathir Bin Mohammad, quoted in *Nucleonics Week*, 5 April 1984, p. 7. The new nuclear suppliers are discussed further in Randy J. Rydell, "Navigating the Archipelago: Nonproliferation Orientations of Emerging Suppliers," in Rodney W. Jones, Cesare Merlini, Joseph F. Pilat, and William C. Potter, eds., *The Nuclear Suppliers and Nonproliferation: International Policy and Choices* (Lexington, Mass.: Lexington Books, 1985), p. 105.

2. *Journal do Brazil*, 14 June 1987, text in Foreign Broadcast Information Service (FBIS), JPRS-TND-87-014, 18 August 1987, p. 62.

3. Agence France Presse, 20 August 1987, cited in FBIS, JPRS-TND-87-016, 4 November 1987, p. 36.

4. *Nucleonics Week*, 20 August 1987, p. 8.

5. *Nucleonics Week*, 22 October 1987, p. 13.

6. "IAEA Approves Argentine Fuel for Teheran Research Reactor," *Nuclear Fuel*, 3 October 1988, p. 13.

7. "Enriched Uranium Export to Algeria Authorized," reported in FBIS, LAT-88-178, 14 September 1988, p. 33.

8. "Argentina/Egypt: Nuclear Pact Signed," *Nucleonics Week*, 15 December 1988, p. 14.

9. For a more specific critique of this literature, see Randy J. Rydell, "Analyzing the Emerging Nuclear Suppliers," Paper presented before the panel "New Thinking on Nuclear Proliferation," American Political Science Association, 1988 Annual Meeting, Washington, D.C., 1 September 1988.

10. Arms Control and Disarmament Agency (ACDA), "Congressional Report of Arms Control and Disarmament Studies," prepared in response to Section 39 of the Arms Control and Disarmament Act, 30 June 1989; and ACDA, *26th Annual Report*, S. PRT. 100–126, Washington, D.C.: U.S. Government Printing Office, May 1988.

11. At least two major attempts have been made to gather, translate, and analyze nuclear export control laws of well-established nuclear suppliers. See Randy

J. Rydell, ed., *Comparative Study of European Nuclear Export Regulations*, 2nd ed., 2 vols., Contract study by Joel Davidow for Lawrence Livermore National Laboratory, Special Projects Division, August 1985 and *The Regulation of Nuclear Trade: Non-Proliferation, Supply, Safety*, 2 vols., (Paris: OECD, Nuclear Energy Agency, 1988), No comparable volume in publication anywhere, to my knowledge, similarly covers the emerging suppliers.

12. Further details on the "product life cycle" approach to market change can be found in Raymond Vernon, "International Investment and International Trade in the Product Cycle," *Quarterly Journal of Economics* (May 1966): 190–207; Louis T. Wells, "A Product Life Cycle for International Trade?" *Journal of Marketing* (July 1968): 1–6; and Jose de la Torre, "Product Life Cycle as a Determinant of Global Marketing Strategies," *Atlanta Economic Review* (September–October 1975): 9–14.

13. Robert Gilpin, *The Political Economy of International Relations* (Princeton, N.J.: Princeton University Press, 1987), p. 85.

3
Emerging Nuclear Suppliers: What's the Beef?

Amy Sands

Efforts to prevent the spread of nuclear weapons have usually taken two tracks: The traditional approach has concentrated on a potential proliferant's perceived need for nuclear technology and possibly weapons; a second approach has targeted the supply side of the proliferation equation. The issue being examined in this book—emerging nuclear suppliers—falls between these two approaches. The potential proliferants have emerged as possible unrestrained suppliers of nuclear materials and technology. They threaten the entire nonproliferation regime by their exporting, not their weapons development.

Who Are the Emerging Suppliers?

Analyzing and understanding the issue of emerging suppliers requires a refined definition of suppliers in general. The simple dichotomy of traditional versus emerging suppliers is no longer an adequate framework for analysis. Suppliers differ significantly in their technical capabilities, experience, and regime involvement, and these distinctions result in different nuclear export policies.

Comparisons of specific technical capabilities, policies, and motivations establish a historical perspective and current framework for a thorough examination of the emerging suppliers issue and threat (see table 3–1). A country with limited nuclear capabilities can be as great a concern as one with extensive abilities if it has few export restrictions and provides materials or technology otherwise unavailable to the potential proliferant.

This work was performed under the auspices of the U.S. Department of Energy by the Lawrence Livermore National Laboratory under contract #W-7405-Eng-48. The views and materials expressed by the author are solely hers and do not necessarily reflect or state those of the University of California or the United States Government.

I would like to thank Richard E. Eddy and Alden H. Mullins of the Lawrence Livermore National Laboratory for their helpful and insightful comments on drafts of this chapter.

Table 3–1
Nuclear Supplier Indicators and Points of Comparison

Indicators	Countries								
	Argentina	India	Israel	France	Federal Republic of Germany (West Germany)	Japan	People's Republic of China	Spain	United States
Historical market share	U	W	W	S	S	S	W	W	S
Financial resources									
Price	W	W	W	S	S	S	M	M	W
Credit terms	W	W	W	S	S	S	W	M	S
Export assistance	W	W	W	S	S	S	W	M	W
Technological capability									
Reactors	U	W	U	S	S	S	U	W	S
Fuel cycle	W	W	M	S	S	S	M	M	S
R&D activities	M	M	S	S	S	S	M	M	S
Services	U	U	U	S	S	S	U	M	S
Reliability	U	U	M	S	S	S	U	M	S
Industrial infrastructure	W	W	M	S	S	S	W	M	S
Political leverage	S	S	W	M	M	M	S	S	M
Export regulations	W	W	W	S	S	S	W-M	M-S	S
International Obligations	W	W	W	S	S	S	M	M-S	S

Key
S = Strong
M = Medium
W = Weak
U = Unknown or not available
Political leverage refers to the amount of influence a supplier might have with a potential buyer.
Export regulations refers to the extent of nuclear export regulations that a supplier country might have.
A double rating for a country reflects movement toward the second rating.

Since the implementation of the Zangger Committee's "trigger list," countries have been added to the list of nuclear suppliers and incorporated into the nonproliferation regime. Italy, Switzerland, and Belgium, though not party to the original trigger list agreement, are fully active in the London Suppliers Group (LSG) and in the international nuclear market-place. These countries are not part of the emerging supplier problem.

Other new nuclear suppliers include those that, though relatively new to the international nuclear marketplace, could challenge the market share of the traditional suppliers because they have advanced nuclear capabilities. Countries such as Japan, China, and Spain fall into this category, as might South Korea and Taiwan, whose capabilities are sophisticated but limited. These states may not be fully incorporated into the supplier regime, but they now claim to accept many of the rules of the regime. Nevertheless, because of the past activities and policies of some of these new but advanced nuclear suppliers, their current activities remain a concern. The capabilities, policies, and behavior of this group of emerging suppliers need to be monitored, examined, and analyzed.

Another concern involves a possible *new* generation of nuclear suppliers and the likelihood that these "emerging suppliers" will not easily, if at all, be coopted into the current nonproliferation regime. For the most part, these new, emerging suppliers are the countries that have been developing indigenous, unsafeguarded capabilities and are often thought of as potential proliferants. These countries, although part of the International Atomic Energy Agency (IAEA) system, have refused to sign the Nuclear Non-Proliferation Treaty (NPT), to participate in regional pacts, and to cooperate fully in safeguards. Several of the states, such as India and Argentina, have declared that the regime is discriminatory and is an effort by the weapons states to maintain their dominance. Thus, some of these new suppliers reject the current nonproliferation regime and are, at times, actors outside its control system; they also have either limited nuclear capabilities or rudimentary ones. Included in this group might be India, Pakistan, Brazil, Argentina, and South Africa.

Emerging nuclear suppliers—defined as including both the new but advanced suppliers and the possible new generation of suppliers—do present a threat to the nonproliferation regime; however, the reality of the threat from their potential exports has sometimes been exaggerated. In seeking business opportunities, potential new suppliers market the most optimistic version of their capabilities. Obtaining a realistic assessment of their actual capabilities—and thus of the threat these new players present to the nonproliferaton regime—requires examining a country's real versus claimed technical capabilities, its international obligations and domestic regulations, its domestic economic and political circumstances, and its current and forecast activities.

Defining a Marketplace of Concern

In attempting to evaluate the threat of the emerging nuclear suppliers, it is crucial to define the scope of activities and the range of materials, equipment, and technology that are of concern. Nuclear trade of any kind could be considered an issue because of its ability to evolve into more sensitive areas or because of the links it encourages between countries outside the nonproliferation regime. However, some ranking of the significance of a transaction is possible and helpful. Clearly, trade in nuclear power plants is not as significant as trade in weapons-grade materials or technology that might be used to fabricate nuclear weapons.

The nuclear marketplace has several different levels, each possibly playing a role in the development of nuclear weapons, but with certain aspects being more critical than others. At the moment, transactions within the nuclear marketplace are concentrating on services, small-scale projects, research and development (R&D) activities, the use of radioactive materials in medicine and agriculture, and training. Although not much commerce in large-scale, costly nuclear power plants and fuel cycle facilities is occurring, some is taking place (for example, in China, South Korea, and possibly Indonesia), and extensive effort is being put into attempting to obtain the few large projects being discussed. Possible categories for these transactions are as follows:

Nuclear power plant

Fuel cycle facility

R&D

Materials

Services

Non-energy-related use of nuclear materials/technology

Optional nuclear weapons use

Sales involving materials, technology, or equipment directly related to nuclear weapons development are unambiguous in their threat to nuclear nonproliferation efforts. The trigger list that was developed by the Zangger Committee to further explain the obligations of suppliers of nuclear materials and technology under the NPT provides a long list of nuclear-related items that require safeguards if they are exported to a non–nuclear weapons state. Without sufficient constraints on their use, these items can be used in the construction of facilities and the development of equipment and materials needed for nuclear weapons development. They also can be necessary aspects of a nuclear energy program. Several of the emerging nuclear suppliers can already provide some of these items, such as enrichment and reprocessing technology, machining capabilities, and specialized equipment for monitoring and evaluating radiation effects. Argentina and China are examples of countries that have actively marketed some of their capabilities in these areas, though with little success.

The area of the most activity in recent years has been in developing the scientific and engineering infrastructure in developing countries so that when these countries have sufficient financial resources, they can support a nuclear power program. The results of this emphasis have been the construction of research centers, the development of lab- or pilot-scale facilities, exploration for uranium and other natural resources, training and personnel exchanges, and the development of capabilities to handle, store, and transport nuclear materials. These activities are not a concern for nuclear nonproliferation efforts in the short term, nor are they indicators of a buyer's long-term nuclear weapons interest. What these types of transactions do permit, albeit gradually and indirectly, is the strengthening of the indigenous nuclear abilities of a country and, eventually, the basis for a nuclear weapons option.

The reality of today's marketplace is that most potential proliferants lack financial resources to pursue large-scale projects, and most suppliers cannot organize alternative funding methods. The emphasis is on small projects that can be afforded or that fall within some international agency's arena of interests. It would be a mistake, however, to underestimate the importance of this "slow period" in nuclear transactions: Countries such as Pakistan do not need large-scale projects to overcome the remaining barriers in their nuclear weapons effort. Specific components, certain materials (for example, maraging steel), or training may provide the missing skills or items.

Why Choose a Newcomer
to the Nuclear Marketplace

Emerging suppliers provide certain advantages to a buyer. These new suppliers might offer attractive and less constraining terms. Services, technology, equipment, or materials could be supplied with minimal safeguards requirements, fewer restrictions on end use, and less cumbersome export licensing procedures. The price for items could also be less than what a traditional supplier might offer.

Buyers also benefit because some emerging suppliers might be willing to do business in politically sensitive areas. A current example of this possibility was Iran, where Argentina's ENACE—jointly owned by the Argentine National Atomic Energy Commission and the West German firm KWU—was negotiating to finish building the Iranian nuclear power plant at Bushehr. Most countries and individual companies refused to do nuclear-related business with Iran until the Iran–Iraq war ended. However, Argentina, acting as the lead negotiator for a consortium of companies, appeared willing to take the flak (political and real) to get the deal.[1] In this case, Argentina would have provided access for KWU to a market possibly denied by West German policies. Iran, on the other hand, appeared willing to rely on Argentina, because it does not have many other options and because it recognizes the technical strength of the other members of the consortium.

New suppliers also offer the buyer additional options for supply routes and sources of materials. A potential proliferant might obtain the majority of its technology and equipment from traditional suppliers but turn to emerging suppliers for specific sensitive materials or technologies. Emerging suppliers can act as gap-fillers in the nuclear fuel cycle, providing buyers a source for otherwise restricted items.

The Problems with Newcomers

All of these benefits must be weighed against the weaknesses of an emerging supplier. An emerging supplier is likely to be limited by its technical capabilities. A reliable supplier is one that not only can build or produce an item domestically but also can export it. Claims of expertise and capabilities may reflect a market strategy more than reality. Argentina is an example of a country that has put substantial effort into promoting itself as supplier of nuclear equipment and technology but whose capabilities are limited at the present. It lacks operational technical experience in a wide range of activities and, as a newcomer to the market, has trouble generating buyer confidence in its products or services.

In addition, buyers may sacrifice timeliness by relying on emerging suppliers that are in the process of developing capabilities or are exporting items for the first time. Delays caused by inexperience, production problems, and lack of materials and manpower could detract from the attractiveness of an emerging supplier. Building a research reactor in another country may not be as easy as building one in your own country because of differences in language, culture, and skills. Algeria and Iran may have to deal with some of these shortcomings in their projects that rely on Argentina as the supplier.[2]

Another constraint on these new suppliers will be the limited financial resources available for supporting exports. Many emerging suppliers do not have extensive domestic financing capabilities and have even had problems paying for their own imports. Looking for funds in international markets may be equally difficult, since they will be competing with traditional suppliers whose economic strength and technical expertise will make them a better risk. Consequently, for any major deals, emerging suppliers will be at a clear disadvantage when they try to obtain financial backing.

A final concern for buyers is that their credibility as a state interested in peaceful nuclear development could be jeopardized by using emerging suppliers that have fewer export constraints. Regardless of the official justification for buying from Argentina or India, such a purchase could cause other countries to be suspicious of the motives of the buyer and to question nuclear exports to that state in the future.

In summary, despite an unproven record, limited and uncertain technical capabilities, and possibly inadequate financial assistance, emerging suppliers offer certain attractions to buyers. They provide alternative sources for sensitive items, with fewer restrictions. They also provide alternative supply routes that companies and buyers may be more than willing to use. These additional entanglements and options create a situation today that facilitates the concealment, if desired, of purchases and technology transfer. Undoubtedly, buyers exist that are willing to risk lower quality and possible delays for fewer constraints and access to restricted materials and technology.

Considerations for the New Nuclear Suppliers

Why Develop Nuclear Capabilities?

The emerging suppliers' nuclear programs were developed because of a mixture of perceived development needs and prestige, desired energy self-reliance, and potential security options. Many of these programs were initiated with the full support and encouragement of the United States and other traditional nuclear suppliers. In the mid-1970s, when concerns over proliferation increased, access to nuclear technology became a much more sensitive issue: Controls were placed on certain exports and end uses; there was implicit denial of sensitive nuclear materials to certain states; and the IAEA safeguards and monitoring system was expanded and refined.

Throughout all of these efforts to prevent nuclear proliferation, the interest in developing civilian nuclear energy programs continued to be encouraged and assisted. The nuclear weapons states and advanced industrial states seemed to want to hook developing countries with the promise of nuclear energy's development benefits without encouraging them to develop the indigenous technical expertise. In other words, developing countries were expected to remain dependent on the original suppliers.

As might be expected, several developing countries saw this as an issue of sovereignty and long ago decided to develop their own nuclear capabilities. Relying on the nonproliferation regime's claim that it was not nuclear energy but weapons development that was being limited, such countries as India, South Korea, and Argentina have taken full advantage of the nuclear cooperation, training, and technology transfer allowed via IAEA programs and permitted by the NPT. Several countries intensified their own efforts to develop a complete fuel cycle and nuclear self-sufficiency when the United States unilaterally tightened its nuclear export controls to require full-scope safeguards on its nuclear exports. Countries did not want to be vulnerable to American policy shifts.

Why Export?

Countries export nuclear technology and materials primarily to make money—that is, foreign exchange—and thereby support the domestic nuclear industry's development and survival. In the case of many emerging suppliers, their domestic markets are not currently large enough to justify the capabilities being developed, nor do they have or expect to have the demand for such capabilities in the near future. Consequently, exporting becomes an integral part of the future of the emerging suppliers' nuclear program, just as it has in most traditional suppliers.

Lacking experience and proven technical capabilities, emerging suppliers promote their nuclear exports with a variety of tactics. They can underprice their products to get a foothold in the market. They also might undertake transactions in politically uncertain areas to show support for their "brothers," to prevent the domination of traditional suppliers, or for purely commercial reasons. Argentina has already built a pilot fuel fabrication plant in Chile and has contracted to build a research reactor in Algeria.[3] South Africa has long been an exporter of uranium to West European countries, Japan, and Taiwan.[4] What would prevent Pakistan from helping Saudi Arabia or even Libya at some point in the future?

Emerging suppliers may not always find it in their best interest, however, to provide sensitive nuclear items to potential customers. First, emerging suppliers remain dependent on foreigners for various types of technology, materials, and assistance. Even China, a recognized nuclear weapons state, has acknowledged its need for advanced nuclear technology for its civilian energy program and has tempered its international nuclear transactions to fall more within the nonproliferation regime's umbrella. Going too far in providing sensitive nuclear materials or technology to potential proliferants might result in an emerging supplier's being cut off from much-needed foreign technology itself.

Second, emerging nuclear suppliers may not see any political advantage from selling its nuclear technology if it is perceived as a national asset not to be passed on lightly.[5] The supplier's national security and political interests may play a greater role in limiting to whom and under what circumstances nuclear technology and materials are exported. Argentina might require more control on nuclear items exported to Chile than to Iran, for example, or it might decide against exporting anything. Just as traditional suppliers balance political and commercial factors in deciding what business to pursue, emerging suppliers may also be sensitive to trade-offs that promote security over commercial gains.

Finally, having newly acquired technical capabilities and limited financial resources, an emerging nuclear supplier might not fully understand or know its own limits. With too strong an export push, a country could overextend its own resources. Most emerging suppliers do not have much depth in skilled personnel, particularly in the middle management and engineering areas, nor do they have extensive funds. Any delays or complications would increase costs and use resources needed elsewhere. To commit to foreign projects that drain these already scarce resources could hurt a country's domestic nuclear program and industry.

What's the Beef?

The Global Concerns: A Regime Stalled?

The threat to the nonproliferation regime posed by emerging suppliers results from the regime's lack of or insufficient change in the face of the changing dynamic of the international nuclear marketplace. The efficacy of the regime is being threatened by the diffusion of technical capabilities, which lessens technological constraints as barriers to proliferation. As James Keeley pointed out: "Changing supply conditions . . . alter the politics of nonproliferation."[6]

The limited number of potential buyers and possible deals has combined with the increase in the number of suppliers to produce a buyers' market in nuclear technology and equipment. When many of the new suppliers are not fully integrated into the regime's consensus, their commitment to and compliance with the regime's rules are undermined. Alternative sources of supply lessen the vulnerability of buyers to possible sanctions imposed by the London Suppliers Group (LSG) and could lessen a buyer's need to accept voluntary safeguards and cooperation with the current regime. In addition, traditional suppliers, concerned that their market share is threatened by these new sources, could weaken in their commitment to the LSG guidelines.

Another concern involves regulation of nuclear export transactions. Because transactions in the nuclear marketplace increasingly consist of multiple actors from various states, efforts to regulate them effectively are becoming more difficult, especially as companies resort to innovative business practices to finalize deals. Emerging supplier countries often have loose export restrictions and political policies that can be exploited to complete international deals. They may be less restricted by supplier guidelines and other international agreements, such as Coordinating Committee for Multilateral Controls (COCOM) restrictions. The countries with weaker export control systems, whether purposely or because of inexperience, and economic policies oriented toward obtaining foreign exchange could become the proliferant country's perfect partner in the procurement process.

The underlying concern about emerging nuclear suppliers, whether or not they are advanced, is that in today's market, their freedom of activity may undermine the basis of the supplier regime and, eventually, the nonproliferation regime. With all of the new sources for materials and technology now available, countries dedicated to obtaining nuclear equipment, materials, or technology while avoiding safeguards will have less of a problem doing so.

Some Specific Concerns Caused By Emerging Suppliers

In addition to being a threat to the nonproliferation regime as a whole, emerging suppliers also pose specific threats in such areas as safety and security. First, in terms of safety, many new nuclear suppliers have not developed sufficient quality assurance programs and have not paid as much attention to the issue of safety as have the traditional suppliers. According to a report of the U.S. government's General Accounting Office (GAO), the safety of most nuclear power plants in operation or being built in developing countries is questionable, because these countries "lack trained personnel to draft nuclear safety standards to train nuclear safety personnel."[7] If safety concerns are not integrated into nuclear programs, equipment and materials that are exported create potential points of danger and accidents. In addition, emerging suppliers frequently do not have the experience to cope with the various cultural and economic limitations that may confront them when they export to other countries. Inadequate training, partly due to language problems, could result in misunderstandings and potential crises.

The security issue has several facets. Part of the concern centers on the capabilities of the emerging suppliers to provide the necessary protection to materials and equipment being stored or exported. Although physical security has been considered by most nuclear suppliers at domestic sites, they may not have sufficient personnel who are trained to protect sensitive nuclear materials when they are enroute to a purchaser. Thus, trying to get into Argentina's uranium enrichment facility at Pilcanyieu may be as difficult as getting into the United States's Oak Ridge National Laboratory,[8] but in transporting and storing equipment, emerging suppliers are dependent on the more advanced states for the necessary equipment (such as shipping casks) to transport items safely and securely and for the required training.

Another aspect of nuclear security concerns that is aggravated by the new suppliers is that there are additional nuclear materials and facilities that could be targets for black market transactions, smuggling, and terrorism. The vulnerability of traditional suppliers' nuclear shipments or facilities to terrorism has been a concern for some time; now the concern must be broadened to include all suppliers and countries with nuclear facilities. The opportunity for diversion of poorly protected or unsafeguarded sensitive nuclear materials is increased by the presence of this new set of suppliers that have activities at home and abroad.[9]

Responding to the Emerging Supplier Challenge

The current problems of the nonproliferation regime reflect the tensions resulting from the historic prestige attached to nuclear technology and weapons, the perceived security benefits of having nuclear weapons, the parallel development of nuclear weapons and energy programs, and the increasing concern by traditional suppliers about the diffusion of sensitive nuclear technology. From the developing states' perspective, it appeared to be all right for Japan, Italy, and even Spain to become reasonably self-sufficient nuclear states, but not for Brazil, South Korea, or Iraq. In a way, "the political realities of the regime may themselves provide an incentive for proliferation,"[10] especially now that the effort to limit proliferation appears to include an effort to prevent states from obtaining a "nuclear weapons option" as well as a nuclear weapon. Thus, states that show interest in developing a complete fuel cycle become suspect, especially if they have not signed the NPT.

Dealing with the quandary of having potential suppliers of sensitive nuclear materials and technology outside the nonproliferation system will require more information and analysis as well as multidimensional responses. One response that is likely to strengthen the nonproliferation regime is one directed at the specific issues of safeguards, security, and safety. By developing more extensive international safety and security programs that emerging suppliers would participate in and benefit from, concerns over nuclear accidents and terrorism can be lessened. Safeguards might be justified as a means of monitoring materials to prevent diversion to terrorist or black market activities.

Using this safety incentive, the new suppliers would become better integrated into the regime for pragmatic reasons, without having to address the often more difficult political question of supporting the current nonproliferation regime. Involvement by emerging suppliers would also provide access to their programs and some leverage over them, albeit limited, and would initiate a process of cooperation that could facilitate later efforts aimed at integrating all suppliers.

The suggestions about safety, security, safeguards, and export controls are piecemeal approaches to responding to the challenge presented by emerging nuclear suppliers. The development of incentives to encourage responsible export behavior by new suppliers may be effective in the short term, since most emerging suppliers remain dependent on traditional suppliers for components of their own fuel cycle. Although they are vulnerable to pressures, being ostracized will not necessarily stop or even slow their programs or prevent the development of nuclear weapons—remember China—but it clearly would slow down progress significantly.

The emerging suppliers have to be recognized as credible suppliers whose opinions and needs should be integrated into supplier guidelines.

Even though, at present, the problem arising from the emerging suppliers is limited to specific aspects of the nuclear fuel cycle and specific political circumstances, ignoring the issue any longer threatens the supplier regime and, eventually, nonproliferation efforts. An effective supplier regime needs to address the concern about unregulated access to sensitive nuclear technology as well as the purchaser's legitimate desire for nuclear technology.

The challenge of emerging suppliers may be the catalyst either to reforming the nonproliferation regime or to destroying it. As long as emerging nuclear suppliers are outcasts from the supplier regime, they present a serious destabilizing force to nonproliferation efforts. Their ability and willingness to circumvent LSG guidelines and to offer items with fewer restrictions could undermine the current shaky consensus. Their being outcasts permits them to question the legitimacy of the regime and to act against it. Before their capabilities catch up to their promises and they become credible alternative sources of nuclear technology and materials, the supplier regime must be adapted and expanded to conform to the realities of today's complex international nuclear marketplace.

Notes

1. "Argentina and Iran," *Foreign Report*, 2 April 1987; and James Dorsey, "Argentina Sells Arms, Nuclear Aid to Iran," *Washington Times*, 22 April 1987, p. 6.

2. Leonard S. Spector, *Going Nuclear* (Cambridge, Mass.: Ballinger, 1987), p. 188.

3. Ibid.

4. Thomas Neff, *The International Uranium Market* (Cambridge, Mass.: Ballinger, 1984), pp. 181–184.

5. Frances Seghers, "Little Agreement Reached During Western Supplier Nations Meeting," *Nucleonics Week*, 19 July 1984.

6. James Keeley, "Containing the Blast: Some Problems of the Non-Proliferation Regime," in Robert Boardman and James F. Keeley, eds., *Nuclear Exports and World Politics: Policy and Regime* (New York: St. Martin's Press, 1983), p. 223.

7. Bennett Ramberg, "Learning from Chernobyl," *Foreign Affairs* (Winter 1986–87).

8. Adrian Van Horst, "Argentina: Uranium Enrichment Plant," *GENTE* 958 (12 December 1983).

9. Ramberg, "Learning from Chernobyl."

10. Keeley, "Containing the Blast," p. 223.

Bibliography

Books

Boardman, Robert, and James F. Keeley, eds. *Nuclear Exports and World Politics: Policy and Regime*. New York: St. Martin's Press, 1983.

Jones, Rodney W., Cesare Merlini, Joseph F. Pilat, and William C. Potter, eds. *The Nuclear Suppliers and Nonproliferation: International Policy and Choices*. Lexington, Mass.: Lexington Books, 1985.

Poulose, T.T. *Nuclear proliferation and the Third World*. Atlantic Highland, N.J.: Humanities Press, 1982.

Simpson, John, and Anthony G. McGrew, eds. *The International Nuclear Non-Proliferation System: Challenges and Choices*. New York: St. Martin's Press, 1984.

Spector, Leonard S. *The New Nuclear Nations*. New York: Random House, 1985.

———. *Going Nuclear*. Cambridge, Mass.: Ballinger, 1987.

Walker, William, and Mans Lonnroth. *Nuclear Power Struggles: Industrial Competition and Proliferation Control*. London: Allen and Unwin, 1983.

Yager, Joseph A. *International Cooperation in Nuclear Energy*. Washington, D.C.: Brookings, 1981.

Papers and Reports

Donnelly, Warren H. "Evolution of US Nuclear Export Controls." Report #83-119S, Congressional Research Service, June 1983.

Donnelly, Warren H., and Joseph F. Pilat. "Nuclear Export Strategies to Restrain the Further Spread of Nuclear Weapons in the 1980's." Report #83-118S, Congressional Research Service, June 1983.

Pilat, Joseph F., and Warren H. Donnelly. "Policies for Nuclear Exports, Cooperation, and Non-Proliferation of 7 Nuclear Supplier States." Report #82-100S, Congressional Research Service, May 1982.

Journal Articles

"Argentina and Iran." *Foreign Report*, 2 April 1987.

Dorsey James. "Argentina Sells Arms, Nuclear Aid to Iran," *Washington Times*, 22 April 1987, p. 6.

Ebinger, Charles K. "The Demise of Nuclear Energy." *Washington Quarterly* 6, no. 1. (Winter 1983).

"Framatome Can Bid. . ." *Nucleonics Week*, 23 December 1982.

"A Nuclear-Armed Latin America?" Editorial, *Washington Post*, 8 March 1982.

Perera, Judith; "Argentina's Nuclear Red Herring." *New Scientist*, 8 December 1983, pp. 726–27.

Ramberg, Bennett. "Learning from Chernobyl." *Foreign Affairs* (Winter 1986–87).

Seghers, Frances. "Little Agreement Reached During Western Supplier Nations Meeting." *Nucleonics Week*, 19 July 1984.

Van Horst, Adrian; "Argentina: Uranium Enrichment Plant," *GENTE* 958 (12 December 1983).

4

The Major Suppliers:
A Baseline for Comparison

Joseph Pilat

The existing nonproliferation regime is, in essence, a regime of regulated nuclear supply. Not surprisingly, the regime has been most strongly influenced by the nuclear "haves"—the major nuclear supplier states, which include four of the five announced nuclear powers. Although the regime was not particularly contentious during its early decades, since the mid-1970s the regime has been castigated by the nuclear "have-nots," who have bitterly opposed the regime—in particular, the creation of and the controls over nuclear exports imposed by the Nuclear Suppliers Group (NSG). As recently evidenced by the Committee on Assurances of Supply (CAS) and the recent U.N. Conference on International Cooperation in the Peaceful Uses of Nuclear Energy (PUNE), this critique has continued, and there are serious questions about the future of the NSG guidelines and the supply regime for which they serve as the principal "rules of the game." Are existing supply arrangements effective? Can the NSG, the Zangger Committee, the CAS, and other international forums become constituent elements of any future supply regime? Will they be capable of meeting the challenges of the future? In particular, can they provide a guide for responsible behavior for emerging nuclear suppliers and, perhaps, ensure their full entry into supplier institutions?

The Major Suppliers: International Commitments

At present, the policies of nuclear cooperation and trade of the major nuclear suppliers reflect various interests, influences, and informal and formal undertakings and commitments. Among these, the formal commitments of the Treaty on the Non-Proliferation of Nuclear Weapons (NPT) and the informal understandings and voluntary undertakings of the Nuclear Suppliers Group guidelines are the common (and dominant) denominators of policy (if not also of behavior).

The NPT commits each member state to the goal of limiting further proliferation of nuclear weapons and other nuclear explosive devices but not of the materials, technology, and industrial base that could indirectly increase a state's capacity to produce nuclear explosive devices. Articles I and II commit nuclear-weapon states (NWS) and non–nuclear-weapons states (NNWS), respectively, not to engage in activities that would result in the spread of nuclear weapons. Under the provisions of Article III, non–nuclear-weapons states also agree to verification of their no-weapons pledges by international inspection. In addition, Article III proscribes the export of source or special fissionable material or equipment or material especially designed or prepared for the processing, use, or production of special fissionable material to any non–nuclear-weapons state for peaceful purposes, unless the source or special fissionable material shall be subject to IAEA safeguards. The informal Zangger Committee, named for its Swiss chairman, first met in 1970 and, following four years of periodic meetings, was able to agree in principle to a list of items that would "trigger" the imposition of safeguards upon their export in accordance with Article III(2)(b) of the NPT. Published by the IAEA in September 1974, the list is known as INFCIRC/209. During the Reagan administration, the United States played a major role in an effort to upgrade the Zangger list, which resulted in an exchange of notes agreeing to tighten controls for components for gas centrifuge enrichment and reprocessing and negotiations on inclusion on the list of items related to other sensitive technologies.

As for cooperation in peaceful uses of nuclear energy, which is a fundamental aspect of supply policy, the NPT specifies that all states have an "inalienable right" to use nuclear energy, and nuclear suppliers are expected to cooperate. Specifically, Article IV provides:

1. Nothing in this Treaty shall be interpreted as affecting the inalienable right of all the Parties to the Treaty to develop research, production and use of nuclear energy for peaceful purposes without discrimination and in conformity with Articles I and II of this Treaty.

2. All the Parties to the Treaty undertake to facilitate, and have the right to participate in, the fullest possible exchange of equipment, materials and scientific and technological information for the peaceful uses of nuclear energy. Parties to the Treaty in a position to do so shall also cooperate in contributing alone or together with other States or international organizations to the further development of the applications of nuclear energy for peaceful purposes, especially in the territories of non-nuclear-weapon States Party to the Treaty, with due consideration for the needs of the developing areas of the world.

The Nuclear Suppliers Group, or the London Club, was organized by the United States during the Ford administration in an attempt to buttress the NPT by controlling, if not preventing, the export of certain sensitive nuclear items. To this end, the group secretly agreed on voluntary guidelines for the transfer of nuclear technology, which were subsequently communicated to the IAEA and published in INFCIRC/254. Initially composed of the major nuclear supplier countries of the world, including Canada, France, the Federal Republic of Germany (FRG), Japan, the United Kingdom, and the USSR, the group was subsequently joined by the Netherlands, Sweden, Switzerland, the German Democratic Republic (GDR), Poland, Czechoslovakia, Italy, and Belgium.[1] Australia, Luxembourg, Denmark, Greece, Ireland, Finland, Hungary, and Bulgaria gave also formally notified the IAEA of their adherence to INFCIRC/254, as has an important emerging supplier, South Africa, in INFCIRC/314. To date, there has been no agreement among the original fifteen on whether these additional states are included in the "Club."

The NSG guidelines are a set of identical but unilaterally adopted voluntary undertakings to use restraint in the transfer or retransfer of sensitive nuclear technology, equipment, and materials. The supplier states have agreed to require certain conditions for export of items on the "trigger list," which includes source and special fissionable material; nuclear reactors and certain reactors components; nonnuclear materials for reactors—notably, heavy water and nuclear-grade graphite; reprocessing plants and equipment therefor; fuel fabrication plants, heavy-water plants, and equipment therefor; and equipment for the separation of isotopes of uranium. The conditions include assurances of nonexplosive use by the recipient, effective physical protection for nuclear materials, and IAEA safeguards agreements, as well as other measures also intended to limit the spread of nuclear weapons.

These international commitments provide the framework for the national policies of the major nuclear suppliers and the foundation for such supplier consensus as exists. This consensus does not extend to comprehensive safeguards (safeguards on all nuclear materials and facilities within a country) as a condition of significant exports; to prior-consent provisions for reprocessing or plutonium use; to agreement on handling dual-use items and technologies; or to an absolute prohibition on the export of enrichment or reprocessing technologies and equipment. Moreover, there are differences in the manner in which the traditional supplier states implement their nuclear supply undertakings; these differences are deeply rooted and have resulted in divergent behavior.

Major Supplier States: National Policies and Laws

The manner in which each of the major suppliers interprets and implements its international commitments reflects differing interests and perspectives concerning, among other matters, the specific nuclear trading interests of the major suppliers and their views of international trade. The European and Japanese suppliers have a greater reliance on international trade than the United States does and tend to see it in terms of political and strategic as well as economic benefits. They hold the interdependencies created by international commerce to be crucial instruments in managing their relations with other states. Of particular relevance to nuclear supply and nonproliferation policy are the special strategic trade relationships between each of these states and various countries and regions in the Third World. In the same vein, the approach of all these states to nuclear supply is also shaped by their differing attitudes toward the proliferation danger, which reflect their unique national security, economic, and political interests and perspectives. Nonproliferation is a declared objective of all of these states. Nevertheless, although the European and Japanese suppliers now hold nonproliferation to be in their national interests, some of them have perceived themselves to be "victims," through U.S. denial of equipment and technology, of the nonproliferation policies of the United States and are unlikely to develop a perspective on nonproliferation identical to that of the United States. Most of the major suppliers are not nuclear-weapons states, and their direct military-strategic interest in proliferation is largely limited to potential effects of a proliferated world on the American nuclear umbrella. France and the United Kingdom, as nuclear-weapons states, do have strategic interests in proliferation, but they are scarcely identical to those of the United States.

In addition, there are significant procedural differences. Among the major suppliers, requirements for licensing nuclear exports and the natures and institutional settings of their nuclear export licensing reviews vary widely and reflect differing political and legal systems; policy perspectives; trade, security, and foreign policy interests; and industry–government relationships. The following sections discuss national policies, laws, and regulations of the major supplier states.[2]

Belgium

Belgium is an exporter of reactor components and other nuclear equipment, technology, and materials and is a participant in Eurodif. Belgian nuclear nonproliferation and supply policies are grounded in its adherence to the Nuclear Suppliers Group guidelines, the NPT, and Euratom. Nuclear exports come under a 1981 law devoted to this subject and designed to ensure the implementation of Belgium's international nonproliferation agreements. Although the law has not been enacted, it is apparently being administered as if it were. Under the law, exports of nuclear materials, equipment, or technology are to be for "peaceful purposes and subject to the required controls." These controls are, presumably, those required by domestic law and international treaty. The law establishes the Advisory Committee on the Exportation of Nuclear Materials and Plant and of Nuclear Technological Data—with representatives of the ministers for economic affairs, foreign affairs, foreign trade, justice, public health, environment, and scientific policy—which investigates and reports on violations and recommends action on export licenses, which are decided by the minister responsible for energy. The Belgians have established a trigger list of equipment, materials, and technology subject to their export licensing regime; it is consistent with the NSG and explicitly includes technology as a licensable item.

Canada

Canada is a major supplier of natural uranium. Canada also exports pressurized heavy-water reactors (PHWRs), heavy-water production technology, and nuclear power technology. Canada is a party to the NPT, and it relies on the NPT and associated IAEA safeguards, along with additional national elements, to assure that its nonproliferation policy is comprehensive.[3]

Specific Canadian nuclear export requirements appear in policy statements before Canada's House of Commons in 1974 and 1976. In December 1974, the following principles were expressed:

1. All nuclear material and equipment would be covered by safeguards over the lifetime of the material and equipment.
2. Future generations of fissile material produced from or with Canadian-supplied material would similarly be safeguarded.
3. Binding assurances would be required that Canadian-supplied material or equipment would not be used to produce any sort of nuclear explosive device.
4. Safeguards would extend to any equipment making use of Canadian technology.
5. All nuclear material, and any material subsequently generated from it, would be bound by the same restrictions, regardless of its origin, if it were produced or processed in facilities supplied by Canada.
6. Potential Canadian exporters of nuclear material or equipment were advised to ascertain from the Atomic Energy Control Board (AECB) and the minister for external affairs that there were no safeguards impediments before making an offer of supply to a prospective customer.[4]

In a statement in December 1976, Canada's secretary of state for external affairs announced a requirement of full-scope safeguards.[5] Canada also requires specific bilateral guarantees, pursuant to the safeguards policy announced in December 1974. Since 1976, then, all of Canada's nuclear exports have required a "double guarantee" to the IAEA and to Canada. Although the Canadian government has emphasized its commitment to an effective international order that ultimately would subsume all bilateral agreements,[6] it relies on stringent bilateral accords to supplement international measures for preventing recipient states from misusing Canadian nuclear material, equipment, and technology. Prior to authorizing foreign nuclear cooperation, the Canadian government reviews the ramifications of such cooperation against a background of a number of elements, including energy requirements and political factors.[7]

Section 17 of the Atomic Energy Control Act of 1946 established the Atomic Energy Control Board, which has "regulation powers over the research, production, transportation and use of substances relating to atomic energy, and over cooperation and maintenance contacts with other countries."[8] Under the Export and Import Permits Act, an export license is required for any item on the Export Control List, which includes nuclear materials and equipment.[9] Atomic Energy Control Board regulations must be complied with in order to export nuclear materials or equipment.[10]

The licensing of nuclear exports falls under the Export and Import Permits Act of 1973, which is administered by the Department of Industry, Trade and Commerce. The ministers for external affairs; energy, mines, and resources; and industry, trade, and commerce have certain responsibilities for international nuclear cooperation and are empowered by the act to approve new reactor sales overseas. In the Canadian parliamentary system, concurrence by the three ministers would be expected. On occasion these ministers have decided that certain sensitive nuclear matters, particularly those involving policy, be reviewed by a cabinet committee or even by the full cabinet. Such cases, however, are relatively rare.[11]

Canada requires rights of prior consent for reprocessing, enrichment over 20 percent, or retransfer of nuclear material subject to Canadian control. Like Australia, Canada has developed an approach to exercise this control on a long-term, predictable basis. In 1981, Canada and Euratom agreed to an annex to their 1978 uranium supply agreement, providing a conditional blanket approval for reprocessing and storage of spent fuel within the European Community (EC), within the framework of the current and planned nuclear energy program of the EC. A similar arrangement has been agreed upon with Sweden. A 1959 agreement, which was renewed in 1978, allowed retransfers of Canadian-controlled material within the EC without prior approval, but retransfers from the EC to third countries required Canadian consent.[12]

The Federal Republic of Germany

The Federal Republic of Germany (FRG, or West Germany) is a major supplier of reactors, reactor components and other nuclear equipment, technology, and materials. With the United Kingdom and the Netherlands, it is part of the multinational uranium enrichment consortium, Urenco. West Germany is also an importer of uranium, enriched uranium, and some equipment. Its nuclear foreign policy reflects its position as both a major nuclear supplier and a substantial nuclear importer.

The FRG renounced the manufacture and possession of nuclear weapons three decades ago, and it supports nonproliferation efforts. West Germany adheres to the provisions of the NPT, the Nuclear Suppliers Group, and Euratom regarding nuclear trade and cooperation, as well as to national legislation that requires that a nuclear export license be denied if the export impairs the security of the FRG or is detrimental to peaceful international relations. West Germany has stated that it accords priority to nonproliferation policy over commercial interests in the event of a conflict.

In the view of the FRG, there is no need to make the NSG guidelines more restrictive, only more effective; and although they have adhered to the voluntary NSG guidelines for nuclear exports, which they hold to be reasonable, the West Germans have said that they would prefer multinational, nondiscriminatory, and binding agreements.[13] West Germany does not require full-scope safeguards; however, its nonproliferation policy goes beyond the guidelines of the Nuclear Suppliers Group. The FRG has unilaterally renounced the export of reprocessing facilities and technologies, although the earlier agreement to transfer sensitive facilities to Brazil was not affected by this moratorium of indefinite duration. Moreover, West Germany not only requires the assurance of peaceful intentions but also that the general nonproliferation posture of the recipient country warrant confidence as to its intentions.

West German laws applicable to nuclear exports include the Foreign Trade Law of 1961, as amended. Paragraph 7 provides for restrictions on exports if they adversely affect national security, German foreign relations, or peaceful international relations. The Atomic Energy Statute requires licenses for import or export on nuclear fuel and provides for the restriction of nuclear fuel exports under similar criteria—that is, that the nuclear fuel to be exported must not be used in a manner that would endanger the international obligations of the FRG in the field of nuclear energy or endanger its internal or external security. The Atomic Energy Statute does not place restrictions on the export of nuclear equipment and technology. However, nuclear materials and equipment that require an export license are listed in the Annex to the Regulation for the Implementation of the

Foreign Trade Act, issued in 1961.[14] The contents of this annex are decided on an administrative basis by the government. However, with the determination of these contents, the government cooperates with parliament on the basis of the Foreign Trade Law. These contents have frequently been amended, with bilateral and multilateral treaties and negotiations taken into account in such amendments.

Responsibility for carrying out West German laws and regulations for nuclear exports is assigned to the Federal Agency for Foreign Trade, which is under the authority of the Federal Ministry of Economics. The Federal Agency for Foreign Trade works in close cooperation with other federal ministries including the Foreign Office, the Ministry of Research and Technology, the Ministry of the Interior, and the Chancellory. As indicated, implementation takes into account the NPT, the NSG guidelines, and West German bilateral agreements for nuclear cooperation. Individual cases are judged on their merits. The West German government has stated that the specific situation in each importing country must be taken into account, along with the provisions of the NPT, in nuclear export decisions. According to a government spokesman:

> Any national program for peaceful use of nuclear energy must be based on the special circumstances of the country involved . . . [albeit] national nuclear-energy programs must find themselves in accord with the Non-Proliferation Treaty.[15]

The FRG commitment to cooperation in peaceful nuclear energy, as expressed in Article IV of the NPT, is a pillar of Germany foreign nuclear policy. The FRG upholds the right of every country to develop peaceful nuclear energy. As the West German delegate to the thirty-first General Conference of the IAEA, in September 1987, stated:

> All interested countries should have access to the technologies for the peaceful uses of nuclear energy. The Agency is the very institution which is in a position to implement programmes for the peaceful use of nuclear power and nuclear technology which are tailored to the needs of developing countries. The realization of technical assistance projects will continue to be one of the Agency's most important tasks.
>
> My country appreciates that further progress has been achieved in this field. The funds available have again been increased—most of the increase being voluntary contributions by countries demonstrating their good will—while at the same time the planning and realization of technical cooperation projects have been improved. We are sure that the evaluation activities have helped to secure this success, and we will be grateful for any further efforts the Secretariat will undertake to evaluate projects.
>
> My country attaches the highest importance to technical assistance and has, therefore, always provided considerable funds for footnote A

projects, fellowships, training courses etc. in addition to contributions to TACF. Last year, for instance, we were able to contribute more extra-budgetary funds than any other member State. We intend to continue to do our best.

West Germany views its nuclear exports not simply as a commercial exchange, but as a way of binding recipient countries into an international regime of peaceful cooperation. The FRG, according to officials, refuses to trade with unreliable partners and insists that a recipient country accept a nonproliferation obligation in any nuclear trade agreement. Given this criterion, presumably not every country in the NPT would be an acceptable trading partner.

France

France is a leading exporter of nuclear equipment, materials, and technology. As Walker and Lonnroth argued: "France is heading for a commanding position in the world nuclear industry, with the largest share of the export market and leadership in the fuel cycle."[16]

France is not a signatory to the NPT nor, apparently, does it intend to become one. But France had pledged in 1968, before the United Nations, to abide by the treaty's rules. France was among the founding fathers of the London Group, and, as such, follows the Nuclear Suppliers Group guidelines. France supports the irreplaceable role of the IAEA and resists any attempt to politicize the agency. All French nuclear exports to non–nuclear weapons states are put under IAEA safeguards. On the other hand, France does not require full-scope or comprehensive safeguards as a condition for exports of nuclear facilities, materials, or technology. France does not consider it realistic to demand such safeguards, although French officials have stated they would like to see all NNWSs voluntarily accept comprehensive safeguards. Finally, in this vein, France took a very active part throughout the International Nuclear Fuel Cycle Evaluation (INFCE), co-chairing Group 2. Thus, although France is not an NPT signatory, it is guided by the provisions of the NPT in its nuclear export behavior. It is also guided by the NSG guidelines and regards IAEA safeguards as essential for nuclear exports.

In addition to the international commitments, French nonproliferation policy is based on a set of six points published in October 1976 by the Conseil de Politique Nucleaire Exterieure (CPNE), a high-level cabinet council chaired by the president. These points are, in essence:

1. Nuclear power is, for a number of countries, an energy source both competitive and necessary to their development. France is therefore ready to contribute to the implementation of its peaceful uses.

2. France will retain full mastery of its nuclear export policy, while complying with its international commitments in this field.

3. France will not favor the proliferation of nuclear weapons. Within its nuclear export policy, it will reinforce the appropriate measures and guarantees concerning equipment, materials, and technologies.

4. France will guarantee the reliability of supply of nuclear fuel for the nuclear plants it sells and will answer to the legitimate needs of technology transfer. France will perform fuel cycle services requested and is prepared to study with interested parties bilateral or multilateral agreements to that effect.

5. The French government deems it indispensable that all the suppliers of nuclear equipment, materials, or technologies refrain from favoring proliferation through commercial competition.

6. The French government is prepared to discuss these problems with the other suppliers as well as with nonsuppliers involved in significant nuclear programs.

In December 1976, the fourth point was clarified to indicate that the French government decided no longer to authorize—until further notice— bilateral contracts pertaining to the sale to third countries of industrial facilities for spent-fuel reprocessing.

The CPNE, which acts on individual cases, has final responsibility for nuclear export policy, although it is the Ministry of Finance that issues export licenses.[17] Establishing criteria for the import and export of nuclear materials in France is essentially an administrative matter. Although France has applicable legislation—that is, Law 80-572 of 25 July 1980—the legislation does not itself establish export lists or criteria; it leaves such matters to administrative decrees by the Council of State.[18]

These principles of French nuclear export policy have been basically noncontroversial and have not been altered. French policy has favored the promotion of peaceful nuclear cooperation, in keeping with Article IV of the NPT. "Like most of the countries possessing nuclear technology, France cooperates with States seeking to avail themselves of the peaceful applications of this form of energy."[19] This position supports the need of the French nuclear industry for exports as well as the French desire to lead in cooperation with the Third World.

Italy

Although Italy does not supply reactors, it is an important supplier of certain specialized reactor components and other nuclear equipment, technology, and materials. It could supply nuclear fuel fabrication and reprocessing technology.

The conduct of the Italian government and industry in the area of nonproliferation and nuclear cooperation is based on the Statute of the IAEA, the Non-Proliferation Treaty, and Euratom. With respect to nuclear exports, Italy is bound, under Article III(2) of the NPT, not to supply non–nuclear-weapons states with certain materials and equipment unless they are under NPT or equivalent safeguards. In compliance with that obligation, Italy participates, together with a number of nuclear exporting countries, in the series of arrangements and understandings known as the Zangger "trigger list" and the NSG guidelines.

It is on the basis of these international commitments and policies that the competent organs of the Italian state regulate and control foreign nuclear trade. Article 4 of Law No. 1860 of 31 December 1962, on the peaceful uses of nuclear energy, provides the basis for authorizations involving nuclear materials. It recognizes Euratom's rights to ownership and control of nuclear fuel under Article 57 of the treaty and grants to the Ministry of Foreign Trade, with the "consonant opinion" of the Ministry of Industry and Commerce, authorization for exporting nuclear materials. Exports of nuclear equipment are dealt with under a decree issued by the Ministry of Foreign Trade and Finance, which includes a list of items that are controlled.

The Netherlands

The Netherlands supplies specialized nuclear goods and services, including heavy reactor components, and is a participant in Urenco. It is a party to the NPT and a member of Euratom and adheres to the NSG guidelines. The Dutch control nuclear exports by means of their export control law. They have established a trigger list, embodied in the Eight Amendment Decree on the Export of Strategic Goods, 1963. Items on the list, which includes technology, cannot be exported unless the Ministry of Economic Affairs allows their export. The Nuclear Energy Law applies to both the import and the export of nuclear material.

Sweden

Sweden, which has the capability to export reactors, reactor components, and other equipment and technology, is a party to the NPT and the NSG. Sweden's nuclear export policy is governed by its international obligations and national law. The Act on Nuclear Activities, which entered into force on 1 February 1984, requires a license for the export of nuclear material or minerals containing such material; products made from nuclear material or goods containing such material; or equipment or material that has been especially designed or prepared for the processing, use, or production of nuclear material or which is otherwise of essential importance for the production of nuclear explosive devices, to the extent prescribed by the government.

A license is also required for the assignment or transfer of a right to manufacture, outside of Sweden, specially designed equipment that is manufactured within Sweden. The government has prescribed more precise rules for export control contained in the Ordinance on Nuclear Activities, which also entered into force on 1 February 1984.

The equipment and material subject to export control are listed in an appendix to the ordinance. The list includes the items in the Zangger and NSG trigger lists. But Sweden goes beyond the existing guidelines by including technology and some dual-use nuclear-related products. When required, the list is revised by technological developments or international obligations.

Applications for export licenses are submitted to the Swedish Nuclear Power Inspectorate (SKI), the agency responsible for ensuring compliance with the Act on Nuclear Activities and the directives issued pursuant to the act. The SKI obtains the necessary information and statements of comment from companies, authorities, and others and consults, when deemed appropriate, with the Swedish Defense Research Institute (FOA). The SKI then submits the relevant documents, together with its own recommendation on the application, to the Ministry for Industry for consideration—in consultation with the Ministry for Foreign Affairs—and final decision by the government in each individual case. The government's decision is made public. It is the policy of the government to grant licenses for nuclear products and materials only to those non–nuclear weapons states that have ratified the Non-Proliferation Treaty or have accepted comprehensive IAEA safeguards covering all of their nuclear activities.

Switzerland

Switzerland is a supplier of heavy reactor components and heavy-water production. Switzerland is a party to the NPT and the NSG. Its Atomic Energy Act provides the legal basis for export controls covering nuclear material, and the Swiss Federal Executive Council passed an ordinance requiring that exports of all items on a trigger list be controlled. However, the ordinance reflects the Swiss view on such matters, in that any item not on the list is not subject to export licensing. An ordinance of 18 January 1984, Concerning Definitions and Licensing in the Field of Atomic Energy, lays out the licensing requirements, which are derived from the NSG guidelines. Recently, the Swiss parliament amended the Atomic Energy Act to provide for stricter controls over exports of sensitive nuclear technology; and an ordinance implemented by Switzerland's Federal Executive Council, which became effective on 1 January 1988, expanded the trigger list by providing a detailed description of items for centrifuge enrichment and reprocessing.[20] The Federal Office of Energy (FOE) considers the applications, but in certain cases the consent of the Swiss Political Department or the Trade Sector of the Economic Department is required. Among the reasons for denying license applications are the security interests of Switzerland, its international obligations, and the protection of human beings and important legal principles. If a case is of particular political or economic significance, the FOE must obtain the concurrence of the Department of External Affairs and the Office of Foreign Commerce.

The Union of Soviet Socialist Republics

Although Soviet nuclear cooperation has been relatively limited and has taken place largely within the Soviet bloc, during the past decade the USSR has become a global supplier of enrichment services, exporting enriched uranium to Western Europe; and it has supplied research and power reactors to Finland, to its satellites, and to Third World countries. Nuclear cooperation and commerce within its bloc have continued to grow.

The USSR is a nuclear-weapons state party to the NPT; it has thereby agreed not to transfer nuclear weapons or explosive devices to non–nuclear weapons states or to otherwise assist, encourage, or induce their development in these states and to require IAEA safeguards for its exports. It seems committed to limiting the further spread of nuclear weapons. With the United States, it assumed a leading role in the negotiations that led to the NPT. The USSR has adhered to the treaty and has frequently called for nonparties to sign the NPT and for parties to abide by its provisions. In addition to its adherence to the NPT, the USSR has said that it hopes to further the goal of nonproliferation through a variety of means, including improved IAEA safeguards; institutional measures such as multinational fuel centers, international plutonium storage, and spent-fuel management regimes; and arms control measures, including nuclear weapons–free zones.[21] The United States and the Soviet Union differ regarding the impact of arms control on nonproliferation; and Soviet proposals for denuclearized zones, notably for Europe and the Mediterranean, offer strategic advantages for the USSR and are seen by the United States as questionable from the perspective of preventing the spread of nuclear weapons.

The USSR's nuclear export policy is defined by its NPT obligations as well as by its voluntary adherence to NSG guidelines. On 13 January 1982, the USSR Council of Ministers approved the Enactment on the Export of Nuclear Materials, Technologies, Equipment, Installations, Special Nonnuclear Materials and Services, which provides for the regulation of Soviet nuclear exports for peaceful purposes to non–nuclear-weapons states in accordance with the NSG guidelines. The enactments states, in part:

Soviet nuclear exports to countries not in possession of nuclear weapons may take place, provided such countries undertake that the exported articles they acquire, as well as the nuclear and special non-nuclear materials, installations and equipment made on the basis of the exported articles or as a result of their application:

a) shall not be used for the manufacture of nuclear weapons or other nuclear explosive devices, or be used to attain any military aim;

b) shall be under the control (safeguards) of the International Atomic Energy Agency (IAEA) during the entire period of their actual utilization;

c) shall be given physical protection at a level not lower than that recommended by the IAEA;

d) will be re-exported (exported) or transferred from the jurisdiction of the recipient country only on the terms provided for in the Enactment; re-export or transfer of export articles proper will take place with the written consent of the relevant Soviet foreign trade organization (in the event of multistage re-export, such a consent may be obtained both directly from the Soviet foreign trade organization and through the intermediate re-exporters).

On the implementation of these obligations, the enactment goes on to say that they "must be formalized by the competent government bodies of the recipient countries by assuming such obligations under the existing multilateral or bilateral treaties, agreements, contracts and other contract law acts in which the Soviet Union or the relevant Soviet bodies and organizations participate." If there is a violation of the obligations by the recipient country, the enactment calls for a suspension of nuclear exports to that country "until the said violation is eliminated." At the same time as the suspension, the Soviet Union "shall take measures in accordance with the appropriate rules of international law and the USSR's international treaties to ensure the fulfillment by the recipient country of the obligation it has assumed." Although this provision would appear to be far-reaching and to involve the possibility of using even the military instrument in the service of nonproliferation policy, the reference to the Ministry of Foreign Trade and the USSR State Committee for Foreign Economic Relations—possibly (if necessary) along with the Ministry of Foreign Affairs and the State Committee on the Utilization of Atomic Energy—as the bodies that would undertake such punitive measures suggests that the Soviets have only economic and perhaps diplomatic actions in mind. Moreover, it requires an important additional export condition for certain recipients—that is, the maintenance of control over spent fuel through the requirement that it be returned to the USSR. As the Soviet delegate to the Second NPT Review Conference put it:

Those countries which have constructed their nuclear power stations with the assistance and participation of the USSR have agreements with the

Soviet Union on guaranteed supplies of nuclear fuel to these plants for the whole period of their operation, as well as on the *return of the irradiated fuel to the USSR.*[22]

This requirement applies only to Comecon countries. Fuel enriched in the USSR for Western customers does not carry this condition. Nonetheless, the USSR is the only supplier to have such a requirement for any of its customers.

Through their voluntary compliance with the NSG guidelines, the Soviets have agreed to use restraint in the transfer of such sensitive technology as that for enrichment and reprocessing. They have not indicated a willingness unilaterally to proscribe the export of these technologies, but it is unlikely that they would do so in present circumstances. As a way to meet the perceived needs of various nations for enrichment and reprocessing without technology transfers, the Soviets say they favor multinational fuel centers.[23] However, there is no evidence of substantive support for such centers.

As for safeguards requirements for nuclear exports, the USSR follows the NSG guidelines. In the context of London Club discussions in the late 1970s, the Soviet Union advocated full-scope safeguards for all nuclear exports,[24] but the USSR was and remains unwilling to impose this requirement unilaterally. Libya and North Korea became parties to the NPT prior to the conclusion of an agreement with the Soviets for power and research reactors. This suggests that the USSR may require accession to the NPT (and thus full-scope safeguards) as a condition for nuclear exports of certain types or to certain countries. That this requirement, if operative, is not absolute is indicated by heavy-water sales to India[25] as well as by the construction of a nuclear power plant in Cuba.[26]

With the exception of an early sale of a natural uranium, heavy-water-moderated reactor to Czechoslovakia, the USSR exports only light-water reactors, which are considered by many nonproliferation experts to be more proliferation-resistant than other types of reactors. The USSR has said it supplies only low-enriched uranium; and the enrichment services it offers provide only low-enriched uranium.[27] There are indications that the USSR exports highly enriched uranium, notable for its use in Polish and Czechoslovakian research reactors, but that the Soviets have recently begun to develop alternative fuels.

As an NPT party, the USSR is committed to promoting peaceful nuclear cooperation. Until recently, however, cooperation has largely been limited to Comecon countries and some "client states" outside the Soviet bloc. Now the Soviets are involved in relatively wide-ranging cooperation in technical and scientific ventures, including research and development, training, and technical assistance, both through the IAEA and through bilateral and multilateral arrangements.[28] Assistance to and cooperation with the developing world appears especially important to the Soviet Union. According to the statement of Soviet delegate at the thirty-first IAEA General Conference (September 1987):

> The Soviet Union has always attached paramount significance to such an important area of the Agency's activities as technical assistance and cooperation with its Member States. We are pleased to note the steady growth of the Agency's activities in the transfer of experience, expertise, technology and equipment for the peaceful uses of atomic energy with the aim to further social and economic development of recipient countries.
>
> Appropriations for technical assistance will be increased in 1988 by 12%. The Soviet delegation supports this increase and continues to believe that the principles of financing the Technical Assistance and Cooperation Fund on a voluntary basis and in national currencies should remain unchanged. The system of financing on the basis of indicative planning figures adopted by the Agency has proven its effectiveness providing a reliable forecasting and guaranteed financing of the Agency's technical assistance and cooperation activities.
>
> The policy of principle adopted by the USSR with regard to the cooperation with developing countries is reflected in continuing growth of our country's voluntary contributions to the Technical Assistance and Cooperation Fund. . . .
>
> These voluntary contributions are realized through the provision of the Soviet equipment, materials, instrumentation and facilities and also through training scientists from the developing Member States at various training courses conducted in the USSR.

The United Kingdom

Although the United Kingdom sold two Magnox-type reactors overseas in the 1960s, the British nuclear industry has since been unable to break into the world nuclear reactor market. The British have sold research and training reactors, however, and offer nuclear components and reprocessing services. The British nuclear industry is a member of the trilateral enrichment consortium, Urenco.

The United Kingdom is a nuclear-weapons state party to the NPT; it has agreed not to transfer nuclear weapons or explosive devices to non–nuclear-weapons states or to otherwise assist, encourage, or induce their development in NNWSs, and to require IAEA safeguards for its exports. The British have acted in a manner consistent with curbing the spread, or proliferation, of nuclear weapons. It has reiterated its interest in developing a safer, more solid international nonproliferation regime centered on the NPT and the universal application of IAEA safeguards.[29]

Exports of nuclear materials, technology, or equipment from the United Kingdom are undertaken within the framework of the NPT and the

NSG guidelines. One of the original members of the Nuclear Suppliers Group, the United Kingdom was one of the nuclear suppliers that attempted unsuccessfully in the mid-1970s to obtain agreement on full-scope safeguards as a condition of export. However, the British have not imposed this requirement unilaterally.

Applicable British legislation includes Section I of the Import, Export and Customs Powers (Defense) Act of 1939, under which the Statutory Instrument of the Export of Goods (Control) Order of 1978 has been made. Article 2 of this order prohibits the export of certain specified nuclear materials and equipment to any destination whatsoever without a license.

Several departments and agencies are involved with British nuclear export policy. The most important are the Foreign and Commonwealth Office, the Department of Energy, and the Department of Trade. The Department of Trade also has responsibility for administering the Export of Goods (Control) Order and issuing export licenses.[30] There are no statutory criteria for exports. The law gives the secretary discretion in determining whether exports are to be issued. Exports are considered on a case-by-case basis in accordance with the United Kingdom government's nonproliferation policies and its international undertakings.[31]

Although the United Kingdom's approach to nuclear trade and the transfer of nuclear technology has been cautious and relatively restrictive, the British are nevertheless committed to nuclear cooperation for peaceful purposes. The NPT, they have said, is the best framework for the peaceful development of nuclear power to meet global energy requirements; indeed, the NPT is understood to require the promotion of nuclear energy for peaceful purposes.[32] Additionally, nuclear energy is seen as "a significant and vital aid in promoting the economics of the underdeveloped countries, particularly in the fields of medicine, agriculture, and electricity generation."[33] The United Kingdom fully supports Article IV of the NPT and the IAEA's promotional activities or technical assistance. As stated by the British delegate at the thirty-first General Conference of the IAEA:

> Determined though we are to prevent the spread of nuclear weapons, we are also anxious that peaceful nuclear technology is not something that the developed world keeps for itself.
>
> That is why the United Kingdom will continue to support the Agency's Technical Assistance and Cooperation Fund. As well as pledging our contribution of $1.8 million to the Fund for 1988, we will once again make an additional contribution for worthwhile projects in Non-Proliferation Treaty Member States.

The United States

The United States is a nuclear weapons state party to the NPT; it has agreed not to transfer nuclear weapons or explosive devices to non–nuclear-weapons states or to otherwise assist, encourage, or induce their development in NNWS and to require IAEA safeguards for its exports. The United States adheres to the international standards for nuclear commerce as set forth in the Zangger list and the Nuclear Suppliers Group guidelines. Not only has the United States incorporated these standards in its national laws and regulations governing the exports of nuclear materials, equipment, and technology, but it has also instituted additional requirements for U.S. nuclear export policy. Among these requirements, the most important is the legal requirement that American trading partners place all their nuclear activities under IAEA safeguards as a condition of continued significant U.S. nuclear exports. Requiring comprehensive safeguards recognizes the risks posed by unsafeguarded activities in non–nuclear-weapons states. The United States has urged other suppliers to require comprehensive safeguards as a condition of significant nuclear exports.

The United States also imposes controls going beyond international standards with its requirement for prior consent over the disposition of nuclear materials and materials subject to U.S. agreements for cooperation and its special controls on the export and retransfer of weapons-usable materials. In 1982, the United States announced a policy offering advanced, long-term consent for Japan and Euratom, in the context of renegotiated agreements for cooperation.

Exports of sensitive nuclear technology receive special treatment in the United States, which has long exercised great restraint in the export of enrichment, reprocessing, and heavy-water technology. President Reagan announced that the United States would continue, as a matter of policy, to inhibit the transfer of sensitive nuclear materials, equipment, and technology, particularly where the danger of proliferation exists.

In the same vein, the United States has established a system to control the export of dual-use items, which have legitimate commercial uses but could also provide significant assistance to the development of a nuclear explosives program. All such items require a validated export license and are carefully reviewed to determine whether they would present a proliferation risk. If an export is determined to pose such a risk, it is denied. Prior to approving the export of dual-use items, the United States imposes various requirements.

Finally, the United States is the only nuclear supplier that has put in place a system of legally mandated sanctions that require the termination of economic and military assistance in the event of certain cooperation involving enrichment or reprocessing and the termination of nuclear cooperation with any non–nuclear-weapons state that explodes a nuclear device, terminates or abrogates a safeguards agreement, or materially violates a safeguards agreement or a peaceful nuclear cooperation agreement with the United States or engages in efforts to manufacture a nuclear explosive device. In addition, U.S. law prohibits the United States from engaging in nuclear cooperation with any nation that assists a non–nuclear weapons state to manufacture or acquire a nuclear explosive device.

The Future of the Supply Regime

The differences in interests, interpretation, and implementation among the supplier states, along with commercial competition and inadequately regulated industry actions, have been exploited by states seeking nuclear weapons or the capabilities to produce them. One recent example is noteworthy. West German and Swiss authorities have been investigating alleged export violations involving the theft of Urenco enrichment technology and the attempted transfer of that technology and equipment to Pakistan. Leybold officials in the FRG and Switzerland were alleged to have aided the production of enrichment equipment destined for export to Pakistan. In January 1986, Swiss customs authorities confiscated three autoclaves and other equipment especially designed by the Swiss firm Mettalwerke Buchs AG and other centrifuge equipment, along with the blueprints used to produce them. These were allegedly stolen from URANIT GmbH, the West German partner in Urenco, by officials from Leybold-Hereaeus. In May 1987, following a raid by West German customs authorities, the Aachen state prosecutor's office announced that it was conducting a criminal investigation of Leybold-Hereaeus, suspected of illegally providing assistance to the uranium enrichment activities of Pakistan.[34] As we look to the future of the supply regime and the supplier institutions in which it is embodied, there are a number of disturbing trends that could exacerbate such supplier problems.

Challenges to the Supply Regime

First, the political rifts in the IAEA/NPT system are extremely corrosive. Although the thirty-first General Conference of the IAEA, meeting in September 1987, was able to defer for a year a recommendation by the June Board to suspend South Africa from the agency, it did pass, by a large majority, a resolution that kept this contentious, divisive, and extraneous political issue alive. It remained alive after the 1988 General Conference. This was also the effect of the General Conference's resolutions on Israeli nuclear arms in 1987 and 1988. In addition to such issues, differences have developed over technology transfers, assurances of nuclear supply, and other issues that indirectly affect or are seen to affect nuclear supply questions (for example, adequacy of safeguards, arms control, and disarmament efforts of nuclear-weapons states), as well as over extraneous political issues (such as apartheid).

A second problem involves the stagnation of the international nuclear market, with the possibility that nonproliferation controls will be sacrificed to obtain advantages in commercial competition. It may be argued with some validity that if the world nuclear market continues to stagnate, and nuclear trade recedes to a trickle in coming decades, supply problems may become less and less important or may even disappear altogether. And it would appear that the nuclear market slump and the existence of established "rules of the game" enshrined in the NPT/IAEA regime and the Nuclear Suppliers Group guidelines have served to reduce possible pressures and ameliorate potential problems of nuclear trade for a decade. However, with increasing underutilization of nuclear reactor production and uranium enrichment capacity, there will be increasing economic pressures to export, even to states with questionable nonproliferation credentials, if they can pay.

Third, there is likely to be a further loss of the U.S. share of nuclear trade and, consequently, U.S. influence in nonproliferation matters. It is true that U.S. technological leadership and a virtual monopoly over exports of nuclear goods and services to non-Communist countries allowed the U.S. concept of nonproliferation policy to prevail through American influence and initiatives for the creation of international institutions. However, we are witnessing the loss of U.S. influence in international nuclear councils, deriving from the perhaps inevitable decline of the U.S. share in the international nuclear market and leadership in nuclear technologies. According to Ambassador Kennedy:

> We no longer possess the degree of influence in the nuclear field—scientific or commercial—that we once enjoyed. Indeed, none of today's suppliers does. As mastery of the technology has become more widespread, the ability of any one nation to influence others through a nuclear supply relationship, let alone dictate their nuclear energy choices, has diminished.[35]

Of course, there are national means of influence beyond nuclear cooperation, using economic, political, diplomatic, and military instruments. However, the use of such instruments would, of necessity, be difficult and, if other U.S. interests came into play, might not be seen as a viable option in a given case.

Fourth, differences over such issues as problem countries and peaceful nuclear explosions could, in the long term, undermine U.S.–Soviet cooperation in this area. The mutual interests and cooperation on nonproliferation policy between the United States and the Soviet Union have certainly played a significant role in the development of the international regime to date. The U.S.–Soviet cooperation on nonproliferation policy has persisted through chills and thaws of East–West relations. And consultation occurs, at present, in a number of bilateral and multilateral forums, the most prominent being the IAEA Board of Governors and General Conference meetings, the meetings of the Zangger Committee, and the regular consultations between Ambassador Kennedy and other senior nonproliferation experts and their Soviet counterparts from the Foreign Ministry and the State Committee for the Utilization of Atomic Energy. For the most part, these bilateral consultations have been apparently without polemic, particularly on the technical issues such as IAEA safeguards.

Currently, as historically, the most effective and enduring cooperation has involved technical matters within the purview of the IAEA. Political issues—particularly those involving nuclear weapons aspirations of allies or friendly countries—have, with few exceptions, been contentious, sensitive, and less conducive to bilateral U.S.–Soviet discussion. If proliferation issues become more politicized, traditional U.S.–Soviet differences may be exacerbated as either the Soviet Union or the United States seeks political advantage, especially since the very different geopolitical situations of the superpowers suggest that a threat to one is not necessarily a threat to the other, although it might very well be a threat to the other's interests. For example, if U.S. nonproliferation efforts in its traditional spheres of influence (for example, Latin America) appear ineffective to the Soviets, or if proliferation appears inevitable (as in South Asia), the Soviets might attempt to take advantage of the situation either to increase nuclear trade or to weaken the United States geopolitically. To the extent that it can do so while minimizing risks to itself, it may pursue this path. As these and other differences could appear and bear on the issue of emerging suppliers, it may not be possible in the future for U.S.–Soviet cooperation to deal effectively with this issue.

A fifth tendency is the growing presence in the international nuclear market of a number of those major nuclear suppliers that have not manifested a willingness to assume nonproliferation responsibilities commensurate with their importance in international nuclear commerce.[36]

Finally, direct challenges to the supply regime dominated by the major suppliers are posed by those states that do not fully accept the fundamental premises and the formal undertakings of the regime—that is, the so-called problem countries. Among these problem states, Argentina, Brazil, India, Israel, Pakistan, and South Africa appear to many observers to be particularly worrisome because of their advanced capabilities and suspected intentions—capabilities sometimes surreptitiously obtained from Western supplier states and intentions revealed by their efforts to avoid supplier regime restrictions. Not only do the problem countries challenge the existing supply regime at present by refusing to accept its undertakings fully, which could restrict imports as well as indigenous nuclear development programs, but as potential future suppliers, these countries could seriously undermine the regime.

At present, there may be no immediate reason for excessive concern. The prospective market is small, and the great majority of potential buyers are bound to accept full-scope safeguards on any imported, as well as indigenous, nuclear technology. There are only a few countries with the capability to export nuclear equipment, technology, and materials on a scale comparable to that of the major suppliers; and very few can supply such critical materials as enriched uranium and heavy water, let alone sensitive equipment and technologies. The emerging suppliers have diverse political perspectives and include both NPT and non-NPT states; their chances of organizing are minimal. Many of these countries require, or have publicly stated that they would require, safeguards on their nuclear exports, and their record of behavior has largely evidenced responsibility.

Nonetheless, the emergence of second-tier suppliers and their role in the future supply regime pose dangers to the supply regime grounded in the NPT and the NSG guidelines. It has been argued that because the NSG placed undue and unreasonable emphasis on preventing weapons proliferation, some states may feel unnecessarily burdened by safeguards requirements of the NSG and may turn to the emerging suppliers. If it is true that the emerging suppliers have proffered support for some elements of the existing supply regime, we cannot forget that many have refused to accept either the NPT or the Treaty of Tlatelolco. The emerging suppliers have explicitly challenged the regime, arguing that it is ineffective, violated by the nuclear-weapons states and the nuclear suppliers, and discriminatory.[37]

Moreover, many emerging suppliers are hostile to the regime partly because they inevitably perceive the proliferation danger differently from either the United States or the other major suppliers. Their view of themselves as the victims of the nonproliferation policies of the nuclear supplier states is especially vivid, and they have bitterly denounced the "nuclear colonialism" of the "Caucasian club" and the existence of "atomic apartheid."

Toward a New Supply Consensus?

The implications of these trends and the altered situation they portend are troubling; they threaten not only the NSG consensus but also the IAEA and the NPT, the pillars of the nonproliferation regime. There is an abiding belief among supplier states that the regime provides a more or less sound foundation for nuclear export and nonproliferation policy. Despite the supply controversies of the past decade and the perceived necessity of responding to the challenges of today and tomorrow, there are few major supplier states that do not hold that the existing regime is legitimate and necessary and that the principal supply mechanisms should not be abandoned. However, there appears to be a general recognition among major suppliers that existing supply mechanisms will have to be improved if the supply regime is to remain viable and the idea of regulated and responsible supply is to serve the world of the future. This view was epitomized by Ambassador Kennedy, who noted that the existing international nuclear regime is "clearly not perfect, and it never will be, [but it] is functioning effectively."[38] According to Kennedy: "We want to make that regime and the institutions, norms, and practices which comprise it, stronger, more complete, and more effective."[39] It is possible to refine and improve the existing supplier consensus, and the need for action is clear. Indeed, there are ongoing efforts to refine and upgrade the Zangger trigger list, which now includes centrifuge enrichment and other sensitive nuclear technologies; these improvements will probably be reflected in the NSG trigger list at some point. And there are ongoing discussions with emerging suppliers, aimed at encouraging them to develop effective export control procedures, consistent with minimum international norms. It is not clear how far such a "dual track" can be pursued—whether the objective of strengthening the supply regime and preventing its being undermined by the emerging suppliers can be accomplished without effectively precluding their entry into the regime or undermining the possibility of inducing them to behave in a manner consistent with the regime.

Are the existing NSG guidelines an appropriate guide for the behavior of the emerging suppliers? As we are well aware, the Nuclear Suppliers Group guidelines require that exports be subject to safeguards, a condition that is found in Article III(2) of the NPT and that appears to be widely acceptable to the emerging suppliers (albeit not in the NPT context) for equipment and material. Other provisions of the guidelines are less tangible. How does one assess "restraint" or assign value to assurances of "non-explosive use"? Although these provisions of the guidelines undoubtedly influence the behavior of the major suppliers—now, if not always in the recent past—they are interpreted and implemented in different ways by these states, which largely share nonproliferation perspectives based on the NPT. Would they influence the emerging suppliers in the same manner or at all? The answer is by no means clear. The only emerging supplier state that has announced its intention to adhere to the guidelines, South Africa, is not party to the NPT, although it has indicated that it will enter into "negotiations" with the nuclear-weapons states on its possible adherence to the treaty, and some talks have occurred. If it does not become an NPT party, which is virtually certain, and if, as a result, it is effectively expelled by the IAEA at some time, it may not carry out its stated intention with respect to the guidelines. And although the outcome of PUNE was ultimately favorable from the perspective of the regime, the behavior of the states that challenged the fundamental tenets of the regime at the conference underscored the problems of the supply regime and the difficulty of broadening the supplier consensus. It would appear that such actions argue against expanding the Nuclear Suppliers Group. Announcements by emerging suppliers that they would require IAEA safeguards on their nuclear exports to non–nuclear-weapons states may bring these countries' policies closer to the NSG norm. By themselves, the guidelines do not create a standard of state behavior that is comparable to national law and policy in the United States, Canada, Australia, and other countries. It is the context of the NPT—with the great majority of states accepting the requirement for safeguards on all of their nuclear facilities, and all of the major supplier states (though unwilling to require full-scope safeguards on a condition of supply) NPT parties or willing to act as if they were—that lessens the impact of the limited consensus embodied in the guidelines. Without the formal and informal supply structures that depend to a greater or lesser extent on the NPT or similar treaty commitments, it is not clear that the behavior of the emerging suppliers will be comparable to that of the traditional suppliers. Thus, the entry of these states (particularly the NPT holdouts) into the supply regime is unlikely to change their behavior, and it could preclude the possibility of improving the regime. In this vein, it is by no means clear that consensus is possible on requiring full-scope safeguards as a condition of future nuclear supply, even among the major suppliers. However, if this is the objective—and it would appear to have been put forward as a consensual goal at the 1985 NPT Review Conference—it may be counterproductive to expand the NSG to include countries such as Argentina and India, which are categorically opposed to full-scope safeguards.

Is it possible both to enhance and to expand the regime? If not, is the regime bound for extinction, having failed to adapt to changing global realities? These questions are at the heart of differences among the members of the NSG and between them and the emerging suppliers and key recipient states. Such tensions over desirable directions of present and future supply policy are evident, and they may worsen over time. All states recognize the necessity of change. However, there are differences over the nature, scope, and tempo of the changes perceived to be necessary. On one side stand the major suppliers, which believe that current policies are legitimate and necessary and basically adequate and which wish to avoid any disruption or erosion of the regime that might follow from inviting new members or initiating radically new policies for the regime. On the other side are those that argue for alternative supply mechanisms and, perhaps, for new initiatives in the nuclear energy or arms control areas. They feel that in the long term, modest, incremental measures will not be sufficient, and they argue for major changes that directly or indirectly challenge the scope and structure of what they view as a discriminatory regime.

At the root of these divergent approaches to change are deeply held views of global politics, development, the relations between nuclear "have" and "have-not" states, and the role and relationship of existing nuclear arsenals, arms control, and nonproliferation. More direct nuclear supply issues are affected by controversies over the benefits and opportunities offered by peaceful application of nuclear energy and over which activities are and are not peaceful. In this context, there is disagreement (political, not technical) over peaceful nuclear explosions and their relationship to nuclear weapons. And there are differences over sensitive nuclear technologies, with disputes over the question of whether to make enriched uranium and separated plutonium available to states that do or do not have an apparent need for these materials for advanced nuclear research or power programs. There are those who argue that dispersal of these products exacerbates the dangers of nuclear proliferation and terrorism and that their spread should be severely restricted; they argue that if sensitive nuclear materials are to be made available, this should be done only under appropriate safeguards, and they assert that only such measures will keep other countries from developing sensitive nuclear technologies themselves. But there are those who argue that they have an intrinsic right to such technologies, asserting that any controls other than nominal safeguards are unnecessary and unnecessarily limiting and that technology transfers should facilitate rather than preclude indigenous development efforts.

It would appear that these uncertainties, complexities, and ambiguities could be exacerbated if the emerging suppliers enter the market in a significant way, even if they insist on safeguards for their exports, but do not back away from their challenge to the commitments of the NPT, Tlatelolco, or other elements of the nonproliferation regime. If this occurs, efforts to prevent proliferation could become more ineffective and could undermine the establishment of a broad consensus on rules of the game for nuclear supply. However, it is clear that such consensus is necessary if the supply and nonproliferation regimes are to be effective in the 1990s and beyond.

Precisely because the supply regime is resented by a large number of Third World states, which argue that its provisions are discriminatory, there is a recognized need to reach a broader international consensus. The CAS (if it has a future, and it is now merely clinging to life) or similar institutional arrangements may be a means of broadening international participation in the regime. Lewis Dunn has suggested this possibility.[40] Even critics of the supply regime, such as Ram Subramanian, have held some hope that an equitable consensus on nuclear supply might be established through the CAS and, in his view, through a renegotiation of the NPT. Of this he said:

When the STS [second-tier suppliers] enters the scene in a big way and breaks the monopoly of the NSG, the only medium presently available for negotiations is the IAEA's CAS. However, the stumbling block in these types of negotiations would be the difference in perspectives of the two sides with regard to the issue of non-proliferation. The only reliable manner in which a regime consistent with the aims of the CAS can be established is by renegotiating the NPT, sometime in the 1990s. This process of renegotiation should aim to remove the discriminatory provisions of the treaty. If this does not happen, the chances are that the present regime will face stiff opposition from some states within and without.[41]

Multilateral supply arrangements are not a panacea for proliferation; however, multilateral management or joint ventures and multilateral control regimes have made and can continue to make a distinct contribution to nonproliferation. In the view of Carlton Stoiber, former director of the Office of Nuclear Export and Import Control, U.S. Department of State:

> They must be developed carefully, with a due regard for the legitimate interests of both nuclear suppliers and recipients. If we avoid overly-ambitious global schemes, and begin modestly, with arrangements which have a clear economic or policy rationale; and then extend the range of covered activities and participation in a step-by-step fashion as these measures prove their worth, there is every reason to hope that multilateral supplier arrangements will become an increasingly valuable instrument for peaceful nuclear development and nonproliferation in the future.[42]

Clearly, these are modest proposals, and they are unlikely to create the desired level of consensus. Without such consensus, we will be faced with the choice of a divided supply regime or contiguous, diverse supply regimes—or, perhaps, the choice of no effective supply regime at all in the years to come.

Notes

1. Japan's nuclear industry will likely export only components and services for some time; however, in the future, Japan could become a competitive supplier of nuclear steam supply systems and fuel cycle services, technology, and equipment. Japan's potential as a nuclear supplier was recognized by its inclusion among the original seven members of the NSG in the mid-1970s.

2. For a fuller discussion of the nuclear export regulations of Belgium, France, the FRG, Italy, the Netherlands, Switzerland, and the United Kingdom, to which the following country sections are indebted, see Lawrence Livermore National Laboratory, *The Comparative Analysis of European Nuclear Export Regulations*, 2nd ed., 2 vols. (Livermore, Calif.: Lawrence Livermore National Laboratory, August 1985).

3. On the NPT/IAEA system and its relation to Canadian national policy, one official has stated:

> Canada since December 1978 has required that all of its non-nuclear-weapon states (NNWS) partners must have made an "NPT or equivalent" commitment to nonproliferation and have submitted nuclear material in all of their nuclear activities (current and future) to international safeguards. . . . Canada recognized, on the basis of its efforts during the 1974–76 period, as well as on the basis of reactions to the NPT itself, that there are a number of countries which for many reasons will find it extremely difficult to adhere to the treaty. Moreover, certain states may prefer regional treaties designed to promote the same nonproliferation objective as the NPT without some of the perceived weaknesses of the NPT. The Treaty of Tlatelolco is an example. At the same time Canada was aware of the dangers of opening the door to *similar* commitments and carefully chose the term *equivalent.* What makes a commitment equivalent to the NPT? The essential features are that: (1) it should be a binding commitment to the international community or a significant regional grouping thereof, not a bilateral commitment dependent on an evolving political relationship between two or several countries; (2) it should include the "no nuclear weapons or nuclear explosive device" commitment of article 2 of the NPT; (3) it should include the acceptance of international safeguards as set forth in article 3(1) of the NPT; and (4) it should contain a commitment concerning nuclear exports by the country as set forth in article 3(2) of the NPT. If these basic elements are not preserved, then the comprehensive political commitment and safeguards undertaking of an effective nonproliferation regime are lost; moreover, by introducing more gradations of such commitments and undertakings, the currency of the NPT is debased.

Mark J. Moher, "Nuclear Suppliers and Nonproliferation: A Canadian Perspective," in Rodney W. Jones, Cesare Merlini, Joseph F. Pilat, and William C. Potter, eds., *The Nuclear Suppliers and Nonproliferation: International Policy Choices* (Lexington, Mass.: Lexington Books, 1985), pp. 45–46.

4. See Robert W. Morrison and Edward F. Wonder, *Canada's Nuclear Export Policy* (Carleton International Studies, 1978), p. 63.

5. Statement on motions made in the House of Commons by the secretary of state for external affairs, 22 December 1976.

6. Ibid.

7. Letter from the Directorate of Fuel Cycle and Materials Regulation, AECB, 11 December 1981. See *Overview of Nuclear Export Policies of Major Foreign Nuclear Suppliers*, U.S. General Accounting Office, ID-77-60, 21 October 1977, p. 50.

8. Ibid.

9. Hunt, "Canadian Policy and the Export of Nuclear Energy," *University of Toronto Law Journal* 27 (1977): 70.

10. Ibid., p. 71.

11. Department of External Affairs, Canada, 1 December 1981. See also *Overview of Nuclear Export Policies*, p. 53.

12. Ibid., p. 71

13. Statement of Armin Gurenwald, German federal government spokesman, Bonn, 7 April 1977.

14. *Bundesgesetzblatt*, J., 1961, p. 1381.

15. Gurenwald statement.

16. William Walker and Mons Lonnroth, *Nuclear Power Struggles: Industrial Competition and Proliferation Control* (London: Allen and Unwin, 1983), p. 174.

17. *Overview of Nuclear Export Policies*, pp. 35–36.

18. Articles 1 and 2, Loi no. 80-572 du 25 Juillet 1980, "Sur ca protection et le controle des matieres nucleaires," *Gazette du palais*, 1980 2e sem., p. 526.

19. Statement of the French government, July 1980.

20. *Nucleonics Week*, 19 November 1987.

21. See, for example, statement by Dr. I.G. Morozov, head of the USSR delegation at the Second Review Conference of the Parties to the Treaty of the Non-Proliferation of Nuclear Weapons, 12 August 1980; see also Gloria Duffy, *Soviet Nuclear Energy: Domestic and International Policies*, prepared by Rand for U.S. Department of Energy, R-2382-DOE (Santa Monica, Calif.: Rand, December 1979), pp. 21–22.

22. Morozov statement, p. 10.

23. Ibid., p. 9.

24. *Washington Post*, 12 January 1978.

25. See Duffy, *Soviet Nuclear Energy*, pp. 22–24.

26. *Latin* (Buenos Aires), 8 April 1981.

27. IAEA, GC(XXIII)/OR. 213, p. 8; and GC(XXIV)/OR. 220, p. 16.

28. Morozov statement, p. 10.

29. See, for example, "Nuclear Non-Proliferation," *Survey of Current Affairs* 10, no. 9 (September 1980).

30. See *Overview of Nuclear Export Policies*, p. 41.

31. See Ibid., pp. 44–45.

32. "Nuclear Non-Proliferation," p. 268; see also p. 266.

33. IAEA, GC(XXIII)/OR. 213, p. 18

34. See *Nucleonics Week*, 7 May 1987; *Nuclear Fuel*, 4 May 1987.

35. Richard Kennedy, "Nuclear Trade: Reliable Supply and Mutual Obligations," in Jones et al., *The Nuclear Suppliers and Nonproliferation*, p. 30.

36. See Joseph F. Pilat, "The French, Germans, and Japanese and the Future of the Nuclear Supply Regime," in Jones et al., *The Nuclear Suppliers and Nonproliferation*, pp. 81–92.

37. The experience of PUNE, where such attacks were heard again and again, is illustrative. A vicious attack on the NPT was launched by Iran, an NPT party, which asserted that the treaty was ineffective and subject to numerous violations. In a PUNE document, Iran specifically charged:

1. The NPT has not prevented the vertical proliferation of nuclear weapons.
    . . .
2. The NPT has not prevented the Nuclear Weapons tests. The USSR Nuclear Test Moratorium was a positive move but not succeeded as the result of lack of cooperation by USA.
3. The NPT has not prevented the spread of nuclear weapons, namely the deployment of nuclear arsenals in Non-Nuclear Weapon States (spatial proliferation).
4. The NPT has not facilitated the international cooperation in the peaceful uses of nuclear energy.
5. The objectives of NPT specially articles I, II, IV and VI have been violated by State parties.

6. The NPT has not been able to facilitate the establishment of genuine Nuclear Weapon-Free zone in the world.

7. The Outer Space, the common heritage of mankind, is seriously threatened by so-called U.S. Strategic Defense Initiative (SDI) which is an attempt towards the militarization of space.

8. The claim that no more weapon State is added to existing five States, since NPT entered into force, is to divert the attention from the fact that there are States such as occupying regime of Palestine, so called Israel, and the racist regime of South Africa which have been granted full access to nuclear weapon technology and materials by some of the nuclear weapon States, specially USA. . . .

9. The NPT has not been able to prevent the militarization of International Waters made by nuclear submarines.

Such criticism by an NPT party, even though it is not an emerging supplier, is significant. The attack was not challenged by the emerging suppliers, some of whom were effective opinion leaders at the conference. Silence implied consent—especially from states that had, themselves, leveled such attacks before and that were prepared to engage in nuclear trade with Iran.

By the third week of PUNE, there was an interesting development that also reveals antipathy for the nuclear supply regime. It had by then become clear that there would be no agreement on the "principles" and "ways and means" of nuclear supply preferred by the G-77, which would have undermined the existing supply regime. Neither the Eastern nor the Western states would succumb to G-77 pressures, and there were no objectives or achievements precious to the United States, the Soviets, or any of their allies that would force them to compromise on fundamental nonproliferation principles. It was then that the representative of an emerging supplier proposed an apparent compromise that, if accepted, would have had a devastating effect on the regime. Rather than denounce the NPT, he recognized that many states held to its principles. But, he argued, there are fundamental differences between NPT and non-NPT states over such issues as the meaning of nonproliferation and what constitutes peaceful uses (for example, PNEs), legally binding nonproliferation commitments, and discrimination. He proposed a chapeau for proposed principles and ways and means that would recognize and institutionalize these different positions and effectively accord equal status to positions shared by over a hundred states on the one hand and only five or six on the other hand. His proposal read as follows:

1. Recognizing that international cooperation in the peaceful uses of nuclear energy and non-proliferation of nuclear weapons are inter-related and inter-dependent objectives, the following principles which are formulated to guide the relationship between States should therefore be read in that context and as an indivisible whole.

2. States which have obligations arising from their commitments to treaties such as Tlatelolco, the NPT and the Treaty of Rarotonga or similar instruments, understand the term non-proliferation in accordance with those treaties.

3. Some other states, which are not parties to any such non-proliferation treaties, understand the term non-proliferation in terms of their national declarations of non-proliferation policy. In their view, proliferation of nuclear weapons includes manufacture, acquisition or storage of nuclear weapons.

4. States with such treaty commitments understand their adherence to the terms of these treaties to constitute internationally binding commitments.

5. Some other states, which do not have such treaty commitments, consider that unilateral public declarations of state policy constitute equally valid commitments of non-proliferation.

6. States with non-proliferation treaty commitments understand the term peaceful use of nuclear energy to exclude not only nuclear weapons but also any other explosive devices.

7. Some other states, which do not have such treaty commitments, understand the term peaceful uses of nuclear energy as not ruling out nuclear explosive devices for peaceful purposes.

8. All states have the sovereign right to develop, acquire and use nuclear energy for peaceful purposes in accordance with their needs, interests and priorities.

9. All states have the sovereign right to give or withhold assistance in this field, in accordance with their understanding of the term peaceful uses of nuclear energy.

This "compromise" was seen for what it was and, with no hope of being accepted by consensus, it was withdrawn.

38. Kennedy, "Nuclear Trade," p. 25.

39. Ibid.

40. Lewis A. Dunn, "The Emerging Nuclear Suppliers: Some Dimensions of the Problem," in Jones et al., *The Nuclear Suppliers and Nuclear Nonproliferation*, p. 126.

41. Ram R. Subramanian, "Second-Tier Suppliers: Threat to the NPT Regime?" in Jones et al., *The Nuclear Suppliers and Nonproliferation*, p. 103.

42. Paper presented at the seminar "Nuclear Suppliers and Nuclear Nonproliferation," Washington, D.C., 28–29 June 1984.

5

Nuclear Delivery Systems in the Threshold States: Assessing the Role of "Second-Tier" Suppliers

Leonard S. Spector

I ndia, Israel, Pakistan, and South Africa are today each capable of building nuclear arms and if they have not done so already, could well be prepared to deploy such weapons in any future war. Although attention has been focused over the years on how these and other emerging nuclear nations have progressed toward the acquisition of nuclear weapons capabilities, it is becoming increasingly important to understand how such capabilities, once acquired, may be militarized—that is, transformed into "small nuclear forces."[1] An early and essential first step in this process is the mating of nuclear weapons with the mean for delivering them to enemy targets.

Over the next decade, the delivery systems potentially available to the new nuclear states will fall into two principal categories: manned aircraft and ballistic missiles.[2] (Cruise missiles are a third possibility, but one that appears more remote at present.) A number of the de facto nuclear-weapons states, along with several other industrializing countries, are today producing jet combat aircraft and military missiles. How serious is the danger that these potential "second-tier" suppliers will contribute to proliferation by engaging in unrestricted commerce in these goods?

With regard to manned aircraft able to deliver early-generation nuclear weapons, the second-tier suppliers are unlikely to play a significant role in most cases because the industrialized suppliers—the United States, the Soviet Union, France, and Great Britain—have largely preempted this market, supplying some of the world's most advanced warplanes to the emerging nuclear powers. Where transfers of ballistic missiles and missile technology are concerned, however, the industrialized countries are becoming more cautious in their export policies, while second-tier commerce in these capabilities is growing substantially. This commerce probably will not contribute significantly to the development of missile delivery systems by the two undeclared nuclear-weapons states with the greatest interest in acquiring such systems—Israel and India—since these countries have developed or are now developing them indigenously. Assistance from industrializing states may, however, make a significant contribution to the missile capabilities of Pakistan and South Africa, two regional powers with nuclear weapons capabilities, and to those of Argentina and Brazil, two states that may shortly acquire such capabilities.

Aircraft Delivery Systems

Advanced aircraft provide the emerging nuclear-weapons states with nuclear delivery systems that can be deployed today. Mated with nuclear weapons, these aircraft can transform the inchoate nuclear capabilities of India, Pakistan, and South Africa into concrete military threats, probably within a matter of months. Given the advanced state of Israel's nuclear weapons program, it is highly probable that Israel has already taken this step. The other potential nuclear powers with less advanced nuclear programs—namely, Argentina, Brazil, Iran, Iraq, Libya, North and South Korea, and Taiwan—could also rapidly adapt jet warplanes in their respective arsenals for nuclear delivery should any of these states eventually develop nuclear arms.

It is generally assumed that the emerging nuclear-weapons states will choose their most advanced combat aircraft as their initial nuclear weapon delivery systems.[3] In theory, these nations might select less sophisticated aircraft and might even use commercial jets if, for example, subterfuge were essential in a particular scenario. However, given the limited number of nuclear weapons that these countries would presumably possess—weapons that would comprise their most potent and costly armaments and that would likely be used only in the most dire circumstances—it seems far more probable that the undeclared nuclear states would rely on those aircraft with the greatest certainty of penetrating enemy air defenses and reaching their targets.[4]

For an aircraft to be considered "nuclear-capable" in this context, it need only have sufficient range to reach potential targets and a sufficient payload capacity to carry an early-generation nuclear weapon.[5] Extensive new information has come to light in recent years suggesting that undeclared nuclear-weapons states' early-generation nuclear bombs are likely to be considerably smaller and lighter than the first weapons developed by the United States, probably weighing no more than 1,000 to 2,000 pounds. Indeed, new Western missile technology export controls (discussed later) assume as a benchmark that a new nuclear state could build a bomb weighing as little as 1,100 pounds. This would be well within the payload capacity of most of the advanced ground-attack aircraft in the arsenals of the undeclared nuclear states to be described here, many of which are equipped to carry several 2,000-pound conventional bombs or drop-tanks of comparable weight.

Recently disclosed information on Sweden's largely secret nuclear-weapons development program of the 1950s and 1960s, for example, indicates that Sweden's prototype nuclear bomb, on which design work was completed by 1958, was to have weighed 1,300 pounds and was aerodynamically shaped to permit it to be carried on the exterior of an aircraft. It was to have had a yield of twenty kilotons. Sweden's nuclear weapons program was terminated in 1968.[6]

Similar results probably could be achieved by Israel, which is thought to have been working on nuclear weapons designs since the mid-1960s and probably has an arsenal of 60 to 100 weapons today, although it is not known to have conducted a test; by India, which tested a single nuclear explosion in 1974 and has stockpiled considerable quantities of nuclear weapons material in the interim; by Pakistan, which probably acquired the essentials for its first atomic bomb in 1986 and is said to have obtained a nuclear weapon design from China, but has not conducted a nuclear test; and by South Africa, which has had the ability to manufacture nuclear weapons since 1980 or 1981, but is not known to have tested.

Indeed, photographs taken by former Israeli technician Mordechai Vanunu—and published in the London *Sunday Times* in 1986—which he claimed were of a model of an Israeli atomic-weapon core, show it to be about seven inches across, indicating a compact weapon, easily within the 1,000- to 2,000-pound range.[7] It has also been reported that Israel has developed a nuclear warhead weighing only 226 pounds.[8] Pakistan, similarly, is said to have developed a device weighing only 400 pounds using a Chinese design, and earlier reports stated that it had attempted to purchase thirteen-inch hemispheres in Western Europe to serve as the skeleton for its nuclear weapon, also suggestive of a relatively small device.[9] India's 1974 nuclear test device, which used plutonium as its core, is said to have been about two and a half feet in diameter and ten feet long—about half the diameter of the first U.S. plutonium bomb—and further miniaturization in the fifteen years since India's test would be well within New Delhi's capabilities.[10] (Little is known about South Africa's possible nuclear weapon designs.)

In selecting a warplane for nuclear missions from its available combat aircraft, a new nuclear-weapons state will seek to optimize a number of factors, especially those that enable an aircraft to penetrate enemy defenses—electronic warfare avionics (target acquisition radar, electronic countermeasures against enemy radar, and navigation systems) and combat characteristics (speed, maneuverability, and armaments).[11] The aircraft's range will also be a key factor.

It is beyond the scope of this chapter to attempt to make fine judgments as to which of the high-performance warplanes in the arsenal of each of the emerging nuclear states would be the most likely to be assigned the mission of nuclear weapons delivery. What is significant here is that the considerable majority of emerging nuclear states possess aircraft manufactured by the first-tier, advanced industrial powers—namely, the United States, the Soviet Union, Great Britain, and France—that are superior to the warplanes being produced by the second-tier suppliers. Accordingly, for such emerging nuclear states—which include Argentina, Brazil, Israel, India, Iran, Iraq, Libya, and North and South Korea—there would be little reason to acquire second-tier aircraft for nuclear delivery purposes. Only South Africa, denied access to new first-tier warplanes by a 1977 United Nations–imposed arms embargo, has relied heavily on aircraft built with the aid of a second-tier supplier—namely, Israel. Taiwan might also look to the second tier in the future because of restrictions on its ability to purchase first-tier systems. And under certain circumstances, Iran might, as well. The analysis that follows will illustrate these points, starting with a review of the warplanes available to the four emerging nuclear states that today are able to deploy nuclear weapons.

All of the aircraft now in the Israeli arsenal have been supplied by the United States or depend critically on U.S.-controlled components. Israel's most capable warplanes for ground-attack missions include the U.S. F-16, the U.S. F-15, the U.S. F-4E (now being upgraded with advanced avionics), and the Israeli-built Kfir, which uses the U.S.-licensed General Electric J-79 engine.[12] All can carry a 2,000-pound bomb easily. Israel demonstrated the strategic bombing potential of its F-16s and F-15s—and its ability to extend their range through aerial refueling—when it destroyed Iraq's principal nuclear reactor outside Baghdad in 1981 and the Palestine Liberation Organization's headquarters in Tunis in 1985, targets that were approximately 600 miles and 1,500 miles, respectively, from Israel.

The top rank of fighter-bombers in India's air force includes the British-French Jaguar; the Soviet MiG-29, MiG-27, and MiG-23; and the French Mirage 2000. Any of these could readily carry an early-generation nuclear device to targets throughout Pakistan, and one report in late 1988 claimed that India had, in fact, designated the MiG-23 and MiG-27 for this role.[13] Pakistan's top strike aircraft, in turn, are the U.S. F-16, the French Mirage V, and the somewhat older Mirage IIIEP. These aircraft could reach key cities and military targets throughout northwest India.[14]

For Israel, India, and Pakistan, there is little question that the capabilities of the aforementioned top-of-the-line U.S., French, British, and Soviet aircraft easily surpass those of domestically produced aircraft or those that might be purchased today from less industrialized countries. Indeed, the only warplanes produced outside the Soviet Union and the industrialized states of the West that deserve serious comparison are the Israeli Kfir and the recently deployed South African Cheetah—apparently an Israeli-assisted upgrade of the Mirage III, similar to the Kfir but lacking its more powerful and more fuel-efficient General Electric J-79 engine.[15]

The Kfir is a close rival to first-tier warplanes, but the aircraft's General Electric J-79 engine is produced under U.S. license, and Israel must obtain U.S. approval before exporting the aircraft. Thus, for the purposes of this analysis, the Kfir is not, strictly speaking, a second-tier warplane: Whether it ultimately contributes to a nuclear weapons delivery capability in the developing world will be decided by the United States, not by the second-tier supplier. Even in the Israeli arsenal, the Kfir is considered inferior to the U.S. F-16 and F-15 in the areas of avionics, sustained velocity, and combat capability (effectiveness), and it was not Israel's choice for the aforementioned bombing raids against Baghdad and Tunis.

It is possible that Israel might build a less capable version of the Kfir using an unrestricted engine, such as the French SNECMA Atar 9K-50, which powers the South African Cheetah. South Africa's Atlas Aircraft Corporation was licensed by France to produce the engine prior to the 1977 UN arms embargo. Similarly, South Africa might consider exporting Cheetahs (although there is some question as to whether Pretoria is able to produce the entire aircraft itself or is capable only of modifying existing Mirage airframes).

It is hard to imagine India or Pakistan purchasing aircraft from either of these countries, however, given their existing relations and the political significance that such a deal would carry. Both South Asian states, moreover, already possess Western and Soviet aircraft superior to such "export versions" of the Kfir.

A number of new supersonic warplanes are under development in the second-tier countries, including the Chinese J-8II, the Indian Light Combat Aircraft (LCA), and the Taiwanese Ching-Kuo. The J-8II utilizes American avionics, and Washington has refused to permit exports of the aircraft with this equipment. China is seeking comparable unrestricted avionics so that the aircraft may be sold abroad in the mid-1990s. Pakistan is a likely customer, but the J-8II's capabilities are nonetheless likely to fall short of those of the F-16, so that the latter would probably remain Pakistan's first choice for nuclear missions.

With respect to the Indian LCA, the prototype of the aircraft will carry a U.S.-supplied General Electric GE-404 engine; and again, the warplane will therefore be subject to U.S. reexport controls unless India is able to find an unrestricted power plant for the production version of the warplane. Taiwan's Ching-Kuo also relies heavily on U.S. technology and therefore cannot be considered a second-tier warplane free of U.S. export controls.[16] Finally, Brazil recently announced plans for the joint development with China of an advanced supersonic fighter.[17] It is doubtful, however, that when the plane becomes available internationally it will be a match for the top aircraft then available from today's advanced supplier countries.

In sum, second-tier suppliers are unlikely to be more than an incidental factor in the aircraft-based nuclear delivery systems of Israel, India, or Pakistan.

This pattern does not appear to hold in the case of South Africa, however. As mentioned earlier, South Africa has been denied access to the first-tier suppliers by the 1977 UN arms embargo; and in recent years, Israel is believed to have transferred key technology to Pretoria for the Cheetah.[18] This nuclear-capable aircraft significantly augments South Africa's preexisting delivery capabilities, based on the French Mirage F-1AZ, and the older British Canberra and Buccaneer bombers, all acquired before the 1977 embargo.[19] Under U.S. pressure to adhere to the UN embargo, Israel agreed in 1987 not to enter into new military contracts with South Africa, although it will continue to honor existing commitments.[20] Thus, even for South Africa, the second-tier supplier option is apparently being curtailed. (In late 1987, however, the possibility of a novel transfer of Israeli aircraft technology to South Africa emerged, as Pretoria reportedly sought to recruit 600 Israeli technicians who had worked on the development of the Lavi fighter. Israel had canceled the project to build the highly advanced fighter several months earlier as too costly.[21])

Similarly, an analysis of other emerging nuclear states with less advanced nuclear programs indicates that second-tier suppliers are unlikely to contribute significantly to potential aircraft delivery systems in most cases. Argentina and Brazil—countries with fewer incentives to acquire nuclear arms than those emerging nuclear states just discussed but whose nuclear capabilities are growing—have purchased relatively modern but not top-of-the-line U.S. and French aircraft. The capabilities of these warplanes, in the typical pattern just described, nonetheless overshadow those of any produced domestically or by other less industrialized suppliers, with the possible exception of the Kfir (domestic or export version) and the Cheetah. Both countries might consider purchasing these aircraft in the future—along with the Chinese J-8II, the Indian LCA, and the Taiwanese Ching-Kuo (assuming that the United States permitted their retransfer)—but only if Western suppliers declined to transfer more capable warplanes.

If nuclear arms spread to Iran, Iraq, Libya, or North or South Korea, all would presumably rely for nuclear delivery systems on the first-rank aircraft from the West or the Soviet Union now in their arsenals. Iran, however, has been unable to obtain replacements for planes in this category that it has lost in its conflict with Iraq. It is now purchasing the less capable Q-5 from China and might well be a customer for the J-8II if and when it becomes available. It might also consider purchasing the export version of the Kfir or possibly the LCA or the Ching-Kuo, if available.[22]

Advanced Western suppliers have closed off Taiwan's access to new, advanced warplanes for fear of antagonizing Beijing. If Taiwan acquired nuclear arms in the future and its Ching-Kuo project had not progressed, it might consider purchasing the Kfir or the LCA. Again, however, U.S. approval would be required if the aircraft employed U.S. technology. In developing the Ching-Kuo, it may be added, Taiwan might seek Israeli assistance. The two countries are said to have collaborated in the past on other military projects—namely, two missile systems discussed in the next section.

Although second-tier designed and manufactured aircraft are unlikely to be a match for their first-tier counterparts, a separate concern is the possibility that a second-tier market in *coproduced* Western and Soviet warplanes could emerge. India, for example, has been licensed to coproduce the Soviet MiG-21, MiG-23, and MiG-25 as well as the British-French Jaguar; Taiwan, Turkey, and South Korea coproduce U.S. F-5Es; Australia coproduces the Mirage IIIE and F-18A Hornet; and Japan and Singapore coproduce the F-16. For now, it appears that all of these coproduced aircraft are for use exclusively in the air forces of the respective coproducing countries, and because of strict supplier restrictions on retransfers, there have been no export sales of these warplanes by the less industrialized party.

This policy against reexports could change in the years ahead. To wean India away from its program to develop the LCA using U.S.-supplied high technology, the Soviet Union has proposed that India instead modernize its fleet of MiG-21s by replacing the motor with that of the MiG-29, among other steps. As a sweetener, Moscow is said to have agreed to permit India to export the upgraded version of the MiG-21. Presumably, the Soviet Union would still have the final say over such sales, however.[23] The aircraft might be attractive to Iraq, Libya, and North Korea, whose air forces already contain Soviet-made aircraft, but would not likely be of interest to other emerging nuclear states whose air forces are based on Western warplanes.

Supplier retransfer restrictions also apply to warplanes that have been *previously purchased* by industrializing states. The possibility of illicit retransfers of advanced Western or Soviet aircraft by these recipients must nonetheless be considered. Although a black market in these aircraft does not now appear to exist, there is apparently a black market in spare parts to which the second-tier suppliers may be contributing, and at least one attempt to smuggle complete fighter aircraft from the United States to Iran has been reported.[24]

Finally, even though the capabilities of second-tier aircraft are inferior, the emerging nuclear states might nonetheless turn to these suppliers in order to avoid nonproliferation restrictions imposed by the industrialized sellers of warplanes. The advanced suppliers, however, are not known to have imposed explicit restrictions on the possible use of their aircraft with nuclear arms, making recourse to other potential suppliers for this reason unnecessary. This appears to be a gap of growing importance in the international nonproliferation regime.[25]

In sum, for the foreseeable future, it appears unlikely that any of the emerging nuclear states, except South Africa and possibly Taiwan and Iran—whose access to first-tier technology is restricted for political reasons—will rely on warplanes available from the second-tier suppliers as nuclear delivery systems.

Ballistic Missile Delivery Systems

Unlike advanced ground-attack warplanes, which are already in the arsenals of the undeclared nuclear states and may be easily adapted to nuclear delivery, the acquisition of nuclear-armed ballistic missiles by the emerging nuclear states remains a somewhat more distant threat—except in the case of Israel, which is thought to have developed a short-range nuclear missile by the early 1970s and is said to have deployed a more advanced version in the early 1980s. Nonetheless, there are strong indications that additional emerging nuclear states are seeking to acquire similar capabilities.

In principle, ballistic missiles can make a militarily significant contribution to a new nuclear power's delivery capability when the alternative of using jet warplanes is unsatisfactory because their range is insufficient to reach essential targets and/or because their ability to penetrate enemy air defenses is in doubt.[26] In addition, ballistic missiles can strengthen a national nuclear deterrent by diversifying delivery capabilities, helping to ensure the survivability of nuclear forces and thus the certainty of retaliation.

Before analyzing the role of second-tier suppliers of nuclear-capable missiles and related technology in assisting the missile delivery systems of the emerging nuclear powers, some consideration must be given to definitions. For the purposes of this discussion, first-tier suppliers of missiles and related technology will be those advanced industrialized nations that either possess sophisticated space or missile programs or are able to manufacture key equipment needed for such programs. Under this definition, the first-tier suppliers include the Soviet Union and a group of seven advanced Western states—Canada, France, Great Britain, Italy, Japan, the United States, and West Germany—that announced in April 1987 that they had adopted new controls over the export of missiles and related technology.

These restrictions are known collectively as the Missile Technology Control Regime (MTCR).[27] A majority of the seven members of the group have a history of exporting technology or equipment for space or missile programs to less industrialized countries. (As of early 1989, the Soviet Union had not joined the regime.)

China, though a nuclear-weapons state with a considerable and long-standing missile capability, will be considered a second-tier supplier on the grounds that it lags behind the first-tier states in terms of overall industrialization and that, unlike most of the first-tier group, it has only recently become a major exporter of relevant equipment or technology.

Other states that will be considered actual or potential second-tier suppliers, all of which have ongoing missile or space-launcher programs, are Argentina, Brazil, Egypt, India, Iran, Iraq, Israel, North Korea, Pakistan, South Africa, South Korea, and Taiwan.[28] Libya—which, according to some reports, is financing the development of certain Brazilian missiles and which is alleged to have retransferred Soviet-made SCUD-B missiles to Iran—will also be considered a second-tier supplier.

A second definitional question to be resolved is what constitutes a "nuclear-capable" missile. The Missile Technology Control Regime deems only those missiles with a range of more than 190 miles (300 kilometers) and a payload of more than 1,100 pounds (500 kilograms) to be nuclear-capable. This definition was adopted for practical reasons, because it was believed that a regime that attempted to regulate rockets and missiles with capabilities below these thresholds, which might extend to unguided artillery rockets and the like, could not be effectively implemented. It would be a mistake to assume, however, that only missiles with the range noted can have strategic importance in regional conflicts or that no emerging nuclear state will be able to build a nuclear warhead weighing less than 1,100 pounds.

In the Middle East, for example, missiles with ranges far less than 190 miles could easily reach Israel's major cities if fired from border regions in Egypt, Jordan, Syria, or Lebanon. Shorter-range missiles could also threaten major cities in South Asia: Lahore, for example—Pakistan's second largest city—lies only about twenty miles from the Indo-Pakistani border; the Pakistani capital of Islamabad lies within sixty miles of the border; and the Indian cities of Amritsar and Srinagar, both with populations of more than half a million persons, lie within forty miles of the border.

With respect to the payload criterion, similarly, two emerging nuclear states are reported to have developed nuclear devices weighing considerably less than the 1,100-pound MTCR threshold: Israel, which is said to have built nuclear warheads weighing only 226 pounds, and Pakistan, which is said to be developing nuclear explosives weighing only 400 pounds.[29] Moreover, a number of American- and Soviet-made missiles in the hands of emerging nuclear states—including the U.S. Lance, deployed by Israel, and the Soviet SS-21, deployed by Syria—though presumably armed only with conventional warheads by these regional powers, carry nuclear warheads in the superpowers' respective arsenals. These missiles are thus undeniably nuclear-capable, even though they are not considered so by the MTCR because their respective ranges and/or payloads fall below the regime's thresholds.

Notwithstanding these limitations in the MTCR framework, it is clear that missiles with greater range and payload are generally of more concern than those with lesser range and payload because of the formers' ability to strike a wider range of targets and because of the greater ease with which they can be outfitted with nuclear warheads by emerging nuclear states. For this reason—and because the thresholds of the MTCR are now codified in Western export controls—the following discussion will concentrate on missiles that have a range of more than 190 miles and payloads of more than 1,100 pounds, while also recognizing the nuclear potential of less capable rockets available to the emerging nuclear states.

Several major routes are available to emerging nuclear states that seek to acquire nuclear-capable ballistic missiles. First, such states may develop these missiles indigenously, either through dedicated military programs or as the offshoot of peaceful space research programs. Historically, the less industrialized states with "indigenous" missile and space programs have relied heavily on assistance obtained from more advanced nations, especially the United States, France, West Germany, and the Soviet Union.[30] This assistance has run the gamut from officially sanctioned cooperation to illicitly acquired technology and equipment. Today, this trend is changing somewhat, and indigenous missile programs in virtually all of the emerging nuclear states, except Israel and India, are relying increasingly on collaborative efforts with other industrializing countries—countries that are often nuclear aspirants themselves.

A second, alternative route to the acquisition of nuclear-capable missiles is for an emerging nuclear state to obtain complete, conventionally armed missiles (and associated launching hardware, training, and so forth) from others and then adapt them to nuclear use. To date, no emerging nuclear state is known to have exercised this option.[31] It is likely to become increasingly attractive, however, as second-tier suppliers begin to offer powerful, conventionally armed, short- and medium-range missiles on the international market. In the past, such armaments were available only from the Soviet Union and, on a much more limited basis, from the United States. Moreover, the two superpowers had offered them only to their respective regional allies, principally in the Middle East, presumably under strict controls precluding their nuclearization.

Adding complexity to this changing situation is that (as noted earlier in connection with Libya) there appears to be a "secondary market" in nuclear-capable missiles, in which countries that have acquired complete missiles from one supplier—whether of the first or second tier—are offering the weapons to others, thereby becoming second-tier suppliers themselves. (As of this writing, it may be noted, no U.S.-origin missiles are known to have appeared on the secondary market.[32])

To assess the contribution that second-tier suppliers may make to the spread of nuclear-armed missiles, it is necessary to draw the likely connections between particular emerging nuclear states and second-tier missile suppliers that might assist each of them, respectively, to acquire such systems. As indicated in the first part of this chapter—addressing aircraft delivery systems—for the next decade, only six industrializing countries will have sufficiently advanced nuclear capabilities to permit them to mate nuclear arms with ballistic missiles: Israel, India, Pakistan, and South Africa (which already have the ability to manufacture nuclear arms) and Argentina and Brazil (which are on the verge of acquiring that capability). Iran, Iraq, and Libya, along with North and South Korea and Taiwan, are unlikely to cross the nuclear weapons threshold during the next decade. Given the more distant nuclear threat they pose, these states will be discussed only passingly, even though all of them have acquired or are acquiring important missile systems.

All of the six most advanced emerging nuclear states have embarked on programs that have led or may lead to the development of indigenously built nuclear missiles. How important will assistance from other second-tier missile states be in each of these instances? As will be detailed here, Israel and India have the most sophisticated missile/space programs in the developing world. For this reason and because of a variety of political inhibitions, they are likely to benefit only marginally from aid supplied by other second-tier states. Pakistan, South Africa, Argentina, and Brazil, on the other hand, are likely to be far more reliant on external assistance, and there is already considerable evidence indicating that less industrialized suppliers are contributing to missile programs in all four of these countries.

Israel

As mentioned earlier, it has long been rumored that Israel developed a missile, known as the Jericho, during the 1960s. Allegedly, the missile was built to Israeli specifications by the French armorer, Dassault. Its range was said to be 250 to 300 miles and its payload 1,000 to 1,500 pounds.[33] Supposedly, fourteen Jerichos were delivered to Israel before the French suspended military assistance in the aftermath of the 1967 Arab–Israeli war; thereafter, Israel began to produce them indigenously. Because of their payload, the missiles have been considered nuclear-capable, and there have been reports that Israel readied them for use in the early stages of the 1973 Arab–Israeli conflict.[34]

In the late 1970s, Israel is believed to have developed a more advanced surface-to-surface ballistic missile, known in the Western press as the Jericho II.[35] According to the usually reliable *Aerospace Daily*, the missile was deployed in 1981, has a range of 400 miles, and has an inertial guidance system, making it far more accurate than its predecessor.[36] There have been repeated reports that key parts for the missile, including fuel compounds, inertial guidance system components, and the shells of the rockets themselves, were illicitly exported from the United States.[37]

In May 1987, Israel tested an advanced version of the Jericho II to a distance of 500 miles. News reports quoting U.S. officials stated that the missile had a planned range of more than 900 miles, making it capable of striking targets in the southern Soviet Union.[38] Moscow thereafter issued a number of warnings to Jerusalem against deploying the rocket, appearing to confirm the Western press accounts.[39]

On 19 September 1988, Israel publicly revealed its considerable missile capabilities for the first time by launching its first space satellite, known as Ofek 1 (Horizon 1). Israeli officials announced that a previously unknown rocket, the Shavit II (Comet II), was used to launch the spacecraft. American officials subsequently indicated that the rocket was a Jericho II missile augmented by a third stage and that it was the same basic system as the one that Israel had fired 500 miles into the Mediterranean in May 1987. In the wake of the satellite launch, U.S. government analyses, apparently revising the July 1987 assessment, estimated that the Shavit II would have a range of 3,000 to 4,500 miles if used as a missile, giving it an intercontinental reach. A second test of the missile version of the rocket was reported in November 1988.[40]

Given these considerable accomplishments, it is unlikely that Israel will need to rely significantly on aid from other second-tier missile supplier states, as virtually all other second-tier programs are less advanced. Nonetheless, there have been rumors that Israel collaborated with South Africa and Taiwan in the development of antiship cruise missiles (the various Israeli versions are known as the Gabriel series); that Israel cooperated with Taiwan in developing a sixty-mile-range surface-to-surface missile (supposedly based on the Lance system that the United States had previously provided Israel); and that Israel and South Africa have a joint missile-testing range on Marion Island in the Antarctic.[41] None of these allegations indicates whether the other parties contributed technical expertise or equipment to these joint projects or merely helped finance them.

Israel is also reported to have assisted the People's Republic of China in developing advanced missile guidance systems, raising the possibility that

Israel might have obtained other rocket technology from China in return.[42] On balance, however, Israel would appear to have little need for substantial assistance from other second-tier states.

India

India has followed a different path from Israel's in developing its missile capabilities. India invested initially in a peaceful space program (which, until the launch of the Israeli Ofek 1, was the most advanced in the developing world) and only subsequently moved to develop ballistic missiles. In July 1980, India became the world's sixth nation to place a satellite in space—the seventy-seven-pound Rohini, using an indigenous space launch vehicle, the four-stage, solid-propellant SLV-3. India repeated its success in April 1983, using the SLV-3 to place a ninety-three-pound satellite into orbit.

According to various estimates, India's SLV-3 could be converted into an intermediate-range ballistic missile with a payload of about 1,000 pounds and a range of 500 to 1,000 miles.[43] A more powerful launch vehicle, the ASLV—capable of placing a 330-pound satellite into low earth orbit—crashed on its first two tests on 24 March 1987 and 13 July 1988. A polar satellite launch vehicle capable of lofting a 2,200-pound payload into orbit is also being developed.[44] India's space program has benefited from extensive official cooperation with the Soviet Union, the United States, France, and other European nations, and the SLV-3 is said to be similiar to the U.S. Scout sounding rocket.[45]

India is also working on at least two military ballistic missiles. It is currently flight-testing the Prithvi, a short-range surface-to-surface missile with a ready nuclear potential. In addition, on May 22, 1989, India tested an intermediate-range ballistic missile, known as the Agni, for the first time.[46] The Prithvi has a range of 155 miles and a one-ton payload, and the Agni, a range of 1,550 miles. Its payload has also been estimated, at one ton, sufficient to carry a nuclear warhead.

There are no reports indicating that other second-tier missile suppliers have provided assistance to India, and for now, it is difficult to identify any likely candidates for this role. India has generally looked to the advanced suppliers or to indigenous production, rather than to other industrializing states, to meet its military needs, and it appears to be seeking to develop an autonomous nuclear and missile/space capability at least in part in order to project itself as a major power. Given this and the absence to date of any reported reliance on assistance from second-tier missile states, it appears unlikely that New Delhi might turn for such aid even to those states in this class with which India has amicable relations, such as Brazil, Argentina, or North Korea.[47]

Pakistan

Pakistan's space program, though it has accelerated since 1981, remains many years behind India's. Islamabad announced plans to launch its first satellite in 1988, but it had not taken this step as of late 1989. On February 5, 1989, however, Chief of the Army Staff, General Mirza Aslam Beg disclosed that Pakistan had recently tested two "indigenously-developed" short-range military missiles, the Haft ("deadly") I and Haft II. The former has a range of 50 miles, while the Haft II has a range of 185 miles. Beg noted that "these are extremely accurate systems and can carry a payload of over 500 kilograms [1,100 pounds]."[48] Pakistan is said to have sought the assistance of the West German aerospace firm OTRAG (Orbital Transport und Raketen Aktien Geselschaft). During the late 1970s and early 1980s, OTRAG briefly set up test facilities in Zaire and Libya to develop an unsophisticated launch vehicle with a 200-mile range.[49] In theory, OTRAG could offer skilled manpower for Pakistan's rocket-development efforts.

The People's Republic of China, Pakistan's long-standing ally, may also have provided assistance. China, it may be noted, is believed to have provided Pakistan with the design of a nuclear weapon in the early 1980s. Significantly, the design was said to be that of the device China detonated in its fourth nuclear test, which was the test of a nuclear missile warhead.[50] This could accelerate Pakistan's acquisition of nuclear-armed missiles.

For the future, a wide range of second-tier suppliers might assist Pakistani missile efforts in a variety of ways. Most obviously, Pakistan might seek to purchase missiles from China, which has been offering two missiles for sale internationally—the M-9 and the M-11, with payloads of more than a ton and ranges of about 400 miles and 100 to 200 miles, respectively.[51] (After the international uproar caused by China's sale of intermediate-range CSS-2 missiles to Saudi Arabia in 1988, it is unlikely that Beijing would transfer this system to Pakistan.[52])

Pakistan could also turn to more than a half-dozen other second-tier suppliers that are developing their own ballistic missiles or that might be prepared to sell Islamabad missiles they had obtained from others. The following are among these potential suppliers:

Argentina, which is developing the Condor II/Badr 2000 with Egypt.

Brazil, which is developing the Avibras SS-300 and the Orbita MB/EE-600.

Egypt, which has Soviet SCUD-Bs in its arsenal and is said to be developing an improved version with North Korean assistance and to be collaborating with Argentina (and reportedly Iraq) on the Condor II/Badr 2000.

Iraq, which is manufacturing two extended-range SCUD-B's, the Al-Abbas and the Al-Huseyn, and which soon may acquire the Condor II/Badr 2000 and the Brazilian Avibras-300, both noted earlier.

Iran, which reportedly possesses a sizable number of North Korean copies of the SCUD-B and has a number of indigenous missiles under development.

Libya, which possesses Soviet-origin SCUD-Bs (some of which it has reportedly sold to Iran) and which may be financing the Brazilian MB/EE-600.

North Korea, which manufactures the SCUD-B and which may shortly be able to offer the advanced version it is said to be building with Egypt.

All of the foregoing systems would be deemed nuclear-capable under the Missile Technology Control Regime, with the exception of the Iraqi Al-Abbas and Al-Huseyn, which are said to be SCUD-Bs whose payload has been reduced below 1,100 pounds in order to extend their range beyond the normal 190 miles.[53]

If, rather than purchasing missiles, Pakistan sought to bolster the resources of its indigenous missile program, help might again be available from virtually all of the second-tier suppliers just mentioned. Several additional industrializing states that possess considerable competence in military rocket technology, even though they have not developed missiles deemed nuclear-capable under the Missile Technology Control Regime, might also be prepared to share know-how with Pakistan. These include South Korea, which has developed short-range surface-to-surface missiles apparently based on the U.S. Nike-Hercules, and Taiwan, which has developed the Ching Feng (Green Bee), apparently based on the U.S. Lance.[54]

To date, the only alleged link between the Pakistani missile program and assistance from a second-tier supplier is the possibility that Islamabad has received technical aid from China. Nonetheless, as the foregoing summary makes clear, many avenues would be open to Pakistan if it sought to advance its program through resort to the second-tier missile states.

South Africa

South Africa has announced its intention to develop surface-to-surface missiles, though little is known about its program. There have been repeated allegations that the program is being pursued in collaboration with Israel and that the two countries are building a missile test site on Marion Island in the Antarctic.[55] Pretoria may also have received Jericho missiles from

Israel; and, as mentioned earlier, Pretoria is also alleged to have cooperated with Taiwan and Israel in the development of antiship cruise missiles.

Given the country's continuing diplomatic isolation and the 1977 UN arms embargo against it, additional second-tier suppliers are unlikely to be prepared to offer technical assistance or missile systems to South Africa. Indeed, even Israel has pledged not to enter into new arms contracts with Pretoria.[56] Thus, South Africa has probably benefited considerably from cooperation with a handful of friendly second-tier states, but this group is unlikely to grow and, indeed, some of these contacts could be curtailed.

Argentina

As mentioned in the discussion of Pakistan, Argentina is developing the Condor II in collaboration with Egypt (where the missile is known as the Badr 2000). Iraq is alleged to be financing the project. The rocket is to have a 500- to 600-mile range and a 1,000-pound payload, making it effectively a nuclear-capable missile under the Missile Technology Control Regime. Given its participants, this project represents one of the most salient instances of mutual assistance among the second-tier states.

Nonetheless, the arrest in June 1988 of an Egyptian-born American for attempting to smuggle key equipment for the project to Egypt demonstrates that the effort remains at least partly dependent on supplies from first-tier states.[57] Moreover, there have been reports that the portion of the project based in Argentina has received important—and possibly illegal—assistance from the West German firm of Messerschmidt-Boelkow-Blohm.[58] It remains to be seen whether these missile programs—and similar efforts in other second-tier states—can be sustained without such supplies, as the Missile Technology Control Regime increasingly restricts access to such supplies.[59]

Brazil

Over the past decade and a half, Brazil has launched a series of sounding rockets with increasing payloads and ranges. These have subsequently been modified into surface-to-surface military missiles, which have been offered for sale on the international market.[60] The largest Brazilian missile currently available is the SS-60 (based on the Sonda III sounding rocket), which carries only a 330-pound payload. However, Brazil has had a number of successful launches of the Sonda IV sounding rocket, which carries an 1,100-pound payload and has a range beyond 200 miles.[61] By the mid-1990s, this rocket is to be converted into a 375-mile-range military version, known as the Orbita MB/EE-600, for sale to foreign customers.[62] Flight tests of the SS-300—a missile comparable to the SCUD-B, with a 190-mile range and a 2,200-pound payload—are expected in 1989.⁶³ Libya is said to be financing the development of the missile, and Iraq is said to be underwriting the rocket.⁶⁴ Longer-range systems are also under development, including one with a 625-mile capability.

Brazil's space program has benefited from extensive official cooperation with the United States, Canada, the European Space Agency, and the Soviet Union; and a number of Western European firms are said to have assisted in the development of components for the Sonda IV.⁶⁵ The only major reported instance of interaction between Brazil and another second-tier missile supplier country, apart from the aforementioned possible Libyan and Iraqi financing for the missiles, is a 1986 agreement with the People's Republic of China under which Brazil is reportedly to receive advanced technology on liquid rocket fuels and rocket guidance systems in return for providing solid-fuel technology to Beijing.⁶⁶

As assistance from advanced states is curtailed because of the Missile Technology Control Regime, it is reasonable to expect that Brazil will seek to expand its technical collaboration with other industrializing states. Iraq may prove a particularly important partner in this regard—notwithstanding the support it is said to be giving to Brazil's regional rival, Argentina, by underwriting the Argentine-Egyptian Condor II/Badr 2000 project. As noted earlier, Iraq appears to be developing a considerable expertise of its own in the missile field, which could provide the basis for collaboration in this area; at the same time, Baghdad appears to have substantial links to Brazil, both as a long-standing purchaser of Brazilian armaments and, more recently, as financier of the Brazilian Orbita MB/EE-600 missile system.

In sum, the potential role of second-tier missile supplier states in aiding the acquisition by the emerging nuclear states of nuclear-capable missiles is likely to be highly varied, depending significantly on the particular emerging nuclear state involved. Perhaps not surprisingly, the emerging nuclear states with the most advanced nuclear weapons capabilities also happen to be those with the most advanced missile programs; these powers appear to be the least likely to look to the second-tier supplier states for assistance in the latter field. The less advanced emerging nuclear states, however, may be expected to turn increasingly to the second-tier missile suppliers. Although political considerations are likely to be an important constraint on collaboration in a number of cases, these second-tier relationships will inevitably pose an increasing proliferation risk in the years ahead.

Conclusions

For the near term, the most dangerous purveyors of nuclear delivery capabilities to the vast majority of emerging nuclear states are not the industrializing nations but the major powers whose transfers of advanced warplanes offer highly capable, easily adapted, and unrestricted nuclear delivery systems. Missiles present a different picture. Second-tier missile transfers and technical collaboration may significantly accelerate the ability of a number of key regional powers to deploy nuclear-armed missiles in the years ahead.

In 1974, the industrialized nations that were the principal suppliers of nuclear material and equipment established rules restricting transfers of such commodities. These restrictions are also being challenged by a group of emerging second-tier nuclear supplier countries. The nuclear supply regime, however, has been in place for fifteen years, and its strictures have created a norm of behavior. Indeed, many of the emerging nuclear supplier states are formally embracing this preexisting code of conduct. By comparison, the rules governing delivery system transfers are in their infancy, and whether they will ever mature into a comprehensive international regulatory regime remains in doubt.

Notes

1. See Rodney W. Jones, ed., *Small Nuclear Forces and U.S. Security Policy* (Lexington, Mass.: Lexington Books, 1984).

2. The term *ballistic missile* refers to a missile that is self-propelled and guided, with a range of many miles. Ballistic missiles carry their own fuel and oxidizer propellants, as opposed to aircraft and cruise missiles, which must stay in the atmosphere and get their oxidizer—oxygen—from it. Ballistic missiles also do not generally need aerodynamic control surfaces, because they travel in a free-falling trajectory under the influence of gravity. Arthur F. Manfredi et al., "Ballistic Missile Proliferation Potential in the Third World," (Washington, D.C.: Congressional Research Service, 1986), p. 1.

3. This assessment appears widely in the literature. See, for example, International Institute for Strategic Studies, *Strategic Survey* (London:IISS, 1974), pp. 37, 38; Jones, *Small Nuclear Forces*; Peter Pry, *Israel's Nuclear Arsenal* (Boulder, Colo.: Westview Press, 1984), p. 99; Richard Burt, "Nuclear Proliferation and the Spread of New, Conventional Weapons Technology," in Stephanie G. Neuman and Robert E. Harkavy, eds. *Arms Transfers in the Modern World* (New York: Praeger, 1979).

4. This is not to say that the most capable warplane in a country's air force will automatically be selected for the nuclear delivery role. Among other factors, military planners would have to weigh the costs of withholding such aircraft from conventional combat in order to ensure their availability for strategic nuclear missions. Top aircraft could also be used as escorts for less capable bombers. On balance, however, given the limited options available to emerging nuclear states, the clear superiority of advanced-supplier aircraft over those offered by second-tier suppliers, and the fundamental importance of successful delivery once the decision to use nuclear weapons had been made, there is good reason to assume that the new nuclear countries would prefer to rely on the high-performance warplanes supplied

by the United States, the USSR, Great Britain, and France than on less capable alternatives.

5. In the forces of the declared nuclear weapons states, the term *nuclear-capable* is used differently to denote aircraft that have been specially equipped for nuclear missions with electronic circuits that permit nuclear weapons to be armed in flight and combination locks, known in the United States as "permissive action links" (PALs), that prevent such arming from taking place until the pilot receives the correct combination from the proper authority. Thomas B. Cochran, William M. Arkin, and Milton M. Hoenig, *U.S. Nuclear Forces and Capabilities*, (Cambridge, Mass: Ballinger, 1984), pp. 30–31. The discussion here has been considerably simplified. No nuclear weapons state supplier of military aircraft is believed to sell aircraft with these nuclear circuits, however. Whether an emerging nuclear state would want to install such circuits on its own is uncertain, but Sweden's 1958 bomb design contained an arming mechanism, suggesting that in-air arming was probably contemplated. A new nuclear state could provide for in-air arming today by slightly modifying circuits for conventional munitions—circuits that are included on American and possibly other aircraft. As for PALs, states with only a handful of nuclear weapons, which presumably would be under the close control of top civilian leaders, might be prepared to forgo this safeguard, which is important to the United States in part because of the great number of U.S. weapons deployed around the world. Indeed, the United States itself did not adopt PALs until 1962. See Donald R. Cotter, "Peacetime Operations: Safety and Security," in Ashton Carter et al., eds., *Managing Nuclear Weapons* (Washington, D.C.: Brookings Institution, 1987), p. 49.

6. Christer Larsson, "Build a Bomb!" *Ny Teknik*, 25 April 1985.

7. "Revealed: The Secrets of Israel's Nuclear Arsenal," *Sunday Times* (London), 5 October 1986. As described below, Israel may, in fact, have developed a 226-pound warhead.

8. Interview with Richard Sale, reporter for the *Aerospace Daily*, NBC "Nightly News," 30 July 1985. (Sale quoted an American scientist who claimed to have been involved in developing the Israeli warhead.)

9. Hedrick Smith, "A Bomb Ticks in Pakistan", *New York Times Magazine*, 6 March 1988, p. 38; Egmont R. Koch and Simon Henderson, "Auf Dunklen Wegen zur Atommacht," *Der Stern*, 30 April 1986, p. 154.

10. Interview with an Indian journalist familiar with details of 1974 device.

11. See, for example, Pry, *Israel's Nuclear Arsenal*, ch. 3.

12. For a list of aircraft in the Israeli Air Force, see International Institute for Strategic Studies, *The Military Balance, 1988–1989* (London: IISS, 1988). All of these aircraft, with the exception of the A-4, are capable of speeds in excess of Mach 2, and the F-15 and F-16 have the most advanced avionics in the group. Israel's aging subsonic U.S. A-4N/Js could, in principle, be used for nuclear missions, but they are far less capable than the more advanced aircraft noted above.

13. For a list of aircraft in the Indian Air Force, see IISS, *The Military Balance*. Concerning the India's alleged selection of the MiG-23 and MiG-27 as nuclear delivery systems, see "India: Fixed-Wing Nuclear Delivery by Mid-1989," *Defense and Foreign Affairs Weekly*, 3–9 October 1988.

14. For a list of aircraft in the Pakistani Air Force, see IISS, *The Military Balance*.

15. Glenn Frankel, "Israeli Economy Depends on No-Questions-Asked Arms Sales," *Washington Post*, 12 December 1986. China produces several supersonic aircraft, including the Q-5, J-6, and J-7, but these are considered antiquated by current standards. A more advanced war plane, the J-8II, with some similarities to the MiG-23, is under development and is discussed below.

16. "Taiwan's Ching-Kuo Fighter," *Jane's Defence Weekly*, 7 January 1989, p. 4.

17. "PRC to Develop Fighter Plane with Embriser," *O Globo*, 27 March 1987, translated in *Foreign Broadcast Information Service (FBIS)/Latin America*, 7 April 1987, p. D-1.

18. "Israel Offers Re-Engined Kfir," *Flight International*, 25 April 1987, p. 10.

19. For a list of aircraft in the South African Air Force, see IISS, *The Military Balance*.

20. "Israel Will Curb Arms For Pretoria," *New York Times*, 19 March 1987.

21. Hirsh Goodman, "RSA Seeking to Lure Lavi Engineers, Technicians," *Jerusalem Post*, 9 November 1987; *FBIS/Near East-South Asia*, 10 November 1987, p. 44. South Africa has denied engaging in the recruitment effort.

22. Iran's possible purchase of Israeli aircraft should not be ruled out, despite Teheran's stated hostility toward Israel. In recent years, Iran appears to have obtained spare parts for some of its U.S. aircraft and other armaments from Israel, in part with U.S. acquiescence. Kenneth B. Timmermann "Shrinking Market Costs Bring Shift in Fighter Production," *International Herald Tribune*, 18 June 1987; *Report of the President's Special Review Board* (Tower Commission Report) (Washington, D.C.: Government Printing Office, 16 February 1987), p. III-4.

23. See K.K. Sharma, "Moscow Offers to Upgrade Indian MiGs," *Financial Times*, 20 December 1988.

24. "A $2.5 Billion Arms Ring for Iran Broken, U.S. Says," *Christian Science Monitor*, 23 April 1986.

25. For a detailed discussion of possible initiatives for restricting the use of these advanced aircraft for nuclear delivery missions, see Leonard S. Spector, *The Undeclared Bomb* (Cambridge, Mass.: Ballinger, 1988), ch. 2.

26. See, generally, Aaron Karp, "Ballistic Missiles in the Third World," *International Security* (Winter 1984–85): 166.

27. See "Missile Technology Control Regime: Fact Sheet to Accompany Public Announcement" (Washington, D.C.: U.S. Department of Defense, 16 April 1987). The regulations are aimed at slowing the spread of unmanned delivery capabilities—including ballistic missiles, space launch vehicles, sounding rockets, and "air-breathing" vehicles, including drones and cruise missiles—with a range of more than 190 miles and a payload of more than 1,100 pounds. The regulations establish two categories of controlled items. Category I items, which are the most sensitive and are subject to the strictest controls, include complete rockets and air vehicles; complete subsystems (for example, rocket stages, reentry vehicles, and solid- or liquid-fuel rocket engines); specially designed production equipment and facilities; and technology for design and production. The export rules provide that there will be no transfers of production facilities and that there will be a strong presumption of denial for transfers of other items in this category. If a transfer is contemplated, binding government-to-government assurances regarding end use and

prohibiting retransfer are to be required. No verification mechanisms are specified, however. Category II items are, in effect, dual-use commodities that are also used, for example, in civil or military aviation: propulsion components, propellants and constituents, missile structural composites, flight instruments and inertial navigation equipment, and the like. Importantly, the new rules state that they are not intended to interfere with peaceful space programs, necessitating difficult judgments in specific cases.

28. For a detailed discussion of the missile and, where applicable, space programs of these states, see Robert D. Shuey et al., "Missile Proliferation: Survey of Emerging Missile Forces," CRS Report 88-642 F (Washington, D.C.: Congressional Research Service, 3 October 1988) [hereafter cited as "CRS Missile Survey"]. (The report is updated periodically.) Highlights of a number of these programs are given in the text.

29. Interview with Richard Sale; Smith, "A Bomb Ticks in Pakistan."

30. Spector, *The Undeclared Bomb*, ch. 2.

31. It is at least conceivable, however, that Israel has secretly equipped U.S.-supplied Lance short-range missiles with nuclear warheads. Great Britain, a nuclear-weapons state, it may be added, has purchased Polaris missiles from the United States and fitted them with British-made nuclear warheads. These missiles (and the U.S. D-5 missiles Britain is currently purchasing) were designed as nuclear systems and sold without warheads, with the understanding that they would be nuclearized.

32. As discussed later, however, Israel is said to have assisted Taiwan in developing a short-range ballistic missile based on the U.S. Lance, which had been previously supplied to Israel.

33. Michael Dunn, "Israel: Jericho II and the Nuclear Arsenal," *Defense And Foreign Affairs Daily*, 9 May 1985.

34. "How Israel Got the Bomb," *Time*, 12 April 1976, p.39; Dunn, "Israel."

35. Elaine Sciolino, "Documents Detail Israeli Missile Deal with Shah," *New York Times*, 1 April 1986.

36. "Israel Said to Deploy Jericho Missile," *Aerospace Daily*, 1 May 1985; "Nuclear Efforts Of Israel, Pakistan Prompt Meeting of U.S. Group," *Aerospace Daily*, 7 May 1985. Current and former Reagan administration officials have privately confirmed the missile's existence.

37. "Nuclear Efforts of Israel, Pakistan Prompt Meeting"; and Richard Sale and Geoffrey Aronson, "Exporting Nuclear Triggers: The Strange Case of Richard Smyth," *Middle East Report* (May–June 1987).

38. Thomas W. Netter, "Israel Reported to Test New, Longer-Range Missile," *New York Times*, 22 July 1987.

39. "USSR Warns against Jericho Missile Development," Jerusalem Television Service, 1800 GMT, 23 July 1987, translated in *FBIS/Middle East and South Asia*, 24 July 1987, p. L-1; S.I. Waxman, "Soviets Assail Testing of Israeli Missile," *Washington Post*, 1 August 1987.

40. Stephen Broening, "Israel Could Build Missiles to Hit Soviets, U.S. Thinks," *Baltimore Sun*, 23 November 1988; "Israel in Second Test of Jericho IRBM," *Jane's Defence Weekly*, 19 November 1988; Leonard S. Spector, "Satellite Strategy," *Christian Science Monitor*, 17 November 1988.

41. "CRS Missile Survey," pp. 82–83; "Recent Developments Concerning Relations Between Israel and South Africa," Special Report of the Special Committee Against Apartheid, United Nations General Assembly, 42d Session, Agenda Item 33, 26 October 1987, p. 9; Martin Bailey, "South Africa's Island Bombshell," *Observer*, 28 December 1986. Israel is also said to have collaborated with Iran in the development of the Jericho II during the late 1970s, before the Iranian revolution, although Iran's contribution may have been principally financial rather than technical. See Sciolino, "Documents Detail Israeli Missile Deal."

42. David Ottaway, "Israelis Aided China on Missiles," *Washington Post*, 23 May 1988.

43. Jerrold F. Elkin and Brian Fredericks, "Military Applications of India's Space Program," *Air University Review* (May–June 1983). "India's Rockets Could Meet Military Ambitions," *New Scientist*, 26 August 1982, p. 555.

44. Steven Weissman, "Launching of a Satellite Rocket Fails in India," *New York Times*, 14 July 1988; Manfredi et al., "Ballistic Missile Potential." Modifying the SLV-3 for use as a ballistic missile nuclear delivery system would require replacing the fourth stage and payload with a nuclear warhead and reentry vehicle. See "India's Launch Vehicle Program Moves Ahead," *Space World* (December 1983). See, also, Elkin and Fredericks, "Military Applications of India's Space Program," p. 60.

45. Aaron Karp, "Space Technology in the Third World," *Space Policy* (May 1986): 157; Maurice Eisenstein, "Third World Missiles and Nuclear Proliferation," *Washington Quarterly* (Summer 1982): 113.

46. "Indian Missile Tests," *Jane's Defense Weekly*, 16 May 1987, p. 9; Richard M. Weintraub, "India Succeeds in Missile Test Launching," *Washington Post*, 26 February, 1988; Barbara Crossette, "India Reports Successful Test of Mid-Range Missile," *New York Times*, 23 May 1989; David White, "Indian Missile Test Raises Fears of Arms Proliferation," *London Sunday Times*, 25 May 1989.

47. Other second-tier suppliers appear to be even more unlikely trading partners. India would hardly turn to Islamic states, such as Egypt, Iran, or Iraq, for key strategic systems, given that one of India's principal antagonists is Pakistan. New Delhi would also undoubtedly have political qualms about looking to Israel or South Africa for assistance on such important weapons. The PRC and India are, of course, potential adversaries.

48. "Progress on Space Research," *Pakistan and Gulf Economist*, 13–19 October 1984; Azim Kidwai, "Muslim Middle East Moves to Exploit Space," *Pakistan and Gulf Economist*, 15–21 May 1982; Gerald M. Steinberg, "Two Missiles in Every Garage," *Bulletin of the Atomic Scientists* (October 1983); "Pak Might Launch Satellite in '88," *News India* (quoting Karachi Radio), 11 September 1987; *Press Trust of India*, 12 May 1987. "Pakistan Claims Long-Range Rocket Ability," *Washington Times*, 6 February 1989; "Pakistan in Missile Build Claim," *Jane's Defense Weekly*, 18 February 1989; Mushahid Hussain, "Missive Missile: Claims of Major Breakthrough," *India Today*, 15 March 1989.

49. Karp, "Ballistic Missiles in the Third World."

50. Leslie Gelb, "Peking Said to Balk at Nuclear Pledges," *New York Times*, 23 June 1984; "China—Fourth Nuclear Test; Firing of Guided Missile with Nuclear Warhead," *Keesing's Contemporary Archives* (1966): 21685.

51. Michael Gordon, "Syria Is Studying New Missile Deal," *New York Times*, 22 June 1988; IISS, *Military Balance 1987–1988* (London: IISS, 1987), p. 146; "China's M-11 Revealed," *Jane's Defence Weekly*, 9 April 1988, p. 655. China has apparently given the United States assurances that it will not sell the M-9 or M-11 in the Middle East, but it is not clear whether these assurances would rule out sales to Pakistan. See Daniel Southerland, "China Assures Carlucci on Mideast Arms Sales," *Washington Post*, 8 September 1988.

52. It remains possible, however, that Pakistan might collaborate with Saudi Arabia to develop nuclear warheads for the missile.

53. For details of the capabilities of these various systems, see "CRS Missile Survey"; W. Seth Carus, "Policy Focus: Missiles in the Middle East—A New Threat to Stability," Research Memorandum No. 6 (Washington, D.C.: Washington Institute for Near East Policy, June 1988); Steve Weissman and Herbert Krosney, *The Islamic Bomb* (New York: Times Books, 1981), pp. 211–212; "Iraq Severs Relations with Libya," *Financial Times*, 27 June 1985. Iran claims to be building a version of the SCUD-B itself, see "Minister on Missile Manufacture," IRNA 0800 GMT, 8 November 1987; *FBIS/Near East and South Asia*, 9 November 1987. p. 61.

54. "CRS Missile Survey," pp. 79–85.

55. *South African Sunday Times*, 20 July 1986; "South Africa May Reportedly Test Atomic Weapons," United Press International, 28 December 1986, AM cycle.

56. See note 20.

57. Richard W. Stevenson, "Egyptian Official Is Accused of Role in Smuggling," *New York Times*, 25 October 1988.

58. Tony Walker, "Argentina, Egypt in Long-Range Missile Project," *Financial Times*, 21 December 1987.

59. Iraq's development of the extended-range SCUD-Bs, used extensively against Iran, is said to have been aided by firms in a number of advanced nations. Numerous West German firms, for example, are said to have assisted Iraq in building an advanced rocket research and development laboratory at Mosul University, known as the Saad 16 facility. See "A Civilian Project of Mosul University," *Der Stern*, 26 January 1989.

60. Manfredi et al., "Ballistic Missile Proliferation."

61. Ibid.

62. Eustaquis de Freitas, "Tactical Missile Development Reported," *O Globo*, 3 January 1988, translated in *FBIS/Latin America*, 5 January 1988, p. 21.

63. Ibid.; Christopher F. Foss, "New Family of Brazilian Missiles in Production," *Jane's Defence Weekly*, 17 January 1987.

64. "Warning on Missiles for Iraq," *Financial Times*, 16 December 1987; de Freitas, "Tactical Missile Development Reported"; Alan Elsner, "Arms Expert Says Iraq Could Soon Have Ballistic Missiles," Reuters, 15 December 1987, AM cycle; Karp, "Ballistic Missile Development"; John Barham, "Brazil Ignores U.S. Protest Over Arms for Libya," *Sunday Times* (London), 31 January 1988.

65. Spector, *The Undeclared Bomb*, p. 41; "CRS Missile Survey," p. 93.

66. "O Globo: Nuclear Missiles Possible in Five Years," *O Globo*, 13 January 1986, translated in *FBIS/Latin America*, 16 January 1986, p. D-1.

II
Country Case Studies

6
Argentina

Sara Tanis
Bennett Ramberg

Argentina's Nuclear Capability

Argentina has embarked on an ambitious domestic nuclear research and energy program. The venture promises to provide the nation with the infrastructure to play an important role in the nuclear export market in the years ahead.

Buenos Aires built its program on a foundation of international support and assistance that overlay an emerging sophisticated industrial and scientific establishment. The foreign contribution sensitized Argentina to opportunities in the global market.

At present, Argentina operates two heavy-water/natural uranium reactors, Atucha I and Embalse. Producing, respectively, 320 MW(e) and 600 MW(e), they supply roughly 10 percent of the country's electricity. With a capacity factor of 84 percent, Atucha I is among the best operated plants in the world. Plans call for a third, 745 MW(e) power plant, Atucha II, to go on line in the early 1990s. During this period, construction also may begin on three 300 MW(e) plants, although the country's foreign indebtedness plus cost overruns in earlier construction will place a heavy burden on these plans.[1]

To minimize foreign political and economic leverage, Argentina made a concerted effort to diversify the exporters on which it relied. West Germany's Siemens and Krafwerk Union joined Austria's Voest Alpine to build the first and third plants; Canada provided Embalse. Imports included pressure vessels, turbine generators, filters, primary coolant pumps, nuclear instrumentation, electric motors, and special valves, some of which came from Spain and Italy. West Germany's RBU supplied machinery for a fuel fabrication facility, and Switzerland's Sulzer Brothers furnished a heavy water plant. Small amounts of heavy water came from China.[2] The Soviet Union assisted the construction of a fuel tubing installation. The wherewithal for Argentina's reprocessing facility, now entering its final stages of construction, came from Europe and the United States.

Along with imported technology came a high learning curve. The resulting domestic infrastructure includes the skeleton for a comprehensive nuclear fuel cycle intended to provide nuclear independence.[3] Four mills process the products of three active mines that hold a portion of Argentina's estimated 18,900 metric tons of uranium reserves. Argentina's atomic energy agency, CNEA, operates uranium purification and conversion plants, a pilot gaseous diffusion facility and reprocessing installation, a fuel fabrication factory, seven research reactors, and one heavy-water plant, with another under construction. Argentina also operates a small enrichment plant, which will have a capacity to produce 250 kilograms of 20 percent enriched uranium. In addition, pilot plants produce zirconium sponges, zircalloy tubes, heavy water, and waste management. With the acquisition

Table 6–1
Major Industrial Firms in Argentina Relevant to the Nuclear Industry

Companies	Provisions
Astarsa	Vessels, heat exchangers, tanks, cranes
Ind. Metalurgicas Pescarmona S.A.	
Gases Industriales	
Cometarsa	
Salcor Caren	
Est. Met. Universal	
Afne	
Lockwood	
Motomecanica Arg.	Valves, pumps, and accessories
Spitzner	
Comp. Sud. de Bombas	
Met. Bellucci	
Intecva	
Francovich	
Byron Jackson	
Cameron	
Worthington	
Worcester	
Invap S.E.	Special nuclear provisions
Conuar S.A.	
Fae S.A.	
Ind. Pirelli S.A.	Electrical and electronic components
Ema. Siam Elect.	
Zoloda	
Elcomat	
Siemens	
Indelqui	
Foxboro	
Jover	
Iecsa, Astarsa, Nuclar, Techint, Argatom, Degremont, etc.	Detail engineering, erection works
Enace S.A.	Architects, engineers

of these capabilities Argentina feels it has reached a point where it can play an active role in the international market.[4]

In a symbiotic relationship, Argentina's private sector works with the government in the drive toward nuclear autarky. Roughly 200 firms deal with CNEA.[5] Small firms (up to ten employees) and medium-sized companies (up to 200 employees) comprise the majority. Among the small concerns, about sixty generate $1 million to $5 million dollars in business in nuclear plant electronics and, to a lesser extent, metallurgical and construction activities. Another fifteen to twenty medium-sized companies annually conduct roughly $50 million in business in these spheres. The largest concerns, about twenty engineering construction and metallurgy establishments, bill out about $100 million a year.[6]

With numerous potential suppliers, CNEA confronts the difficult task of equitably and profitably allocating contracts that are both competitive with the international market and consistent with the pursuit of self-reliance. To make its job easier, in the early 1980s, CNEA set about to identify the most important firms.[7] Table 6–1 lists the principal providers of vessels, heat exchangers, tanks, cranes, valves, pumps, electrical components, engineering designs, and so on.

To promote the domestic market as well as nuclear exports, private concerns formed a lobby, Comite Empresarial, within Buenos Aires' nuclear

Table 6–2
Percentages of National Participation in Nuclear Projects

Project	Basis of Participation Estimate	Direct Costs of the Plant (1)	(1) + Other Costs from the Proprietary (2)	(2) + First Core and Initial Heavy Water (3)
Atucha I	Contractual values[a]	36.78	41.96	37.72
	Medium values[b]	24.67	30.85	27.75
Embalse		51.15	56.04	49.02
Atucha II		54.70	58.88	63.03
Fourth nuclear power plant	Pressure tube type[c]	77.34	79.60	82.15
	Pressure vessel type[c]	73.28	75.48	77.96

[a]This methodology is considered more representative than the alternative.

[b]According to the available information, compared to the original contract.

[c]For both types, this participation is considered the same, independent of the technological accessibility. The value for the pressure tube type doesn't coincide with the feasibility study realized in 1983–84. In this study, the value obtained was 78.1 percent instead of 82.15 percent. There are no new figures available for the pressure vessel type. J.O. Cosentino and B. Murmis, "Central Nuclear Embalse," *Realidad Energerica*, no. 2 (1984): 15.

professional society, the Argentine Association of Nuclear Technology (an organization akin to the American Nuclear Society).[8] The association, which holds annual scientific meetings, co-organized international conferences in 1978 and 1982 in Iran and Argentina that focused on nuclear technology transfer. Argentina's growing nuclear prowess revealed itself at the second convocation in the delivery of twenty-one papers on a variety of subjects.[9] Publication of such nuclear journals as *Argentina Nuclear, Proyecto Energetico, Energia,* and *Informe Industrial* further marks the intellectual maturing of the Argentine nuclear program.

Table 6–2 presents the fruits of growing domestic sophistication. Whereas national resources contributed to 36 percent of the Atucha I, they furnished 54 percent to Atucha II. The figure will expand substantially in future construction. The experience Argentina gains as a result will increase its competitiveness in international markets.

Argentina as an International Exporter: Motives, Incentives, and Disincentives

National pride characterizes Argentina's nuclear program. It carries a message to the world: Argentina has emerged to become not simply a supplier of agricultural products but a reliable international competitor in nuclear commerce.

From the Buenos Aires vantage point, nuclear energy affords a number of benefits. It contributes to such spin-off technologies as advanced materials, information systems, the production and application of halogens, and nickeling techniques, among others. The program serves to sharpen Argentina's international entrepreneurial skills. In this endeavor, the country's secretary for industrial and external commerce plays an important role. Private as well as government financial institutions complement its efforts through the supply of capital. Banco Provincia de Buenos Aires took the lead when it included nuclear technology among its first ventures to support Argentina's technology exports.[10] The action encouraged other Argentine banks—notably, the country's central bank—to do the same.

Argentina's position as the most advanced Latin American state in nuclear technology galvanizes its effort to seek markets in the Western Hemisphere. From a bureaucratic and commercial point of view, decision makers have a vested interest in promoting the program beyond the country's frontiers. Pride alone is not the only reason. Policymakers see the program as a means to address trade imbalances and to acquire foreign exchange. And because Argentina is itself a developing nation, it feels that kindred countries will find working with it attractive.

The antecedents for Argentina's involvement in the international nuclear market go back to the late 1950s, when CNEA and the Cuyo University created a school of physics in the Bariloche Center. Offering advanced graduate education, it provided scholarships to Latin American students.

In 1962, the Department of Metallurgy started the Pan-American Course in Nuclear Metallurgy, later expanded to general metallurgy and materials science. In 1967, with the encouragement of the Western Hemispheric Presidents meeting in Punta del Este, Argentina created the Multinational Program in Metallurgy.[11] Focusing on human resource development and joint research, the course offerings include an introduction to physical metallurgy, thermodynamics, instruments, crystallography, x-ray diffraction, defects in metals, diffusion, mechanical properties, solidification, phase transformation, mechanical working, electron microscopy, microanalysis, steel corrosion, fracture mechanics, welding, nondestructive testing, quality control, and ceramics. Specialized groups provide four weeks of practical training. The program also includes two-week visits to relevant factories throughout the country.

The Multinational Program provided the seed for a regional program on nondestructive testing, coordinated by CNEA. Supported by the IAEA, UNIDO, the OAS, Italy, West Germany, and Canada, seventeen Latin American countries participate. Coverage includes such nondestructive techniques as liquid penetrates, ultrasonics, radiography, acoustic emission, and thermography, which can be used by both operators and inspectors of nuclear plants. The program also provides information on national certification systems.

With other training courses on nuclear plant operation, solid-state physics, radiation protection, and so on, Argentina believes that exposure of Latin Americans and others to its technology and personnel is the most efficient and economical means to introduce the international community to the country's nuclear capabilities. Buenos Aires sees the students who attend the offerings as its best ambassadors to sell the world on its nuclear technology.

In addition to multilateral endeavors, Argentina has entered into a number of bilateral agreements to exchange knowledge and technology on the nuclear fuel cycle, radiological protection, nuclear safety, safeguards, and power reactor components. The most important agreements include the following.

Bilateral Agreements

Algeria. In 1985, Algeria negotiated three contracts with Argentina to procure fuel elements for a subcritical facility, a research reactor to produce radioisotopes, and a pilot nuclear fuel plant.[12] Although there is some civil engineering collaboration between CNEA and its subsidiary, Invap S.A., and Algerian companies, Argentine firms conduct most of the plant, equipment, and architectural engineering. The contracts also include Argentine training of Algerian personnel. In 1988, Buenos Aires shipped 80 kilograms of Uranium enriched to 19.7% to Algeria which fueled an Argentine-imported research reactor. The reactor commenced operations in 1989.

Brazil. In 1980, Argentina entered into negotiations with Brazil for the exchange of nuclear technology and know-how. The resulting accord allows Brazil's NUCLEP to provide parts for Argentina's Atucha II pressure vessel and 10,000 meters of zircalloy tubing. A 1984 accord provides for exchange of information on the fuel cycle, enrichment,[13] safety, nuclear instrumentation, plasma technology, and fast reactors, and an accord with Brazil's Nuclebras includes an exchange of information and assistance on nuclear reactor technology.[14]

In February 1985, the two Latin American neighbors reached agreement in principle on mutual inspection of nuclear facilities to verify peaceful intent.[15] In the realm of safety, a 1986 convention provided for notification and assistance in the event of nuclear accident. Also in 1985, to address security concerns, the two parties signed a joint declaration reaffirming a commitment to develop nuclear energy for peaceful purposes.[16] More recently, in September 1987, collaboration extended to sharing information on uranium enrichment.

Peru. In 1980, Argentina entered into an agreement with Peru.[17] Under its terms, Buenos Aires provides Lima with two research reactors, the largest being 10MW(t); a radiological protection laboratory; and auxiliary installations. The facilities are under construction. Sponsored by the Central Bank of Peru, Argentine companies provide most of the engineering, equipment, and training of Peru's IPEN personnel through courses and hands-on job experience. Fuel for the plants will come from Argentina's Pilcaniyeu enrichment facility. In addition, Argentina will aid Lima in the production of radioisotopes for agricultural, medical, and industrial purposes.[18] Argentina will also help Peru map its uranium reserves and construct a pilot plant that will be able to process thirty tons of uranium per year.

Rumania. Argentina's relationship with Rumania emerged as a result of contacts developed at IAEA-sponsored meetings on fuel manufacturing and the fuel cycle generally. In 1986, Buenos Aires exported to Bucharest a specially designed welding machine for fuel tubing, which had been developed for the domestic market.

Turkey. Like those with Rumania, Argentine contacts with Turkey emerged from interchanges at IAEA-sponsored meetings. Argentine engineers provide Turkey with technical assistance and training in Ankara's ongoing construction of one power reactor. Through INVAP, Argentina also furnished Turkey with a furnace to sinter UO_2 pellets. In 1988 the two countries signed a fifteen-year cooperation agreement.

Yugoslavia. Technical-informational assistance to several Yugoslav nuclear research centers characterizes Argentina's current role. Plans are more ambitious. They include Argentine offers to design and construct a pilot uranium ore-processing plan, a fuel element pilot plant, and a heavy-water plant.

Italy. A private concern in Argentina, Techint, conducted engineering work on behalf of Italian firms for the French Superphoenix breeder reactor.

Iran. Argentina has negotiated an agreement with Iran to reshape the core of its small research reactor to permit the utilization of uranium enriched up to 20 percent in lieu of the current 93 percent requirements.

Israel. Rumors have abounded for years that Argentina entered into transactions with Israel.[19] The reports concern the supply of raw material. A former CNEA official confirmed that Buenos Aires delivered a metric ton of yellowcake in the mid-1960s. By the mid-1970s, links may have extended to cooperation in nuclear fuel cycle development. Under the Alfonsin regime, all nuclear ties reportedly came to a halt, although Israel has raised the possibility of future nuclear commerce.

Pakistan and Libya. Both Pakistan and Libya have approached Argentina for assistance. To date, Buenos Aires has provided noncritical components and technologies to enhance nuclear safety and radiological protection.

Czechoslovakia. Czechoslovakia has proposed joint marketing of Argentine goods to Latin America and Europe.[20] The inquiry came as the two countries discussed joint development of Argentina's uranium reserves and fuel cycle technology.

West Germany. Argentina's Enace has engaged Germany's KWU in a joint venture to design a pressurized heavy-water reactor (PHWR) using state-of-the-art technology.[21] The success of Atucha I stimulated the undertaking.

Pending Ventures

In addition to the foregoing agreements, Argentine pursuits include a number of other ventures. Enace S.A., Techint S.A., and Argatom are among

Argentine companies that have prepared offers with Spain's ENSA and West Germany's KWU to complete construction of Iran's two Bushehr plants.[22] They also have offered to provide engineering and technology for Egypt's planned nuclear plants to be situated about 150 miles east of Alexandria. In Latin America, Argentina is in negotiation with Colombia and Uruguay to furnish facilities similar to those it provided Peru. In 1986, Argentina signed a nuclear cooperation agreement with Cuba. In East Asia, INVAP entered into a like compact with China as it did in Africa with Nigeria.[23] Table 6–3 provides additional information on these and other agreements.

Transhipping

Argentina has shunned the role of transshipper, taking the position that it aims to promote its own technology, not the capabilities of others.

Conclusions

In comparison to such traditional nuclear suppliers as Germany, France, and the United States, Argentina's involvement in the international nuclear market is modest. The program generates about $100 million of business. Nonetheless, Buenos Aires has ambitions to play a more formidable role. However, its ability for the moment has inherent limits. Lack of capital to finance projects is a major impediment. There also are technological restraints, such as the inability to provide steam generators and large reactor cores. As a result, Buenos Aires has focused its attention on the supply of basic technological information, research reactors, and ancillary services for other vendors of nuclear plants.

Argentina's Nuclear Export Safeguard Requirements and Structures

Although Argentina has not codified its nuclear export practices (such codification is being written), procedures have been routinized.

For an export to take place, the importer must contact CNEA, which, in turn, reports the request to the office of Argentina's president and the Department of Nuclear Affairs and Disarmament in the Ministry of Foreign Affairs. Under Presidential Decree No. 376/86, signed 13 March 1986, the ministry bears the responsibility to assess the implications of nuclear exports on nonproliferation. The department coordinates its evaluation with CNEA, which communicates the assessment to the president. Parliament enters decision making when regulations must be modified to consummate transactions. Figures 6–1 and 6–2 illustrate this decision-making process.

Table 6–3
Argentina's Nuclear Cooperation Agreements

Country	Date of Origin	Type of Cooperation	Sources
Algeria	3-12-84 ratified 27-04-87	Research	Ley 23424
Bolivia	19-03-1970	Research-minerals-protection energy	Ley 18814
Brazil	17-05-80 17-05-80 CNEA and Nuclebras 17-05-80 CNEA and CNEN	Research-fuel cycle-radioisotopes Energy-minerals-zircalloy-fuel production power reactors Research-radioisotopes-licensing	Internal CNEA
Canada	30-01-1976 (10 years) Now renegotiating	Research-energy-technology	Internal CNEA
Colombia	15-09-1967	Research-minerals-radiation-protection-energy	Internal CNEA
Chile	17-03-1974 13-11-1976	Research-reactors-radiation-protection-radioiosotopes-other applications	Internal CNEA
Cuba	8-11-1986	Food irradiation-nuclear instrumentation-nuclear-physics-waste management-metallurgy-minerals	Internal CNEA
Ecuador	5-04-1976	Research-isotopes-minerals-radiation protection	Internal CNEA
Federal Republic of Germany	8-10-1981 31-3-1969 29-7-1971 CNEA y GfK	Radiation-protection-licensing-basic research and development physics-nuclear accelerators-reactors fuel cycle	Internal CNEA
India	28-05-1974	Research	Internal CNEA
Korea	11-02-1980 CNEA and Korea Electric Co	Nuclear power	Internal CNEA
Paraguay	20-07-1967	Research-energy	Internal CNEA
Peru	25-05-1968	Research-energy-radiation-protection Other basic fields	Internal CNEA
Spain	30-11-1978	Fuel cycle-nuclear power reactors equipments-radioisotopes and radiation	Internal CNEA
United States	22-06-1962 8-06-1964 25-07-1969	Research reactors	
Uruguay	08-07-1968	Research, energy, radiation protection	Law 17938 approved 21-10-1968
Venezuela	8-08-1979	Research reactors, radioisotopes, minerals, nuclear technology	Internal CNEA
Yugoslavia	23-09-1982	Research reactors, nuclear power reactors, radioisotopes, radiation protection	Law 23387
Peoples Republic of China	15-04-1985	Research reactors, safety, radioisotopes NPP-engineering, fabrication and supply of components, waste management, radiation protection	To be approved by Argentine law

Figure 6–1. Organization Flowchart for Nuclear Export Decisions

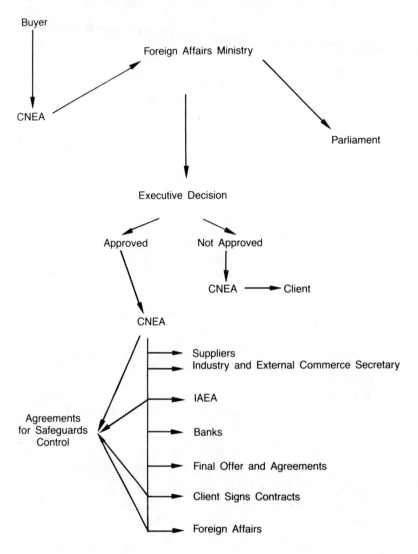

When an export meets with approval—not a foregone conclusion, as some have been denied—CNEA will execute the contract for sale on condition that the importer certifies in writing that it will use the imports only for peaceful purposes and that it enter into a safeguard agreement with the International Atomic Energy Agency. Argentina requires that all exports be covered by IAEA safeguards under INFCIRC/66/rev2.[24]

Figure 6–2. Distribution of Responsibilities of the Different Partners

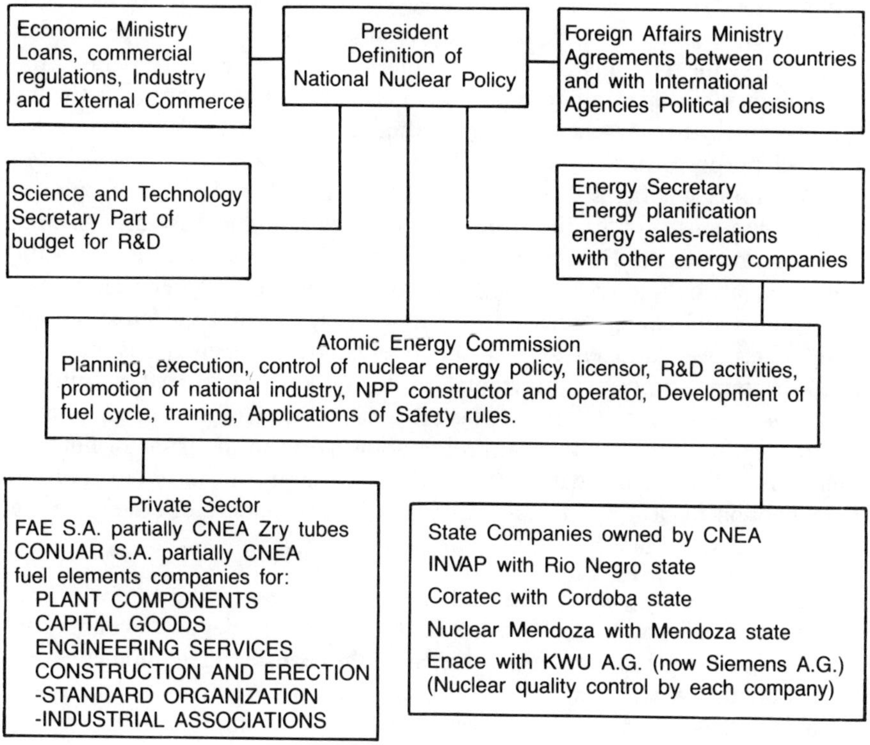

Economic Ministry Loans, commercial regulations, Industry and External Commerce	President Definition of National Nuclear Policy	Foreign Affairs Ministry Agreements between countries and with International Agencies Political decisions
Science and Technology Secretary Part of budget for R&D		Energy Secretary Energy planification energy sales-relations with other energy companies

Atomic Energy Commission
Planning, execution, control of nuclear energy policy, licensor, R&D activities, promotion of national industry, NPP constructor and operator, Development of fuel cycle, training, Applications of Safety rules.

Private Sector FAE S.A. partially CNEA Zry tubes CONUAR S.A. partially CNEA fuel elements companies for: PLANT COMPONENTS CAPITAL GOODS ENGINEERING SERVICES CONSTRUCTION AND ERECTION -STANDARD ORGANIZATION -INDUSTRIAL ASSOCIATIONS	State Companies owned by CNEA INVAP with Rio Negro state Coratec with Cordoba state Nuclear Mendoza with Mendoza state Enace with KWU A.G. (now Siemens A.G.) (Nuclear quality control by each company)

Efforts under way to codify procedures will formalize objectives and standards for both the domestic market and exports. Plans call for authority to be given to CNEA to execute nonproliferation review procedures.

Argentina and the Nuclear Nonproliferation Regime

Argentina's commitment to nonproliferation was born in ambiguity, given the involvement of a Nazi scientist, Ronald Richter, who declared in 1951 that the country had acquired the capability to build a hydrogen weapon.[25] Although the announcement was a hoax, a nuclear weapons hue always has clouded Argentina's program in the minds of proliferation analysts.

Publicly, every Argentine leader has dismissed speculation that the country is bent on acquiring nuclear weapons, although it has admitted to the capability.[26] Still, though muted since Alfonsin assumed the presidency, suspicions remain. Buenos Aires' unwillingness to sign the Nuclear Non-Proliferation Treaty and ratify the Treaty of Tlateloco fuels the concern. The secretive pursuit of domestic plutonium and enrichment production capabilities, the prominence of the military in directing the program, the unwillingness to open all facilities to international inspection and, finally, the insistence that Argentina reserves the right to test nuclear devices for peaceful purposes further cast a pall over the program.

Argentina justifies its policies on the grounds that although it opposes nuclear weapons proliferation—indeed, a policy it uttered as early as May 1950 in Presidential Decree No. 10936—it rejects the tools used by the international community to achieve that objective. From its perspective, the NPT and the London Nuclear Suppliers Groups (NSG) guidelines represent superpower duplicity.[27] On the one hand, the Americans and the Russians try to prevent "horizontal proliferation" (the spread of nuclear weapons to other countries); on the other hand, they engage in an insatiable nuclear arms race—"vertical proliferation." And in the name of nonproliferation, they, along with other NSG suppliers endeavor to keep a monopoly on nuclear supply and, thereby, the dependence of others. In the words of Castro Madero:

> Secretly, ignoring the IAEA and without listening to the countries in receipt of that technology, the Club established safeguards conditions that were more rigid as regards the transfer of equipment, materials and services. . . . In fact this implied a flagrant violation of Article 4 of the NPT, as well as being an attempt to maintain hegemony in the industrial field and dependence on the part of the countries receiving nuclear supplies.[28]

While excoriating the NSG suppliers, Argentina, in practice, acts almost as if it were a member. It places all of its exports under IAEA safeguards, although it does not require full-scope safeguards. In 1986, it announced that it would restrict exports of enrichment and reprocessing technology unless they were part of a larger sale of nuclear equipment, presumably because this would demonstrate that a country intended to use such facilities for nuclear energy.[29] Finally, to reduce tensions with Brazil, Buenos Aires has entered into discussions to open the facilities of both countries to mutual inspection.

Conclusions

The commercial nuclear export activity of Argentina at this time is modest. To date, the country has not exported any big-ticket items. Its most significant nuclear exports are research reactors. Nonetheless, its potential is growing. In one sense, it has a natural market in Latin America, which it has cultivated over the years through a variety of training programs. Whether the inroads it has made in Peru in particular are a harbinger for the rest of the continent is uncertain at this time, given the competition that Buenos Aires will inevitably confront from traditional suppliers. As Etel Solingen points out in this volume (chapter 7), Argnetina does not face any substantial competition from its only potential Latin competitor, Brazil.

For Argentina, the international nuclear energy market affords some unique opportunities. As the country acquires greater nuclear know-how, it will be able to compete with the traditional suppliers in some limited areas. This is a matter of considerable pride. But more than pride and prestige, from the point of view of Argentine policymakers, nuclear energy in the long term will help improve the country's balance of payments. It will also create new commercial markets.

There is no evidence in the public literature to suggest that Argentina has been anything but responsible as a nuclear exporter. This responsibility seems to be growing, as recent public announcements suggest that Buenos Aires will restrain its export of sensitive nuclear technologies. Ironically, given its criticism of the NSG suppliers, Argentina appears to have largely adopted their norms through the requirement that safeguards be placed over all exports. It is apparent that the present civilian government in Buenos Aires has fostered a more forthcoming attitude toward the international nuclear regime. Codification of developing norms, therefore, is important and is a direction the country is now prepared to take. Whether this will be sufficient routinization to overcome other inclinations of future governments is something we can only hope for. It is therefore incumbent on traditional suppliers to invite Argentina's participation in the development of future supplier standards to reinforce the nonproliferation norm.

Notes

1. For a review of the problems Argentina has had in financing Atucha II, see "ENACD Director Discusses Major Nuclear Challenges," *Clarin*, 31 May 1985, p. 18, in JPRS-TND85-013, 24 July 1985, p. 8; "Argentina," *Nuclear Engineering International* (June 1987): 47.

2. "Argentina to Tender for Heavy Water After June Purchase from China," *Nucleonics Week*, 25 September 1986, p. 5.

3. For an informative elaboration of Argentina's goal of nuclear independence, see Castro Madero's rationale for Bueno Aires' acquisition of an enrichment capability in *La Nacion*, 18–19 June 1984.

4. For elaboration, see Leonard S. Spector, *Going Nuclear* (Cambridge, Mass.: Ballinger, 1987) pp. 193–97.

5. J. Katz, *Desarrollo y Crisis de la Capacidad Tecnologica Latinoamerica*, 1986, available from Sara Tanis.

6. S.V. Tanis, *Evaluacion de la Capacidad Industrial Atgentina y Desarrollo de los Proveedores para Instalaciones Nucleares*, IAEA-SR-124/8, available from Sara Tanis.

7. CNEA, *Formulario CNEA*, No. 176, available from Sara Tanis.

8. Private communication from Raul Boix Amat (ex-president of Argentine Association of Nuclear Technology), available from Sara Tanis.

9. *Transactions of the First and Second International Conferences on Transfer of Nuclear Technology*, 1978, 1982, available from Sara Tanis.

10. Banco Provincia Buenos Aires, "Seminario Internacional Sobre Capital de Riesgo de Innovacion Tecnologica y Pequena y Mediana Empresa," various papers, *Serie Technologica*, 1986

11. Proyecto Multinacional de Metalurgia OEA-CNEA, "Resumen de Actividates, 1969–1974," Internal publication published by the project, available from Sara Tanis.

12. "Research Reactor for Algeria," TELAM, 0000 GMT, 27 May 1985, in JPRS-TND-85, 26 June 1985, p. 14.

13. "Program with Argentina" EFE, 2330 GMT, 10 September 1986, in JPRS-TND-86-021, 2 October 1986, p. 19.

14. Declaracion Conjunta Sobre Politica Nuclear del Gobierno de la Republica Argentina y el Gobierno de la Republica Federative de Brasil, 10 de Diciembre de 1986, y sus Anexos al Protocolo Nol. 11, available from Sara Tanis.

15. "Mutual Inspection Agreement Mapped Out," *Nuclear News* (May 1985): 86; "Alfonsin-Sarney Meeting Includes Inspection Talk," *Nuclear News* (January 1986): 82.

16. "Alfonsin, Sarney Sign Nuclear Declaration," TELAM, 1533 GMT, 30 November 1985, in JPRS-TND-001, 9 January 1986, p. 20.

17. J. Barreda Delgado, "Peru: Transferencia de Tecnologia, un Consejo Para el Proyecto Argentino," in *El Desarrollo Nuclear Argentino*, 1985, available from Sara Tanis.

18. "Argentina to Aid Peru in Production of Radioisotopes," *El Comercio*, 19 December 1985, p. A-6, in JPRS-TND-86-003, 4 February 1986, p. 5.

19. "Argentine Officials Deny Rumors of Nuclear Trade with Israel," *Nucleonics Week*, 29 May 1986, pp. 6–7.

20. "Argentina," *Nucleonics Week*, 17 November 1985, p. 12.

21. "PHWR 200—An Attractive Option for Developing Countries," *Nuclear Engineering International* (May 1986): 33.

22. "Iran Seeking Way to Finish Bushehr Plant but Bonn Denies Exports," *Nucleonics Week*, 30 October 1986, p. 5.

23. "Caputo on Nuclear Accord with PRC, Other Issues," TELAM, 456 GMT, 16 April 1985, in JPRS-TND-009, 23 May 1985, p. 42; "Argentina/Nigeria: Cooperation Agreement Signed," *Nucleonics Week*, 22 September 1988, p. 13.

24. J. Martinez Favini, *Derecho y Politica Nuclear*, available from Sara Tanis.

25. For a history of Argentina's nuclear program, see Douglas L. Tweedale, "Argentina," in James Everett Katz and Onkar S. Marwah, eds., *Nuclear Power in Developing Countries* (Lexington, Mass.: Lexington Books, 1982) pp. 79–96; and

Daniel Poneman, *Nuclear Power in the Developing World* (London: Allen and Unwin, 1982), pp. 68–83.

26. "Nuclear Program Said Capable of Atomic Bomb" *Folha de Sao Paulo*, 4 November 1986, p. 6, in JPKS-TND-86-026, 3 December 1986, p. 25.

27. J.C. Carasales, *El Desarme de los Desarmados: Argentina y el Tratado de No Proliferacion de Armas Nucleares* (Buenos Aires: Pleamar, 1987).

28. Quoted in Antonio Sanchez-Gijon, "Argentina," in Harald Muller, ed., *A European Non-Proliferation Policy: Prospects and Problems* (Oxford: Oxford University Press, 1987), pp 391–92.

29. "Argentina Won't Export Sensitive Technologies Without Safeguards," *Nucleonics Week*, 27 Feburary 1987, p. 7.

7
Brazil: Technology, Countertrade, and Nuclear Exports

Etel Solingen

T echnological advances by newly industrialized countries (NICs) have become a central concern of the recent literature on the political economy of development. Striking a fatal blow to dependency thinking, in so far as it had diagnosed a "structural" barrier to technological development, these countries have absorbed foreign technology and have developed a very impressive domestic technological capacity. Moreover, their exports have evolved from a traditional reliance on raw materials and unprocessed goods to include increasingly sophisticated manufactured goods and technology itself. The capabilities, motivations, and structures behind nuclear exports must be examined in light of these secular trends.

Technology, trade, debt, and competitiveness dominate Brazilian foreign policy. President Sarney's speech announcing the achievements of Brazil's "parallel nuclear program" reflected the centrality of nuclear exports:

> In the future as today, nuclear energy will constitute one of the major markets in the industrialized world. We should prepare for that future, in order to share in it, by developing technology, producing reactors, and selling fuel; in other words, by, on an equal footing, seeking out new spaces and creating wealth domestically to improve our people's standard of living.[1]

This exploratory analysis of the country's emergence as a nuclear supplier focuses on six major areas: (1) the balance of motivations and constraints underlying Brazil's nuclear export potential; (2) areas of extant capabilities that would allow the country to play a significant role as a

I would like to thank UCLA's Center for International and Strategic Affairs, the University of California's Institute on Global Conflict and Cooperation, and UCLA's Latin American Center for their support. I also thank Scott Thollefson and Jan K. Black for their helpful criticism.

nuclear supplier; (3) formal and informal structures beneath nuclear export policy; (4) patterns of nuclear trade as reflected in past transactions; (5) prospects for continuity and change; (6) generalizability of findings to other emerging suppliers.

Brazil's first power plant (Angra 1) was purchased from Westinghouse in 1971 and has been fully operational only since 1987, due to technical difficulties. In 1975 an agreement between the state firm Nuclebrás and West Germany's Kraftwerk Union (KWU) established the following provisions: (1) eight 1100 MW(e) pressurized water reactors (PWRs); (2) prospecting, extraction, and processing of uranium minerals; (3) production of reactors and components; (4) enrichment and reprocessing technologies (See Appendix 1). IAEA safeguards, applying also to replicas of the enrichment and reprocessing plants, accompanied the agreement.

None of the power plants is operating yet and the whole structure in existence since 1975 was transformed in 1988, with the dissolution of Nuclebrás and transfer of all power plants (including the two scheduled to operate in the mid-1990s) and the engineering subsidiary NUCLEN to the state utility Eletrobrás. The heavy components subsidiary NUCLEP and NUCLEMON were privatized, the fuel elements plant transferred to Uranium of Brazil, and NUSTEP and NUCLAM dissolved. The commercial reprocessing plant has been postponed indefinitely. Figure 7–1 contrasts the old sectoral organization with the one introduced in 1988.

Beyond capabilities acquired through the agreement with West Germany's KWU, Brazil has been involved in the development of national nuclear technologies through the so-called parallel program, which is not subject to international safeguards.[2] An announcement that Brazil was capable of laboratory-scale production of plutonium in 1986 was followed by the inauguration of a gas centrifuge uranium enrichment plant in 1988.[3] Before turning to a more detailed analysis of capabilities, let us first review the potential calculus of risks and opportunities underlying nuclear exports.

Motivations and Constraints

The first part of this section examines technological, commercial, and political incentives for engaging in nuclear exports. The second part suggests possible constraints, such as market mechanisms, financial bottlenecks, and political and moral considerations. Legal barriers, particularly those related to the sensitive aspect of nuclear technology, will be discussed separately later in this chapter.

The Technological Dimension

A major incentive in Brazil's drive toward nuclear exports must be found in the broader context of its foreign economic policy. "Deteriorating terms of

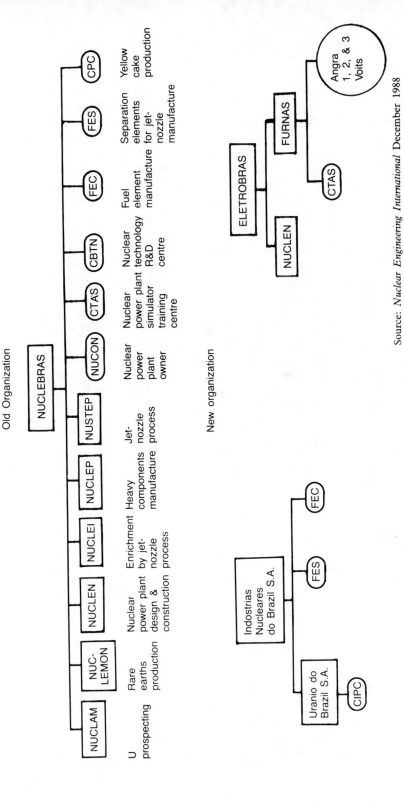

Old Organization

NUCLAM	NUC-LEMON	NUCLEN	NUCLEI	NUCLEP	NUSTEP
U prospecting	Rare earths production	Nuclear power plant design & construction	Enrichment by jet-nozzle process	Heavy components manufacture	Jet-nozzle process

NUCLEBRAS

NUCON	CTAS	CBTN	FEC	FES	CPC
Nuclear power plant owner	Nuclear power plant simulator training centre	Nuclear power plant technology R&D centre	Fuel element manufacture	Separation elements for jet-nozzle manufacture	Yellow cake production

New organization

Indostrias Nucleares do Brazil S.A.
— FEC
— FES

Uranio do Brazil S.A.
— CIPC

ELETROBRAS
— NUCLEN
— FURNAS
  — CTAS
  — Angra 1, 2, & 3 Voits

Source: *Nuclear Engineering International* December 1988

Figure 7–1. Sectoral Organization

trade" and dependency on exports of unprocessed goods have been at the core of the debate over development. They have, to a large extent, given rise to early theories of "dependency" (Raúl Prebisch and the Economic Commission for Latin America group) and "unequal exchange" (Emmanuel, 1969). Technology exports are often considered an indicator of changes in comparative advantage resulting from industrialization and technological development (Dahlman and Sercovich, 1984). Beyond actual revenues, technology exports are associated with the external benefit of strengthening the growth of domestic capabilities, often referred to as "learning by exporting" and "learning by teaching" effects.[4] In an attempt to change its exports structure, Brazil has targeted "increasingly narrower slices of industrial products requiring relatively more sophisticated technology" (WBCS, 1980). Nuclear exports, therefore, must be studied in the context of this shift from exports of raw materials to manufactures, to sophisticated equipment, to technical services, to patents and licenses.

The view that processed exports are preferable to unprocessed ones for a country's economic development is quite widespread (Firebaugh and Bullock, 1986) and became an underpinning of Brazil's so-called economic miracle of 1969–74. However, the role of exports has remained a bone of contention between advocates of import substitution and those favoring export-led industrialization. Brazil maintained the world's third-largest positive trade balance in 1988, reaching $19 billion. Exports of capital goods, engineering, and construction projects—encouraged through fiscal and financial incentives—tend to account for most of Brazil's technology exports.[5] The 1975 decision to establish Nuclep (Nuclebras' joint venture with KWU—see figure 7–2), with an eye on potential exports of heavy components, fits neatly into this set of priorities.

The concern for acquiring technological competence in the nuclear area arose as early as 1947, when the Commission for the Study and Control of Strategic Minerals was created within the National Security Council (Morel, 1979). The demand for "specific compensations" became a cornerstone of Brazilian nuclear export policy in the early 1950s. Conceived and promoted by Admiral Alvaro Alberto, director of the Conselho Nacional de Pesquisas (CNPq), this policy required that the United States provide Brazil with technology in exchange for uranium exports. This early emphasis on technology absorption was geared not only to offset political dependencies but also to ensure Brazil's own ability to become a supplier in an oligopolistic market.

The general tendency to expand Brazilian exports in project design, geological and mineral prospecting and research, and engineering and construction services could promote the particular case of nuclear exports in these areas. These priorities imply an ability to put together, schedule, and supervise large-scale projects. The importance attached to this objective can

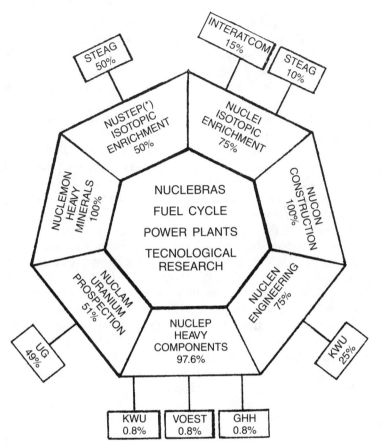

Source: Nuclebras, *Annual Report* 1984, (Adapted)

Figure 7–2. Nucleabras and Subsidiaries

be inferred, perhaps, from Brazil's willingness to cooperate with Argentina in advancing common technological objectives and improving their joint export potential.[6]

The Commercial Dimension

The need for foreign exchange is a straightforward incentive for engaging in export activities, particularly in light of Brazil's $117 billion foreign debt (in 1988), the highest in the Third World. Exports of uranium, power plant components, and nuclear engineering services were declared a main objective of the 1975 agreements.[7] The potential for uranium exports, including enriched uranium, was mentioned at the outset (in 1976) as a justification for continued investment in uranium exploitation. Sales of yellowcake to Turkey were justified as a way of financing the production of enriched uranium. In advancing the construction of a new uranium enrichment plant, the minister of mines and energy, Cesar Cals, stated that in the 1990s, countries with an effective capacity to exploit and enrich uranium "will have more strength in the world than the present oil producers."[8] Moreover, enriched uranium exports would, according to Cals, finance Brazil's nuclear program.

The domestic economic crisis of the late 1970s and early 1980s was reflected in widespread idle capacity in industry. This contraction of domestic markets gave strong impetus to capital goods exports.[9] Against this background, the minister of mines and energy, Shigeaki Ueki, advanced the idea of Brazilian exports of nuclear reactors in 1978.[10] Production of all heavy components of the nuclear steam supply system became the domain of Nuclebrás' subsidiary Nuclep, a joint venture with West German firms. The suspension of six (of the eight) plants originally projected paralyzed Nuclep, designed to produce components for at least one power plant a year shortly after it entered production in 1980.[11] Thus, the possibility of exports not only became a compelling solution for Nuclebrás managers, but served political considerations as well. Nuclep's creation became a bone of contention between state technocrats and private entrepreneurs, who regarded the subsidiary as a competitor in the custom-made capital goods sector. Turning it to satisfy potential foreign demand could deflate some of the pressure against increased "*estatização*."[12]

Commercial considerations enter the analysis of nuclear export potential in yet another way. Various compensatory trade mechanisms, which reduce the amount of foreign exchange required to purchase equipment and services, have become a pervasive feature of international economic transactions. Countertrade arrangements are estimated today to cover roughly one-third of world trade, up from less than one-tenth in the mid-1960s (Neuman, 1985). Compensation agreements, for instance, commit the original exporter of technical aid to accept repayment with related output. Buyback arrangements require the foreign seller of machinery to purchase part of the output. Brazil has required suppliers of mining machinery to buy at least half of the output.

The recently dissolved joint venture Nuclam (see figure 7–2) ensured the German technology supplier the equivalent of 20 percent of uranium reserves, with a potential increase to 49 percent, conditional on Brazil's approval.[13] Similar arrangements with Japanese firms are being considered for Nuclemon's rare-earth processing activities. Other compensatory mechanisms facilitating nuclear trade included attracting foreign financing (French and German) for uranium concentrate plants in exchange for a percentage of the output. Through another type of transaction—leasing—

Brazil obtained yellowcake from West Germany, the United Kingdom, France, and Argentina and repaid them when its own uranium concentrate plant began operating.

Brazil has been particularly active in pursuing barter transactions, often in exchange for Middle Eastern and African oil. A 1978 agreement provided for the exchange of Venezuelan oil for Brazilian technical assistance in radioactive mineral prospecting and planning of nuclear plant construction.[14] The possibility of exchanging nuclear equipment and assistance for oil was also discussed. The proliferation of barter agreements in the post-1974 era may have significant implications for nuclear trade (which I discuss later in this chapter). The tendency to engage in barter deals, which facilitate trade, may be strengthened by Brazil's foreign balance of payments difficulties. It is not yet clear, however, whether the pattern may result in lowering the threshold of reluctance to export certain technologies. Brazil's relations with Iraq provide an example of how bilateral interdependence can strengthen tendencies to barter—in this case, oil for arms and uranium. As early as 1975, Brazil commited itself to supply Iraq with low-enriched uranium, safety technology, the IAEA's nuclear information system, and personnel training (Redick, 1981). Although certain "issue linkages" are created through these forms of countertrade, they tend to be dynamic. Thus, on the one hand, significant new oil discoveries in Brazil have diminished considerably the pressures for external procurement of energy sources that characterized Brazil's foreign economic policy in the 1970s. On the other hand, pressures for debt-for-exports conversions may turn certain exports into instruments for managing Brazil's foreign debt.

The Political Dimension

Domestic and international political and strategic factors can play as both incentives and constraints. Brazil's aspiration to a leading regional and international status has been analyzed extensively (Quester, 1979; Redick, 1981; Selcher, 1981; Wesson, 1981; Roett, 1985). Domestically, the country's transition from military rule since 1985—led by President José Sarney, of the military-backed Liberal Front Party culminated in the drafting and approval of a new constitution in 1988, stating that "all nuclear activities on the nation's territory shall be permitted for peaceful purposes only and with the approval of the National Congress" (Spector, 1988). This provision does not necessarily imply technical oversight by the congress. The complexity of the domestic politics level of analysis requires the disaggregation of motivations across a number of actors: the military, the powerful Foreign Ministry (Itamaraty), nuclear sectoral agencies, industrial entrepreneurs, the scientific community, and political parties. Defining the nature and strength of these actors and their reflection in the Brazilian state is no simple task. The attempt to do so becomes entangled in a debate—among statist, pluralist, and Marxist interpretations of the state—that is beyond the scope of this chapter.[15]

It is safe to argue, however, that the record of Brazilian industrial entrepreneurs in the nuclear sector has been, to a large extent, a reflection of broader patterns of state–private sector interaction in the last twenty years. National industry adjusted to its role as a junior partner in the "triple alliance" between state, private local, and foreign capital between 1964 and 1974. Its influence increased toward the latter part of the 1970s, as it coordinated the attack on uncontrolled *estatização*. The creation of the state firm Nuclep (discussed earlier) provided a major rallying point for national industrial and engineering firms reacting against such market-displacing behavior on the part of the state.

Brazil's powerful and diversified industry of the 1980s provides a solid foundation for the production of power plant components. Although industrialists have not appeared eager to invest in nuclear-related exports in the past, given the policy uncertainty of the nuclear program, the privatization of Nuclep (the heavy components plant designed with an eye on foreign demand) could change their investment calculus. Firms in the areas of project design, engineering, and construction of turnkey plants (predominantly in the front end of the fuel cycle) have been most active thus far. Some firms have increased their involvement with the Nuclear Energy Commission (CNEN) since 1980, in the development of new processes and products.[16] Entrepreneurial opportunities will be affected in the future not only by market uncertainties but also by the extent and nature of state inducements, in the form of fiscal benefits, credit, subsidies, and other measures. In turn, the increased political power of private industrialists in the 1980s may influence the nature and extent of state intervention in this area.

Another corporate actor, the military, is ridden with internal cleavages regarding most political and economic issues, and nuclear priorities are no exception. Disagreement between officers who favored cooperation with Argentina and those who opposed it has recently been reported.[17] It is not yet clear how these conflicts may affect policy regarding nuclear exports. Possibly, with some marginal differences regarding the question of safeguards, the consensus may favor such activities, given the element of prestige attached to them and their association with high technology, a long-time motto of the armed forces' approach to security and development. As the military's role in the new political reality is far from weakened, it is not inconceivable that civilian leaders would yield to a variety of political and economic conditions as a payoff for keeping the military away from direct political control of the state. Such trade-offs may include continuous support for the conventional arms industry, which makes commercial sense to at least some civilian politicians, and possibly for nuclear-related projects.[18]

Constraints: Nuclear Markets and Financial Bottlenecks

Various considerations here are influenced by the conditions of the international nuclear market: Will it continue to be depressed in the short and medium terms, with potential for expansion in the long one? What are the real and perceived effects of Chernobyl regarding continued demand for nuclear power? Who are the potential buyers of which items? Will Brazil be able to compete with traditional suppliers? Under what conditions would it be favored in international bids, in light of its "newcomer" status? The uncertainty regarding market conditions notwithstanding, it is important to integrate the following considerations in the analysis of demand. Beyond the respective energy calculus of potential buyers, developing countries continue to regard nuclear technology as having positive synergistic effects on a country's economic, scientific, and technological infrastructure. Although largely an assumption of mythical proportions, the perception of nuclear technology as a developmental panacea may well offset market-related constraints.[19]

The incentives of state and private exporters will nevertheless be significantly affected by international economic factors, including the prospects of competing with traditional suppliers and the dynamics of comparative advantage. The latter may tilt toward countries such as Argentina and Brazil in engineering services (given the low-overhead cost of managerial and technical staff). In equipment, however, Brazil may be able to compete only if costs can be reduced enough (through elimination of superfluous "baroqueness," for instance) to offset the technological leadership of traditional suppliers. Dual-use items, including electronic equipment and instrumentation, will be less influenced by purely nuclear markets.

In general, three major considerations should be taken into account regarding domestic and international economic conditions. First, from the point of view of prospective demand, potential buyers are no less constrained by their external debt than Brazil is. Nuclep's bids for two Mexican plants, for instance, fell victim to Mexico's freeze of its nuclear program as a consequence of its own economic crisis. Capital costs for a 600–900 MW(e) plant were theoretically about $2 billion in 1985, yet actual costs have risen to over $4 billion in Argentina (Atucha 2) and $5 billion in Brazil (Angra 2 and 3).[20]

Second, from the supplier's perspective, Brazilian firms provide a diversified basket of industrial exports, in which the proportion of nuclear-related items is very small. It may be argued that local firms are less focused on nuclear exports than is the case, for instance, in Argentina, where a number of enterprises—active through the Argentine Association for Nuclear Technology—concentrate mostly in nuclear products and services.[21]

Finally, the motivation and ability to export is intricately related to the availability of financing. This may not always present a problem, as with the 1984 sale of an uranium concentrate plant to Somalia, financed by the Somali-Arab Mining Company.[22] On another occasion, however, Nuclebrás could not approve the sale of 370 tons of yellowcake per year (1985–89) to a U.S. firm and another shipment to Turkey because of financial difficulties within the uranium concentrate plant and the Planning Secretariat's unwillingness to authorize new investments.[23] The ability to provide at least partial financing will tend to vary according to the scope of export projects. Small facilities, some engineering services, and selected equipment may find greater access to national financial sources (such as the National Bank for Social and Economic Development—BNDES) than large-scale projects.

A recent shift in World Bank policy, reflected in its role in the Turkish nuclear program, may herald a greater willingness on its part to cofinance nuclear power projects with other bilateral and commercial sources or at least to facilitate financing mechanisms and guarantees.[24] The expansion in the number of suppliers may make it easier to apply the basic rules of competitive bidding.[25] Yet the expansion of traditional suppliers' nuclear exports was largely related to their capability to link prospective sales to attractive financial arrangements. These included bilateral loans and suppliers' credits backed by supplier states eager to assist their own exporters. It is doubtful that Brazil will be able to generate this kind of financial leverage, at least in the near future. In addition, advocates of nuclear exports will need to convince their own entrepreneurs and public technocrats (including central banks and development banks)—in their search for subsidies, fiscal incentives, and income tax deductions—of the feasibility of such exports.[26] This point shifts our attention to broader political considerations.

Political Restraint

Domestically, the new constitutional era will undoubtedly be felt in aspects of the nuclear program that involve budgetary commitments and legislative approval. Thus, given the emerging tension in Brazil's political life induced by the need to address the country's morally reprobate (and politically explosive) social problems, it will be hard to conceive broad-based support for investments associated with the nuclear program. The public image of the nuclear program has increasingly been one of wastefulness, inefficiency, and failure, accounting for about 4 percent of the foreign debt in 1984.[27] Political parties, particularly those on the left, may tend to articulate popular dissatisfaction and limit investments in programs often associated with military uses and perceived to siphon off resources from social priorities. The first Latin American conference of democratic political parties condemned the presence and production of nuclear weapons in Latin America, but nuclear policy has not yet gained a prominent place in the major divisive issues among political parties.[28]

Internationally, other kinds of considerations may influence Brazil's calculus regarding nuclear exports. It is hard to assess, for instance, reactions from other countries, the extent to which continued links with traditional suppliers of technology would be jeopardized in this event, or how critical those links may continue to be for Brazil. On the one hand, the staggering foreign debt may increase the country's vulnerability vis-à-vis external sources of financial and technical assistance. On the other hand, beyond the intrinsic merits (or lack thereof) of establishing issue linkages, the unfolding of the debt crisis seems to suggest that the relative leverage of creditors and debtors is a far more dynamic structure than was initially anticipated. Domestic reactions to direct or subtle attempts by banks or creditor states to link these two issue areas will be predominantly defiant, with the unintended result of closing the ranks among otherwise antagonistic actors along nationalistic lines. The attempt to link Brazil's access to international capital may precipitate greater calamities—including dooming the lifes of millions to poverty and the prospects of democratic reconstruction—than those which nonproliferation efforts are designed to prevent.

Moral Concerns

Antinuclear protests in Brazil have increased in the last two years in the wake of Chernobyl and a local nuclear accident in Goiania, where an abandoned hospital irradiation machine caused several deaths in 1987. They were supported by the Workers' party (which won municipal elections in São Paulo in 1988 and had a strong showing nationwide), the Greens, scientists, and environmentalists. Brazilian scientists have also played a central role in advancing moral arguments against military uses of nuclear technology and in denouncing the technological and economic characteristics of their country's nuclear program, which they associate with the perpetuation of technological dependency. Most of them, however, do not seem to condemn nuclear technology as such. On the one hand, the Brazilian Physics Society signed a pledge with its Argentine counterpart in 1986 not to partake in any military-related nuclear project and supported mutual inspections to ensure the peaceful nature of their respective programs.

On the other hand, cooperation with the southern neighbor—particularly in joint nuclear technology development, with prospects for exports—may gain considerable support within the scientific community.

Given that community's traditional stands in defense of developing countries' access to any technology available worldwide, including nuclear technology, it would be hard to conceive of strong opposition to nuclear exports. Such a posture would bear too close a resemblance to what had been, until now, a doctrine mostly associated with traditional suppliers. Scientists have been among the most ardent critics of what they consider an attempt to freeze the current international economic and technological stratification. Antisuperpower rhetoric runs even higher among groups of scientists and other intellectuals than among government bureaucrats.

In another kind of "dove's dilemma," therefore, scientists in nuclear NICs will be required to support nuclear exports by their governments and firms if they are to maintain consistency with their own arguments, ardently espoused when their countries played the role of recipients.[29] Yet given their genuine concern for keeping nuclear technology in the realm of civilian uses, they may well be facing the dilemma that expanded capabilities raise—namely, the potential misuse of the technology by irresponsible leaders or regimes. It is worth noting that many among activist scientists from traditional supplier states do not face this paradox of consistency: They have always opposed their countries' nuclear exports and tend to forcibly challenge nuclear power as an energy alternative worldwide.

Capabilities: Materials, Products, and Services

Materials

Brazil has the fifth largest uranium reserve worldwide, with 8 percent of world reserves, estimated to be enough to supply forty-eight pressurized water reactors (PWRs)—1,300 MW—for thirty years (although the country may have only three operating PWRs by the end of the century).[30] Production of uranium concentrate (yellowcake) could reach 3,600 tons per year in the decade of 1985–95.[31] The yellowcake plant at Poços de Caldas, inaugurated in 1982, exported 180 and 88 tons, respectively, to France and Argentina in 1984 and 60 tons to the United Kingdom in 1985.[32] Proposals to supply Turkey with 150 tons annually for five years and a U.S. firm with 370 tons per year (1985–89) failed because of Nuclebras' financial constraints.[33] The newly created Brazilian Nuclear Industries plans two new plants at Itaiaia (with a capacity of up to 600 tons per year) and Lagoa Real to expand exports to uranium-poor European and Asian countries.

Brazil has the world's largest thorium reserves and may begin exporting it to China in the context of a joint development of thorium-fueled fast breeder reactors, established in 1988. With 90 percent of the world's niobium reserves (a value of $500 billion), Brazil exports $100 million worth annually. There is a concern with endangering reserves of strategic metals, on the one hand, and excluding domestic firms from a potentially profitable market, on the other.[34] The National Security Council reportedly requested replacement of powdered niobium exports with a more processed niobium metal or high-energy conductor cables, for which Brazil has advanced know-how. The possibility of nationalizing the Brazilian Mining and Metallurgy Company (CBMM), a Brazilian-American consortium engaged in niobium exports, was being studied.[35] The future competitiveness of niobium may be affected by new progress in superconductor technology.

The recently privatized Nuclemon and other firms (private and public) are involved in mineral processing of monazitic sands and rare earths.[36] Nuclemon exported over $1 million worth of goods to the United States, Austria, Netherlands, France, and Japan in 1983—an increase of 222 percent over the previous year. In addition, beryllium oxide, previously an imported item, was exported to the United States in 1985. Export quotas were placed for beryllium, lithium, niobium, and zirconium, among others.[37] Recent negotiations to obtain Japanese technology in the processing of rare earths in exchange for guaranteed long-term supplies may expand Nuclemon's capacity. The acquisition of mining, milling, and processing capabilities allowed Brazil to begin exporting whole turnkey plants in the fuel cycle area, a core objective in a platform encouraging technology-intensive exports.

The National Nuclear Energy Commission has developed uranium hexafluoride (UF_6) conversion technology with prospects for further commercialization of the process of conversion of yellowcake into UF_6 and of UF_6 itself, and it inaugurated a uranium enrichment plant in 1988 (see Appendix 7A).[38] In all of these areas, developing countries represent the only potential markets, but prospects for foreign demand are tenuous under current conditions of overcapacity in enrichment services.[39] A fuel element plant has been in operation (with KWU technology) since 1982. With a nominal annual capacity of 100 tons, appropriate for the first charge of a 1,300 MW(e) reactor, it has not received any orders because of delays in power plant construction.[40]

Products and Components

Brazil's capability to export manufactures and heavy machinery at the highest level of processing is not a potential but a reality.[41] Equipment and instrumentation for the Argonaut and other research reactors were developed and built in Brazil.[42] National industry was responsible for 90 percent of the yellowcake production complex and fuel element plant and 40 percent of the jet nozzle uranium-enrichment demonstration plant. In 1984, Nuclebras' engineering subsidiary Nuclen identified 780 Brazilian firms interested in supplying materials, equipment, and services for nuclear plants.[43] Over 30 percent of the electromechanical components for the first two KWU power plants were supplied by about forty Brazilian firms, thirty in the mechanical area and ten in electrical equipment. These included some of Brazil's largest manufacturers of heavy equipment, such as Confab, Cobrasma, Bardella, Jaguare, Romi, and Dedini. Table 7–1 describes national private participation in electromechanical supplies (by area) for Brazil's own nuclear power plants, as envisaged in 1975. The table underscores the actual capabilities of Brazilian industry in turbogenerators and other supplies. Participation shares were largely affected by the availability of "suppliers' credits" and by KWU's influence within the joint venture Nuclen, which ensured KWU and its associated firms a significant proportion of electromechanical supplies (Solingen, 1989). Table 7–2 lists major capital goods, engineering, and construction firms involved in the nuclear program; the nature of their participation; and their technological links. The technological growth of Brazil's industry in the last decade may diminish the value of these tables as an approximation of more current industrial capabilities. The recently privatized heavy component plant Nuclep (800 employees) can produce one entire set (with potential for three) of reactor components per year.[44] Given the contraction of Brazil's program

Table 7–1
National Participation in Electromechanical Supplies (As defined in 1975 accord between Nuclebras and KWU). (*Source: C.P.I., Vol. III:132*).

Components	Plants 1–2	Plant 3	Plant 4	Plants 5–6	Plants 7–8
Turbo-generator	10	15	20	25	30
Heavy components	—	70	100	100	100
Electrical equipment	85	87	90	93	95
Piping	15	20	25	50	65
Instrum. and Control	5	10	60	70	90
Pumps	40	45	47	50	50
Special steel struct.	100	100	100	100	100
Heat exchangers	80	90	100	100	100
Ventil., air-cond.	100	100	100	100	100
Spec. reactor Compon.	—	10	30	40	50
Rolling bridges	100	100	100	100	100
Valves	10	20	30	40	50
Tanks	90	100	100	100	100
Miscelaneous	70	75	80	85	90
Total share of national nuclear components	30	47	60	65	70

Table 7–2
Capital Goods, Engineering, and Construction Firms—Supplies for Nuclear Program and Technology Transfer

Firm	Component/Service	Licensor/Technical Assistance
Capital Goods		
Cobrasm	Heat exchangers	Balcke Duerr
	Surface condensers	KWV
	Quality assurance	NJS
	Boilers, auxiliary steam-generator equipm.	
Confab	Heat exchangers	Thyssen
	Containment vessels and access locks to cont. vessels	
	Reactor and fuel pits linings	Noell
	Support for the reactor, steam generators, main pumps	Noell
	piping	
	Atmospheric tanks and pressure vessels	KWU
	Degasification systems	
	Radioactive wastes decontamination systems	Balcke-Duerr
		Luwa
Treu	Filter-exchange machines.	Thyssen-Henschel
	Vertical centrifugal pumps	Balcke-Duerr
	Silencers	Blohm & Voss
	Filters, heat exchangers, press. vessels and tanks,	
	containers for nuclear fuel transportation	Atlantik GmbH.
Bardella	Water purificaiton system	Bamag
	Overhead crane for turbo-generator room; polar crane	
	for ass./maint. of reactors	
	Semi-gantry crane for containment vessel	Noell
		Grunzweig & Hartmann
Ebse	Piping/secondary circuit	Servatious
	Silencers, press. vessels	GmbH
Engineering		
Promon	Structural design/main power plant foundations	Hochtief A.G.
	Civil engineering/reactor, auxiliary, switchgear	Dyckerhoff &
	Preliminary design/piping systems	Widman
		(Mannesman)
Natron	Structural design/piping	Kraftlangen
	Detailed des., procurem., construction,	Heidl.
	erection/Yellow-cake plant (Pocos)	
		Pechiney-Ugine Kuhlmann
Engevix	Structural design/turbine generator building	Dyckerhoff &
	Uranium hexafluoride plant	Widman (Dividag)
Assembly		
Montreal Eng.	Mechan./electr. assembly	Mannesman
Construction		
Odebrecht	Civil works	Hochtieff

Source: Annual Reports (all firms); KWU, *Noticias Nucleares,* 10/13/1983; Rosa et al., 1984:79.

from eight to two plants and Nuclep's consequent idle capacity, "nucleo-crats" have encouraged exports of heavy reactor components. NUCLEP's potential as the largest boiler factory in Latin America and the only inte-grated heavy components producer (multinationals tend to rely on diverse subsuppliers) is enhanced by its unique maritime terminal, allowing move-ment of pieces weighing up to 1,000 tons.[45]

Regarding dual-use items, Brazil's increased capacity in the area of instrumentation and control may be of some significance. The protective "informatics" policy may not have brought about all expected results, par-ticularly if one uses the level of technological sophistication of the indus-try's output as a benchmark. It has, however, allowed the development of a certain local competence in electronics, which may be relevant particularly to instrumentation and control. Finally, in the area of delivery systems, Brazil sold Astros II rockets to Iran and Iraq; and the production of the SS-300, a solid-fuel 300-mile-range ballistic missile, and a longer-range nuclear-capable SS-1000, is expected in the 1990s.[46] Solid-fuel technology developed in Brazil has been sold to China.

Services and Know-How

In mineral prospecting, the Brazilian Mineral Resources Prospecting Com-pany (not a Nuclebras subsidiary) has been selling its services to Libya since 1980, including discovery of uranium in Libyan territory, personnel training, and aerial geophysics.[47] Nuclebras has trained technicians from developing countries in mining and consultancy services and, together with a private firm, won a bid for the design and construction of a uranium concentrate plant in Somalia.[48] Brazilian firms can also provide exploration equipment for radioactive minerals.[49]

Many engineers trained by Nuclebras' subsidiary Nuclen, 200 at least, left the firm for the private sector.[50] Clearly, expertise in many areas of nuclear plant design—including conventional systems, steam generators, heat exchangers, quality assurance, materials technology, and instrumenta-tion and control—has been gained and could potentially be reassembled or exported. Brazilian firms may now be capable of exporting engineering services for nuclear plants in areas such as site selection, structural design (including special seismic analysis), special piping, complete design of non-nuclear portions of nuclear plants, and field engineering.[51] Finally, CNEN has been interested in exporting technology for licensing nuclear installa-tions since 1969.

Summing up, Brazil has the potential to become a supplier of a wide range of products and services, including guidance in negotiating strategies vis-à-vis nuclear vendors. Widespread criticism of the inefficiency and mis-takes of its domestic program led to corrective steps that may strengthen foreign perceptions of its potential, mainly in the eyes of Third World customers, as a reliable industrial partner.

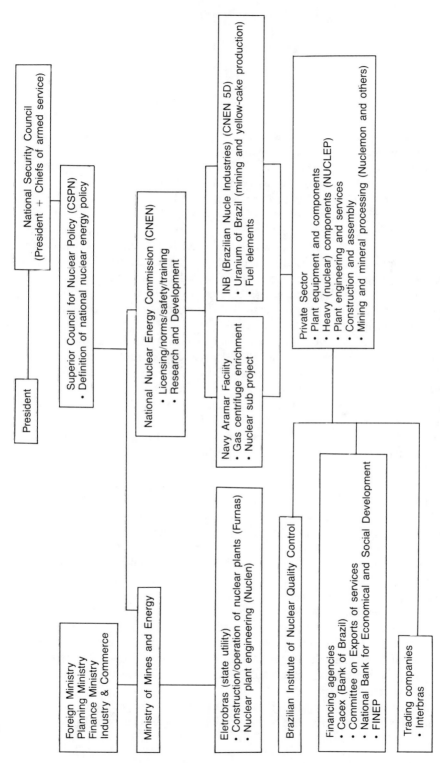

Figure 7–3. Organizational Flow Chart for the Nuclear Sector

Formal Structures and Declaratory Policy

Structures

The 1962 Law on National Nuclear Energy Policy established that foreign negotiations and treaties regarding the sale of nuclear materials and services, financing, and the like, are a monopoly of the national Nuclear Energy Commission (CNEN), formally an administratively and financially autonomous agency. Figure 7–3 reflects a recent institutional shift whereby CNEN, formerly under the Ministry of Mines and Energy, became subordinated to the Superior Council for Nuclear Policy, which includes representatives of nineteen ministries, CNEN, Brazil's Nuclear Industries (INB), and three private citizens, including physicist José Goldemberg, prominent among critics of the 1975 agreements.[52] CNEN is now responsible for executing nuclear policy in areas formerly under Nuclebrás. The military-dominated National Security Council (CSN), which supervised and advised the president on nuclear policy, was eliminated by the new constitution but reinstated by President Sarney with a different name—the Secretariat for National Defense.[53]

It is unclear in what ways these changes may affect formal procedures related to nuclear exports. The 1974 legislation on nuclear policy (Law 6.189/74) established CNEN's responsibility for overseeing international agreements and commitments "of any type" in relation to nuclear energy (Article 9).[54] A 1988 presidential decree instructed the ministers of finance, mines and energy, planning, and the CSN (including CNEN) to discuss uranium exports to Japan and France.[55] It may be safe to assume that nuclear exports will require approval of the president of the republic and the CSN.

This brief review of the formal structure of nuclear agencies may underscore the role of other informal, bureaucratic mechanisms that are routinely involved in decision making but on which scant information is available concerning nuclear matters. It is conceivable, for instance, that the foreign Ministry, Itamaraty, may play a critical role, given its history of involvement in nuclear policymaking in Brazil. For dual-use items, we can expect that the closer and more obvious their association to purely nuclear uses, the greater the intervention of Itamaraty and the nuclear agencies.[56] Itamaraty's leverage vis-à-vis the economic ministries (planning, finance, mines and energy, industry and commerce) and associated agencies (Bank of Brazil, the central bank) has declined in recent years.[57] Technocrats from the economic agencies have been far from enthusiastic about the domestic nuclear program and its exorbitant costs, and their role in foreign trade may grow (Selcher, 1984).

Decision making regarding nuclear exports can be inferred, to some extent, from export licensing of conventional weapons, in which there are three levels of export controls. Orders must be processed through CACEX, the foreign trade section of Bank of Brazil, then approved by the CSN, and finally facilitated by the interagency Program for Military Exports, which coordinates production and negotiates credit lines (Lock, 1986). There are significant structural differences between the nuclear and conventional sectors, however. A wide array of economic and political forces is behind conventional arms exports, an industry characterized by a working relationship between state and private interests. This was not a strong feature of the nuclear program in its earlier stages, although increased cooperation between CNEN and private industry has resulted in a variety of new products and processes.[58]

Without the benefit of detailed studies of nuclear decision making in Brazil, I suggest that nuclear exports, as other nuclear-related policy issues, will be largely influenced by four major considerations. The first is the nature of prevailing economic-technocratic orientations within the state's bureaucracy. Even at the height of military rule (1964–85), civilian technocrats, rather than their military partners, defined the characteristics of the agreements with KWU (Solingen, 1989). The second consideration is the changes in the fundamental structure of Brazil's political system. The new constitution (1988) redefined relations between the congress and the executive, introducing greater legislative oversight into a bureaucracy traditionally accustomed to carrying out executive decrees. Third, nuclear exports may be conditioned by the way new political structures define civil–military relations.[59] Even civilian regimes imbued with the highest democratic values may consider themselves compelled to accept military monopoly over certain issue areas for their own survival's sake. Finally, the increased political weight of private sector interests, to which state bureaucrats will be forced to pay greater attention, will be reflected in any calculus regarding nuclear exports.

Legal Compliance and Declaratory Policy

Brazil has consistently resisted pressures to sign the non-proliferation treaty (NPT), claiming (1) that it legitimizes (and freezes) the existing international distribution of power; (2) that it provides no effective barrier for vertical proliferation by nuclear weapons countries; and (3) that it overlooks efficient protection for nonnuclear weapons states.[60] The country is not technically bound by the Tlatelolco Treaty,[61] but it has declared commitment to its principles (Redick, 1984) and has ratified the Limited Test Ban Treaty.

Given its position vis-à-vis the international nonproliferation regime, what can we expect Brazil's posture to be as a nuclear technology supplier? The 1975 agreement between the governments of Brazil and West Germany established (Article 3) that (1) the approval of both parties will be required when considering export permits (for fertile or special fissile materials, equipment and materials for processing fuel, or technology know-how) to third parties; (2) The agreement to transfer any of the foregoing items will be accompanied by an acceptance, on the part of the recipient, of IAEA safeguards, to ensure nondiversion for military uses.[62] Article 4 specifies the need for mutual consultations in approving exports of sensitive materials to nonnuclear weapon states. The following items trigger immediate application of safeguards: (1) ^{235}U enriched over 20 percent, ^{233}U, and plutonium, except for laboratory samples; (2) fuel element plants processing any of these; (3) reprocessing plants; and (4) enrichment plants. These safeguards will remain in place even after the expiration of the Brazilian-German accord (Soares, 1976).

In the past, KWU exercised considerable control of joint ventures in Nuclebras through a variety of special clauses and requirements. At Nuclen (engineering) and Nuclep (heavy components), for instance, the directorship could not veto a decision by the German-controlled technical committee.[63] This structure implied that KWU's approval was required in the negotiation of any licensing, sublicensing, or technical cooperation agreements.[64] The potential export of Nuclep's components, for instance, would be subject to approval by the German members of the consortium.[65]

In addition to limitations on licensing and technical cooperation, there was a recognition of KWU as sole supplier of technology and equipment—often called a tie-out clause—in new projects involving Nuclen (Section 12.6.2).[66] The free use by Nuclen of reports, drawings, specifications, technical instructions, computer programs, and so forth, after the expiration of the agreement was assured (Lepecki, 1985). According to German research and technology minister Hans-Hilger Haunschild, all export licenses requested by Brazil for nuclear reactors and fuel elements, uranium enrichment plants and hardware, and blueprints of reprocessing installations were granted.[67] The legal principles that will regulate export of nuclear materials and equipment developed by CNEN's independent program have not been made public yet.[68]

It is not clear whether Brazil will require from recipients either a verbal pledge to abstain from military uses or a formal agreement not to retransfer materials or technology to third countries, unless they accept similar constraints. A 1985 umbrella cooperation agreement with China demanded (Article 6) IAEA safeguards on exports of any fissionable materoal and restrictions on reexports to third parties.[69] In general, it can be said that declaratory policies regarding international nuclear behavior have enjoyed a remarkable degree of continuity. The new republic (following the 1985 election of a civilian president) brought no departures from previous postures—other than, perhaps, a more active implementation of prior commitments undertaken by the last military president regarding cooperation with Argentina (Redick, 1981). There is no intention to relay information about mutual inspections with Argentina to the IAEA or to join the London Nuclear Suppliers Group.[70]

From Potential to Action: Patterns of Nuclear Trade

Brazil has scientific and technical nuclear cooperation agreements with Venezuela, the People's Republic of China (PRC), Argentina, Bolivia, Chile, Colombia, India, Iraq, the United States, Italy, Israel, Egypt, Paraguay, Portugal, the Federal Republic of Germany (FRG), Spain, and Ecuador. Like many other bilateral agreements on scientific cooperation, these are no more than a show of goodwill, with little operational implications.

Strategic minerals were Brazil's first nuclear exports; as early as 1945, it supplied the United States with 5,000 tons annually of monazitic sands, for a period of three years (Morel, 1979). Advocates of a nationalistic policy of "specific compensations" demanded technology in exchange for uranium, thorium, and derivatives. However, the newly created Commission for Strategic Minerals Exports within the Ministry of Foreign Affairs opposed these initiatives, favored granting the United States preferential status over other potential nuclear partners, and gained control over nuclear policy in the 1950s. A 1972 treaty established the exchange of Brazilian natural uranium for U.S. enriched uranium, with IAEA safeguards.

Some of the more recent commercially relevant transactions, discussed in a previous section on capabilities, are summarized in table 7–3. Exports of products extracted from mineral processing of monazitic sands and rare earths have increased considerably, with developed countries—such as the United States, Japan, and Austria—as major clients. The exchange of uranium for technology and financing has been quite common. Exports of yellowcake to France, Argentina, and the United Kingdom (88, 180, and 60 tons respectively) in 1984–85 were partial payments on the debt incurred when these countries supplied Brazil with yellowcake; they did not result in foreign exchange. Financial difficulties in Nuclebras precluded the sale of 370 tons ($22.2 million) per year (1985–89) to a U.S. firm and 150 tons per year to Turkey (potentially for a fifteen-year period starting in 1988).[71]

Given the lack of financing to develop other uranium concentrate plants and the fact that the one at Poços de Caldas has been operating at one-third of its capacity, the ability to fulfill foreign demand is limited. French financing of a new yellowcake plant at Itatiaia is to be repaid in "ore currency," and a similar arrangement was being negotiated with Urangesellchaft (FRG) to finance a new uranium concentrate plant in

Table 7–3
Brazil's Nuclear Exports

Export category	Supplier		Recipient	Technology source		Transnat'l assoc.	Date	Transactn. Value
Materials	S.	P.		B.	F.			
a) Ores (monazite rutile, ilmenite)	X		U.S.	X			1945–8	
b) Pure elements (rare earths, etc)	X	X		X		X	annual	$100M.
	X		France, Japan,	X			) About $1 M.) (annual)/1983)	
			US,	X				
			Austria,	X				
			Netherlands	X				
c) Beryllium oxide		X	US	X			1985	
d) Uranium ore, thorium, zirconium								
e) U_3O_8 (yellowcake)	X	France	French			1984	) return	
	X		Argentina	French			1984	) for
	X		U.K.	French			1985	) lease
e) Low Enriched Uranium	X		Iraq	X			1979	(barter?)
	X		Argentina	W. German			1988	$1.4 M.
Research Reactors Equipm/Instrum.								
Power Reactors A) Nuclear Steam Supply System	X		Argentina	W. German			1984	$2 M.
b) Auxiliary Sys.								
Fuel Cycle/Plants a) Mining/Milling								
b) Yellowcake	X	X	Somalia	X			1984	$360,000
c) Conversion (UF_6)								
d) Enrichment								
e) Fuel element								
f) Reprocessing								
g) HW								
Services a) Fuel cycle	?	X	Libya	X			1980–	$15M.
b) Engineering								
c) Construction								
d) Training	X		Iraq				1979–	(barter)
	X		Spain				1983	$200,000
Negotiations Not Leading to Transactions	X(U_3O_8)		Turkey	French			1984	
	X(U_3O_8)		U.S.	French			1984	
	X(Techn. reactors?)		Egypt	?			1986	
	X (explor.)		Algeria	X			1985	$25 M.

Table 7–3 continued

Export category	Supplier	Recipient	Technology source	Transnat'l assoc.	Date	Transactn. Value
	X(heavy comadponts.)Mexico	Mexico	)			)
		Turkey	)			
			KWU		1984–6	)
		Egypt	)			)
		China	)			)
	X(reactor oper. train, equipm) Venezuela	Venezuela			1978–9	
	X(enrichm technology) Nigeria	Nigeria	?		1987	

Notes: S = State   P = Private   B = Brazilian   F = Foreign
Source: FBIS, JPRS Report, *Nuclear Developments*, 1980–1988.

exchange for part of its output. Uranium exports to Japan and France are now being considered. The commercial success of uranium sales has been used to justify the continuation of other nuclear programs by using these revenues to fund them.[72] The objective, however, is to shift away from uranium ore to processed exports, with greater value-added. Brazil has offered to supply Argentina with slightly enriched uranium for "spiking" Atucha 1's fuel; in turn, Argentina would provide low- and medium-enriched uranium for Brazil's Angra 1 and three research reactors.[73] Finally, the possibility of exchanging Nigerian uranium for Brazilian uranium enrichment technology has been discussed.[74]

In 1984, in conjunction with its German partner, KWU, Nuclep exported the ($2 million) lower portion of the reactor vessel for Argentina's third nuclear plant (Atucha 2), was included as subcontractor in tenders for the reactor and pressure vessels in Turkey and Egypt, and participated in a direct bid for two nuclear plants in Mexico.[75] This pattern suggests that exports in this area may be contingent on KWU's (now absorbed by Siemens AG) own commercial considerations and leverage and mostly reflect transactions among the multinational's affiliates.[76] With a 25 percent share in both Nuclen (Brazil) and Enace (Argentina), KWU has exercised considerable influence on the joint ventures in nuclear engineering. Finally, some private firms expanded their exports of conventional products—some of which required special levels of resistance to variations in temperature and pressure—as a result of their involvement in the nuclear program.[77]

As in the case of capital goods, the lack of domestic demand stepped up a drive for exports among engineering firms. One firm won a $280 million contract in 1982 for the preparation of the complete basic and front-end engineering package and definitive estimate for a turnkey supply of a yellowcake plant in Somalia.[78] The firm had no prior export experience and had been responsible for detailed design of the yellowcake mining complex at Pocos de Caldas. Nuclebras coordinated between the engineering and the construction firms, offering its own laboratories to define technical parameters, equipment, and other services.[79]

The nuclear agreement with Iraq involved the supply of low-enriched uranium, safety technology, and training of Iraqi personnel in exchange for Iraqi oil.[80] A $15 million agreement on prospecting and mining services led a Brazilian firm to discover uranium reserves in Libya in 1984.[81] Technical assistance has been provided to Spain in the form of training for reactor operators. A 1986 cooperation agreement with Egypt called for Brazil's export of technology, equipment, and possibly complete power plants to Egypt and led to a bid for that country's second and third plants. In the areas of mining, milling, and processing, Nuclebras has trained technicians from developing countries and has consulted for foreign clients.[82] In sum, the export record so far suggests several major patterns.

Technology Acquisition and Export Potential

First, those sectors least associated with technology transfer from KWU and related German firms appear, thus far, to have been relatively more successful regarding exports. No doubt such success is primarily related to the international market for the specific good or service. Nevertheless, in the context of a nuclear program, it does illuminate potential trade-offs between levels of investment (usually high for technology transfer agreements) and export potential across different (nuclear) industrial areas. It may be interesting to examine, by looking at other cases, the proposition that sectors that show greater intensity of imported technology tend to contribute to only a small fraction of exports.[83] CNEN's development of instrumentation technology for research and other reactors, which it transferred to the private sector with an eye on potential exports, may reflect such an interpretation of the role of domestic versus foreign technology in exports.[84]

Second, export potential has apparently been increased by some firms' involvement with Brazil's first and only operating reactor, Westinghouse's Angra 1, defined as a turnkey transaction (presumably placing lesser emphasis on technology absorption).[85] This outcome challenges propositions that associate this mode of technology transfer with a "technological enclave" that is not capable of generating localized technological mastery. The entrance of these firms into world markets may also be influenced by an intangible gain from producing for the nuclear sector—a "prestige linkage," by which prospective clients deduce from that involvement the firm's technological sophistication and reliability.

The Role of Nuclear Agencies

In the process of restructuring the nuclear sector, nuclear agencies may be tempted to gain greater domestic political influence by providing concrete achievements in external markets. Nuclebras and CNEN have been active in the past in promoting exports of goods and services by Brazilian firms, as in the agreement with Somalia. I have also referred to CNEN's efforts in promoting exports of nuclear materials, reactor fuel, technology, and instrumentation and control equipment, all obtained through an independent program not tied to the agreement with KWU. In 1988, CNEN president Rex Nazare declared Brazil's intention to participate in the international fuel cycle market, a major target of CNEN's newly created subsidiary, Uranium of Brazil.[86] The leverage of nuclear agencies to advance expansion into the external market may be limited by broader political and economic considerations. These agencies may be also checked by their relative institutional weakness vis-à-vis other powerful state agencies.

Transnational Partnerships

Joint ventures are regarded as useful by traditional suppliers when they can capture host-country technical expertise, thus reducing R&D costs, spreading the risk, and exploiting local governmental incentives to R&D activities (Mytelka, 1987). Joint ventures in mining and processing and power plant engineering and components may provide local firms with increased opportunities and some constraints. These partnerships may facilitate access to the marketing system of an experienced supplier, but they may also curtail domestic control of technology transfer and commercial policy.[87] In the past, as the major architect-engineer, KWU had considerable influence in shaping exports of heavy components by Nuclep as a subcontractor.[88] Whether Nuclep's exports after privatization will remain linked to KWU's own commercial considerations may depend, in part, on the latter's agreement to transfer its Nuclep shares (2 percent) to Brazil's Nuclear Industries. We may point, however, to the following observations regarding transnational partnerships. First, these arrangements do not appear to decrease with higher levels of technical competence, as the Argentine case suggests.[89] Second, heavy foreign indebtedness increased debt-for-equity swaps, leaving creditors with greater shares in joint ventures. It is not yet clear whether any of the nuclear partnerships with West Germany will be affected. Finally, increased technological cooperation with Argentina may be a strategy to reduce dependence on multinationals in the nuclear sector, which is perceived to perpetuate a vertical (north–south) international division of labor.

Continuity and Change

Brazil's nuclear export activities have been relatively limited, although the experience of recent years may point to a broadened range of transactions in the future. The dearth of public statements regarding the political, strategic, bureaucratic, and economic dimensions of nuclear exports constrains our ability to take stock, let alone forecast future trends. To some extent, it can be argued that policies regarding nuclear exports will tend to be affected, beyond political and strategic considerations, by broader foreign economic policies and prevailing attitudes toward import substitution and export-led growth.[90] Given the centrality of the foreign debt crisis for Brazil, this consideration acquires particular saliency. From an international perspective, export incentive programs and protection of local markets, invoking technological-developmental goals (such as in the electronics sector), have brought Brazil in direct collision with the United States and the Europeans. Brazil's (and other NICs') attempts to expand the export of services—particularly in engineering, consultancy, construction, and turnkey projects—while protecting their own markets are a central bone of contention at current General Agreement on Tariffs and Trade (GATT—Uruguay Round) negotiations. In the nuclear sector, these export efforts were reflected in sales of prospecting, mining, engineering, construction, and technical services. All of these have a multiplier effect on capital goods exports.

It may be too early to assess the effects of the 1988 restructuring of the nuclear sector. Privatization may increase rationalization of production of nuclear components and may enhance sensitivity to demand factors, to which state firms have been somewhat oblivious, given their own bureaucratic inertia. Increased domestic criticism of the nuclear power program on economic, technological, political, and safety grounds may force Brazil to turn whatever capacity there may be to foreign markets. The prospects of a left-leaning or a right-wing populist victory in the 1989 presidential elections—reflected in the 1988 municipal elections results—may affect all of these factors in opposite directions. Nuclear policy, however, may remain the domain of the armed forces—reflecting, along with many other items in the 1988 constitution, their unabated power to shape the boundaries of Brazil's political life.

Potential Third World customers may continue to be Middle Eastern and African countries. The developing world provides an excellent market because the technology exported by newly industrialized countries is generally more appropriate to the former's relative factor endowments and skill requirements. Beyond increased links with regional oil producers (Mexico and Venezuela) and former Portuguese colonies (Angola, in particular), Brazil has strengthened its ties with Nigeria, Algeria, Iraq, Libya, and Saudi Arabia, largely through "weapons for oil" arrangements.[91] By 1980 Iraq, Nigeria, and Venezuela alone accounted for about 60 percent of all Brazilian engineering exports.[92] Although commercial interests in these countries may continue—as they provide significant markets for Brazilian manufactures, engineering, and construction services—exchange based on oil dependencies will tend to decline, given Brazil's doubling of domestic reserves in the 1980s.

It was a cornerstone of the bilateral protocols with Argentina that cooperation would be extended to other Latin American nations with "the same objectives."[93] Protocol 17, signed in Brasilia in 1986, provided for cooperation in sensors, electronics and nuclear instrumentation, and enrichment of stable isotopes and joint development of a new family of research reactor fuel rods and test materials for pure and applied physics. It also envisaged future cooperation in plasma physics research and a study of the feasibility of developing a small (100 MW or less) fast breeder reactor by the year 2011.[94] Potential cooperation in the production of a "compact" reactor (300–400 MW) has been advanced, and Brazil may not be too far from the point of view of engineering capabilities and manufacturing, from designing one.[95] An immediate application of smaller reactors may be in nuclear-powered submarines.[96] Brazil's and Argentina's nuclear engineering agencies, Nuclen and Enace, signed an agreement to cooperate in nuclear plant design, engineering, and services.

Negotiations have also taken place between private firm representatives of the two countries, including engineering, equipment manufacturing, and assembly firms; potential exchanges for Brazil's Angra 2 and Argentina's Atucha 2 were estimated at $10 million on each side.[97] Although Brazil may be ahead in equipment technology, Argentina is more advanced in the architecture of nuclear plants.[98] A proposal for the standardization of nuclear plants was justified as facilitating sales to third countries. The prospects for effectively implementing commercial nuclear ventures between Brazil and Argentina may be hindered by common financial constraints. Yet recent Argentine–Brazilian cooperation—including mutual presidential visits to sensitive facilities—may lay the foundations for a regional regime with characteristics of restraint. Initial steps taken mostly in the area of bilateral safeguards and safety considerations may be expanded to include a system of export controls. How this system may react in the presence of less restrictive behavior on the part of extraregional traditional and emerging suppliers is hard to predict.

It is unclear whether Brazil will behave differently than traditional suppliers in its nuclear exports.[99] On the one hand, the records of West Germany, France, Belgium, and others seem to suggest that "exercise of restraint" is too undefined a guideline. The U.S. record in nuclear exports shows relatively greater restraint since 1978, but U.S. leverage in condemning other suppliers of military-related technology for sensitive exchanges with "crazy states" has been undermined by the Iran Contra scandal.[100] On the other hand, the attempt by recipients to extract concessions by demanding technological assistance and increased indigenization of components and engineering services is a universal one. Brazil has used it itself in its negotiations with suppliers, and there is no reason to assume that in becoming a supplier, it will ignore the realities of commercial trends. Moreover, local subcontracting can be used as a means to avoid heavy fixed investment and increase the supplier's attractiveness as a nuclear partner (Walker and Lonnroth, 1983).

Pragmatism has been a cornerstone of Brazil's foreign policy throughout a number of successive political regimes. As with other traditional and emerging suppliers, Brazil's reluctance to provide materials and assistance to conflict areas or "pariah" states has not been a characteristic of its foreign trade and policy. Nor do trends in conventional weapons and missile technology point to a particularly discriminating approach, as exports to Iran, Iraq, and Libya suggest.[101] Potential nuclear clients are bound to be other Third World countries, regardless of their ideological leanings. The 1986 Argentine–Cuban agreement for nuclear cooperation and other Brazilian–Cuban negotiations point to the region's decreased emphasis on ideological barriers to economic and technological cooperation.[102] The possibility of joint (or unilateral) Brazilian–Argentine nuclear exports to Cuba is more easily conceivable in the international political and economic environment of the 1990s than ever before.[103] Disputes with the United States concerning trade, conventional arms exports, and nuclear policy are regarded, along with their risks, as opportunities to advance Brazil's international objectives.

A right-wing populist victory in the November 1989 elections may attempt to maintain the vision of Brazil as a scientific and technological giant among developing nations, fostered by the military predecessors. The Foreign Ministry (Itamaraty) and the Ministry of Science and Technology have been active in promoting bilateral and multilateral agreements in data processing, microelectronics, biotechnology, and atomic energy. Given appropriate market conditions, Brazil's close commercial and political ties with the most feasible clients in Africa and the Middle East may grant it considerable competitive advantage over other suppliers. Never before has Brazil's policy of "responsible pragmatism," formulated in the 1970s, been put to such a clear test as the one nuclear exports may trigger.

Technology, Offsets, and the Political Economy of Newly Industrialized Countries' Nuclear Exports

What can we learn from Brazil's experience that may be of broader applicability to other emerging suppliers? Given Brazil's specific endowments and level of industrial development, at least some generalizations may be valid for other NICs. First, as recent experience suggests, NICs have succeeded in reversing their traditional dependency on unprocessed exports. At the heart of this turnabout is the growth of their indigenous technological capacity. Nuclear technology is considered a showcase for this upgraded status. During the inauguration of Brazil's heavy components plant, Nuclep, Nuclebras director Paulo N. Batista emphasized with pride the fact that this was the first Third World factory of nuclear plants.

Exports with high technology content are preferred because they may improve the terms of trade, they can lead to fast economic growth, and they are perceived to hold a better promise for the creation of forward and backward linkages in the economy than primary products (Firebaugh and Bullock, 1986). However, evidence that these relationships hold is far from conclusive in a generic sense, let alone for the nuclear sector. But the aura and prestige surrounding nuclear exports may blur the ability to weight these effects adequately.

Past patterns suggest that—given traditional suppliers' leadership in power plant engineering, equipment, and machinery—the NICs' niche in nuclear markets may be limited, in the short term, to research reactors and fuel cycle activities, particularly in the technologically less sophisticated areas of prospecting, mining, and yellowcake production, and to selected capital goods and engineering services. The potential for NICs to compete with established suppliers, however, should be evaluated in the context of a changing web of technological capabilities in the international system, where gaps tend to narrow and widen as a function of the rate of change of the technology in question, dedicated industrial efforts, and the growth of human-embodied resources.

Second, although in the specific case of Brazil some forms of countertrade may decrease (notably, barter agreements related to oil), the general tendency to resort to variations of "offsets" may continue, with important consequences for the conduct of nuclear trade.[104] Given a growing awareness in the international technology transfer regime, recipients of technology tend to bargain for increasing shares of licensed production, local subcontracting, and joint ventures. These provide the recipients with an opportunity to promote faster and more effective absorption of technology and production capabilities; to strengthen their industrial structure in manpower, quality assurance, and production techniques; and to improve their balance of payments and employment levels.

Some of the emerging nuclear suppliers (Korea, Taiwan, India, Pakistan, Argentina, and Brazil) have been most active in negotiating offset agreements with technology suppliers, in both the conventional and the nuclear realms. As suppliers, it will be hard for them not to acknowledge and abide by these commercial practices.[105] Given the current international debt and shortages of foreign exchange of at least some of the emerging suppliers, as well as their potential clients, the use of countertrade as an instrument for expanding exports may intensify. The need to obtain vital imports may increase suppliers' vulnerability to conditional arrangements, thus lowering the threshold of domestic resistance to engaging in nuclear exports. If conventional arms exports are suggestive of potential trends, it is important to note the willingness of arms producers (including Brazil, Egypt, and others) to exchange military hardware for raw materials.[105]

Offsets can serve a political function for both nuclear suppliers and recipients. From the point of view of suppliers, they may provide political, strategic, and symbolic benefits, such as "promotion of (southern) collective self-reliance," increased international prestige, and a tacit legitimization of their nuclear programs. Argentina's declaratory policy regarding nuclear exports bears some of these characteristics.[106] From the recipient's point of view, the use of countertrade mechanisms—with an emphasis on employment and developmental spin-offs—may strengthen domestic political acceptance of capital-intensive programs such as nuclear technology. In sum, emerging suppliers will be affected by the same trends toward indigenization that turned them from recipients into exporters.[107] Moreover, a willingness to agree to compensatory agreements of this nature will tend to increase competition among suppliers for a competitive edge, weakening the concept of restraint as a guideline in nuclear trade.

Third, emerging suppliers' patterns of state–industry relationships will tend to resemble the "active" state model—coordinating export efforts, as in France and Canada—more than the less visible, albeit supportive (West German) or "antagonistic" (U.S.), models in which the state has resorted to export controls despite objections by private firms. In general, it appears that there may be less policy incompatibility (between private firms and state bureaucracies) regarding nuclear exports among most emerging suppliers than is the case for the traditional suppliers.[108] Despite this potential for a "happy convergence," private sector interests in nuclear exports have not been as evident or as politically vocal in Brazil as in Argentina, at least until now. Changes in this area may be reinforced by a perceived prestige effect that production for a nuclear program tends to accrue in the eyes of potential clients, nuclear and nonnuclear.

Finally, this overview of the potential determinants of nuclear exports in Brazil advances a certain analytic perspective. International political, economic, technological, and financial conditions provide an array of opportunities and constraints for emerging suppliers. I have pointed at countertrade mechanisms and transnational associations as examples, and others are also worth exploring. The final calculus, however, seems to be largely influenced by the domestic configuration of politically relevant actors, including private entrepreneurs, the military, and state agencies. Their relative structural or conjunctural strength in the fluid environment of Brazilian politics is an elusive yet most critical angle to pursue in the study of foreign policy in general and nuclear policy in particular.

Notes

1. Speech delivered in Brasilia, Planalto Palace, 4 September 1987.
2. The parallel program has reportedly received between $1 billion and $3 billion annually. *Veja*, 22 April 1987.
3. The Ipero facility was to reach 20 percent enrichment levels in 1988. *Nucleonics Week*, 14 April 1988. Laser enrichment is presumably being studied at the Aerospace Technology Center and IPEN. *FBIS World Wide Report: Latin America* [henceforth *FBIS*], 23 May 1985, p. 60; 24 September 1984, p. 48; *Nuclear News* (February 1987):51.
4. The terms are quoted in Araoz and Sercovich (1977) and attributed to M. Kamenetzky.
5. The total value of exports in 1988 reached $33 billion (Latin American Regional Reports: Brazil, 5 January 1989). From 1966 to 1979, the share of capital goods exports from Brazil increased from 1.8 percent to 14.7 percent of total exports (WBCS, 1980); and by 1982, capital goods exports exceeded imports. The value of exports, which accounted for 25 percent of total capital goods production, was over twenty-six times that of 1970 (Erber et al., 1984:24–25). Exports included plants for iron and steel making and for textile, paper, and pulp making; engineering products, turbine equipment, and power, agricultural, and metal-working machinery; construction and engineering services (hydroelectric projects, highways, railways, mining); turnkey plants; and industrial processes (Mitra, 1979).
6. Technological efficiency is cited as one of the stimuli to the cooperation agreements between the two countries. *Integración Latinoamericana* (April 1987):5.
7. See interview with Nuclebras president Paulo Nogueira Batista in *Manchete*, 14 August 1976, pp. 152–53.
8. *O Globo*, 16 July 1976, p. 18; *O Estado de São Pauo*, 23 September 1981 and 20 October 1984, p. 24. His statement did not anticipate the remarkable decline of oil producers' bargaining power.
9. ABDIB *Informa* 1984, p. 3. In custom-built capital goods, within which many nuclear components fall, exports amounted to $800 million in 1983.
10. *Folha de São Paulo*, 30 July 1978, p. 58.
11. The first two sets of heavy components (for plants 1 and 2) were to be supplied by KWU.

12. *Estatizacao* refers to the uncontrolled growth of the state sector and, particularly since the 1970s, has been a major political issue in Brazil.

13. Nuclam could, if it chose to, use UG as its exporting agent for the remaining 51 percent. See Comissão Parlamentar de Inquérito do Senado Federal Sobre o Acordo Nuclear do Brasil com a Republica Federal da Alemanha [henceforth *CPI*], Vol. III. (Brasilia, 1984).

14. *O Estado de São Paulo*, 24 November 1978, p. 25.

15. This extremely important area of inquiry can benefit greatly from further research. An analysis of U.S. behavior in nuclear exports from this vantage point, by Jacobsen and Hofhansel (1984), points to increased leverage of influential corporate interests over state objectives in moments of "policy crisis" between state and private actors. For a comprehensive analysis of relevant actors in Brazil's foreign policy see Schneider (1976).

16. *O Estado de São Paulo*, 25 February 1986, p. 2. This independent, small-scale program involves about 150 mostly small and medium-sized firms. *Exame*, 14 October 1987, pp. 57–58.

17. *Agence France Presse* (Paris), 18 August 1986.

18. President Sarney's subordination of the Nuclear Energy Commission to the presidency and the military-dominated National Security Council (NSC) may be an indication of such trade-offs. *Veja*, 19 November 1986, p. 50. Placing nuclear budgets for the "parallel program" beyond the finance minister's, let alone legislative, scrutiny may be another. *Veja*, 9 September 1987, pp. 18–27. According to the same source, the NSC had sponsored the transfer of uranium to Iraq. According to Schneider (1976), the Foreign Ministry had a limited voice in Brazil's arms sales' policy.

19. For a systematic study of the industrial-technological impacts of nuclear programs, see Solingen (1989).

20. *O Estado de São Paulo*, 18 September 1986. A total of about $10 billion in foreign exchange is made available for all LDCs each year for the energy sector. *IAEA Bulletin* 27, no. 4 (1985):54.

21. The weight of nuclear-related products and services among Brazilian firms that participated in the program is marginal. At the height of their involvement, the nuclear program accounted for 40 to 50 percent of total revenues for capital goods firms and between 5 and 25 percent for engineering firms. Beyond the three- to five-year link to nuclear-related projects, the bulk of their business was in other energy, infrastructural, and chemical sectors (Solingen, 1989).

22. One-third of this firm is owned by the Amman-based Arab Mining Company, with participation of Saudi Arabia and Iraq. *FBIS*, 14 November 1984, p. 34; 26 February 1985, p. 56.

23. *FBIS*, 4 December 1984, p. 31.

24. *Nucleonics Week*, 17 October 1985, p. 9. However, the World Bank's role in a loan to Brazil's state utility Electrobras, which might have indirectly involved support for nuclear power plant construction, ignited considerable protest on the part of Washington-based environmental and nonproliferation groups, leading to the loan's cancellation (*Nucleonics Week*, 22 September 1988).

25. International lending institutions and commercial banks, however, are likely to examine a buyer's creditworthiness with great care, considerably limiting the potential range of prospective buyers.

26. Aircraft and military equipment have been exempted from the Industrial Products Tax (IPI) and the Merchandise Circulation Tax (ICM), while benefiting from income tax deductions and credit premiums from official banks at special interest rates. See R.A. Hudson, "The Brazilian Way to Technological Independence: Foreign Joint Ventures and the Aircraft Industry," *Inter-American Economic Affairs* 37, no. 2 (1983):23–44.

27. The total debt was estimated at $4 billion in 1984. (*O Estado de São Paulo*, 10 June 1984, 20 December 1985, 1 November 1986. Not a single KWU plant is operating, despite a $7 billion investment (by 1986). Effective transfer of enrichment and reprocessing technologies has not taken place. *FBIS*, 1 July 1986, p. 34.

28. *FBIS*, 12 April 1986.

29. The "dove's dilemma" originally referred to the use of conventional arms transfers as a nonproliferation strategy (Dunn, 1981).

30. Known reserves increased by 2,630 percent, from 11,000 tons in 1975 to 301,490 tons in 1983.

31. *O Globo*, 29 October 1983, p. 16; 22 September 1986, p. 15; *FBIS*, 17 November 1986; *Mundo Eléctrico* (December 1984):23.

32. Until Angra 2 and 3 go into operation, Brazil cannot absorb current production capacity. *O Estado de São Paulo*, 7 September 1988.

33. *Brazilian News Agency*, 15 February 1985; *Gazeta Mercantil*, 6 November 1984; *O Estado de São Paulo*, 6 November 1984, p. 34; 7 September 1988.

34. *O Globo*, 22 September 1986, p. 15; *EFE*, 4 August 1986. Niobium, a superconductor mineral, is used to transmit energy produced by nuclear plants.

35. The same firm intended to export tungsten, molybdenum, tantalum, and hafnium, which may be used in nuclear reactors for naval propulsion. The president of a Brazilian metal-processing firm denounced niobium exports by a binational concern, claiming that his own firm could use niobium to produce a superconducting alloy, which could be exported at hundreds of times the price of the raw material. *FBIS*, 17 February 1987.

36. *Gazeta Mercantil*, 21–22 October 1984, p. 11. *O Estado de São Paulo*, 14 January 1984, p. 22. Exports of rare earths may take a revolutionary course, as they have recently proved to be a key element in the production of an entire class of superconducting materials.

37. Beryllium can be used in the manufacture of the core of a nuclear weapon.

38. These facilities for production of UF_6 are unsafeguarded. *Nuclear Engineering* (March 1987); *Folha de São Paulo*, 7 September 1986, p. 11.

39. See *CPI*, Vol. VI, III, p. 415. Enriched uranium produced in Rezende has little chance of even approaching an internationally competitive price because of the greater cost of enrichment through jet nozzle, compared to diffusion or ultracentrifuge. CPI, Vol. VI, p. 66). However, a recent Brazilian offer included the exchange of low-enriched uranium from Rezende for low- and medium-enriched uranium from Argentina's Pilcaniyeu plant, to suit different needs. Brazil announced its capacity to enrich uranium through high-speed ultracentrifuges in 1987. *Economist Foreign Report*, 24 September 1987.

40. Structural parts and uranium pellets are supplied by the German firm RBU, and the plant is restricted to the loading, welding, and final assembly of UO_2 pellets. Backward integration (local pellet fabrication and UO_2 reconversion) is planned.

41. The percentage of highly processed manufactures over total exports grew from 2 percent to 13 percent from 1970 to 1980. This category includes aircraft, ships, heavy machinery, and electrical machinery, among others (Firebaugh and Bullock, 1986:343).

42. *FBIS*, 2 October 1986.

43. A third of these firms were in the mechanical sector, another third in materials, and the rest in electrical equipment and components, including instrumentation and control.

44. Each set includes one pressure vessel, four steam generators, one pressurizer, eight accumulators, and a reactor core.

45. *FBIS*, 9 February 1984.

46. *Washington Post*, 28 March 1988.

47. *Gazeta Mercantil*, 6 November 1984, p. 14.

48. *Folha de São Paulo*, 27 September 1984, p. 10.

49. This equipment includes scintillation detectors, gamma counters, and profilers. Nuclebras, *O Avanço da Prospeccão e Pesquisa du Uranio no Brasil*, n.d.

50. *O Estado de São Paulo*, 18 November 1984, p. 43; Spitalnik and Fonseca (1985).

51. Rosa et al. (1984:221). Two engineering firms in the "nuclear consortium" were able to compete successfully for detailed design and construction supervisoon of sections of the Baghdad metro.

52. *Nuclear Engineering International* (December 1988).

53. CSN receives information on all aspects of the nuclear program, including private sector capabilities and new technologies, from the National Information Service (SNI). *CPI*, Vol. III, p. 171; *O Globo*, 17 March 1975, p. 12. On the SNI see Góes (1988).

54. Soares (1976). CNEN has also been in charge of research projects—notably, those of the "parallel program," geared to the development of independent capabilities—as well as university research.

55. *Folha de São Paulo*, 1 June 1988.

56. Itamaraty has also played a prominent "marketing" role for Brazilian products and services in many areas.

57. Among trading organizations, Interbras, a subsidiary of Petrobras, has been prominent in negotiating countertrade agreements with oil suppliers, facilitating sales of Brazilian equipment and engineering services.

58. *O Estado de São Paulo*, 25 February 1986.

59. The transitional administration of Sarney has often been accused of accepting a continued military veto power over an array of policy issues.

60. See former president E. Geisel's introduction to a white paper on Brazil's nuclear policy (1977) in Goldemberg (1985).

61. The treaty does not enter into force unless all countries ratify it (Article 28.1), but countries can waive this requirement (Article 28.2). Although Brazil signed and ratified the treaty, it has not chosen to waive the requirement of Article 28.1.

62. *CPI*, Vol. III, p. 88; *Jornal do Brasil*, 26 August 1980.

63. The technical responsibility was to be transferred to Nuclebras as majority partner in December 1986, according to the *CPI*, Vol. III, p. 126.

64. *CPI*, Vol. III, pp. 122–24.

65. Free use of patents and information transferred to Nuclep was made possible only after the fabrication of the sixth set of heavy components (for the sixth plant). *CPI*, Vol. II, p. 126; Vol. IV, p. 73. This stage may never materialize, because only the first two plants (of eight) have survived the program's radical contraction. By 1996, the technology supplied by KWU would be considered obsolete.

66. Tie-out clauses forbid the acquisition of complementary or competing technologies from other than the supplier (Frame, 1983).

67. These licenses are valid for two years, so they are generally not requested too far in advance. *O Estado de São Paulo*, 24 October 1978, p. 7.

68. *Exame*, 14 October 1987, pp. 57–58.

69. *FBIS*, 29 February 1988. A 1980 agreement with Iraq called for adherence to the safeguard provisions of the Brazil–West Germany–IAEA agreement (*Nucleonics Week*, 17 January 1980).

70. *Nucleonics Week*, 27 March 1986, p. 9; *O Estado de São Paulo*, 2 March 1988.

71. *FBIS*, 4 December 1984, p. 32.

72. *FBIS*, 14 May 1984, p. 24; 14 August 1986, p. 12; 13 July 1988; 3 September 1988.

73. *Nucleonics Week*, 30 July 1987. The exchange reflects a rationalization of nuclear trade, since Brazil's 0.85 percent enriched uranium cannot be used in its own plants (greater investments in enrichment would be required), whereas Argentina has an overcapacity in enrichment and uses heavy-water reactors, which do not require enriched uranium.

74. *O Estado de São Paulo*, 11 September 1987, p. 6.

75. *FBIS*, 9 February 84, pp. 36–37. Even for Nuclep's manager, A. Amaral Osorio, the prospects for exports did not seem encouraging. Bids prepared for Peru and Mexico were canceled because of the deactivation of these countries' programs. *O Estado de São Paulo*, 23 October 1983.

76. Nuclep's export to Argentina was arranged by KWU, which is also a partner in the Argentine program. Nuclebras and KWU agreed, also, that Nuclep's approval would be required for exports of nuclear material or services in Latin America. *Brazil Energy*, 12 October 1981, p. 10.

77. These included boilers, heat exchangers, pressure vessels, steel pipes for oil and gas lines, and other oil refinery equipment. Despite the existence of export restrictions, German suppliers approved export licenses in a number of areas.

78. In addition to an effort at absorbing basic design technology supplied by a French consortium, the facilities included a sulfuric acid plant designed with the Brazilian firm's own proprietary technology. *Gazeta Mercantil*, 27 September 1984, p. 13. Overall, including marketing of equipment by other firms, the contract was estimated at $600,000. *FBIS*, 14 November 1984, p. 34.

79. In general, there are few governmental incentives, in other areas, to strengthen engineering exports.

80. *Jornal do Brasil*, 27 September 1979. Other Brazilian sources reported an eight-ton uranium shipment to Iraq. *Brazil Energy*, 24 June 1981, p. 1.

81. *FBIS*, 14 January 1985, p. 41.

82. *Correio Brasiliense*, 12 April 1983; *FBIS*, 13 June 1986, p. 15; Nuclebras, *Uranio, Garantia Brasileira de Independencia Energetica*, n.d.

83. There is a broader theoretical relevance to this finding for the debate over external sector performance as a function of technological variables (see Fajnsylber, 1977).

84. *O Estado de São Paulo*, 30 December 1983, p. 27. These efforts increased after new restrictions were imposed on foreign purchases. Among the items ready to transfer to the private sector were supplementary equipment for various nuclear measures, digital fluorometers for mineral analysis, and multinational analyzers.

85. Promon, accounting for 49 percent of all engineering effort (excluding the nuclear systems) for Angra 1, performed the complete mechanical, electrical, structural, and architectural detailed design of the turbogenerator building and its systems, other nuclear-related and "balance of plant" (nonnuclear) areas, and systems for the utility Furnas (Gasparian and Calvet Filho, 1979).

86. CNEN officials proclaim the international nuclear fuel market to be $15 billion per year and the nuclear technology market another $100 billion per year. *Exame*, 14 October 1987, pp. 57–58.

87. In 1984, CNEN announced a contract with a British firm for distributing Brazilian-made 100-curie iridium-192 (^{192}Ir) waffles to Argentina, Bolivia, Colombia, Chile, and Venezuela. *O Estado de São Paulo*, 19 January 1984, p. 8.

88. The 1975 agreements between Nuclebras and KWU established the need to consult with Nuclep for any material or service to be sold in Latin America, pointing to potential Brazilian participation in any such transaction *Brazil Energy*, 10 December 1981, p. 10.

89. Argentina's Enace (CNEA/KWU) bid for Iran's and Egypt's power reactors, in conjunction with Spain's ENSA and West Germany's KWU.

90. In the decade following 1964, outward-oriented policies led to the abolition of state export taxes, simplified administrative export procedures, and export tax incentives and subsidized credits (Baer and Von Doellinger, 1978). In the early 1980s, commercial policies have been characterized by an "antiexport" bias. See William G. Tyler, "The Anti-Export Bias in Commercial Policies and Export Performance: Some Evidence from the Recent Brazilian Experience," *World Bank Reprint Series* 273 (1983):98.

91. Countertrade arrangements are a prime feature of Brazil's relations with Iran and Nigeria. The latter, an NPT signatory, is Brazil's third-largest trading partner ($2.3 billion volume in 1985), after the United States and Iraq. Algeria, Angola, Mozambique, and Qatar are among Brazil's non-NPT trading partners, and Saudi Arabia has recently pledged to join the treaty.

92. "Engenharia e Consultoria no Brasil e no Grupo Andino: Possiveis Areas de Cooperação," Serie Estudios para o Planejamento 25 (Brasilia: Projeto de Pesquisa Conjunta IPEA/CEPAL, Instituto de Planejamento Economico e Social, 1984), p. 45.

93. *Nucleonics Week*, 5 December 1985, p. 9.

94. *Integración Latinoamericana*, 4 (1987):90. Research on breeder reactors is conducted at the Advanced Studies Institute (IEA), subordinated to the Airspace Technical Center in Sao Jose dos Campos. *FBIS*, 2 October 1986. The joint breeder project was to begin as early as February 1987. *FBIS*, January 1987.

95. Brazil lacks, however, the experience of India or Argentina in reactor design and operation and in direct supervision of project development and management. India has developed a 235 MW unit, and Argentina has recently launched its 380 MW(e) Argos PHWR.

96. Brazil's navy minister confirmed that a "nuclear submarine propulsion system" is being developed in Ipero. *FBIS*, 3 December 1986. The model for a nuclear submarine compact reactor is being developed at IPEN and would be built, presumably, in the second half of the 1990s. *Veja*, 20 August 1986; *Folha de São Paulo*, 23 August 1986.

97. Several Brazilian firms that supplied the nuclear program (Cobrasma, Odebrecht, Metaleve) were among the most active participants in some of these meetings. *Integración Latinoamericana*, 4 (1987):63; *FBIS*, 28 April 1988; *Nuclear Engineering International*, May 1988.

98. *Nucleonics Week*, 24 July 1986, 11 December 1986, 15 January 1987; *FBIS*, 3 December 1986.

99. Brazil has recently been approached to join a ban on exports of sensitive missile technology, signed by the United States, the United Kingdom, West Germany, Japan, Italy, Canada, and France but it refused to do so. *New York Times*, 17 April 1987.

100. The concept of "crazy states" was coined by Y. Dror (1971). This argument is particularly relevant to Argentine–Iranian cooperation, including Argentine sales of 20 percent enriched uranium to Iran. *Jornal do Brasil*, 14 June 1987, p. 21.

101. However, South Africa, Rhodesia, and Somalia were refused arms sales (Selcher, 1984) for reasons of political expediency (i.e. relations with black African states).

102. Brazil reestablished diplomatic relations with Cuba in 1986, with strong support from the business community, twenty-two years after severing formal ties.

103. It may be interesting to watch Soviet reactions to such a scenario, given Gorbachev's new approach to the Third World, Soviet–Cuban relations, and the USSR's traditional postures regarding diffusion of nuclear technology. On Soviet nonproliferation policy, see Potter (1985).

104. In his efforts at promoting nuclear energy, Edward Teller expressed in a visit to Indonesia in 1975 that the country may be willing to exchange oil for reactors: "up to 1/2 million barrels a day for 20 reactors." J.M. Huacuz V., "El Debate Nuclear y sus Implicaciones en America Latina," *Interciencia* 2, no. 5 (1977):264–74.

105. In fact, Brazilian arms sales to Saudi Arabia involved a number of offsets (Neuman, 1985).

106. Witness, also, actual behavior, such as proposed barter arrangements with Yugoslavia (pilot plants for fuel cycle and heavy water in exchange for goods).

107. Nuclear trade enjoys a special status under the GATT and other multilateral trade arrangements, escaping restrictions on governmental intervention. Subsidies, preferential treatment for domestic suppliers, and fiscal measures are the norm (Walker and Lonnroth, 1983).

108. State leadership, however, may improve control over export conditions related to safeguards. Emerging suppliers may feel more compelled than traditional suppliers to behave responsibly, to justify their claim to political maturity and moral equivalence.

References

Araoz, A., and F.C. Sercovich. 1977. *Oferta de Tecnología Comercializable*, Serie Ciencia y Tecnología No. 4. Buenos Aires: CISEA.

Baer, W., and C. Von Doellinger. 1978. "Determinants of Brazil's Foreign Economic Policy." In J. Grunwald, ed., *Latin America and World Economy: A Changing International Order*. Beverly Hills, Calif.: Sage, pp. 147–61.

Chudnovsky, D., and M. Nagao. 1983. *Capital Goods Production in the Third World*. New York: St. Martin's Press.

Dahlman, C., and F.C. Sercovich. 1984. "Local Development and Exports of Technology," World Bank Staff Working Papers No. 667. Washington D.C.: World Bank.

Dror, Y. 1971. *Crazy States: A Counterconventional Strategic Problem*. Lexington, Mass.: Heath Lexington Books.

Dunn, Lewis A. 1981. "Some Reflections on the dove's dilemma?" *International Organization* 35, Number 1 (Winter):181–92.

Emmanuel, A. 1969. *Unequal Exchange: A Study of the Imperialism of Trade*. New York: Monthly Review Press.

Erber, F., et al. 1984. *A Politica Tecnologica da Segunda Metade dos Anos Oitenta*. Rio de Janeiro: Instituto de Economia Industrial.

Fajnsylber, F. 1977. "Oligopolio, Empresas Transnacionais e Estilos de Desenvolvimento. *Cadernos CEBRAP* 19.

Firebaugh, G., and B.P. Bullock. 1986. "Level of Processing of Exports: Estimates for Developing Nations. *International Studies Quarterly* 30, no. 3:333–50.

Frame, D.J. 1983. *International Business and Global Technology*. Lexington, Mass.: Lexington Books.

Gasparian, A.E., and H. Calvet Filho. 1979. "The Role of Brazilian Architect Engineering Firms in the Transfer and Development of Nuclear Power Plant Technology." Paper presented at the Pan American Nuclear Technology Exchange Conference. Hollywood, Florida.

Góes, Walder de. 1988. "Military and Political Transition." In Chacel, J.M., P.S. Falk, and D.V. Fleischer, eds., *Brazil's Economic and Political Future*. Boulder: Westview Press.

Goldemberg, Jose. 1985. "Brazil." In Joseph Goldblat, ed., *Nonproliferation: The Why and the Wherefore*. London: Taylor and Francis, p. 817.

Jacobsen, J.K., and C. Hofhansel. 1984. "Safeguards and Profits: Civilian Nuclear Exports, Neo-Marxism, and the Statist Approach." *International Studies Quarterly* 28:195–218.

Jones, W.R., C. Merlini, J. Pilat, and W.C. Potter, eds. 1985. *The Nuclear Suppliers and Nonproliferation: International Policy Choices*. Lexington, Mass.: Lexington Books.

Lepecki, W.P.S. 1985. "The Brazilian Nuclear Program and the Technology Transfer from the F.R.G. to Brazil." Paper presented at the Second International Course on Nuclear Physics and Reactors. Bogota, Colombia.

Lock, P. 1986. "Brazil: Arms for Export." In M. Brzoska and T. Ohlson, eds., *Arms Production in the Third World*. London: Taylor and Francis. Mitra, J.D. 1979. "The Capital Goods Sector in LDCs: A Case Study for State Intervention," World Bank Staff Working Papers No. 343. Washington D.C.: World Bank.

Morel, R.L. de. 1979. *Ciencia e Estado: A Política Científica no Brasil*. São Paulo: T.A. Queiroz.

Myers, David J. 1984. "Brazil: Reluctant Pursuit of the Nuclear Option." Orbis (Winter):881–911.

Mytelka, L.K. 1987. "Knowledge-Intensive Production and the Changing Internationalization Strategies of Multinational Firms." In J.A. Caporaso, ed., *A Changing International Division of Labor*. Boulder, Colo.: Lynne Rienner, pp. 43–70.

Neuman, S.G. 1985. "Coproduction, Barter, and Countertrade: Offsets in the International Arms Market." *Orbis* (Spring):183–213.

Potter, W.C. 1985. "The Soviet Union and Nonproliferation." *Slavic Review* (Fall):468–88.

Quester, George H. 1979. "Brazil and Latin American Nuclear Proliferation," CISA Working Paper 17. Los Angeles: UCLA, Center for International and Strategic Affairs.

Redick, John. 1981. "The Tlatelolco Regime and Nonproliferation in Latin America." *International Organization* 35, no. 1 (Winter):103–34.

———. 1984. "Nonproliferation and Latin America: Some Current Policy Options." Paper presented at the Conference on Nonproliferation: Attitudes and Motivations, SIPRI, October 18–19.

Roett, Riordan. 1985. "Brazil and the United States: Beyond the Debt Crisis." *Journal of Interamerican Studies and World Affairs* 27, no.1:1–17.

Rosa, L.P., et al. 1984. *Technological and Economic Impact of the Brazilian Nuclear Program*. Rio de Janeiro: COPPE, UFRJ, Area Interdiciplinar de Energia.

Schneider, Ronald M. 1976. *Brazil—Foreign Policy of a Future World Power*. Boulder, Colo.: Westview Press.

Selcher, Wayne, ed. 1981. *Brazil in the International System: The Rise of a Middle Power*. Boulder, Colo.: Westview Press.

———. 1984. "Brazil's Foreign Policy: More Actors and Expanding Agendas." In J.K. Lincoln and E.G. Ferris eds., *The Dynamics of Latin American Foreign Policies: Challenges for the 1980s*. Boulder, Colo.: Westview Press, pp. 101–24.

Sercovich, F.C. 1978. "Design Engineering and Endogenous Technical Change." Working Paper No. 19. Buenos Aires: BID/CEPAL.

Soares, G.F.S. 1976. "O Acordo de Cooperação Nuclear Brasil–Alemanha Federal." *Revista Forense* 253:207–32.

Solingen, E. 1989. "Technology and the Industrializing State: Domestic Structures and Institutional Constrants in Brazil and Argentina." In preparation.

Spector, Leonard S. 1988. *The Undeclared Bomb*. Cambridge, Mass.: Ballinger.

Spitalnik, J., and G. Fonseca. 1985. "Training in Brazil." presented at the Fifth Pacific Basin Nuclear Conference, Seoul, Korea, May.

Villela, A.V., and W. Baer. 1980. *O Setor Privado Nacional: Problemas e Políticas para seu Fortalecimento*. Rio de Janeiro: IPEA/INPES.

Walker, W. and M. Lönnroth. 1983. *Nuclear Power Struggles: Industrial Competition and Proliferation Control*. Winchester, Mass.: Allen & Unwin.

Wesson, Robert. 1981. *The US and Brazil: Limits of Influence*. New York: Praeger.

World Bank Country Study (WBCS). 1980. *Brazil: Industrial Policies and Manfactured Exports*. Washington D.C.: World Bank.

Appendix 7
Brazilian nuclear program: Current capabilities (1987).

	SITE	LOCATION	STATUS	TYPE	SIZE	OPERATION	DESIGN
RESEARCH REACTORS	Institute of Atomic Energy	Sao Paulo	Critical S	Pool	5 MWT	1957	Babcock & Wilcox
	Institute of Radioactive Research	Belo Horizonte	Critical S	Tank	100 KWT	1960	General Dynamics
	Institute of Nuclear Engineering	Rio de Janeiro	Critical S	Tank Arg.	10 KWT	1965	Brazil (on US Argonne)
	Aerospace Technology Institute	Sao Jose Dos Campos	Sub-Critical			?	Brazil
	Nuclear Energy Center	Pernambuco	Sub-Critical			?	Brazil
POWER REACTORS	Angra I	Rio de Janeiro	Critical S	PWR	626 MWE	1985	Westinghouse
	Angra II	Rio de Janeiro		PWR	1245 MWE	1992	Estimated KWU
	Angra III	Rio de Janeiro	PWR	1245 MWE	1997	Estimated KWU	
	6 Additional reactor projects on hold.						
HEAVY COMPONENTS FACTORY	NUCLEP (Joint venture Nuclebras-KWU)	Itaguai				1980	KWU

Source: FBIS, 1978–1983; Nucleonics Week, 1978–1987; C.P.I., 1983, Nuclebras, Annual Reports (1983–86).

Appendix 7 (Cont.)

FUEL CYCLE FACILITIES	LOCATION	SAFEGROS	BASIC DESIGN	OPERATION
URANIUM MINING and CONCENTRATE (yellowcake)	Pocos de Caldas	S	Pechiney Ugine-Kuhlman	1982
	Itatiaia Pilot plant	U	Brazil(?)	1986
CONVERSION (UF6)	Resende	S	Pechiney Ugine-Kuhlman	Postponed
	IPEN (Sao Paulo) Pilot plant	U	Brazil	1984
ENRICH-MENT — Jet Nozzle	Resende Demonstration Plant	S	NUCLEI (Steag, Interatom, Muclebras)	1992 (?)
	Resende Industrial Plant	S		
Ultra-centrifuge	IPEN / Pilot plant Aramar	U / U	Brazil / Brazil	1986 (?) / 1988
FUEL ELEMENT ASSEMBLY	Resende	S	KWU-RBU	1982
REPROCESSING	Resende Pilot plant	S	KEWA UHED	Postponed
	IPEN Sao Paulo	96F	Brazil	1986

Key
S = Safeguarded
U = Unsafeguarded
SSF = Safeguarded for safeguarded fuel only.

8

India:
Groping for a Supplier Policy

Rodney W. Jones

Interest has grown recently in the issues of "third tier" or "emerging" nuclear suppliers.[1] These are states that could export nuclear equipment, services, or technology but are outside the export control framework of the London Nuclear Suppliers Group (NSG). The concern is that they may conduct nuclear trade without adequate safeguards, thus weakening the nonproliferation regime or even contributing to nuclear proliferation. The volume of nuclear sales by emerging suppliers is still minuscule, and it is unclear how far their export practices will diverge from the NSG framework.[2] This case study of Indian nuclear supplier capability and practice is an effort to discern the type of path India is likely to adopt.

India probably is the best-established Third World nation to build civilian nuclear plants and elements of the nuclear fuel cycle.[3] India is well ahead of the People's Republic of China (PRC) in *civilian* nuclear power development. With six operational nuclear power reactors as of 1988, including two built almost entirely at home, India outranks both Argentina and Brazil. Both South Korea and Taiwan have greatly outdistanced India in installed nuclear power[4] but have accepted dependence on foreign suppliers for most nuclear equipment and have refrained from developing full nuclear fuel cycles. Hence, India probably exceeds both South Korea and Taiwan in nuclear industrial capabilities.

India has the potential, therefore, to become the most prominent Third World nuclear supplier.[5] This is one but not the only reason that India is an interesting case. India resembles France in experience and attitudes. Early French nuclear policies were the least conformist of the major Western suppliers, as evidenced by France's refusal to join the NPT. Before 1979, France also was reluctant to join multilateral coordination of nuclear export controls.

I am indebted to Joseph Yager and T.V. Paul for their comments on this chapter during its preparation.

Like France in the early days, India perceives itself to be victimized by the nonproliferation policies of the major powers and so justifies its non-conforming international policies.[6] Like France, India has aimed to become commercially self-reliant in nuclear technology, even when the cost-effectiveness has been dubious. If India someday promotes nuclear exports vigorously, as France has done, it will matter greatly whether India emulates earlier French policies or, instead, moves close to the NSG framework, just as France finally did.

This case study examines four aspects of India's nuclear activity for clues to India's potential role as an emerging nuclear supplier: (1) foreign transactions; (2) nuclear decision making; (3) policy norms; and (4) nuclear industrial capabilities.

Transactions

The vast majority of India's foreign nuclear transactions have been imports, not exports. India has imported nuclear technology, equipment, materials, and services to build nuclear research and power programs. From the start, India sought self-reliance in these programs—to keep them free from long-term foreign financial or technical dependence.

India's goal of autarky dictated a multisource acquisition strategy, playing on the political and commercial competition between the major suppliers.[7] India's payoffs from this strategy were high in the "Atoms for Peace" era of the 1950s and 1960s but shrank after India's explosion of a nuclear device in 1974. As a result, India is still in an import-for-indigenous-development mode, requires all of its nuclear industrial output for domestic purposes, and shows only sporadic interest in nuclear export opportunities.

Nuclear Cooperation Agreements

India enjoys agreements for peaceful nuclear cooperation with the countries listed in tables 8–1 and 8–2.[8] India has a large number of such agreements with advanced nuclear supplier countries, both in the West (ten) and in the Soviet bloc (six), plus Yugoslavia.

Until recently, India relied almost exclusively on Western suppliers for major nuclear equipment, fuel, and technical service inputs. But India also used the prospect of Soviet supply alternatives to expedite U.S., Canadian, and British decisions to aid India in nuclear research and power development in the 1950s and 1960s. At the same time, India maneuvered among Western competitors to win supply on exceptionally favorable terms, including less stringent safeguards.[9]

India has made nuclear cooperation agreements with at least fifteen

Table 8–1
India's Nuclear Cooperation Agreements—Advanced Countries

Affiliation/Country	Date of Origin	Type of Cooperation	Sources
Western World			
Belgium	1/30/65	research	(1,2)
Canada	4/20/56	research reactor	(3)
	11/15/63*,12/16/66*	power	(3)
Denmark	2/18/63	research	(1)
FRG (W. Germany)	10/5/71, 5/19/72	research/hvy water	(1,2,4)
	2/7/74	safety/medicine	(2,3,4)
France	6/23/65	research	(1)
	4/3/69, 7/22/69	heavy water facility	(1,4)
	5/7/71, 3/72	breeder cooperation	(3,4)
Italy	—	—	(1)
Spain	3/27/65	research	(1)
Sweden	—	research	(4)
United Kingdom	12/23/55	research	(3)
United States	10/25/63, 12/7/63	power/fuel	(1,2,3)
	12/7/71	IAEA safeguards	(1,2,3)
Soviet Bloc			
Czechoslovakia	1/01/67	research	(1,2)
GDR (E. Germany)	6/19/74, 6/12/82	research	(1,3)
Hungary	10/9/61	research	(1,2)
Poland	—	—	(2)
Romania	3/18/72	research	(1,2)
USSR**	10/6/61, 1968, 1/22/71	research	(1,2,3,4)
	1/22/76	hvy water/safeguards	(4)
	1/22/79	research	(2,3,4)
	10/20/88	power/fuel/spent fuel	(5)
Yugoslavia	—	—	(2)

Sources:

1 *Nuclear Proliferation Factbook*, 1977, pp. 275–78.

2 Graham Chronology, citing Prime Minister Indira Gandhi's statement in Parliament, *Foreign Broadcast Information Service* (FBIS), August 8, 1980.

3 Graham Chronology.

4 G.G. Mirchandani and P.K.S. Namboodiri, *Nuclear India: A Technological Assessment*, 1981, pp. 133–145.

5 Cited *infra*, *Washington Post*, Nov. 21, 1988, pp. A15, A21.

* The first agreement expired in 1971; the second agreement was terminated along with all nuclear cooperation on May 18, 1976.

** This table deals with peaceful (civilian) nuclear cooperation agreements. In late 1987, the Soviet Union and India consummated an agreement for Indian lease of Soviet nuclear-powered submarines.

developing countries—six or seven in Asia, six in the Middle East, and three in Latin America. With its Asian and Middle East partners, India normally would expect to be the seller. But its Latin American partners, Brazil and Argentina, are sufficiently advanced to offer two-way cooperation or even assistance to India. In Asia, India appears to have no nuclear

Table 8–2
India's Nuclear Cooperation Agreements—Developing Countries

Region/Country	Date of Origin	Type of Cooperation	Sources
Asia			
Afghanistan	12/12/65	research	(1,2)
Bangladesh	8/27/73	research	(1)
Indonesia	—	research	(4)
Malaysia	—	research	(4)
Philippines	3/14/69	research	(1)
Sri Lanka	1/–/86	research	(5)
Middle East			
Algeria	—	—	(2)
Egypt	7/10/62	research	(1)
	1981, 5/14/84	—	(3)
Iran	2/25/77, 8/19/82	—	(3)
Iraq	3/28/74	research	(1,2)
Libya	7/19/78	technical aid	(2,3)
Syria	—	—	(2)
Latin America			
Argentina	5/28/74	research	(1,2,3)
Brazil	9/23/68, 6/5/74	—	(3)
	3/08/84	—	(3)
Cuba	5/30/85	—	(3)

Sources:
1 *Nuclear Proliferation Factbook*, 1977, pp. 275–78.
2 Graham Chronology, citing Prime Minister Indira Gandhi's statement in Parliament, *Foreign Braodcast Information Service* (FBIS), August 8, 1980.
3 Graham Chronology.
4 G.G. Mirchandani and P.K.S. Namboodiri, *Nuclear India: A Technological Assessment*, 1981, pp. 133–145.
5 *Nuclear Engineering International*, "Regional Prospects," January 1986.

cooperation with South Korea and Taiwan, two states with relatively advanced nuclear power programs. Not surprisingly, India has no formal nuclear cooperation with the PRC or Pakistan, two other Asian states with significant nuclear programs.

Several Indian nuclear relationships with developing countries are politically sensitive. In Asia, the documented one with Indonesia and the undocumented one with Vietnam could fall into that category. In the Middle East, they include relationships with Libya, Iran, Iraq, and Syria. In the Latin American region, India's cooperation with Brazil and Argentina may be sensitive on nonproliferation grounds and that with Cuba on political grounds.

Major Indian Nuclear Import Relationships

In India's nuclear research sector, the United States, Canada, the United Kingdom, and France have all played a supply role. France supported

India's experimental fast breeder reactor program, and India's plutonium reprocessing capability was derived largely from French and U.S. scientific and industrial sources (see table 8–3).

The United States and Canada have been the principal suppliers of nuclear hardware and fuel for India's nuclear power program. India's indigenous nuclear power plants are based essentially on the Canadian-designed, heavy-water-moderated, natural-uranium-fueled (CANDU) reactors. Indian development of fuel fabrication facilities also drew on Canadian technical assistance. Canada was India's main source for heavy water until 1976, when Canada suspended cooperation in lieu of Indian acceptance of comprehensive safeguards.

Seeking self-reliance in heavy-water production, India engaged West German, French, Swiss, and Japanese sources to construct facilities for this purpose as adjuncts to chemical fertilizer plants in India. The completion and operation of these facilities has followed a bumpy course.[10]

In 1976, the Soviet Union replaced Canada as India's main foreign supplier of heavy water. Operating the CANDU reactors in Rajasthan depended subsequently on this Soviet-supplied heavy water. Despite initial vacillation, Moscow finally insisted on stringent IAEA safeguards conditions on the equipment and on any nuclear material exposed to this heavy water in India.[11]

India's shortages of domestically produced, unsafeguarded heavy water caused delays into the mid-1980s in bringing the newly built Madras power reactors and the Dhruva (R-5) research reactor on line. India was determined to keep its homemade reactors free of safeguards. For the same reasons, India may have imported, through shady channels, several shipments of heavy water originating in China,[12] the USSR, and Norway.[13]

With West German assistance in 1972, India apparently investigated the feasibility of using the Becker nozzle uranium enrichment technology.[14] Plans for gas-centrifuge enrichment had been featured in India's 1970 Department of Atomic Energy Plan (the "Sarabhai profile"),[15] and a low-key R&D program was maintained thereafter. Recently, Indian sources revealed that a laboratory scale centrifuge facility was completed in 1984 at the Bhabha Atomic Research Center (BARC) site in Trombay, with about 100 centrifuges.[16]

Instead of ramping up this BARC facility to about 1,500 centrifuges, as first planned, the Indian Atomic Energy Commission (IAEC) is said to have begun construction of a 5,000 centrifuge facility at the Rare Materials Plant (RMP) at Ratanhalli, near Mysore, in Karnataka.[17] Reportedly, "a special purchase cell has been set up [presumably in the Department of Atomic Energy] to import a range of components [including] electronic and mechanical devices for controlling motor speeds."[18] Where India will obtain these components is unclear, but it may be worth keeping an eye on the sources Pakistan went to in its covert acquisition program.[19]

Table 8–3
Principal Indian Nuclear Import Relationships

Supplier	Reactors			Materials				Sensitive Facilities		Other Facilities	
	Research	Power	Advanced	Low Enriched Uranium	High Enriched Uranium	Plutonium	Heavy Water	Reprocess	Enrichment	Fuel Fabr.	Heavy Water
Canada	X	X		X			X			X	X
France	X	O	X	X	O	O		X			X
W. Germany			X						O		X
Japan										X	X
Norway							X[1]				
Sweden		O									
Switzerland											X
U.K.	X				X						X
U.S.A.		X		X	X	X	X	X			X
U.S.S.R.		X		X			X				
China (PRC)							X[1]				O

Key

x denotes actual assistance or cooperation occured

o denotes that assistance or cooperation was offered or solicited, but did not occur.

Sources: CRS, *Nuclear Proliferation Factbook*, 1977; Mirchandani and Namboodiri, *Nuclear India*, 1981, pp. 133–145.

[1] Gary Milhollin of the Wisconsin Law Project has compiled evidence that Alfred Hempel, owner of Rohstoff Einfuhr and other nuclear brokerage firms, illegally diverted various quantities of heavy water from Norway, the Soviet Union and China to India. See, for instance, Gary Milhollin, "Bonn's Proliferation Policy," *New York Times*, Jan. 4, 1989; John J. Fialka, "How 'Heavy Water' Seeps Through Cracks of Nuclear Regulation," *Wall Street Journal*, Jan. 3, 1989; and S. Hazarika, "Norway Planning to Ban Export of Heavy Water, *New York Times*, Nov. 12, 1988, p. A12.

India's major nuclear import relationships with the United States and Canada were severely strained by the 1974 detonation of a nuclear device. Canada severed nuclear cooperation with India in 1976. American nuclear cooperation with India, which revolved mainly around the U.S.–supplied Tarapur power plant, was suspended for all practical purposes by 1979, after India refused to accommodate changes made in U.S. nuclear export laws in 1978 and France agreed to take over the supply of Tarapur fuel.

All other major suppliers became at least a little more restrictive in nuclear exports to India after 1974. Both France and the USSR were willing to continue to export nuclear items to India without requiring NPT or full-scope safeguards, yet both have tightened certain other conditions: The Soviet Union, as mentioned earlier, required IAEA safeguards as a condition for supply of heavy water, and France declined to supply highly enriched uranium to India for the fuel core of the experimental fast breeder reactor at Kalpakkam, even though this reactor was built with French assistance.

India continues to import mechanical and electronic components for its nuclear reactors,[20] enriched uranium for Tarapur, and heavy water for CANDU reactors, and it appears to have geared up to import components for an enrichment facility. Although India has made steady progress in reducing dependence on foreign equipment imports for the CANDU-type power reactors planned by the IAEC, Indian-built reactors apparently are not performing as well as would be hoped and are increasingly out of date in design. India will have to import from advanced suppliers in order to modernize its reactor designs, satisfy world-standard safety requirements, or acquire state-of-the-art production capabilities for major nuclear reactor components.

During Soviet leader Gorbachev's visit to India in November 1988, a formal agreement was signed for Soviet supply of twin 1,000-MW power reactors.[21] The Soviet Union had offered to sell power reactors to India on previous occasions.[22] India first seriously considered this possibility in the early 1980s, and there were reports in 1987 that a Soviet power plant supply agreement was all but final.[23] India had also explored the possibility of French assistance with power reactor production in the mid-1980s,[24] and Sweden had declined earlier Indian overtures.[25] The agreement to buy Soviet nuclear power plants suggests, among other things,[26] that India finally concluded that it must buy abroad to expand nuclear power on a reliable basis, raising questions about its former claims of self-sufficiency.

Indian Nuclear Export Activities and Relationships

The record of Indian nuclear export activities (see table 8–4) shows that they are sporadic and limited. India has exported nuclear items mainly to

Table 8–4
Indian Nuclear Export Inquiries and Transactions

Region/Recipient Country	Date of Action	Type of Transaction	Source
Asia			
Bangladesh	n.a.	India agreed to build a 1 MW research reactor.	(5)
Indonesia	late 1970s	India supplied on turnkey basis a Cobalt-60 batch irradiator at Indonesia's nuclear research center.	(5)
Malaysia	n.a.	India offered to set up an atomic power plant.	(5)
Philippines	n.a.	In collaboration with IAEA, India set up a neutron crystal spectrometer in a facility for nuclear physics training.	(5)
Sri Lanka	Aug. 1985	Inquiry from Sri Lanka as to whether India could help build an Apsara-type reactor (swimming pool research reactor fueled by enriched uranium, Apsara being 1 MWt).	(2,4c)
	Jan. 1986	Indo-Sri Lanka agreement for Indian assistance in developing a research reactor.	(8a)
Middle East			
Egypt	n.a.	Indian assistance with ore extraction and isotopes.	(6)
Iraq	1977 (?)	Bid to construct "hot cells".	(3)
	n.a.	Site study	(6)
	n.a.	Remote handling equipment.	
Libya	1978–79	Engineering and construction contract bids for infra-structure projects; Libyan request for sensitive technology (plotonium reprocessing) entertained, but finally rejected.	(1,3)
		Indo-Libyan agreement covered Indian assistance with uranium extraction and conversion to fuel; reprocessing; waste management; and perhaps a HWR research reactor. India offered design for a uranium extraction plant, but Libya dropped the agreement.	(6)
	1978–79	Libyan solicitation of nuclear explosive know-how and technology; rejected.	(2)
Iran	1977–78	Technical exchange visits	(6)
	1982	Iran asked India for help to	(2,4a)

Table 8–4 continued

Region/Recipient Country	Date of Action	Type of Transaction	Source
		complete Bushehr power plant project.	
		Discussion, but not concrete Indian action.	(6)
Saudi Arabia	n.a.	India approached for a zero-energy (research) assembly; Riyadh declined because price too high.	(6)
Latin America Argentina	1984	India reportedly discussed cooperation in heavy water technology.	(2,4b)
		Proposed exchange of technical information on HWR for information on Plutonium extraction.	(6)
Brazil	1985–86	Technical exchange involving uranium enrichment.	(7)
	1986	Brazilian nuclear official (of Indian extraction) requested Indian cooperation in fast breeder reactor (FBR) technology.	(8)

Sources:

1. Rodney W. Jones, *Nuclear Proliferation* (1981), pp. 52–53 (citing *The Economist*, Nov. 17, 1979, p. 72).

2. Graham Chronology.

3. Weissman and Krosney, *The Islamic Bomb* (1981).

4. *Nucleonics Week*, (a) Sept. 2, 1982; (b) NOv. 29, 1984; (c) Sept. 5, 1985.

5. G.G. Mirchandani and P.K.S. Namboodiri, *Nuclear India: A Technological Assessment*, 1981, pp. 133–145.

6. Author's interviews with Indian officials in New Delhi and Bombay, September 1987.

7. Information supplied to author at Bellagio conference, June 1987.

8. *Worldwide Report*, Aug. 2, 1986, p. 17.

8a. *Nuclear Engineering International*, "Regional Prospects", January 1986.

Third World countries, typically involving assistance to budding research programs by training of foreign personnel in Indian universities or nuclear research institutions. India's actual nuclear export transactions—those completed, not just contemplated—generally have not involved transfer of major nuclear equipment, sensitive technology, or significant quantities of fissionable materials. Possible exceptions to this general rule could occur with supply of a research reactor to Sri Lanka and may have been envisaged in a deal with Libya (discussed below).

Evidence of Indian efforts to enter the market to sell nuclear research reactors (for example, to Sri Lanka and Bangladesh) or nuclear power equipment and services (for example, to Malaysia, Iran, and Egypt) is sketchy and may be unreliable. It is insufficient thus far to establish a definite trend. Rather, it suggests that India is neither inclined nor ready to promote nuclear exports. India's nuclear industrial capability probably is fully committed to the needs of the home market.

This need not prevent India from entering contracts for nuclear power services to an internationally isolated country, such as Iran during the 1980s, which might seek an alternative nuclear supplier within the developing world. India could even make room in its industrial production to bid to supply one or two nuclear power projects in a developing country for prestige or for political or economic gains.

Hoping to establish a secure supply of Middle East petroleum after the 1973 oil crisis, India's Janata government negotiated an economic agreement with Libya in 1977–78 that promised nuclear assistance.[27] It also paved the way for India to bid on potentially lucrative engineering and construction projects in Libya and involved Libyan promises to supply crude oil on favorable terms. Libyan officials apparently asked for reprocessing technology and perhaps even nuclear explosive information from India. India finally rebuffed Libya's nuclear overtures, and Libya canceled the oil supply agreement.

This episode should be treated with caution. The way the story is now being told in India suggests that the Morarji Desai government blundered, against the advice of atomic energy officials, into a relationship with Libya that obligated India to help Libya develop sensitive nuclear technology or facilities. This story may be overstated as a result of partisan attacks on Desai and other Janata leaders by members of a successor government.[28] Prime Minister Desai's international nuclear policy broke with the mainstream in certain other respects and provoked considerable domestic opposition from the weapons lobby.[29]

The more important point raised by this case, and by the report of Indian willingness to bid on Iraqi acquisition of hot cell facilities, is the possible Indian vulnerability to pressure from the Middle East oil suppliers. It would be ironic if India could be viewed as easily as Pakistan or another Muslim country as the progenitor of an Islamic bomb.

In the final analysis, the list of actual Indian nuclear export transactions is rather short. The volume of India's nuclear export activities thus appears to be very small.

The Structure of Indian Nuclear Decision Making

This chapter explores the commercial aspects of Indian nuclear decision making for clues to the shape of a future nuclear export policy. Much has been published on India's domestic nuclear power program and nuclear issues in foreign relations. But little has been written about Indian decision making on nuclear imports, let alone on Indian nuclear exports. The discussion here consists of inferences about the main players and responsibilities in the process from the structure of Indian institutions that bear on nuclear policy and programs; therefore, it must be regarded as tentative.

National Policy

The policy structure for nuclear affairs in India remains highly centralized, despite years of bureaucratic differentiation. The prime minister personally acts as the cabinet minister in charge of atomic energy. The chief atomic scientist or engineer usually serves directly under the prime minister, both as secretary of the Department of Atomic Energy (DAE) and as chairman of the Indian Atomic Energy Commission (IAEC).[30] The relationship was institutionalized under Prime Minister Jawaharlal Nehru with Dr. Homi Bhabha, father of the Indian nuclear program, and remains formally intact today.[31]

In the early years, the high-level access of the DAE/IAEC chief was used to carve out an autonomous sphere of management for the nuclear research and power programs. Over the years, the DAE/IAEC constellation of activities, sites, and organizations became an impressive bureaucratic and industrial empire. By one recent estimate, it consumes about one-third of the Indian public resources devoted to research and development (R&D).[32] Moreover, the DAE/IAEC complex is beginning to exercise a quasi-managerial role over public and private sector industrial firms that supply the nuclear sector (a matter to be discussed further here).

Major Tensions in National Policy and Programs

Historically, the IAEC has faced bureaucratic competition mainly from the "foreign office"— the Ministry of External Affairs (MEA)—and the "resource planners"—the Ministry of Finance and the Planning Commission. The IAEC chiefs have also found their access at the highest levels constrained, however, by the addition of new layers of bureaucracy around the prime minister and, over time, by the attenuation of personal relationships that once had made that access unusually effective.

The MEA has played a major role in articulating India's diplomatic and international legal posture on nuclear matters in the United Nations and arms control and disarmament arenas and in International Atomic Energy Agency (IAEA) affairs. The MEA has also been where India's detailed positions in agreements for cooperation in peaceful nuclear activities and acceptance (or rejection) of certain nuclear safeguards conditions have been hammered out.

The policy guidelines and crucial decisions on these matters have been made at the cabinet or subcabinet level. In the 1960s, for example, crucial decisions concerning the NPT were prepared in the Emergency Committee of the Cabinet (ECC), a subcommittee formed in response to the Chinese invasion of 1962 and consisting of key cabinet ministers and coordinate department secretaries.[33] In the ECC, the DAE secretary could count on being heard on nuclear policy issues, particularly on technical aspects.

For more than a decade, however, the ECC has ceased to be pivotal. It was essentially superseded by the Political Affairs Committee of the cabinet, whose responsibilities have been principally of a domestic political and internal security nature.

Meanwhile, under both Indira Gandhi and Rajiv Gandhi, the locus of decision making on sensitive foreign relations and nuclear policy issues has gravitated away from cabinet committees and the formally responsible departments into the prime minister's "secretariat." The prime minister's secretariat is functionally similar to the U.S. White House staff but is recruited, in the Indian case, almost exclusively from among permanent civil servants. The prime minister's secretariat today interposes an additional layer of personnel, not only between the prime minister and subcabinet officials in every department but also between the prime minister and most cabinet ministers.

Traditionally, the DAE secretary and staff would have had the initiative in (1) defining the technical requirements for imports of equipment to support the nuclear research and power programs; (2) surveying logical supplier sources and assessing likely terms of supply; (3) selecting Indian technical personnel to help staff international committees and agencies such as the IAEA; and (4) formulating the technical rationale for India's policy positions on issues of international nuclear cooperation, such as safeguards terms. The DAE secretary would also be the originator of budget estimates and proposals to support the atomic energy programs or to pursue foreign procurements. Thus, the DAE historically must have played a significant role in India's nuclear import decision making and international policy on safeguards and the NPT.

The Indian foreign office (the MEA) developed political and legal expertise in international nuclear affairs, with staffers in UN posts and in international conference forums. The MEA took the lead in dealing with the political and foreign relations aspects of international nuclear cooperation, including negotiations with advanced supplier governments in establishing agreements for cooperation. The MEA undoubtedly guarded Indian sovereignty in negotiating nuclear agreements. But once they are negotiated, the MEA has had the obligation to see that agreements are implemented and complied with internally, even if they constrained the DAE's programs—as, for example, with IAEA safeguards.

How would this relationship affect questions concerning emerging Indian nuclear exports? Since nuclear cooperation and trade, even when strictly peaceful in nature, tend to involve sensitive political questions, the MEA would usually be involved, with the right to concur, in major nuclear transactions between India and another party (though perhaps not minor ones, such as routine visits of scientists or minor training and educational exchanges). The MEA would also be the likely initiator of science and technology agreements for cooperation with other countries in cases where these agreements could be viewed as means of improving bilateral relations. Similarly, the MEA probably would prompt the prime minister to overrule DAE proposals for procurement of nuclear items, or for the export of same, if such action would adversely affect Indian political relations abroad.

To the extent that policy guidelines or rules governing India's nuclear export practices have already been set down or will be elaborated, the MEA presumably has the formal lead, polling the DAE and IAEC for technical advice and inputs. However, interviews conducted in India suggested that the decision process in the celebrated case of negotiating the July 1978 agreement with Libya for nuclear cooperation was ad hoc. Reportedly, the lead in concluding an agreement in principle was made by cabinet ministers who had no experience with or responsibility for nuclear or foreign policy. The prime minister's office, which was drawn in to formalize the agreement, solicited IAEC comments on only selected provisions of the agreement. In response, the IAEC forwarded a memorandum that formalized, perhaps for the first time, principles limiting the scope of Indian nuclear exports to a politically sensitive developing country.

The IAEC memo proposed that India consider itself ready to provide nuclear technical assistance in ore extraction, low-level wastes, and health and safety but refrain from supplying assistance or technology for fuel fabrication, reprocessing, and high-level wastes. This IAEC advice was overruled in the written agreement concluded with Libya. The agreement had a wider scope, which would have covered Indian assistance in, among other things, reprocessing. When it became clear that Libya intended to invoke the agreement by requesting help with sensitive technology, the IAEC reportedly objected and ultimately prevailed. A strategy of delay and substitution was adopted to avoid the onus of failing to comply with the agreement but to make it nonetheless ineffectual.

The tension with resource planners arises from DAE/IAEC demands for favored financial treatment in India's national investment picture in the development of science, technology, and energy sources. Although the definition of India's nuclear technology import requirements normally would originate in the DAE/IAEC, the foreign exchange and budgetary implications have been scrutinized and adjudicated by other players in the Planning Commission, the Ministry of Finance, and probably the Reserve Bank of India.

In taking the broad view of India's energy and industrial development requirements, the Planning Commission became increasingly skeptical of the DAE/IAEC's nuclear energy planning.[34] Planning Commission economists have challenged the cost-effectiveness of nuclear power in the overall energy picture, the cost overruns of nuclear power projects, and the failure to keep up with planned nuclear power installation schedules. The IAEC and BARC have defended the cost-effectiveness of nuclear-generated electricity in regions distant from coal-production sites, particularly western India. But these estimates have suffered a loss of credibility because of delayed production and the rising capital costs of nuclear installations. The final line of defense of the atomic energy advocates has been the promised benefits of technological self-reliance, which is not quantifiable and is harder to dispute.

The question of Indian nuclear exports may someday be driven by internal criticism of the financial drain of the atomic energy program and by DAE/IAEC efforts to defend their programs, not only by completing the construction of power plants more rapidly but by exporting nuclear equipment and services for foreign exchange. At this stage, the domestic nuclear power program theoretically could absorb all and more than the nuclear industry can produce. But incentives to divert some of that equipment to foreign exports—to demonstrate the validity of nuclear power development in India—may be increasing, ironically, just as India seems to be finally on the verge of harnessing its industry to build enough equipment to get the domestic nuclear construction program on track.

Norms in Indian Policy and Implications for Nuclear Commerce

India has selectively joined elements of the international nonproliferation regime. It was a charter member of the IAEA and, although India ultimately refused the Non-Proliferation Treaty (NPT) on the grounds that its provisions were discriminatory, it was a leading proponent of the purposes and many of the concepts that were eventually embodied in that treaty.[35] India also subscribes (subject to agreements it has entered) to IAEA safeguards on imported nuclear materials and equipment. But India does not accept full-scope or NPT-type safeguards on all its facilities, and it explicitly rejects safeguards on material and facilities of indigenous origin.

No effort was made to enroll India or similar nuclear-capable Third World countries in the Nuclear Suppliers Group (London Club). Not surprisingly, Indian commentators have a pejorative view of the NSG, seeing it as a cartel of advanced countries that aims to deny modern technology to developing countries. Apart from the IAEA, India is not a participant in any international organization that attempts to confine nuclear exports to peaceful purposes.

At this stage, therefore, India's policy in the area of controls over nuclear exports is enigmatic—perhaps calculated to be so. India has privately expressed assurances that suggest it has an interest in maintaining a "responsible" reputation. India may have understandings or specific agreements with several traditional supplier countries that would prohibit Indian exports (retransfers) of technology or materials originating with those suppliers. For example, India reportedly offered the United States assurances in 1975 that it would not transfer U.S. nuclear technology to other countries.[36]

An Indian expert, Ram Subramanian, commenting more generally on the shaping factors in export decisions by emerging suppliers, suggested that two factors will be dominant: (1) commercial considerations, such as earning profits or foreign exchange; and (2) local nonproliferation concerns, such as the effects of exports on the proliferation capabilities of a neighbor or rival.[37] The effects, he believes, will not be auspicious for NSG-type export controls: "What [emerging suppliers] may do is outbid the members of the NSG by underpricing nuclear exports in some areas. [They] may water down the principle . . . that 'safeguards shall be triggered by the transfer of technology, and not merely of hardware,' . . ."[38] permitting recipient states to determine end uses independently. He also suggested that emerging suppliers may use unresolved differences of supply approach to bargain for a revision of the NPT in 1995, when the treaty is up for extension.

A key issue that India has not yet publicly addressed is whether it will adopt policies and rules for exports of its indigenous nuclear technology, equipment, or materials in order to place them under appropriate controls. Such controls could consist of Indian criteria of restraint on sensitive exports or on any nuclear exports to sensitive parties, supplier conditions on peaceful end uses defined by India and agreed to by a recipient, or Indian requirements for IAEA safeguards to be applied to exports. At this stage, there is no evidence that India has addressed these questions carefully, let alone resolved them as matters of policy or procedure.

It seems safe to say that India is unlikely, in view of its own opposition to full-scope safeguards, to seek to impose them on a recipient. It would be encouraging if one could show that India is independently committed to insisting on partial IAEA safeguards—that is, safeguards covering the specific items transferred—in any major nuclear exports that it decides to try for. This could mean India's willingness to apply to others the partial IAEA safeguards that it accepted as the recipient of nuclear equipment from advanced supplier countries. Commitments to partial safeguards could evolve into support for more stringent safeguards. French policy on safeguards and exports, incidentally, evolved in much this way. However, there is no official sign from India yet of such an inclination.

The IAEA's experience with India, in contrast, suggests that Indian opposition to safeguards is so deep-seated that it is just as plausible to speculate that India would not require IAEA safeguards on its own exports.[39] Moreover, India could conceal its own requirements if it engaged in nuclear exports, but only to countries that have already accepted full-scope IAEA safeguards. Such recipients would have IAEA safeguards on their imports from any source, including India, whether or not India required them.

Capabilities

The capability for a major nuclear supply role in the international market, at a minimum, tends to be a function of (1) demonstrated success in building and operating nuclear energy facilities, particularly power plants; (2) technical ability to provide fuel, fuel cycle services, and engineering and other operational services to another nuclear program; and (3) the credibility of commitments or contracts entered into.[40] The last point has two dimensions: the availability of sufficient capacity to produce exportable nuclear equipment and material on a predictable schedule; and a reputation for reliability in performing promises entered into commercially.

India is approaching a threshold that could satisfy the first two conditions—that is, technical and industrial capability. But it has no track record as yet on either dimension of condition three—surplus capacity for export or reputation for reliability.

The Indian nuclear program has fallen far behind its expected rate of growth. Homi Bhabha ventured to a conference audience in Bombay in late 1965, just before his untimely death, that India would install one 290 MW(e) capacity power reactor every year, beginning in 1968.[41] Had this happened, India today would have twenty-two such reactors, with a total capacity of 6,380 MW(e), five times the actual current capacity.[42] Later projections were cut back but still overshot results.[43] Reactors built and under construction have all been in the 210–235 MW(e) capacity range, and plans to move up to construction of 500 MW(e) reactors had to be postponed. Early setbacks in these plans centered on the shortcomings of Indian metallurgical firms in fabricating heavy reactor components to appropriate standards for nuclear operation.[44] Later, the cutoff of Canadian assistance and India's problems with heavy water added other sources of delay.

Since about 1979, India's DAE has made concerted efforts to revive the momentum of the nuclear power plant construction program and to take advantage of increasing experience, depth, and sophistication in the country's engineering, heavy equipment, and electronics industries.

The problem-ridden Canadian-origin Rajasthan reactors—220 MW(e) CANDU heavy-water reactors (HWRs) known as RAPP I and II,[45] which were commissioned in 1973 and 1981, respectively—were reported to have been brought finally into regular operation in 1984 and 1985.[46] But interviews in India in September 1987 suggested that RAPP II is still plagued with defects and that DAE decisions then being made might abandon further efforts to salvage it. The CANDU-design but indigenously fabricated 235 MW(e) HWRs at Madras (MAPP I and II) were brought into operation in 1984 and 1985, raising India's operating capacity to about 1,100 MW(e).[47] Several additional nuclear [twin 235 MW(e) reactors] power plants have been under construction at specific sites such as Narora and Kakrapur or are planned for sites in Rajasthan and Karnataka.

The big push in the 1980s is based on plans for "batch" or "series" ordering of standardized reactors from Indian industry to fulfill a DAE fifteen-year plan to achieve 10,000 MW(e) by the year 2000. This calls for building eight more 235 MW(e) reactors based on the improved pattern being installed at Narora and, returning to an earlier concept, ten upsized 500 MW(e) reactors of the same basic design, all estimated to cost (in 1983 prices) about $11.6 billion.[48]

The DAE has worked for several years to cultivate the conditions for series ordering by forging links with public and private engineering companies through the Association of Indian Engineering Industry (AIEI), based in Bombay. In May 1982, the Nuclear Plant and Equipment Division (NPED) was formed within the AIEI in response to DAE encouragement. About the same time, the DAE reorganized its Power Projects Engineering Division into the Nuclear Power Board (NPB), with enhanced powers over power reactor design, construction, operation, and maintenance. In February 1984, links were established between nine newly formed product subgroups of the NPED, each convened by an industry executive and technical representatives in the DAE's NPB, as follows:[49]

NPED Product Subgroup	*Industry Convener*	*NPB Representative*
Special reactor components	G.R. Engineering Works (Bombay)	A. Krishnari
Fuel handling equipment	Walchandnagar Industries (Pune)	A. Natarajan
Heat transfer equipment	Kaveri Engr. Industries (Tiruchirapalli)	M.L. Mitra
Pumps	KSS Pumps (Pune)	G. Ghosh
Valves	Fouress Engineering (Bombay)	G. Ghosh

Instrumentation and control	Instrumentation Ltd. (Kota)	K. Natarajan
Conventional mechanical equipment	Bharat Heavy Plates & Vessels (Bombay)	R.S. Kumar
Electrical equipment	Crompton Greaves (Madras)	N.K. Murty
General services	IAEC (India) Ltd. (Bombay)	Y.P. Abrol
Special nuclear	Lloyd Insulations (Bombay)	G. Ghosh

See table 8–5 for a partial listing of other domestic firms in India that are part of, or have production capabilities relevant to, the nuclear industry of the country.

The Nuclear Power Board's relationships with the engineering firms through this arrangement are meant to ensure a coordinated flow of information on construction plans, standardized component requirements, industrial production and delivery schedules, and quality control. The hope

Table 8–5
Major Industrial firms in India Relevant to Nuclear Industry

Bharat Heavy Electricals (BHEL)
Bharat Heavy Pumps/Compressors
Bharat Steel Tubes
Bush India, Ltd. (computers, electronics)
Eicher Precision Machines, Ltd.
Electronics Corporation of India (ECIL), Ltd.
General Electric Co. (GEC) India
Hindustan Cables, Ltd.
Hindustan Machine Tools (HMT), Ltd.
Incommet India (computers, electronics)
International Computers Indian Manufacturer (ICIM), Ltd.
IPCL, Gujarat (chemicals)
Kirloskar Brothers, Ltd. (machine tools)
Larsen & Toubro, Ltd. (engineering)
Line Products Pvt., Ltd (transformers, reactors)
National Mineral Development Corporation (NMDC)
NGEF, Ltd (pumps and motors)
Saber Tools
Shriram Fertilizers and Chemicals
Steel and Allied Products, Ltd.
Tata Chemicals, Ltd.
Transformers and Electrical, Kerala, Ltd.

is that this will stimulate industrial efficiency and competition, make the NPB's procurements predictable, and allow construction of any given reactor in an eight-year time frame.

Under the new leadership of Prime Minister Rajiv Gandhi, the Indian government has sought to revitalize nuclear ties with certain advanced supplier countries, particularly France, West Germany, and the Soviet Union.[50] India thus hopes to enhance its access to advanced experience with reactor construction and operation, the fuel cycle, nuclear safety, and nuclear waste management. From France, India has sought assistance with HWR technology, hinting that it could develop a reactor export capability in partnership with French organizations.[51] Being skeptical about this, France has encouraged India to cooperate in light-water reactor (LWR) technology, on which France can offer more commercially to help India accelerate its nuclear power expansion.[52]

In the spring of 1985, an understanding was reported to have been reached by Rajiv Gandhi in Moscow that the Soviet Union would supply India with a turnkey 440 MW(e) LWR plant to be built in the vicinity of the current Tarapur power station. It became clear when the prime minister returned to Delhi that his government was " 'trying to sort out' problems with 'safeguards and the Soviet law on this matter.' "[53] As mentioned earlier, the Soviet Union finally signed an agreement with India in November 1988 to provide two large nuclear power reactors, 1,000 MW each, to augment nuclear power plants in South India.

In mid-1987, reports began to surface about Indian negotiations with the Soviet Union to transfer one or more nuclear-powered submarines. Interviews with Indian sources in 1987 indicated that India had started a nuclear submarine reactor program of its own at BARC a decade before, but with unsatisfactory results. Consequently, India decided to import this capability from the Soviet Union, initially in the form of Soviet nuclear-powered submarines, with Indian personnel already in training in the Soviet Union to handle this equipment. In early January 1988, All-India Radio announced that the Soviet Union had "leased" a nuclear-powered submarine to India, with India taking delivery in the Soviet port of Vladivostok.[54]

The transfer of a nuclear-powered submarine is an unprecedented development, with nuclear proliferation[55] as well as strategic connotations. Presumably, the lease arrangement is a step short of sovereign transfer. What would account for so radical a departure by the Soviet Union? Would this not compromise highly sensitive Soviet military information? One hypothesis is that the Soviet Union agreed to this lease arrangement on condition that India purchase Soviet nuclear power reactors.[56]

India's outreach suggests that it actually needs fresh technological inputs to make its own nuclear power program take off; and not only is India beginning to recognize this, but it has started to do something practical about it. This is an admission that optimal nuclear technology development requires international cooperation and acceptance of interdependence, rather than autarky. It also suggests that India is far from ready to export nuclear power equipment.

At the same time, India's return to the nuclear import market could narrow the nuclear power technology and experience gap. In the longer term, this could enhance India's potential for entering the nuclear export market independently. There are also options, at least theoretically, for India to resume importing in a manner that could simultaneously involve it in the export market—through involvement in joint ventures or consortia. Who its partners would be, in that event, probably would make some difference to the types of export practices that India would evolve. If France were a partner, for example, India might adopt the current French practice of negotiating for acceptance of IAEA safeguards on particular nuclear exports and the facilities in which they are used.

It should also be noted that India's accumulating experience with relatively small power reactors—long out of favor in most advanced countries—could position it to compete for a niche in the market among countries that, perhaps for limited power grid reasons, could not sensibly absorb large plants.

It is technically plausible that India could become an independent exporter in specific product or service areas short of major nuclear power projects, such as offering assistance with research reactor construction or research-scale fuel cycle facility development that developing countries might want at early stages in nuclear program development. Arguably, India has had such capabilities for many years. India has not moved aggressively in this area, however, perhaps mainly because it has not been found likely to be commercially profitable,[57] or, in the exceptional Libyan case, because there are major political inhibitions or sensitivities.

The centralized organization of and trends toward standardization of equipment in the Indian nuclear power program suggest that private industrial firms would play an extremely limited role in the promotion of Indian nuclear export deals. This would be in contrast to the role of major industrial corporations in the more market-oriented and decentralized economies of advanced nuclear countries in the West. Industrial firms there, although regulated and scrutinized in many ways, have nonetheless had considerable scope for initiative in soliciting business, helping to arrange financing, organizing technology transfer, and shaping both national and international nuclear policies and controls.

Concluding Observations

India's nuclear export policies today are still vague and undeveloped. Thus, they cannot be readily evaluated. India's nuclear exports to date are too limited in scale and value to form recognizable patterns. Albeit this is evidence in the negative sense, there is little to suggest that India will adopt nuclear export practices that are reckless or intentionally disruptive of nonproliferation controls. There is no firm evidence that India's nuclear export practices are less responsible than those of France and Italy, for example, though the hints that India actually considered assistance with plutonium reprocessing technology to Iraq and had agreed to cooperate in sensitive nuclear areas with Libya raises caution flags.

Apparently, India's nuclear sales so far have consisted of scientific training, radioisotopes for research, very small quantities of special nuclear material, or nonnuclear components that have not, by past conventions, required the application of IAEA safeguards. A test case of an Indian nuclear export that could require IAEA safeguards has not surfaced. Until it does, India probably will avoid declaring policy on the matter. The reported agreement to supply a research reactor to Sri Lanka could raise a test case, however, and thus bears watching.

Even so, India probably will be inclined, if it enters the nuclear export market, to deal with cases one by one, developing policies incrementally. The evolution of those policies might lead toward requirements for partial IAEA safeguards to be applied to a recipient's use of Indian-origin equipment or nuclear material. But this is far from certain. India used to oppose the idea in international circles of safeguards on anything but fissile (nuclear explosive) materials.

Who the chief actors in Indian nuclear export licensing for commerce will be is also unclear at this stage. Any major nuclear export agreements are likely in India's present setup to be initiated by the prime minister's secretariat, not by any department. But the final approval on major nuclear exports (licenses) is likely to be a matter for cabinet-level decision, with some technical review by the DAE/IAEC and political review by MEA.

The initiation of proposals for licensing of minor nuclear exports is likely to start with the IAEC (possibly with a special subcommittee or a specially staffed cell in the DAE created for this purpose) or, in particular cases, with a major entity in the DAE constellation, such as BARC (the chief research center), the Nuclear Fuel Complex, or the Nuclear Power Board. In any case, the IAEC or an element of the DAE is likely to be the central point for developing overall regulations for nuclear export licenses and practices.

Other actors that might be consulted in developing nuclear export licensing regulations or on decisions to approve specific nuclear export transactions, apart from the MEA and the Department of Commerce, probably would be those agencies that play a major role in planning and high-cost technology import decisions:[58] (1) the Reserve Bank of India; (2) the Ministry of Industry's Director General for Technical Development (DGTD); (3) the Ministry of Finance's Bureau of Public Enterprises (BPE); (4) the Project Investment Board (PIB), which coordinates between the Finance Ministry and the Planning Commission on domestic projects; (5) the Department of Science and Technology; (6) the Indian Council of Scientific and Industrial Research; and (7) cognate high-technology departments and commissions, such as the Departments of Electronics and Space and the Electronics Commission.

Notes

1. See Jones et al. (1985).

2. Dunn Ibid., (1985), pp. 119–28.

3. As one indication, the U.S. Congress Joint Committee on Atomic Energy, in its 1976 annual report listing the "nuclear power supply capabilities of various countries," identified only India and Argentina as Third World countries with independent nuclear industrial capabilities. It rated India with six out of seven key capabilities (the exception being uranium enrichment). Argentina had only one (uranium ore processing). See Congressional Research Service (1977), p. 282.

4. In contrast to India's six commissioned nuclear power reactors (three power stations), which totaled only about 1,150 MW(e) capacity and contributed under 3 percent of India's electrical supply in 1986, the Republic of Korea in the same year had four nuclear power plants, with a total capacity of 2865 MW(e), providing 17.7 percent of electrical generating capacity; and Taiwan had six nuclear power plants, with a total capacity of 5,144 MW(e), representing 35.7 percent of total electrical generating capacity.

5. It is not there yet. So far, Argentina and the PRC have been more active than India as nuclear exporters. However, the volume of nuclear exports in each of these cases is still small.

6. On France, see Goldschmidt (1982). On India, see Jones (1985a), pp. 101–24.

7. See, for instance, Kapur (1976).

8. I am indebted to Tom Graham for access to his unpublished chronology, including a compilation of cooperation agreements. See Graham (1986).

9. For the peculiar impact on the safeguards provision in the U.S.–India (Tarapur) Cooperation Agreement of 1963, see Jones (1981), ch. VII.

10. See Mirchandani and Namboodiri (1981), pp. 58–69.

11. The text of the 17 November 1977 trilateral safeguards agreement on Soviet-supplied heavy water to India may be found in Ibid., annexure V, pp. 202–12.

12. For the story compiled from circumstantial but intricate evidence, see Milhollin (1986), pp. 161–75.

13. The story of diversion of these shipments to India through firms owned by Alfred Hempel continues to be elaborated in research by Gary Milhollin and news accounts of European investigations. See, for example, John J. Fialka, "How 'Heavy Water' Seeps Through Cracks of Nuclear Regulation," *Wall Street Journal*, 3 January 1989, p. A1.

14. Reported in Graham (1986).

15. See Wayne A. Wilcox, "Nuclear Weapons Options and the Strategic Environment in South Asia: Arms Control Implications for India, Paper presented at Southern California Arms Control and Foreign Policy Seminar, June 1971, p. 29; and, for Pakistani awareness, M. Afaf, "Nuclear Weaponry and the Indian Scene," *Strategic Studies* (Islamabad) 1, no. 2 (July–September 1977): 47; cited in Jones (1981), pp. 27, 83.

16. Fera and Srinivasan (1986), pp. 2119–20.

17. Ibid.

18. Ibid.

19. See my companion piece on Pakistan in this volume (Chapter 11).

20. India recently ordered, for example, heavy foundry components such as pumps, valves, nozzles, casings, turbine rotors, and engine parts and turbine generator rings from France's Companie Française de Forge et Foundaries (CZF). *Worldwide Report*, 9 July 1986, p. 37.

21. The agreement reportedly "calls for Soviet construction on a turn-key basis of a power station in southern India consisting of two 1,000 MW reactors. In addition . . . Moscow is to provide concessional financing and enriched fuel for the life of the power station. The accord . . . apparently includes mutually agreed limits on a minimum quantity of nuclear fuel and control assemblies and a requirement that spent fuel be returned to the Soviet Union." See Richard M. Weintraub, "Gorbachev Urges Afghan Talks," *Washington Post*, 21 November 1988, pp. A15, A21.

22. An early instance was in March 1960, when the USSR offered large-scale nuclear assistance to India on attractive terms, with indications that a full-size nuclear power project was proposed. The agreement concluded with USSR in October 1961, however, only referred to nuclear research. See Hart (1983), p. 36.

23. Interviews by the author with Ministry of External Affairs officials in New Delhi and IAEC officials in Bombay in September 1987 indicated that unresolved issues over safeguards and disposition of spent fuel remained and that the IAEC had not consented. For an official announcement on 20 April 1986 to the Lok Sabha of Indian "discussions" with the USSR and "preliminary talks" with France for the purchase of a nuclear power plant, see *Times of India*, 1 May 1986, p. 16, cited in *Worldwide Report*, 1 July 1986, p. 52. For earlier reference to safeguards being the "stumbling block" in Indo–Soviet negotiations on PWR supply, see *Nucleonics Week*, 4 July 1985, p. 14E.

24. See previous note and *Times of India*, 16 December 1985, p. 9, cited in *Worldwide Report*, 7 February 1986, p. 67.

25. *Worldwide Report*, 19 May 1986, p. 72.

26. The proximity in timing of the other recent Soviet–Indian nuclear agreement, announced at the end of 1987, to lease to India the first of three or four nuclear-powered submarines (for the training of Indian crews) raises the question of

whether India had to accept the nuclear power plant supply as part of its price for obtaining the nuclear submarines.

27. See Libya, and notes, in Middle East section of table 8–4.

28. Prime Minister Indira Gandhi told the Lok Sabha that the DAE has reservations about certain provisions of the Indo–Libyan nuclear accord signed by former prime minister Morarji Desai and Libyan Staff Major Jalloud in July 1978 and that, beyond an exchange of scientists, there had been no activity under the agreement, which has since lapsed. Report in *The Telegraph* (India), cited in *Worldwide Report*, 24 September 1984, p. 69.

29. See Jones (1985a), pp. 114–15; and B. S. Gupta, *Nuclear Weapons? Policy Options for India* (New Delhi: Sage, 1983), pp. 13ff.

30. The IAEC was chartered under the Atomic Energy Act of 1948, with three tasks: "(1) . . . to protect the interests of the country in . . . atomic energy by exercise of the powers conferred on the Government of India by the . . . Act; (2) to survey [India] for . . . useful minerals [for] atomic energy; and (3) to promote research in their own laboratories and to subsidize such research in existing institutions and universities." Mirchandani and Namboodiri (1981), pp. 27–28. The DAE was established in 1954.

31. Following Bhabha as DAE secretary and IAEC chairman were Dr. Vikram Sarabhai (1966–71), Dr. Homi Sethna (1971–83), Dr. Raja Ramanna (1983–87), and Dr. Malur Srinivasan (incumbent).

32. According to Thomas Graham, the nuclear and space research budget of the central government (which is the overwhelming source of public research funding) in India is about 37 percent of the total research budget and nearly twice the proportion allocated to dedicated (openly defined) "defense" research. See Graham (1984), p. 161.

33. See Jones (1985a), pp. 110–12; and Jha (1983), ch. 17.

34. Hart (1983), p. 35. The DAE was brought into the five-year plan system only with the Third Plan (1961–66).

35. For a historical decision-making review of India's stance on relevant issues, see Jones (1985a), pp. 101–24.

36. Graham (1986), citing Shannon Gurbaxani, "Nuclear Technology Transfer and Its Control: The Indian Case," PhD dissertation, University of New Mexico, Department of Political Science, 1979, p. 178.

37. See Subramanian (1985), pp. 95–104.

38. Ibid., p. 96.

39. For IAEA experience with safeguards in particular countries, see Fischer and Szasz (1985).

40. This is quite apart from factors of economic demand, or political considerations in international relations, which may affect whether a nuclear export capability can be exercised.

41. Mirchandani and Namboodiri (1981), p. 29.

42. This forecast itself was a setback from the even more optimistic 1954 IAEC planning estimate of 8,000 MW(e) nuclear power capacity installed by 1980. Ibid.

43. Targets for installed nuclear power capacity by 1980 were: (1) 5,000 MW(e) estimated by the Energy Survey Committee in 1965; (2) 2,700 MW(e) projected by the Sarabhai profile of 1970; and (3) 1,020 MW(e)—in contrast to

actual in 1980 of 640 MW(e)—by the Fuel Policy Committee Report of 1974. Ibid.

44. Ibid., p. 34.

45. RAPP stands for Rajasthan power plant. The designation RAPS, for Rajasthan power station, is also used. Similar designations are used for other nuclear power plants or stations. The numbers refer to units 1 and 2, early plans usually being for two reactors per station.

46. *Nucleonics Week*, 13 June 1985, p. 11.

47. The theoretical capacity would be higher—about 1,330 MW(e)—but the Tarapur reactors, now aging, are run at much lower than rated capacity.

48. *Nucleonics Week*, 23 May 1985, p. 15.

49. *Nucleonics Week*, 23 May 1985, pp. 16–17.

50. *Nucleonics Week*, 4 July 1985, pp. 13–14.

51. Ibid.

52. Ibid.

53. Ibid.

54. Story in *The Washington Times*, 6 January 1988, based on Reuters service from New Delhi and referring to All-India Radio announcement as well as reports by TASS and *The Hindu* (Madras). See, also, *India Today*, 31 December 1987, pp. 72–74, which discloses that India plans to lease from four to six Soviet SSNs, probably Victor class, at a cost equivalent to about $3 billion (over an unspecified period).

55. See Ben Sanders and John Simpson, "Nuclear Submarines and Non-Proliferation," PPNN Occasional Paper No. 2, Centre for International Policy Studies, University of Southampton, 1988; Tariq Rauf and Marie-France Desjardins, "Canada's Nuclear Subs: A New Proliferation Concern," *Arms Control Today* (December 1988): 13–19.

56. By selling power reactors to India, the Soviet Union may get a foothold in a strategically sensitive Indian domain. This would be particularly so if along with supply of power reactors, the Soviet Union also provides technical and design assistance to make Indian production of its own submarine reactors feasible. The lease of SSNs would give India early operating experience with such reactors. The "lease" arrangement may be a convenient way of guaranteeing return to the Soviet Union of the submarine reactor fuel. At the same time, other motives may be part of the appeal of this arrangement. The price that India is paying to lease these submarines is considerable. Moreover, as *India Today*, 31 December 1987, speculates, Soviet nuclear-powered submarines operated by India in the Indian Ocean could complicate U.S. naval surveillance of Soviet submarines in that region.

57. At least not profitable enough to compete with the dominant DAE concerns, which are to get momentum into the domestic program and extract a flow of equipment on predictable schedules from domestic industrial sources.

58. See Mascarenhas (1982).

References

Congressional Research Service, Library of Congress. 1977. *Nuclear Proliferation Factbook*. Washington, D.C.: U.S. Government Printing Office.

Dunn, Lewis A. 1985. "The Emerging Suppliers: Some Dimensions of the Problem." in Jones *et al.*, eds., *The Nuclear Suppliers and Nonproliferation*, pp. 119–128.

Fera, Ivan, and Kannan Srinivasan. 1986. "Keeping the Nuclear Option Open," *Economic and Political Weekly* (Bombay) 21, no. 49 6 December 1986): 2119–20.

Fischer, David, and P. Szasz, with Jozef Goldblat, eds. 1985. *Safeguarding the Atom.* London and Philadelphia: Taylor and Francis for SIPRI.

Goldschmidt, Bertrand. 1982. *The Atomic Complex: A Worldwide Political History of Nuclear Energy.* La Grange Park, Ill.: American Nuclear Society.

Graham, Thomas W. 1984. "India," in James E. Katz, ed., *Arms Production in Developing Countries* (Lexington, Mass.: Lexington Books.

———. 1986. "South Asian Nuclear Proliferation and National Security Chronology," 10 January 1986 (unpublished).

Hart, David. 1983. *Nuclear Power in India: A Comparative Analysis.* London: George Allen and Unwin 1985.

India International, Inc. 1985. *Doing Business Collaborations in India,* prepared for U.S. Department of State and the Overseas Private Investment Corporation. Washington, D.C., March 1985.

Jha, C.S. 1983. *From Bandung to Tashkent: Glimpses of India's Foreign Policy.* Madras: Sangam Books.

Joeck, Neil, ed. 1986. *Strategic Consequences of Nuclear Proliferation in South Asia.* London: Frank Cass.

Jones, Rodney W. 1981. *Nuclear Proliferation: Islam, the Bomb, and South Asia,* Washington Papers No. 82. Washington, D.C.: Center for Strategic and International Studies.

———. 1985a. "India," in Jozef Goldblat, ed., *Nonproliferation: The Why and Wherefore.* London: Taylor and Francis for SIPRI, ch. 5B, pp. 101–24.

———. 1985b. "Nuclear Supply Policy and South Asia," in Jones et al., eds., *The Nuclear Suppliers and Nonproliferation*, pp. 163–74.

Jones, Rodney W., Cesare Merlini, Joseph F. Pilat, and William C. Potter, eds. 1985. *The Nuclear Suppliers and Nonproliferation: International Policy Choices.* (Lexington, Mass.: Lexington Books.

Kapur, Ashok. 1976. *India's Nuclear Option: Atomic Diplomacy and Decisionmaking.* New York: Praeger.

Mascarenhas, R.C. 1982. *Technology Transfer and Development: India's Hindustan Machine Tools Company.* Boulder, Colo.: Westview Press.

Milhollin, Gary. 1986. "India's Nuclear Cover-up," *Foreign Policy*, No. 64 (Fall 1986): 161–75.

Mirchandani, G.G., and P.K.S. Namboodiri. 1981. *Nuclear India: A Technological Assessment.* Delhi: Vision Books.

Spector, Leonard. 1984. *Nuclear Proliferation Today.* New York: Vintage Books for the (Carnegie Endowment for International Peace.)

———. 1987. *Going Nuclear.* Cambridge, Mass.: Ballinger for the (Carnegie Endowment for International Peace.)

———. 1988. *The Undeclared Bomb.* Cambridge, Mass.: Ballinger for the (Carnegie Endowment for International Peace.)

Subramanian, Ram. 1985. "Second-Tier Suppliers: Threat to the NPT Regime?", in Jones et al., eds., *The Nuclear Suppliers and Nonproliferation*, pp. 95–104.

Subramanian, Ram R., and C. Raja Mohan. 1982. "India." In James E. Katz and Onkar S. Marwah, *Nuclear Power in Developing Countries*. Lexington, Mass.: Lexington Books, pp. 161–80.

9

Israel:
An Unlikely Nuclear Supplier

Gerald M. Steinberg

In the area of nuclear weapons and the development of the potential capability as a nuclear supplier, as in many other issues, Israel stands out as a highly unusual, and indeed unique, case. In contrast to most other states considered in this study, such as Argentina, Brazil, and South Korea, Israel does not have an active civil nuclear energy industry. Despite some meager efforts in this direction, Israel does not operate large civil nuclear power reactors, and no Israeli firms produce commercial nuclear fuel cycle components of significance. Thus, many of the commercial and political factors that contribute to the emergence of "second-tier suppliers" are not salient in the Israeli case.

Israel's status as a potential second tier nuclear supplier is based on its own nuclear weapons program and capability. Israeli scientists and engineers have clearly developed the technical infrastructure and facilities to design, produce, test, and deploy nuclear weapons and appropriate delivery vehicles. While Jerusalem has not acknowledged this status, Israel is generally considered a nuclear or near-nuclear nation. In one sense, the existence of this capability automatically places Israel into the category of a potential nuclear supplies. At the same time, the existence of the capability to produce and deploy nuclear weapons should not be confused with the supply of materials related to the development of nuclear weapons. The two issues, while clearly related, must be considered separately.

The evaluation of the extent to which the role of supplier has been, or might be, actualized is greatly hampered by the sensitivity of the subject of nuclear weapons and related technology. For many years, successive Israeli governments have adopted a policy of deliberate ambiguity regarding the development of a nuclear deterrent. Rumors regarding possible tests or deployments have been met with silence on the part of the government, which will "neither confirm or deny" the existence of a development program or nuclear capability.[1] Information in this area is highly classified,

I would like to thank Brenda Shaffer for helping in the research for this chapter.

and any public exposure of related information is considered a treasonable offense. When a former technician at the Dimona nuclear research complex provided information to the *Sunday Times*, (London) he was returned to Israel to face charges. Thus, reliable information in this area is limited.

Technical Capabilities

The bulk of Israel's nuclear activities are centered around relatively small nuclear reactors at Nahal Soreq and Dimona. The first, at Nahal Soreq, is a 5-megawatt (thermal) swimming-pool type research reactor fueled, until recently, by highly enriched uranium supplied by the United States.

The second reactor and complex—at the Nuclear Research Center (NNRC), located near the city of Dimona in the south of the country—provides the basis for the Israeli nuclear weapons' potential. The central element in this complex is the French-designed reactor, fueled with natural uranium elements and moderated by heavy water. It is technically dual-purpose, producing a relatively limited supply of electricity and, more importantly, a significant supply of plutonium. The reactor was completed in the early 1960s and, according to available reports, has been operating since then. Initially reported to be rated at 25 megawatts, recent reports have suggested that the reactor was upgraded to 150 megawatts (thermal) and is capable of producing 40 kilograms of plutonium annually.[2] The heavy water to operate the plant is believed to have been provided by Norway in 1960, and there is also some speculation regarding the existence of a small heavy-water production plant.[3]

Both the Nahal Soreq and Dimona facilities also have a number of ancillary research activities. The former operates a very small scale chemical separation lab.[4] There has been a great deal of speculation about larger reprocessing facilities at Dimona. According to some reports, the French provided such a facility, or at least the plans, while other sources claim that this was developed independently by Israel.[5] (It is highly probable that, like the reactor itself, the construction of a reprocessing facility would have involved a combination of French and Israeli technology.) Mordechai Vannunu, a former technician at Dimona, told the *Sunday Times* (London) that this complex includes a relatively sizable plutonium extraction plant on the site, as well as producing Lithium 6, tritium, and deuterium.[6]

Israeli Nuclear Expertise

Israel has the largest per capita ratio of scientists and technicians in the world, and many are also among the leaders in their respective fields.[7] A significant number of these scientists and technicians work in the area of nuclear physics and chemistry. The Weizmann Institute, the Technion (Israel's equivalent to MIT), and Israel's four major universities also have high-level nuclear physics and engineering groups. In addition, the Geological Survey of Israel and the Israel Armament Development Authority (Ra-'fael) sponsor some nuclear-related research.

The research of these individuals and groups is sponsored and funded by a number of diverse sources and is generally conducted under the auspices of the Israel Atomic Energy Commission. Topics include reactor safety, physics of high-temperature gas-cooled reactors, computer codes and reactor simulation, fusion-related research, lithium lead blankers, laser-produced plasmas, aspects of plasma-induced shock waves, trace element analysis of silicate rocks, and uranium recovery from phosphoric acid.[8]

Israelis have also developed expertise in areas such as high explosives, shaped charges, precision machining, advanced electronic, monitoring, and remote sensing, chemical separation technology, remote handling, and N-B-C protective equipment.[9]

Nuclear Delivery Vehicles

In its own arsenal, Israel relies heavily on imported weapons, and any current Israeli atomic strike would, in all likelihood, be delivered by aircraft manufactured in the United States, such as the F-15, F-16, and F-4.[10] Israel has also developed a significant indigenous aircraft design and manufacturing capability. According to the *Middle East Military Balance*, the Israel Air Force currently deploys 180 locally designed and produced Kfirs. This aircraft, which is based on the Mirage V airframe and incorporates the U.S. General Electric J-79 engine, has a payload close to 10,000 pounds and a range of almost 1,000 miles. The Kfir has locally designed advanced electronics, avionics, navigation, and defensive systems. These components qualify the Kfir as a nuclear-capable aircraft.[11]

During the past decade, the Israeli Aircraft Industries designed and produced two test models of an advanced combat aircraft known as the Lavi. While primarily designed for ground support operations, the Lavi would also have had the range, payload, and various subsystems necessary for use as a nuclear delivery vehicle.[12] In August 1987, however, the Israeli government acknowledged the high cost of the project and canceled the Lavi.

Israel has also developed extensive missile technology. Most of the products are small tactical missiles such as the sea-to-sea Gabriel and the air-to-air Python, but there are also unofficial reports that Israel has also been developing a surface-to-surface missile, often referred to as the Jericho. According to recent reports, the Jericho 2 has a range of 700 kilometers and is nuclear-capable.[13]

Israel demonstrated its ability to launch a ballistic missile in September 1988, when it placed a small satellite into low Earth orbit. The satellite, *Ofek 1*, weighed 156 kilograms and was launched by a three-stage solid-fueled missile. Neither the Israeli government nor the Israeli Aircraft Industry (IAI) that produced the launcher revealed much about the characteristics of the missile, which was officially named Shavit (Comet). It is likely, however, that this system is similar to and based upon the technology of the Jericho IRBM. Using such a system, Israel has shown the ability to launch a medium-sized nuclear payload to a range of over 3,000 kilometers.

Israeli Participation in International Nuclear Research

Israeli scientists are particularly active in international research programs, including those in the nuclear field. Indeed, since Israeli nuclear research program and facilities are quite limited—particularly when compared to the number of nuclear scientists and engineers—one might say that some of the main centers of Israeli nuclear activities are outside of Israel.

Many of the international exchanges and visits are conducted within the frameworks of cooperation agreements for civil nuclear research which Israel, like other states, conducts via the International Atomic Energy Agency (IAEA) and in bilateral frameworks, which include the United States. Other projects are sponsored directly by the National Research and Development Council (NRDC) and the Israel Atomic Energy Commission. In the past five years, these agencies have supported visits by Israeli nuclear personnel in the United States, Italy, West Germany, France, the United Kingdom, and Denmark. Israelis have also participated actively in IAEA research, and Israeli representatives have presented papers at international meetings such as the International Conference on Nuclear Technology Transfer (Madrid, 1985) and the Symposium on Separation Science and Technology for Energy Applications (Knoxville, Tennessee, October 1985). In 1983, Israel hosted a meeting on Safety and Siting Problems of Nuclear Power Reactors in a Small Country.[14]

Evidence Regarding Transactions

Efforts to assess Israel's activities as a supplier of nuclear equipment, material, and technology are necessarily made difficult by the various layers of ambiguity and disinformation that surround Israel's own military nuclear activities and, in a wider sense, the export of weapons, the dispatch of military advisors to other states, and other forms of international military links.

Despite persistent pressures, successive Israeli governments have refused to acknowledge or specify the nature of the Israeli nuclear weapons capability. In general, Israel has pursued a policy of "deliberate ambiguity," neither seeking to deny the development of a nuclear weapons capability nor explicitly stating the nature of that capability. Israeli officials often seem to encourage speculation and general discussion of the nuclear option, at least in the foreign press, in order to strengthen the deterrence provided by the recognition of a "bomb in the basement."[15]

Discussion of specific, technical details is, however, not encouraged. In 1986, a former technician in the Dimona nuclear complex provided the *Sunday Times* (London) with a detailed description of the Dimona operation and facilities. He was subsequently "involuntarily repatriated" to Israel, arrested, and charged with treason. Since then, government officials and others involved in nuclear activity of any form (including civil research projects and commercial operations, as discussed later) have been even more reluctant to discuss the issues or provide information.

In addition, many external analyses of the Israeli nuclear program and reports of Israeli nuclear assistance to other states are motivated by the political hostility with which Israel has been confronted since 1948. In many cases, disinformation is generated and disseminated in order to delegitimize Israel. Frequently, this (dis)information is reprinted uncritically in the press, as well as in academic publications and reports of various governments and research centers. The central focus of this effort concerns allegations of Israeli links to South Africa, but there are also various attempts to link Israel to Taiwan (thus forming a nexus of "pariah states"), the People's Republic of China, and South Korea. In some cases these reports have a foundation in fact, whereas in many other cases there is no solid evidence and, in fact, the inability to produce evidence—despite great effort—seems to indicate the absence of such transactions.[16] For all these reasons, careful, critical examination of the evidence is needed for each report involving Israel military links with other states, including nuclear links.

Confusion is also increased by the nature of the Israeli policy regarding arms sales and exports of advanced technology and know-how. Israel has extensive commercial, technological, and military links with many states—including a number of industrializing powers that might be considered potential nuclear proliferators—but these links and related transactions are not publicly acknowledged.[17] Some of this ambiguity is designed to avoid Arab economic or political sanctions that might be imposed on states and firms dealing with Israel. Revelations regarding transactions involving South Africa and the People's Republic of China would also be costly in terms of international politics, as well as in domestic politics, and so the extent of those relations are also kept secret by the groups responsible for arms sales.

As discussed in detail later, the decision-making structure for conventional arms sales and military cooperation and assistance to other states is deliberately decentralized. Many transactions are initiated at low levels, and the approval of the political echelon is often not required or encouraged.

Israeli diplomats and Foreign Ministry officials are often not consulted or informed of arms sales or military assistance programs, the members of the Knesset (Israel's legislative body) are not informed, and even requests for information from Cabinet members are routinely denied.[18] This adds an additional layer of ambiguity and further limits the sources of reliable information.

As a result of these factors in combination, evidence is ambiguous, and the study of Israel as an emerging nuclear supplier must be based primarily on its known technical capability. In the absence of reliable information about actual activities, the emphasis is placed on the potential activities derived from these technological capabilities.

Analysis of Transactions

Motivations

Based on technical capability alone, Israel clearly has the potential to be a major nuclear supplier. While Israel did not design or construct the Dimona reactor, according to reports Israel completed the reactor begun by the French and, at a later date, expanded its capacity significantly.[19] Israel has developed uranium extraction and refining systems for relatively small plutonium production reactors, as well as fuel rod cladding, reprocessing, and plutonium separation.[20] Israeli scientists have also contributed to the development of laser and nozzle uranium enrichment techniques, which might make the use of heavy-water-moderated reactors unnecessary for the production of "special nuclear material."[21]

For some years, there has been discussion of the development of civil nuclear power plants in Israel.[22] In the mid-1970s, the United States expressed interest in selling Israel (as well as Egypt) commercial nuclear power plants. Israel, however, was unwilling to accept the safeguard provisions and was also not interested in promoting Egyptian acquisition of nuclear materials and technology. In the early 1980s, France was seen as a possible source of commercial nuclear plants. However, with the general worldwide decline of interest in such plants, as well as lower fossil-fuel costs and greater Israeli access to conventional fuels, plans for commercial nuclear power in Israel were postponed indefinitely. Thus, a potential rise in the Israeli investment in a nuclear infrastructure was avoided.

At the same time, Israel has a very small nuclear industry and infrastructure. The Dimona complex employs 2,700 individuals, and the total additional personnel at Nahal Soreq and the universities can be estimated to be on the same order.[23] The local demand for the products and services of this sector is also limited, and thus Israeli firms have sought to expand through exports.

In general, since the 1970s Israel has attempted to lower the costs of indigenous military and other advanced technological production activities through exports. The major arms producers, such as IAI, IMI, and Rafael, have increased their export activities significantly, with the encouragement and support of the Defense and Commerce ministries and the government in general—although the military has opposed this development, since the products of this industry are increasingly designed to meet the requirements of the export market rather than the needs of the IDF. In the late 1970s, conventional military exports accounted for approximately $1 billion annually, or one-third of total Israeli industrial exports.[24]

Similarly, in the nuclear area the Israeli government has sought to offset the cost of building and maintaining its atomic infrastructure through commercialization. Rotem Industries was created to "commercialize scientific developments of the Negev Nuclear Research Center" at Dimona. Its brochures advertise medical lasers, carbon-membrane gas separation, solution purification, manufacture of tritium, monitoring and control systems, and glove boxes for handling of radioactive materials.[25] Similarly, Isorad Limited was created to sell the products and services of the Nahal Soreq center. Isorad advertises radiation protection, nuclear material handling and waste disposal, high vacuum engineering, training, NMR and ESR techniques, precision machining, glass to metal sealing, and pulsed power technology.[26]

A number of small independent firms offering nuclear services and materials have also developed. Most of these commercial enterprises seek foreign investments, partners, and markets. In return, the Israel firms—in this as in other high-tech enterprises—offer expertise, services, know-how, and an array of hardware and materials for sale or licensed production. INKA Engineering, for example, advertises clear room technology and robotic wet stations.[27]

In addition to the possible economic motivations, the sale of advanced technology and weapons is often perceived by Israeli decision makers to provide a political dividend. In the past, sales of conventional arms to countries such as Iran, Zaire, and even the People's Republic of China could be seen, at least in part, as politically motivated. Accordingly, sales of nuclear know-how, technology, and components to such countries as Argentina, the People's Republic of China, and perhaps even a post-Khomeni Iran might also be seen as politically worthwhile.[28]

Disincentives

Many of the states most actively seeking or likely to seek nuclear weapons are fundamentally opposed to the existence of the Jewish State. Israel is unlikely to assist Libya, Iraq, or an Islamic fundamentalist regime in Iran in acquiring a nuclear capability. As an Islamic state, Pakistan is also considered a potential threat. Israeli decision makers must also consider the possibility that other potential recipients, such as Brazil, Taiwan, or South Korea, might, in turn, sell or transfer the technology to one of the Middle East confrontation states.

Furthermore, Israel is highly dependent on the United States for economic, military, and political support. Israeli governments have been sensitive to Washington's concerns regarding nuclear proliferation, and this concern has helped to contribute to the development of the policy of deliberate ambiguity surrounding Israel's own nuclear capability. Similarly, Jerusalem must be aware that exporting nuclear-related technology or know-how would also engender a stiff American response and endanger the level of support Israel receives from the United States.

In addition, the supply of nuclear know-how and technology is unlikely to be a major source of revenue, particularly in comparison to the level of exports of conventional weapons (approximately $1 billion annually). Thus, the risks of becoming identified as a nuclear supplier state, in most cases, far outweigh the benefits.

These arguments are somewhat less important in relation to dual-capable or gray-area technologies that can be used for both conventional and nuclear missions, such as delivery vehicles. For Israel, as for many other weapons manufacturers and technology exporters, dual-use weapons are not considered separately from conventional weapons, and the fact that they might also be used for nuclear weapons is not of major significance. As noted previously, the Israeli-made Kfir combat aircraft, although primarily a conventional ground support aircraft, can be used to deliver nuclear weapons, and Israel has been actively seeking to export this system for many years. According to some reports, South Africa has purchased the Kfir or has used technology developed for the Kfir in the development of its own Mirage-based combat aircraft, the Cheetah (referred to later on).

For many years, Israeli leaders have announced the objective of developing and maintaining an indigenous capability to produce advanced combat aircraft. Given the cost of this objective—as evidenced in the case of the Lavi effort—it is increasingly apparent that such an indigenous capability is beyond Israel's means. Nevertheless, in order to lower the degree of dependence on a single source of supply, the United States, Israel might consider joint production of combat aircraft with other countries. There have been reports regarding a South African role in the development of the Lavi.[29]

Similarly, Israel has sought partners for the cooperative development of intermediate-and short-range ballistic missiles. In the 1970s, Israel sought Iranian funding for joint development of the Jericho. Documents left behind in Teheran in 1979, and subsequently published in Iran, show that in the 1970s Israeli and Iranian military leaders held negotiations on this project.[30]

There have also been isolated reports of Israeli involvement with Taiwan and South Africa in the joint development of a nuclear-armed ground-launched cruise missile. This report was first published by Jack Anderson in 1980, but like many similar reports, no evidence of this project has surfaced.[31]

Israel and South Africa

For many years, there have been a number of reports that Israelis have been involved in assisting other states in the development of a technological base for the development of nuclear weapons. Most of these reports center on allegations regarding Israeli assistance to South Africa. According to James Adams, a reporter for the *Sunday Times* (London) who has written extensively on the subject, Israel "in the search for friends, has not hesitated to share its nuclear expertise with . . . South Africa."[32] Over the past decade, the UN General Assembly has adopted a number of resolutions concerning relations between Israel and South Africa that "strongly condemned the continuing and increasing collaboration by Israel with the racist regime of South Africa, especially in the military and nuclear fields."[33]

South Africa has provided uranium to many states, and in the 1960s Israel received a relatively small shipment of natural uranium, which was reported to and monitored by the IAEA. However, according to Adams and others, Israel requires South African uranium for the Dimona reactor. Adams states that this relationship was established in 1976 during meetings between South African Prime Minister John Vorster and Israeli Prime Minister Yitzhak Rabin, in which an agreement was concluded to exchange "South African raw material for Israeli manpower in joint projects."[34]

In 1968, Professor Ernst Bergmann, the head of the Israel Atomic Energy Authority, visited South Africa. This visit allegedly established the nature of the technical expertise supplied by Israel. According to Adams, Israeli scientists went to South Africa to assist in the development and construction of the Safari 2 research reactor. In their book on the West German involvement in the South African nuclear program, Rogers and Cervenka also cite "persistent reports" that the enrichment plant at Valindaba had "large numbers of Israelis with experience in their own country's nuclear weapons programme."[35] Other reports suggest that the flow is in the opposite direction, and that Israel may be benefiting from South Africa's development of the jet nozzle nuclear separation process.[36]

A major element of the reports of the Israeli-South African nuclear link concerns the case of the "mysterious flash" that was detected in 1979 in the South Atlantic. While there is still debate about the cause of the flash, which was detected by U.S. Vela satellites, there are persistent allegations that it was triggered by a joint Israeli-South African nuclear test. Here again, however, there is no evidence to support this interpretation.[37]

On the other hand, Israel, along with many other states, has supplied South Africa with conventional military technology and weapons. Israel has supplied South Africa with fast patrol boats and Gabriel ship-to-ship missiles. There are also allegations that South Africa has purchased the Kfir combat aircraft, which, as has already been discussed might be considered dual-capable. According to other reports, and previously noted here, Israeli technology developed for the Kfir might have been used by South Africa to manufacture the Cheetah. The evidence for either case is, however, weak. Similarly, reports that South Africa is involved in the Lavi combat aircraft project or in Jericho missile development must also be considered not credible.

At the same time, it must be noted that South Africa has made a strong effort to induce individual Israelis with training and skills in the aerospace and nuclear fields to move to and work in South Africa. Like many other democratic states, Israel does not have the ability to prevent civilians from accepting lucrative offers and emigrating. The 1987 decision to cancel the Lavi project left about 4,000 unemployed aerospace engineers, and the small scale of the Israeli industry left little prospect of finding a job within the country. South African firms were busy trying to sign on many of these engineers; some public figures in Israel sought to prevent this "brain drain," but with no effect. Thus, it is not surprising to find reports of Israeli technicians at a number of South African facilities. This does not, however, imply that there is any direct or even indirect Israeli government involvement or approval of these relationships.

Intermediate Roles

Israeli activities and imports involving nuclear materials, facilities, and delivery vehicles are carefully monitored. In 1985, it was discovered that Israel had purchased and imported krytons, and the U.S. government investigated and eventually brought charges.[38] Other reports concerning Israeli acquisition of uranium (depleted, natural, and enriched) have also been published widely.[39]

As a result of this careful and intense scrutiny, it would be difficult for Israel to act as a transshipper or intermediary for nuclear equipment or materials. Since Israel has not signed the Nuclear Non-Proliferation Treaty (NPT) and has refused to accept full-scope safeguards, its ability to purchase nuclear-related equipment on the international market is even more limited than many other proto-nuclear weapons states. Under these circumstances, it is difficult to develop credible scenarios whereby Israel might be able to purchase nuclear weapons related equipment or material and transfer it to a third party, even if it should so desire.

Relevant Decision-Making Structures

Israeli conventional arms exports are not centrally coordinated, and government and high-echelon political control is very loose. Israeli arms producers and SIBAT, the agency in the Ministry of Defense responsible for arms sales, have licensed approximately eight hundred retired generals to open offices and, with their associates, to negotiate export agreements. Although formally the Defense Ministry must ultimately approve agreements, functionally the high-level review is often pro forma and rarely results in the denial of applications. The process is structured in a way that gives credence to the claims of Israeli political leaders that they are not involved in decisions to sell weapons to various countries. However, sales with political motivations—involving Iran, for example—often involve and are initiated or coordinated by the political echelon.

As critics have noted, other government agencies are not involved in or informed of arms sales decisions. Even members of the Israeli government have difficulty tracking arms sales to some states, to say nothing of attempts to control or limit these sales.

In addition, it must be recalled that many individuals somehow associated with Israel (former Israeli citizens or residents, for example) often act independently, beyond governmental control. Some of the arms that were sold to Iran were arranged by individual Israelis, operating entirely outside the country and without governmental control or permission. Many former Air Force pilots become "freelancers" after completing their military service, and, as noted, there are reports that South African firms were attempting to hire individual Israeli engineers after the Lavi was canceled. These are all activities that fall outside the government's purview.

If applied to the nuclear area, this loose decentralized system of controls whereby specific arms sales and the exchange of technical know-how can go ahead without high-level political approval could, at least in theory, also enable Israelis to act independently and without government approval. Under such circumstances, it would be possible for Israelis to serve as intermidiaries and transshippers of sensitive nuclear material and equipment. On the other hand, in general, any activity dealing with what Israel considers matters related to nuclear weapons (that is, nuclear materials and facilities, but not necessarily dual-use delivery vehicles) is considered to be outside the normal military sphere. Nuclear matters are carefully monitored and controlled. (Indeed, requests for information concerning civilian commercial nuclear activities from the Nahal Soreq center were referred to "the responsible authorities" for approval.)

Norms and Attitudes to the NPT and Export Controls

Both ethically and politically, Israeli policy generally favors efforts that would strengthen the nuclear nonproliferation regime. Indeed, Israeli leaders believed and portrayed that the destruction of the Iraqi nuclear facilities and the Osiraq reactor were a blow against nuclear weapons proliferation. From their perspective, Israel is a unique case, in which survival of the nation and the Jewish people in the face of overwhelming Arab numerical superiority depends, at least in the long term, on the development of nuclear weapons.[40] Thus, the development of Israel's own nuclear weapons capability has been tentative, and the capability has remained ambiguous in order to preserve, at least in theory, the option of some form of nuclear-free zone in the region. Internally, as well, the Israeli nuclear program has been widely criticized. In the 1960s, as the Dimona reactor was becoming operational, most of the scientists on the Israeli Atomic Energy Commission resigned, apparently in protest of this policy. When reports of the activity at Dimona indicated that the "textile" plant had what appeared to be a reactor containment building around it, a number of Israeli political figures and nuclear scientists objected.[41]

While supporting the concept of nuclear nonproliferation in general, Israel has been a leading critic of the international safeguards system operated by the IAEA and by individual states. In defending its decision to destroy the Iraqi Osiraq nuclear complex in 1981, Israel cited deficiencies in the IAEA safeguard system, to which the reactor was subject, as well as lack of faith in the "assurances" from the French government, which supplied the reactor and related technology and personnel. This view is frequently reflected in Israeli positions at the NPT Review Conferences and at meetings of the IAEA.

At the same time, Jerusalem has encouraged the establishment of a Nuclear Weapons Free Zone (NWFZ) in the Middle East. Since 1974, Israeli representatives at the UN and other international forums have supported a NWFZ based on the Tlatelolco model. Officially, the Israeli government has favored the negotiation of an NWFZ prior, if necessary, to the settlement of the Arab-Israeli conflict and a general peace arrangement in the region. A regional NWFZ, including a mutual system of inspections and safeguards, has been explicitly advocated by Israel.[42]

Israeli attitudes to specific measures designed to impose limits on its status as a second-tier nuclear supplier are likely to be mixed. On the one hand, Israel has generally had negative experiences with such international organizations and institutions, which are usually stacked politically against Israel. For example, the IAEA safeguard system is seen as not only ineffective with respect to inspection of the Arab states, but also biased against Israel. From this perspective, the acceptance of IAEA safeguards would mean that "we would have international inspectors crawling all over us, while the Arab countries would be free to do what they want, as Iraq did."[43] Similarly, Israel is likely to react to any supplier agreements with cynicism as long as the major nuclear suppliers, including France, Italy, and others, are still selling nuclear reactors and other facilities and materials to countries such as Iraq under the guise of "peaceful nuclear programs."

However, Israel would probably support and participate in limitations on the supply of nuclear materials if the limitations were not subject to simple political manipulation, if they extended to all suppliers and recipients without exception, and if they were based on a much strengthened safeguards and inspection system. Political leaders in Israel recognize the dangers inherent in nuclear proliferation and would be willing to contribute to measures that would strengthen the nonproliferation regime, as long as these measures were applied evenly to nuclear suppliers as well as recipients.

Conclusions

A semipopular Israeli publication, *Technologies*, recently published an exposé entitled "Israeli Nuclear Know-How for Sale." The article included a scenario according to which the services of the commercial nuclear services of the Dimona complex were purchased by an American entrepreneur, who then employed the Israeli engineers (who were eventually hired directly by the American-based firm) to develop what was later revealed to be an independent nuclear weapons capability for sale to the highest bidder. In response, David Peleg, managing director of the Israel Atomic Energy Commission, asserted that external funding for industrial applications of nuclear technology "contributes to the preservation of essential capabilities during the current period of budgetary reductions." Nevertheless, he reiterated the importance that the IAEC attaches to maintaining a "proper balance between government funded research and research funded by external factors. In addition, . . . there is no fear of pressures and demands from external investors."[44]

This article and the responses to it demonstrate that there is some recognition and concern in Israel regarding the process by which nuclear expertise is being sold, even for civil commercial purposes.

Yet, as noted above, Israel's overall industrial strategy emphasizes the maximum exploitation of the comparative advantage provided by the Israeli advanced technological base. Economic options are limited by the absence of raw materials, and the Arab boycott has limited potential markets. Furthermore, a high level of imports—largely the result of ongoing defense requirements—and limited export markets—reflecting in part the impact of the Arab boycott—have all contributed to the Israeli emphasis on military exports. The high value-added aspect of technological exports in general and military technology in particular also contribute to this strategy. The arms business is very profitable. Thus, a decision to export nuclear-related or dual-purpose technology would be consistent with Israel's broader policy regarding arms sales and its efforts to offset the cost of maintaining an indigenous advanced military capability through foreign sales.

However, given the sensitivity of the issue of nuclear weapons, it is highly unlikely that the broad policy regarding arms sales would be extended to technology directly applicable to the development of nuclear weapons. As noted, nuclear issues and technology are widely recognized in Israel as a special category, and the normal rules of the game do not apply in this sensitive area.

Israel is also unlikely to become involved in partnerships in the form of "market-sharing" or "division-of-labor" agreements. While, under certain circumstances, such arrangements might be conceivable in the case of Brazil, Argentina, and/or India, the geographic and political isolation of Israel prevent the development of such ties on either a formal or informal basis.

However, in the area of dual-use delivery systems, including aircraft and missiles, it is possible that economic and political motivation would be important factors in policy formation.

A series of recent events, including Israeli involvement in the Iran/Contras arms sales affair, the arrest of a number of Israelis (including former generals) by the United States for attempting to violate U.S. arms export rules by selling arms independently to Iran, and the State Department's report to Congress on arms sales to South Africa, which included detailed discussion of Israeli actions in this area, have all made Israel more aware of the diplomatic sensitivity of the export of arms and military technology in general. Furthermore, the Vannunu affair has also increased Israeli sensitivity to the international implications of nuclear-related activities. Decision-making structures in both areas are likely to be centralized and control is likely to be tightened in the future. As the political echelon is held accountable for decisions and policy in this area, controls are likely to increase and sales of sensitive equipment are likely to decrease.

On the other hand, if political and military developments push Israel toward an overt nuclear weapons capability, and the degree of sensitivity to the uniqueness of nuclear weapons is lessened, some of the constraints on the export of materials and technology might similarly be reduced. The acquisition of nuclear weapons by other states in the region—including Iraq, Iran, Egypt, Libya, and Syria—would clearly result in such an Israeli deployment. More immediately, the use of chemical weapons by Iraq and the development of a similar capability by Syria and Libya may also lead to an overt deployment of a nuclear deterrent in Israel, and thus create or strengthen the incentives to becoming a nuclear supplier.

Finally, the moral issues surrounding nuclear weapons and the status of a potential nuclear supplier are recognized and very salient in the Israeli context. Academics, Jewish religious and moral philosophers, and others recognize that nuclear weapons constitute a separate category. While the trade in conventional weapons, and even the development of a nuclear option, may be necessary evils required to ensure survival, the export of nuclear technology cannot be justified by any rationalization.

Notes

1. The most accurate and comprehensive summary of the development of the Israel nuclear "option" through the 1980s is contained in Shai Feldman, *Israeli Nuclear Deterrence: A Strategy for the 1980s* (New York: Columbia University Press, 1982). For a summary of the various speculations and claims regarding this capability, see Peter Pry, *Israel's Nuclear Arsenal* (Boulder, Colo.: Westview Press, 1984).

2. See "Revealed: The Secrets of Israel's Nuclear Arsenal," *Sunday Times* (London), 5 October 1986, p. 1. Nevertheless, the 1986 edition of *Scientific Research in Israel*, edited by Norman Greenwald and Shlomo Herskovic (Jerusalem: The National Council for Research and Development, 1986), p. 406, reports the maximum output of the reactor as 25 megawatts.

3. The question of the heavy water was recently reopened by Norway. See Michael Gordon, "Norway Questions Israeli Use of Nuclear Material," *New York Times* 17 February 1987, p. 10. See also *Ha' aretz*, 28 December 1986; and United Nations, General Assembly, *Israeli Nuclear Weapons Armament*, Report of the Secretary General, 1981.

4. See Leonard Spector, *Going Nuclear* (Cambridge, Mass.: Ballinger, 1987), p. 144; and Pry, *Israel's Nuclear Arsenal*, p. 66.

5. See Pierre Pean, *Les Deux Bombes* (Paris: Fayard, 1982), cited by Leonard Spector, *Nuclear Proliferation Today* (New York: Vintage, 1984), p. 132.

6. *Sunday Times* (London), 5 October 1986.

7. Leah Sinan and K. Nagaraja Rao, *Supply and Demand for Professional and Technical Manpower in Israel* (Cambridge Mass.: Center for Policy Alternatives, Massachusetts Institute of Technology, 1980), p. 14.

8. Israel Atomic Energy Commission, *Research Laboratories Annual Report-1985*, Tel Aviv, 1985.

9. See Greenwald and Herskovic, eds., *Scientific Research in Israel 1986*, pp. 406–7; Dun and Bradstreet (Israel) Ltd., *Israel Aviation Aerospace and Defence 1985/6*, Tel Aviv; sales brochure, Isorad/Soreq Nuclear Research Center; sales brochure, Rotem Industries Ltd.

10. The different potential Israeli delivery systems are discussed in Feldman, *Israeli Nuclear Deterrence*, and Pry, *Israel's Nuclear Arsenal*.

11. See Mark Heller, ed., *1985 Middle East Military Balance* (Tel Aviv: Jaffee Center for Strategic Studies, 1986).

12. For detailed descriptions of the technical capabilities of the Lavi, see Germain Chambost, "Israel's Lavi: A Technological Target," *International Defense Review* (July 1986): 891; and Peter Hellman, "The Fighter of the Future," *Discover* 7 (July 1986).

13. *Aerospace Daily*, May 1, 1985.

14. "Safety and Siting Problems in a Small Country," *Nuclear News* (March 1984): 98.

15. For a detailed analysis of this policy, see Gerald Steinberg, "Deliberate Ambiguity: Evolution and Evaluation," in Louis Rene Beres, ed., *Security or Armageddon: Israel's Nuclear Strategy* (Lexington Mass.: Lexington Books, 1985).

16. See Gerald Steinberg, "The Mythology of Israeli-South African Nuclear Relations," in Louis Rene Beres, ed., *Security or Armageddon: Israel's Nuclear Strategy* (Lexington, Mass.: Lexington Books, 1986).

17. Aaron Klieman, *Israel's Global Reach: Arms Sales as Diplomacy* (New York: Pergamon-Brassey's, 1985).

18. *Jerusalem Post*, 29 February 1984.

19. See note 2.

20. Shefi Gabbai, "Atomic Israel," *Maariv*, 4 October 1985, based on reports in an article in *Al Ahram* (Egypt).

21. Robert Gillette, "Uranium Enrichment: Rumors of Israeli Progress with Lasers," *Science* 183 (March 1974): 1172–74. Spector also cites references to Israeli use of the Becker nozzle enrichment process *Nuclear Proliferation Today*, p. 378, n63).

22. Uzi Eilam, "The Implementation of the Nuclear Power Plant Programme in Israel," *Nuclear Engineering International* 22 (May 1977): 23, 59–62.

23. *Sunday Times* (London), 5 October 1986.

24. Klieman, *Israel's Global Reach*, pp. 53–70.

25. Sales brochure, Rotem Industries Ltd.

26. Sales brochure, Isorad/Soreq Nuclear Research Center.

27. INKA Engineering sales brochure, Kjar Saba.

28. For a discussion of domestic Israeli attitudes regarding arms sales to these states, see Klieman, *Israel's Global Reach*, pp. 92–123.

29. See James Adams, *The Unnatural Alliance* (London: Quartet Books, 1984).

30. Text of the minutes of a meeting between Israeli Minister of Defense Ezer Weitzman and the Iranian Minister of War Toufanian on 18 July 1977, reproduced by the Iranian government in *Den of Spies* from documents found at the U.S.

Embassy and The Israeli Interests Office, Teheran. The Hebrew translation was published in *Ma'ariv*, 18 April 1986.

31. Jack Anderson, *Washington Post*, 8 December 1980.

32. Adams, *Unnatural Alliance*, p. 165.

33. United Nations, General Assembly, Summary record of the 15th meeting of the Third Committee, 38th sess., 19 October 1983.

34. Adams, *Unnatural Alliance*, p. 180.

35. Zdenek Cervenka and Barbara Rogers, *The Nuclear Axis: Secret Collaboration Between West Germany and South Africa* (New York: New York Times Books, 1978), p. 160.

36. George Quester, "Israel," in Jed C. Snyder and Samuel Wells, eds., *Limiting Nuclear Proliferation* (Cambridge, Mass.: Ballinger, 1985), p. 147.

37. "Blowup," *Technology Review*, October 1980.

38. Wolf Blitzer, "Questions over Krytons," *Jerusalem Post*, 24 May 1985.

39. David Grant, "Israel Didn't Make Nukes, Luxembourg Inspectors Find," *Jerusalem Post*, 14 July 1985.

40. Interview with Moshe Dayan, *Ma'ariv*, 3 December 1976.

41. Apparently as a consequence of the activities at Dimona, in 1961 most members of the Israeli Atomic Energy Commission resigned. See Inbar, "Israeli Basement," p. 104, n26.

42. Avi Becker, "A Regional Non-Proliferation Treaty for the Middle East," in Louis Rene Beres, ed., *Security or Armageddon: Israel's Nuclear Strategy* (Lexington Mass.: Lexington Books, 1985), p. 130.

43. *Jerusalem Post*, 21 February 1984, p. 1, cited in Becker, "Regional Non-Proliferation Treaty," p. 130.

44. "Israeli Nuclear Know-How for Sale," *Technologies* (Israel) 37 (November 1986): 20–23. In Hebrew.

10
Japan

Stephanie Sharron
Warren H. Donnelly

A mong the many new nuclear supplier states, Japan ranks as the most formidable future competitor. Already moving in that direction, its policies and practices can work to reenforce or to change those of both the new and the established suppliers.

Japan's Nuclear Export Activity and Policy

Incentives for Japanese Nuclear Exports

Japan has strong reasons to expand its nuclear cooperation and trade and become a major supplier. It clearly is interested in influencing the policies of the Pacific Rim nations—some of which have energy problems—which are seen as important to its security as well as to its economy.[1] Japan can also expect political and economic benefits from aiding China's fledgling nuclear power industry. Indeed, Japan already has a net of agreements for nuclear cooperation with other countries, including the United States and other major suppliers as well as developing countries. In addition, Japan is committed under the Nuclear Non-Proliferation Treaty (NPT) to cooperate in the peaceful applications of nuclear energy, "especially in the territories of non-nuclear-weapons states party to the Treaty, with due consideration for the needs of the developing areas of the world."[2]

Looking inward, Japan finds other reasons for becoming a nuclear exporter. Following its national policy to reduce its dependence upon foreign suppliers through diversification of fuel and energy resources, Japan sees nuclear power fueled with uranium, and in the future with plutonium, as a way to reduce dependence on imported oil and coal for the generation of electricity. Thus, Japan has built a strong technological foundation for its powerful domestic nuclear manufacturing industry, competent in virtually

The views expressed herein are solely those of the authors.

all aspects of the supply of nuclear power plants, nuclear fuels (including uranium enrichment and its reprocessing of spent fuel to recover its residual uranium and plutonium for further fuel use), and disposal of nuclear wastes. However, this initial surge of nuclear power plant construction has passed its peak, and expected new domestic orders are not enough to keep Japan's nuclear industry occupied. Its underutilized nuclear industry needs foreign orders. As with other nations facing this situation, Japan needs exports to bring in money to help sustain its nuclear industry and to help pay for continuing nuclear research and development.

Moreover, the admirable performance of Japanese nuclear power plants should make them desirable on the world market and give its nuclear engineers a competitive advantage. As its nuclear industries improve and its nuclear exports grow, Japan's voice on matters of nuclear export policy will command more respect abroad.

Disincentives for Japanese Nuclear Exports

Despite Japan's success with nuclear power, it is not yet a major nuclear exporter. Probably the major reason is the long depression in the world market for nuclear power plants, brought on in part by the rapid fall in international oil prices and in part by the major nuclear power accidents at Three Mile Island in the United States in 1979 and at Chernobyl in the Soviet Union in April of 1986. As for markets, Japan can scarcely expect to sell nuclear power plants to the major nuclear power nations.[3] This leaves mainly the developing and new industrial states that would like to increase their supply and use of electricity but probably could not afford conventional financing. For Japan to sell to the Asian, Latin American, or Pacific Rim states, it would probably have to provide some kind of long-term financing that could bypass the debt problems of many of these potential buyers. Also, many of these states lack electrical transmission systems big enough to accommodate the large (1,000 MW(e) capacity) central nuclear power plants now being offered by most major nuclear suppliers.[4] While Japan has shown interest in developing a small nuclear power plant (100–300 MW(e)), it has yet to demonstrate a prototype. At present, only the Soviet Union markets a comparatively small, proven 440 MW(e) unit.

Notable Nuclear Transactions of the 1980s

While Japan's nuclear industry does not yet export major components for nuclear power reactors, its contract to supply a reactor pressure vessel to the People's Republic of China was one of the first notable orders won by a foreign supplier. Perhaps this is the first swallow of spring. More important, through collaboration between Japanese and American manufacturers of nuclear power units, the next generation of units for the U.S. market in effect is being developed and demonstrated in Japan.

Changes in Japan's Nuclear Export Status

During the past two decades Japan has evolved from a major nuclear importer to a potentially formidable nuclear supplier and competitor. It already is a supplier of nuclear technology, equipment and services, and it continues to expand its network of bilateral agreements for nuclear cooperation, which can open the way for further Japanese nuclear competition.

Some insight into official Japanese thinking about nuclear cooperation was apparent at the 20th annual conference of Japan's Atomic Industrial Forum in Tokyo in 1987.[5] There Commissioner Tsuneo Fujinami of Japan's Atomic Energy Commission spoke of a philosophy of nuclear cooperation that would have Japan proceed with cooperation corresponding to the stage of nuclear development of a partner country.[6]

Japanese Safeguards and Requirements for Nuclear Exports

If Japan does move vigorously into the world nuclear market, then the conditions it attaches to its nuclear sales become important for the world's nonproliferation regime.[7]

As a party to the Treaty on the Non-Proliferation of Nuclear Weapons (NPT), Japan has undertaken not to provide source or special fissionable material or equipment, or materials especially designed or prepared for the processing, use, or production of special nuclear material, to any non-nuclear-weapons state for peaceful purposes unless the materials are subject to IAEA safeguards.[8] Although the NPT opened for signature in 1968, Japan did not ratify it until 1976. The following year, Japan subscribed to the statement of conditions for nuclear exports drafted by NPT states in the Zangger Committee and to its list of items that would require IAEA safeguards to apply to such materials.[9]

Japan also subscribes to the Nuclear Suppliers' trigger list of categories of nuclear equipment and materials to which safeguards apply.[10] This list includes complete reactor components and certain important materials, such as heavy water and nuclear-grade graphite, that are essential for the operation of certain types of reactors.

Overall Assessment of Japan's Nuclear Export Activity and Policy

At the moment, Japan is poised to vigorously compete to sell nuclear power reactors abroad once a market revives. It now has the technological and financial strength to supply smaller units on terms attractive to many power-short developing countries, which could greatly expand its infiuence.

Overall, Japan appears to be cautious and prudent in its nuclear export policy and adheres to the requirements of the NPT and the IAEA. On the other hand, as will be seen later, Japan does not favor external intervention by one country in another country's use of nuclear energy. American insistence on post-export controls for U.S. nuclear exports in Japan has been a source of friction between the two countries, particularly for restrictions over Japanese reprocessing of spent fuel subject to U.S. controls and the transportation and use of the recovered plutonium.[11]

Domestic Laws, Regulations And Organization For Nuclear Exports And Cooperation

Japanese Laws Affecting Nuclear Exports and Cooperation

Since the early 1950s, Japan's development of nuclear power and its nuclear imports have rested upon legislation that also provides the basis for growing Japanese nuclear cooperation and exports with other countries. Fundamental is the Atomic Energy Basic Law of 1955.[12] Article 1 of the Basic Law lays out its objective as follows:

> The objective of this Law should be to secure energy resources in the future, to achieve the progress of science and technology and the promotion of industries by fostering the research, development and utilization of atomic energy and thereby to contribute to the welfare of mankind and to the elevation of the national living standard.

Going further, Article 2 states in its basic policy for Japan that:

> The research, development and utilization of atomic energy shall be limited to peaceful purposes and performed independently under democratic management, the results therefrom shall be made public to contribute to international cooperation.

As for control over imported nuclear fuel materials, Article 12 provides that:

> Those who attempt to produce, import, export, possess, hold, transfer, receive, use or transport nuclear fuel materials shall be subject . . . to the regulations to be enforced by the Government.[13]

The Basic Law is supplemented by the Law for the Regulation of Nuclear Source Material, Nuclear Fuel Material and Reactors, commonly called the Regulation Law,[14] and the Prevention Law.[15] The Basic Law and the Regulation Law together with two Cabinet Orders undergird the licensing for nuclear activities in Japan.[16] The Regulation Law regulates the importing of nuclear materials and equipment and the execution of agreements or other international arrangements concerning the research, development, and use of atomic energy for peaceful uses.[17] The Prevention Law regulates the use, sale, disposal, and handling of radioisotopes. These three laws constitute the framework for Japanese nuclear trade. They complement general import and export control laws and also international treaty and other commitments.

Under the Regulation Law, any person wishing to hold or use nuclear fuel material must obtain a permit from the prime minister, who may not give such permission unless four conditions are met.[18] The conditions are:

1. The nuclear fuel material will not be used for non-peaceful purposes;
2. The permission will cause no hindrance to the planned research, development and utilization of atomic energy;
3. The location, structure and equipment of using facilities, storing facilities and disposing facilities are such that they will cause no hindrance from accidents by nuclear fuel or material contaminated by nuclear fuel; and
4. The applicant has technical ability sound enough to use nuclear fuel material competently.[19]

The Regulation Law also deals with internationally controlled material. Any person who wishes to use such materials must also obtain the prime minister's permission.[20] Furthermore, such users must report changes made in the materials and keep records of their use.[21]

When internationally controlled material is to be used for the refining, fabrication, or operation of reactors, advance notice of the kinds, quantity, and period of use of such material must be given to the prime minister and the minister of international trade and industry.[22] The prime minister may order the user to return or transfer this material if the international agreement involved has been superseded, has expired or terminated, or if a supply state exercises an option to recover the material.[23]

Cabinet Orders Affecting Nuclear Imports and Exports

Several Cabinet Orders flesh out Japanese legislation affecting nuclear imports and exports.

Regulation of Imports. Cabinet Order No. 378 in 1949 laid down basic rules for import controls.[24] Nuclear import procedures were specified later in 1979 by the Import Trade Control Regulations of the Ministry of International Trade and Industry (MITI).[25] The minister of international trade and industry designates goods to be governed by an import quota system, as well as the places of origin or shipment areas of goods for which import approval must be obtained. Nuclear and related items subject to import quotas are specified in MITI Notification No. 170 of 1966, as amended by Notification No. 503 of 10 December 1985.[26] Government agencies, however, are not subject to the order.

Persons wishing to obtain an import approval or an import quota allocation must apply to MITI.

Regulation of Exports. Any person wishing to export items listed in Cabinet Order No. 378 for Export Trade Control must obtain a license from MITI. The items listed include many forms of metals, heavy hydrogen, nuclear reactors and their fuel, and various kinds of related equipment.[27] MITI may require an applicant to report on the items concerned so that it can check whether the proposed export conforms to laws and regulations in force.

Organization for Nuclear Power, Cooperation, and Trade

Responsibility for Japan's development of nuclear power and for nuclear cooperation and control is vested in the prime minister, who fulfills these responsibilities with the aid of three advisory bodies, three ministries, and a major extraministerial bureau.[28] Figure 10–1 indicates their place in government.

The Prime Minister and Advisory Bodies. As noted earlier, the Basic Law authorizes the prime minister and his cabinet to regulate all nuclear activities and to establish bodies to perform and manage these activities. Three statutory advisory bodies advise the prime minister on nuclear cooperation and trade.

Established in 1955, the *Atomic Energy Commission* (AEC) advises the prime minister on policy and budgetary issues. Responsible for major nuclear issues of basic principle, the AEC formulates research, industrial, and diplomatic policy. The commission may also make recommendations through the prime minister to ministerial departments and agencies. A number of advisory committees, some of which deal with international nuclear issues and nuclear nonproliferation, assist the AEC.

Once the AEC decides on a nuclear matter, it reports to the prime minister, who is fully expected to respect the decision and act or launch a new policy based upon the AEC report, in accordance with the Atomic Energy Commission Establishment Act. Since the establishment of the

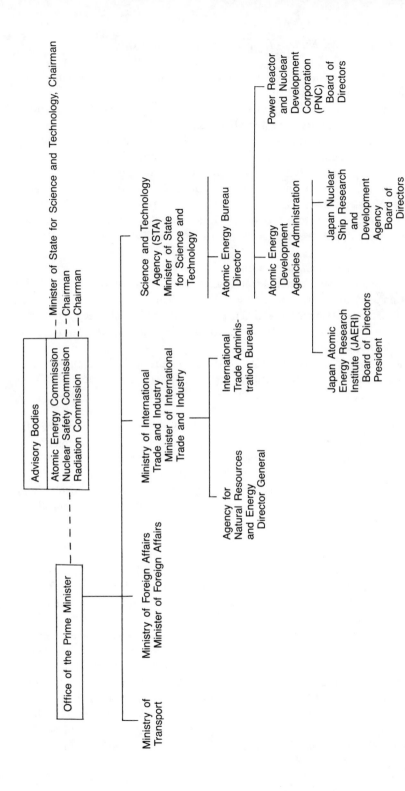

Figure 10–1. Organization of the Government of Japan for Nuclear Cooperation and Commerce

commission more than thirty years ago, no case has arisen where the prime minister has not respected an AEC decision.

The prime minister appoints the five AEC commissioners, including three standing members, one tentative member, and the chairperson. The state minister for science and technology chairs the commission. Persons from the government, the private sector, and academia have been chosen as AEC commissioners. Often representatives of the foreign ministry, the utilities, or the Ministry of International Trade and Industry are appointed.

The *Nuclear Safety Commission* advises the prime minister on safety issues for nuclear reactors. It too is composed of a chairperson and four commissioners appointed by the prime minister and uses advisory committees.

The *Radiation Council* is a third advisory body for the office of the prime minister. The council establishes technical standards for radiation protection and exposure and advises the Nuclear Safety Commission, the Nuclear Safety Bureau of the Science and Technology Agency, and other governmental agencies. It has some voice in setting safety standards for shipments of radioactive materials.

The council consists of up to thirty part-time members appointed by the prime minister from members of government departments or from persons having a special knowledge in this field.

The Ministry of Foreign Affairs. The Ministry of Foreign Affairs officially speaks for the Japanese government in negotiating agreements for nuclear cooperation and in representing Japan's nuclear policies. The Science Affairs and Nuclear Affairs offices within the foreign ministry are involved with nuclear issues. The foreign ministry often consults with MITI to ensure that Japan's export policy is in line with its nonproliferation policies.

The Ministry of International Trade and Industry (MITI). Headed by the minister of international trade and industry, MITI is the main regulatory and promotional agency for peaceful uses of nuclear energy. Regulatory responsibilities are divided between MITI and the Science and Technology Agency (STA). MITI regulates commercial nuclear activities, and STA regulates nuclear research and development. The ministry licenses nuclear imports and exports and has the major responsibility for nuclear cooperation. The London Nuclear Suppliers Group Guidelines and Zangger Committee Guidelines are incorporated into MITI's basic trade restrictions. Since MITI is responsible for the regulation of commercial nuclear technology, MITI oversees the licensing of commercial power reactors as well.

The *Agency for Natural Resources and Energy* (ANRE) is a subordinate agency of MITI. It has general control over research, development, and utilization of nuclear energy within MITI's jurisdiction. The Nuclear Energy Industries Division of ANRE is responsible, in consultation with the Science and Technology Agency, for technical assistance contracts involving nuclear energy. The division also grants permission for receiving import allotments (quotas) of nuclear materials, for transfers of nuclear materials of U.S. origin, and for the use and sale of radioactive isotopes.

The *Strategic-Export Control Office* of MITI is responsible for screening export license applications for potential violations of rules set by the Coordinating Committee for Multilateral Export Controls (COCOM).

The *International Trade Administration Bureau* is in charge of promotion, improvement, and regulation of Japan's exports and imports. Its duties include supervision of organizations related to international trade under the law concerning the Japan External Trade Organization (JETRO)[29] and inspection of the business procedures of trading firms to ensure compliance with the Foreign Exchange and Foreign Trade Control Law.[30] It is also responsible for overall control of approvals related to exports.

The Science and Technology Agency (STA). The Science and Technology Agency is an extraministerial bureau of the prime minister's office. Established in 1956 and headed by the minister of state for science and technology, the STA is the central mechanism for the planning, coordination, and administration of nuclear research and development. In conjunction with the Ministry of Foreign Affairs and MITI, the STA is a leader in international dialogue as well. As Secretariat to the AEC, the STA ensures that nuclear activities are for peaceful purposes and that safeguards are enforced. STA makes these priorities clear during any negotiation of a nuclear cooperation agreement.

The STA has two bureaus: the Atomic Energy Bureau and the Nuclear Safety bureau. The latter was established by a reorganization of the STA in 1975 to separate the agency's regulatory and development functions.

The *Atomic Energy Bureau* formulates basic policies for and promotes the peaceful uses of atomic energy. Its Research and International Affairs Division is responsible for international cooperation and information collection and analysis. The bureau also includes the Atomic Energy Development Agencies Administration, which supervises the Japan Atomic Energy Research Institute (JAERI) and the Japan Nuclear Ship Research and Development Agency.

The *Japan Atomic Energy Research Institute* (JAERI) was established under the Basic Law to undertake research and development for atomic energy under the authority of the prime minister's office. The institute is organized as a separate special corporation. One of its functions is the import, production, and distribution of radioisotopes.

The executive officers of JAERI include a president, a vice-president, and up to seven directors, all appointed by the prime minister in agreement with the Atomic Energy Commission. While funds for JAERI are not restricted to the government, in practice almost all of the funds come from government sources.

A second part of the bureau is the *Japan Nuclear Ship Research and Development Agency*. While the future of Japan's experimental nuclear cargo ship, the *Mutsu*, seems bleak, there is some possibility that nuclear power may prove desirable for cargo and passenger ships if the cost of oil should again increase.

The agency was created under the Basic Law in 1963 as a semipublic corporation.

A third major part of the bureau is the *Power Reactor and Nuclear Fuel Development Corporation* (PNC), which was established in 1967 to do research and development for nuclear fuels and power reactors. It is an independent entity under the authority of the prime minister's office through the Atomic Energy Bureau. PNC is responsible for development of fast breeder and advanced reactors; nuclear fuel technology; fuel reprocessing; uranium ore prospecting; importing and exporting; and purchasing and selling of nuclear source materials and nuclear fuels. PNC is financed by a combination of government and private funds.

The other bureau of the STA, *the Nuclear Safety Bureau*, is responsible for nuclear safety regulation and implementation of comprehensive measures to ensure the safety of nuclear facilities. Its Safeguard Division is in charge of regulations on internationally controlled materials. In particular, the bureau operates the Nuclear Materials Control Center (NMCC), which was established in April 1972. The center supports government work in nonproliferation, especially safeguards. In addition, upon request the center undertakes research and studies on safeguards and physical protection of nuclear material and holds seminars for training engineers and technicians.

The Minister of Transport. Under the Regulation Law, the minister of transport has jurisdiction for all questions involving the licensing of reactors for commercial nuclear ships. He also has jurisdiction, together with the Science and Technology Agency, for the transport of radioactive materials and nuclear fuel by rail, road, ship, and aircraft. These responsibilities involve this ministry in shipments of spent fuel to Europe and the return shipments of plutonium and high-level wastes. The ministry would also be involved if in the future Japan was to offer reprocessing services to other countries.

Japan's Nuclear Supply Commitments Under Treaties And Agreements

Japan's policies for nuclear cooperation and trade reflect its commitments under several treaties and international agreements, including the International Statute of the International Atomic Energy Agency, the Non-Proliferation Treaty, the Convention on the Physical Protection of Nuclear Material, two conventions dealing with responses to major nuclear accidents, and the voluntary Nuclear Suppliers Guidelines.

The Statute of the International Atomic Energy Agency. As a member of the International Atomic Energy Agency and party to its international statute, which established the agency in 1957, Japan supports the proposition that peaceful uses of nuclear energy should be encouraged and can be kept separate from military applications, and that peaceful use commitments for items received through international nuclear cooperation and trade can be verified by international inspection (safeguards) of the agency.

The Non-Proliferation Treaty. As a party to the Nuclear Non-Proliferation Treaty (NPT), Japan endorses the principle that the benefits of peaceful uses of nuclear technology should be available to all parties to the treaty, and that all parties are entitled to participate in the "fullest possible exchange" of scientific information for, and to contribute, alone or in cooperation with other States, to the further development of the application of atomic energy for peaceful purpose.[31] As an NPT party, Japan has also undertaken not to provide source or special fissionable material, or equipment or materials especially designed or prepared for the processing, use, or production of special nuclear material, to any non–nuclear-weapons state for peaceful purposes unless the materials are subject to IAEA safeguards.[32] Through the treaty, Japan also recognizes the "inalienable right" of all NPT parties to research, develop, produce, and use nuclear energy for peaceful purposes without discrimination.[33] It is, in addition, committed to cooperate, either alone or with other states, to the further development of peaceful uses of nuclear energy, "especially in the territories of non–nuclear-weapon states party to the Treaty, with due consideration for the needs of the developing areas of the world."[34]

Japan is a member of the Zangger Committee, established to create an international trigger list of items that require IAEA safeguards under the NPT. The list includes complete reactors, reactor components, and certain other materials, notably heavy water and high-purity graphite.[35]

Japan and the International Convention on the Physical Protection of Nuclear Material. On 27 November 1988, Japan acceded to the Convention on the Physical Protection of Nuclear Material. The result of a U.S. proposal in 1974, this treaty provides for adequate physical security for international shipments of significant quantities of source or special nuclear material. Each party must ensure that during international transport nuclear material is protected at an agreed-upon level while the material is within its territory or on board a ship or aircraft under its jurisdiction. Each party also agrees not to export or import nuclear material or allow its transit through its territory unless assured that the nuclear material will be protected at the agreed levels.

Japan and the Nuclear Accident Conventions. One result of the Chernobyl accident in the Soviet Union in April 1988 was the negotiation of two international conventions dealing with major nuclear power accidents that involve neighboring countries. One requires the prompt reporting of such accidents to other states, and the other commits its parties to cooperate between themselves and the International Atomic Energy Agency to facilitate prompt assistance in the event of a nuclear accident or radiological emergency. Both conventions are now in force.[36] Japan's ratification of both took effect on 10 July 1987.

Bilateral Agreements for Nuclear Cooperation. Japan has followed in the footsteps of the United States by establishing a widespread net of bilaterial agreements for nuclear cooperation. With these in place, its nuclear industry can move quickly as opportunities arise. At present Japan has in effect four diplomatic notes, eleven bilateral government-to-government agreements, and nine other agreements for technical and industrial nuclear cooperation.

Voluntary Commitments: The Nuclear Supplier Guidelines. Beginning in the Ford Administration, the United States organized secret talks in London with nuclear supplier states to seek agreement on additional export controls that went beyond NPT requirements. These culminated in publication of the Voluntary Nuclear Suppliers Guidelines in 1978 by fifteen member states. As noted earlier, Japan subscribes to them. The guidelines provide for a formal assurance from the recipient government explicitly excluding uses that would result in any nuclear explosive devices; effective physical protection by the importing country to prevent any unauthorized use and handling of the material or facilities; and application of IAEA safeguards to the exported item.[37]

Additionally, the guidelines called for restraint in the transfer of sensitive facilities, technology, and weapons-usable material, as well as encouragement of alternatives to national enrichment or reprocessing plants, such as multi-national fuel cycle centers.[38]

Indications of Japanese Attitudes Concerning Nuclear Cooperation

Over the years Japan has tended to follow the nonproliferation and nuclear supply policies of the United States. Nonetheless, there was some resistance in the late 1960s in Japan to joining the NPT, and there has been continuing resistance since the late 1970s to U.S. attempts to control Japan's reprocessing of spent fuels containing U.S. supplied enriched uranium. Japan favors the building of an international consensus among supplier states as preferable to unilateral action by one supplier, and does not favor detailed postexport controls.[39] Recently there have been signs of awakening Japanese interest in becoming a leader rather than a follower of nonproliferation policy.

Statements by government officials, industry organizations, and the public in Japan show common themes as well as some divergences. Generally, the official and industry views support nuclear cooperation, whereas some public groups tend to oppose it.

The fact that Japan did not ratify the NPT until 1976 shows that this treaty presented some problems to the Japanese. AEC Commissioner Masahio Nishibori alluded to these at the 18th annual conference of the Japan Atomic Industrial Forum in 1985.[40] For him, nonproliferation is more a political than a technical question. In this context, the NPT is discriminatory and unequal. It sharply and arbitrarily divides countries into those that have and those that do not have nuclear weapons. According to Commissioner Nishibori, it was not easy for Japan to sign and ratify the NPT, a fact that should always be kept in mind. In particular, the nuclear-weapons states, which occupy a privileged position, must not make light of this stern reality."

From this Japanese viewpoint, nations should first understand the positions of other countries and then work for an international consensus on objectives and rational standards, common systems, and joint measures relating to nuclear activities. In doing this, and only by doing this, can a "sound and wholesome international order of nuclear energy" be established, based on "harmonious solutions to what is pre-eminently a political problem."

Some Official Views

The Atomic Energy Commission. In 1983, the AEC proposed that Japan deal independently with nuclear nonproliferation problems and make further contributions to international cooperation. More to the point, with expectations growing for international nuclear cooperation in both advanced and developing countries, it was "vital for Japan to meet such expectations, not only to promote the development and utilization of nuclear energy smoothly and effectively, but also to fulfill Japan's international obligations as a leading country in nuclear power."[41]

The 1984 AEC report carried the theme of international cooperation a step further when for the first time it mentioned possible exports of nuclear power plants.[42] Looking to developing countries, the 1984 report urged cooperation on use of radiation and isotopes. Furthermore, because of improvements in nuclear energy technology and the growth of its nuclear industry, Japan would be a supplier of nuclear materials and technology, and even nuclear power plants.[43] So it was necessary for Japan's nuclear industry to strengthen its technical foundations and improve the efficiency of its nuclear power plants. Further, because the export of nuclear power plants would involve large funds and risks, it was necessary for the government to consider appropriate financing measures and to create conditions favorable for such exports.[44]

A MITI Advisory Committee Report in 1986. In March 1986, a Subcommittee on Nuclear Power of the MITI Advisory Committee for Energy discussed how to promote nuclear cooperation with developing countries.[45] Its underlying premise was that developing countries were looking toward Japan for cooperation. The report called on Japan's governmental and private organizations to keep in close contact with each other in extending cooperation on a "united government-industry basis," with priority given to cooperation with China, South Korea, and Southeast Asian neighbors.

Some Nuclear Industry Views

The Nuclear Energy Vision Report of 1986. A major report revealing Japanese views on nuclear energy was prepared by a Subcommittee on Nuclear Energy of MITI's Advisory Committee for Energy in September 1986.[46] It signaled a change in outlook. Noting that Japan had caught up with Europe and the United States in nuclear power, the subcommittee argued that it was necessary that the Japanese no longer feel backward, and that they should recognize that Japan has a positive role to play in world development and use of nuclear energy. Indeed, Japan could be pulling ahead: "While the influence of the United States used to be dominant, the international nuclear development scene is now becoming more internally diversified."[47]

Three basic concepts for nuclear cooperation were advanced by the subcommittee. (1) Japan's nuclear cooperation should be limited to peaceful purposes; (2) Japan should meet the increasing expectations for its role in supporting and improving the international system for nuclear energy development; and (3) Japan should promote joint research and development on an equal footing with other nuclear suppliers.

As for the United States, "from an international situation, it seems difficult for the United States to keep the same dominant role in technological development in the nuclear power generating field."[48]

Public Attitudes Toward Nuclear Power

The story of Japanese public attitudes toward nuclear power is long and beyond the scope of this article. Still, something needs to be said. In brief, the situation in Japan resembles that of some other countries. The general public is mildly indifferent to nuclear power, with small but energetic and vocal groups trying to arouse public opposition.

Major political parties have shown divergent views. An analysis by the Social and Economic Congress of Japan in June 1985[49] showed that all parties except the Liberal-Democrats gave a lower place to energy in comparison with other issues.[50] The advisability of nuclear power for the future was controversial for all parties, with the Socialists internally divided. On the whole, the role of nuclear power as an important energy source seemed to be recognized by all parties except the Socialists and the Communists. Looking ahead, the Liberal-Democrats, Democratic Socialists, and Komei favored establishing a full nuclear fuel cycle.[51] The New Liberals, although favoring continued development, stressed the need, along with Komei, to ensure safety. The Communist Party said it did not approve of the Japanese nuclear generation system because it was technically far from perfect. It favored studies for comprehensive research and development and for scrupulous safety review. The Social Democratic Federation favored the Swedish approach of legislating an end to nuclear power.

Japan's Nuclear Capabilities

Probably the most compelling reason to take Japan seriously as a strong future competitor on the world nuclear market is the growing strength of its nuclear power generation and nuclear supply industries. Among the major nuclear power states, Japan appears to have enough projected domestic growth to keep its domestic nuclear manufacturers partially busy until a hoped for upturn in demand for new nuclear power plants appears.

Nuclear Power Generation in Japan

As of 31 July 1988, Japan had thirty-eight operable nuclear power units, with a generating capacity of 28,966 MW(e), in comparison with a world total of 432 units and 326,528 MW(e). These units supplied 31.2 percent of Japan's electricity. In comparison with other countries, this is about midway between Italy, which derived 0.1 percent of its electricity from uranium, and France, where nuclear power supplied 69.8 percent of the total.[52]

The Japanese government maintains a long-term plan for development and utilization of nuclear energy. Prepared by Japan's Atomic Energy Commission for approval by the prime minister, it is updated every five years. The most recent revision came in 1987.[53] This revision shifted emphasis from the rapid expansion of generating capacity featured in the previous 1982 plan toward increased research and development to consolidate Japan's nuclear program and to assure a leading position in nuclear technology. The nuclear generating capacity planned in 1982 for the year 2000 was cut back from 90,000 MW(e) to 53,000 MW(e), which would supply about 40 percent of Japan's electricity. Commercial operation of fast breeder reactors was postponed to 2020, with development emphasis shifted to improvements in safety and reliability and to the use of plutonium in conventional nuclear power plants, with reprocessing the plutonium-mixed oxide fuel fabrication being done in Japan to ensure Japan's plutonium-use policy could be implemented without outside interference.[54] The AEC lowered its projections because of slowed growth in energy-intensive industries and advances in energy conservation.[55]

On the whole, while Japanese nuclear generating capacity will continue to grow, the construction pace for new plants will be slow, and Japan's nuclear construction industry faces a time of stagnation. Japan's three reactor manufacturers have a production capacity of about 6,000 MW(e) a year, but face an annual anticipated order rate of about 2,000 MW(e).[56]

The Outlook for Japan's Nuclear Industry Market

The 1986 Nuclear Energy Vision report for the MITI Advisory Committee for Energy projected a leveling off for new power plant construction, but suggested a substantial increase in the domestic market for technical services for operation, maintenance, and management of power plants and for completion of the fuel cycle. Overall, the report expected the domestic market to increase to 6,700 billion yen ($55.8 billion U.S. at 120 yen/$U.S.) by the year 2030. The cumulative total for this forty-five-year period would come to about 180,000 billion yen ($1,500 billion U.S.). Of this, about 50,000 billion yen ($416 billion U.S.) would be for plant construction, 60,000 billion yen ($500 billion U.S.) for operation, maintenance, and management, and 70,000 billion yen ($583 billion U.S.) for the fuel cycle.[57]

Even when the uncertainties of projections are taken into account, these figures indicate substantial continuing work for Japan's nuclear industry. Yet some observers say these levels will lead to underutilization of the industry and its eventual weakening unless a substantial nuclear export market can be developed.

Japan's Nuclear Supply Industries

Japan's nuclear power industry consists of its electric utilities and a nuclear supply industry. The latter includes three groups: the nuclear equipment supply industry, the nuclear service industry, and the fuel cycle industry. In 1988 the market for the supply industry was about 1,500 billion yen ($12.5 billion U.S.). While the market for light-water-type reactors is already well established in Japan, advanced reactors and the nuclear fuel cycle are still at the research and development stage, with government investments continuing to be important.[58]

Japan's nuclear equipment supply industry is organized around its major reactor suppliers, with their high technology and financial resources. It includes some three hundred enterprises. At its heart are three major industrial groups, each centering on a major reactor manufacturer: Toshiba, Hitachi, and Mitsubishi. Within each group the central manufacturers and affiliated suppliers have a close and rather exclusive relationship, which is a distinguishing feature of Japan's nuclear industry.[59] If new orders continue at about 2,000 MW(e) per year, the major suppliers will be less able to make additional investments, which will make it increasingly difficult for them to maintain their technical development capacity.

Japan's nuclear service industry comprises maintenance and transport services. While the size of its domestic market is not clear, one estimate indicates that for 1983 it had reached an annual level of 100 billion yen ($800 million U.S.).[60]

As for Japan's fuel cycle industry, this is still incomplete and formative. It includes companies that develop and produce centrifuges for Japan's uranium enrichment effort, that are expected to produce equipment for Japan's commercial fuel reprocessing plant, and that fabricate fuel for Japan's conventional nuclear power plants. Because of their significance for Japan's technological standing, the enrichment and reprocessing projects will be described in more detail.

Japan's Enrichment Capacity. An essential element of Japan's policy for nuclear power is to complete the nuclear fuel cycle, which means Japan would acquire an industrial capacity to enrich uranium.[61] The 1986 Nuclear Energy Vision report called for promotion of domestic enrichment, with aggressive efforts to develop new technologies. Japan's enrichment needs will probably be wholly filled by the United States and France until about the year 2000. Then a gradual growth of domestic enrichment is expected to begin, rising to a capacity of about 6,000,000 separative work units (SWUs) per year by 2015, in comparison with an estimated total demand of 12,000,000 SWU per year. After 2015, the ratio of domestically produced enrichment should gradually increase.[62] Typically, a large modern nuclear power plant will require enrichment services of 125,000 to 284,000 SWU per year for its fuel.

A notable step toward the goal of Japanese enrichment came on 26 May 1987, when Japan Nuclear Fuel Industries applied to the Science and Technology Agency for permission to enrich uranium. A plant with an ultimate output of 1.5 million SWU per year is to be built at Rokkasho-mura village, Aomori Prefecture in northern Honshu, Japan. The initial capacity planned is 600,000 SWU per year. Construction started in October 1988, and start-up is expected in 1994.[63]

Japan's Reprocessing Capacity. Another part of Japan's nuclear policy is to encourage the extraction of plutonium from spent nuclear fuel for reuse in fast breeders and in conventional nuclear power reactors. Japan has a pilot reprocessing plant, built with French technology at Tokai-Mura, which is operated by the Power Reactor and Nuclear Fuel Development Corporation. Plans are well along for the construction of a large commercial reprocessing plant at the Rokkashomura site. With a planned reprocessing capacity of 800 metric tons of spent fuel a year, this plant is to be built by Japan Nuclear Fuel Service (JPNFS), which hopes to complete the facility in the 1990s with the help of imported French technology.[64]

Japan's Nuclear Imports

Until well into the 1960s Japan was predominantly an importer of U.S. nuclear power technology and equipment. As Japan's electrical and ship-building industries moved to fill this void, imports of nuclear equipment from the United States declined, although Japan's growing nuclear power industry also began to import more uranium enriched in the United States. In the mid-1980s, Japanese companies still import some U.S. nuclear power technology via joint commercial undertakings with Westinghouse and General Electric, and Japan remains the U.S. Department of Energy's largest buyer of enrichment services. It also continues to depend upon the reprocessing services of France.

Looking ahead, within the decade Japan could begin to reduce its demand for U.S. enrichment services if the large new enrichment plant at Rokkashomura starts up on schedule and is able to supply about one-third of Japan's needs. Likewise, if the reprocessing plant is completed this would reduce, but not eliminate, Japan's dependence upon French and possibly British reprocessing. Japan will probably also continue to depend upon U.S. universities to educate young Japanese in nuclear engineering, as well as looking to U.S. working experience with nuclear power plants for insights to further improve the safety and efficiency of operation of its own nuclear power units.

On the whole, over the past three decades Japan has completed the transition from dependence upon imported nuclear power technology, goods, and services to virtual independence. A blending of U.S. and Japanese nuclear technology holds promise for the next generation of nuclear power reactors, as Japan continues its transition from the status of a major customer for the U.S. nuclear power industry to that of a major competitor itself.

Notes

1. The Pacific Rim states include those bordering on the Pacific Ocean for North and South America and Asia. The major states of the Asian part of the Pacific Rim include Japan, South Korea, Taiwan, Singapore, Hong Kong, Indonesia, Malaysia, Thailand, the Philippines, and China. These Asian Pacific countries now rank with North America and Western Europe as major centers of economic vitality.

2. Nuclear Non-Proliferation Treaty (NPT), Article IV.

3. However, if circumstances cause new orders for nuclear power plants in the United States, where U.S. industries have lost much of their capacity to produce major components for the nuclear part of these plants, it is plausible that Japan might supply them.

4. MW(e): megawatts electric.

5. For a detailed summary of the conference, see the April 1987 issue of *Atoms in Japan.*

6. "Strengthening International Nuclear Cooperation in Asia," (summary of Session 3), *Atoms in Japan* (April 1987): 22.

7. The nonproliferation regime refers to the collection of treaties, bilateral agreements, voluntary understandings of the nuclear suppliers, and inspection by the International Atomic Energy Agency (safeguards) that are collectively intended to prevent the further spread, or proliferation, of nuclear weapons.

8. NPT, Article III-2. Note that the NPT does not require that *all* nuclear activities of an importing non–nuclear-weapons state be under IAEA safeguards, only that the imported items be safeguarded.

9. These voluntary understandings were published in IAEA Information Circular No. 209. Japan's undertaking appears in INFCIRC/209/Add.9, 8 July 1977. The list was prepared by the NPT Exporters Committee headed by Professor C. Zangger of Switzerland, and is often referred to as the Zangger list.

10. In addition to the Zangger list, there is a substantially identical trigger list implemented through the Nuclear Suppliers Group. The NSG trigger list has the

potential advantage of being open to adoption by states which will not join the NPT. Nonetheless, the existence of two lists is sometimes confusing.

11. U.S. post-export controls apply to spent fuel in Japan that contains U.S. enriched uranium. The recently revised agreement for nuclear cooperation extends this control to spent fuel from U.S.-supplied reactors even if the uranium in their fuel was not enriched in the United States. However, the revised agreement provided a thirty-year advance approval for reprocessing.

12. The Atomic Energy Basic Law, Law No. 186, 19 December 1955. The text of this and several related laws were published in Japan in 1965. See *Atomic Energy Laws of Japan* (Tokyo: Atomic Energy Bureau, 1965).

13. "Nuclear fuel materials" are defined in the Basic Law, Article 3, to mean "materials which release a large amount of energy in process of nuclear fission such as uranium, thorium, etc., and which are specified by the Cabinet Order."

14. Law No. 166, 10 June 1957.

15. Law No. 167, 10 June 1957.

16. The two Cabinet Orders are the Ordinance for the Definition of Nuclear Fuel Material, Nuclear Source Material, Reactors, and Radiation (Cabinet Order No. 325, 21 November 1957), and the Ordinance for the Enforcement of the Regulation Law (Cabinet Order No. 324, 21 November 1957).

17. The Japanese law introduces a new term not used in U.S. nuclear law and regulation, namely "internationally controlled material." This is defined by the Regulation Law (Law No. 166) to mean "nuclear source material, nuclear fuel material, . . . or other material or equipment to which safeguards are applied under agreements or other international arrangements." "Nuclear source materials" are "raw materials for nuclear fuel materials, such as uranium ore, thorium ore, etc., and which are to be specified by the Cabinet Order."

18. Article 52 of the Regulation Law provides that: "Any person who wishes to use nuclear fuel material shall . . . obtain the Prime Minister's permission." Certain government agencies are exempted from this requirement.

19. Regulation Law, Article 53.

20. Regulation Law, Article 61-2.

21. Regulation Law, Article 61-4.

22. Regulation Law, Article 61-7.

23. Regulation Law, Article 61-8.

24. The Import Trade Control Order, Cabinet Order No. 378, 1 December 1949.

25. The Import Trade Control Regulations, MITI Ordinance No. 77, December 1979. This supplements the Cabinet's Import Trade Control Order No. 414.

26. Items listed in MITI Notification No. 503 include ores of radioactive elements; various forms of fissile materials, of thorium and uranium; nuclear reactors and their parts; and radiation detection and measuring instruments and their parts and accessories.

27. Nuclear items subject to MITI export controls include nuclear fuel materials and raw materials; reactors and their parts and accessories for electric power or propulsion; generators for neutrons or atomic particles; apparatus for reprocessing radioactive nuclear materials and for uranium enrichment; and flash-X-ray systems and X ray tubes.

28. This section relies heavily upon a 1983 review of national legislation for nuclear energy by the Nuclear Energy Agency of the OECD. See *Nuclear Legislation. Analytical Study. Regulatory and Institutional Framework for Nuclear Activities*, vol. 2. (Paris: Nuclear Energy Agency/OECD, 1983) pp. 174–91.

29. Law No. 95, 26 April 1958. JETRO is a nonprofit organization to promote international trade in line with the government's free-trade policy. Its activities include cooperation to promote imports and to encourage development of trade and industry in developing countries.

30. Law No. 228, 1949.

31. Preamble to the NPT.

32. While some nuclear supplier states have insisted on full-scope safeguards as a condition for their nuclear exports—notably the United States, the United Kingdom, Canada, and Australia—Japan does not.

33. NPT, Article IV-1.

34. NPT, Article IV-2.

35. For details see IAEA Information Circular INFCIRC/209.

36. The Convention on Early Notification of Nuclear Accidents entered into effect on 27 October 1986, while the Convention on Assistance in the Case of a Nuclear Accident entered into effect on 26 February 1987.

37. "Communications Received from Certain Member States Regarding Guidelines for the Export of Nuclear Material, Equipment or Technology. IAEA Information Circular INFCIRC/254, February 1978.

38. Sensitive items refer to those for reprocessing, enrichment, and heavy-water production.

39. Notably the unilateral action by the United States during the Carter Administration and in the Nuclear Non-Proliferation Act of 1978.

40. "Peaceful Uses and Non-Proliferation: Searching for a New Regime," *Atoms in Japan* (April 1985): 33–34.

41. "1983 White Paper on A-Energy Emphasizes Japan's Role in International Cooperation," *Atoms in Japan* (November 1983): 27.

42. "White Paper on Atomic Energy," *Atoms in Japan* (November 1984): 11.

43. Ibid., p. 14.

44. Ibid., p. 15.

45. "MITI Policy of Nuclear Cooperation with Developing Countries Calls for the JAIF and JEPIC To Act as Agents for Receiving Trainees," *Atoms in Japan* (March 1986): 13–16.

46. Advisory Committee for Energy, Ministry of International Trade and Industry, Subcommittee on Nuclear Energy, *Nuclear Energy Vision: Perspectives of Nuclear Energy for the 21st Century*. (Tokyo: Japan Atomic Industrial Forum, 1986).

47. Ibid., p. 77.

48. Ibid., p. 81.

49. The analysis relied on a questionnaire sent to the Liberal-Democratic Party, the Socialist Party of Japan, the Komei Party, the Japan Democratic Socialist Party, the Japanese Communist Party, the New Liberal Club, and the Social Democratic Federation. The results of the survey were summarized in *Atoms in Japan* (July 1985): 21–23.

50. About this finding, the survey commented: "The likelihood is that the

stability of energy supply is yielding to policies more sensitive to the currents of the times, such as stable economic growth, assurance of employment and welfare, educational and administrative forms, technological developments and the foundation for a sophisticated information society." *Atoms in Japan* (July 1985): 21.

51. A full, or complete, nuclear fuel cycle includes uranium enrichment, spent fuel reprocessing, and use of plutonium as a nuclear fuel.

52. *World Nuclear Industry Handbook 1989* (Surrey, England: Nuclear Engineering International, 1988), pp. 10–12.

53. "Lower LWR Target Set; Breeder Delay Agreed," *Nuclear News* (May 1987): 53.

54. "Japan Taking a Lead," *Nuclear Engineering International* (June 1988): 28. This is a veiled reference to U.S.-Japanese controversey over U.S. controls for Japan's recovery, transportation, and use of plutonium recovered from spent fuel containing plutonium subject to the U.S.-Japan nuclear agreement.

55. *Nuclear News* (May 1987): 52.

56. *Nuclear Industry in Japan. Present Status and Future Prospects.* (Tokyo: International Energy Forum, January 1988), p. 4.

57. Advisory Committee for Energy, MITI, *Nuclear Energy Vision*, p. 66.

58. Ibid., p. 5.

59. Ibid., p. 6.

60. Ibid., p. 11.

61. A full, or complete, fuel cycle includes industrial capacities to produce enriched uranium, fabricate nuclear fuel, reprocess spent nuclear fuel, and dispose of radioactive wastes.

62. Advisory Committee for Energy MITI, *Nuclear Energy Vision*, p. 36.

63. "JNFI Applies to STA for Permission to Construct Enrichment Plant," *Atoms in Japan* (May 1987): 22.

64. "Japan Makes Plans for Reprocessing," *Nuclear Engineering International* (July 1984): 21.

11
Pakistan:
Emerging Nuclear Supplier Issues

Rodney W. Jones

In contrast to India, Pakistan is many years away from becoming a commercial nuclear supplier.[1] Pakistan's nuclear technology and industrial base is dwarfed by India's, and even by those of smaller Asian nations such as South Korea and Taiwan. In the face of an embargo by advanced suppliers, Pakistan is still struggling to attract bids to supply equipment for the Chashma nuclear power project—some twenty years after starting the Karachi nuclear power plant (KANUPP), Pakistan's first and only power reactor import to date.

The reason, then, to focus on Pakistan's potential as an emerging nuclear supplier is to ascertain whether it could transfer sensitive nuclear equipment, material, or knowledge to high-proliferation-risk countries. This is technically conceivable, because Pakistan has strived, with partial success, to acquire independent means of enriching uranium and of reprocessing spent fuel for plutonium—the two main paths to nuclear weapons-grade material.

Since Pakistan procured enrichment technology despite an embargo by advanced suppliers, it is natural to ask whether Pakistan would aid other countries facing similar embargoes. Given the new power of Islam in the region, it would be no surprise if Pakistan traded on its nuclear assets in relations with other Muslim nations for leadership, prestige, enhanced security, or profit, at the expense of the nonproliferation regime.

These concerns aside, it is also worth bearing in mind that Pakistan may eventually acquire enough of a nuclear and industrial base to offer peaceful nuclear exports on a commercial basis. Hence, it is important to try to foresee how Pakistan would behave in nuclear export practices.

I am indebted to Joseph Yager, guest scholar and consultant to the Center for National Security Negotiations, for reading and commenting on this paper during its preparation.

The case of Pakistan is important in another way. Pakistan allegedly has received sensitive nuclear technical assistance from the People's Republic of China, another "emerging supplier." Although some of these reports are sensationalist and fail to separate fact from fiction, the study of Pakistan's commercial nuclear activity can shed light on Chinese as well as Pakistani nuclear supplier behavior.

This inquiry focuses on four sets of questions about Pakistan that could shape its potential role as a future nuclear supplier: (1) transactions in the international nuclear market; (2) structure of decision making in nuclear affairs; (3) norms that guide its domestic and international nuclear policies; and (4) capabilities for nuclear export.

Transactions

Like India, Pakistan's long-term goals for developing nuclear technology are based on aspirations for scientific and technological self-reliance, reliable energy supply, and moving closer to nuclear weapons capability. In practice, this tends to mean trying in some measure to keep pace with India. As with India, Pakistan orginally benefited from the relatively suspicion-free atmosphere of the Atoms for Peace programs in the 1950s and 1960s. But with its much smaller resources, Pakistan did not have India's capacity to play advanced nuclear suppliers off against one another.

Moreover, nuclear energy was far lower in Pakistan's early national development priorities than in India's. Although Pakistan's domestic energy resources appear to be poorer than India's, the discovery of natural gas after independence was a boon to Pakistan's urban and industrial development. It relieved the pressure to develop capital-intensive alternatives such as nuclear power.

Pakistani development of nuclear energy capacity thus lagged well behind that of India in the 1950s and early 1960s. The fresh Pakistani emphasis on nuclear technology in the late 1960s and 1970s was driven both by perceptions of the emerging military potential in India's nuclear program (the commissioning of the Indian pilot reprocessing plant in 1965 made a big impression on then Foreign Minister Z.A. Bhutto) and by the chastening experiences of wars with India in 1965 and 1971.

By the time Pakistan's Canadian-supplied reactor at Karachi became operational in 1973, heightened concern over proliferation was beginning to cause the major suppliers to review their policies. India's detonation of a nuclear device in May 1974 made the suppliers more restrictive. It became difficult for countries with nascent nuclear energy programs and shaky nonproliferation credentials to freely import nuclear power equipment. The Indian explosion caused Canada to reevaluate and then to suspend its nuclear cooperation not only with India but also with Pakistan, neither of which had joined the Nuclear Non-Proliferation Treaty (NPT).

Nuclear Cooperation Agreements

The number of countries with which Pakistan has formal agreements for nuclear cooperation[2] (see tables 11–1 and 11–2) are slightly more than half as many as with India, but similarly span several regions.[3] These bilateral agreements include seven advanced Western supplier states, three Soviet bloc nations, and seven developing countries (three in Asia, three in the Middle East, and one in South America).

Formal cooperation agreements, however, do not give the full picture of nuclear transactions, even with advanced suppliers. It is known, for example, that Belgonucleaire played a role in Pakistani acquisition of research-scale reprocessing (as did American and French firms in India's Trombay pilot reprocessing plant)[4] and possibly helped Pakistan build a heavy-water plant, but apparently not under formal cooperation agreements. Some sub-contract transactions, moreover, such as Japan's supply of generating equipment for the KANUPP power plant, may not have been regarded as nuclear components needing such an agreement, or could have been covered indirectly by the bilateral agreement with the primary supplier country, in this case Canada. Pakistan also pursued some nuclear technical exchanges with Iran before its revolution.

Table 11–1
Pakistan's Nuclear Cooperation Agreements—Advanced Countries

Affiliation/Country	Date of Origin	Type of Cooperation	Sources
Western World			
Canada	7/18/60[a]	power	(1)
Denmark	1965	research	(3)
France	10/18/74, 3/17/76	reprocessing	(1,2)
Italy	1966	training	(3)
Spain	7/1966		(3)
United Kingdom	7/3/64, 10/13/64	research	(1)
United States	1955		(2)
Soviet Bloc			
Poland	about 1970		(3)
Romania	1973	research	(2,3)
USSR	5/20/70		(2)

Sources:
1 US Congress 1977
2 Graham Chronology
3 Sinha and Subramanian, *Nuclear Pakistan* (1980).
Note:
[a]The agreement was terminated along with all nuclear cooperation 12/31/76.

Table 11–2

Pakistan's Nuclear Cooperation Agreements—Developing Countries

Region/Country	Date of Origin	Type of Cooperation	Sources
Asia			
China (PRC)	7/30/66[a], 5/26/76	scientific	(2,3)
	1/29/77[a], 6/78[a]	scientific	(2,3)
	9/19/86[b]	research	(4)
Indonesia	4/10/80	research	(2)
Malaysia	4/5/84	research	(2)
Middle East			
Libya	3/74		(2)
Niger	3/6/83	uranium safeguards	(2)
Turkey	about 1970		(3)
Latin America			
Argentina	8/81	research	(2)

Sources:

1 US Congress 1977

2 Graham Chronology

3 Sinha and Subramanian, *Nuclear Pakistan* (1980).

4 *The Muslim* (Islamabad), Sept. 20, 1986, p. 4, cited in *Worldwide Reports*, Nov. 3, 1986, pp. 63–64; Akhtar Ali, *South Asia: Nuclear Stalemate or Conflagration* (Karachi: Research on Armanent and Poverty, 1987), pp. 97–99.

Notes:

[a]Science and Technology agreements were signed on these dates. There has been speculation, but no firm announcement, that nuclear cooperaiton may have been included as part of these agreements.

[b]This PRC-Pakistan agreement reportedly covers cooperaiton in various peaceful uses of nuclear energy—industrial, agricultural, medical, etc. Akhtar Ali suggests that "uranium mining and processing, nuclear waste management and fuel fabrication could . . . be the immediate items on the agenda" and that PRC heavy water production "dovetails with Pakistan's immediate shortages." See note 4 above.

The list of agreements suggests no pattern of deliberately reaching out to other "problem" countries as such. South Korea, Taiwan, South Africa, Iraq, and Brazil, for instance, are not on the list and have not been otherwise reported as having nuclear dealings with Pakistan. Argentina is on the list, but apparently is not an active partner. The two most politically sensitive of the active relationships listed with developing countries are with the People's Republic of China and Libya.

Five of the seven Pakistani agreements with developing nations are with Islamic countries—Indonesia, Malaysia, Libya, Niger, and Turkey—but these, except for Libya, are not centers of initiative in Islamic affairs per se, nor are they involved in the Arab-Israeli conflict. India has far more formal agreements for nuclear cooperation with activist Islamic and Arab countries—including Egypt, Iran, Iraq, Syria, and Algeria, in addition to Libya—than does Pakistan.[5]

In light of this list, and Libya aside, one can easily wonder whether the more activist Islamic and Arab states have not tacitly boycotted Pakistan, even in favor of India, in nuclear trade. Western estimates of the likelihood that Pakistan will become a nuclear supplier to sensitive countries in the Middle East probably has been exaggerated by a failure to take into account political and social barriers in regional relations.

Pakistan's nuclear cooperation with sensitive Middle Eastern countries may surface in another channel, the multilateral structure of the Organization of the Islamic Conference (OIC).[6] We should not jump to the conclusion that this would be a unique situation, however, except in its Islamic flavor. A Latin analogue in the form of the Tlatelolco framework also exists. The Non-Aligned Movement (NAM) offers similar potentials, on a south-versus-north basis, and several other regional associations, such as the Association of South East Asian Nations (ASEAN) in Southeast Asia and the South Asian Association for Regional Cooperation (SAARC) in South Asia, could evolve autonomous nuclear cooperation networks.[7]

Pakistan's primary agreements for nuclear cooperation in the early days, like India's, were with the advanced Western suppliers. But Pakistani technical cooperation with China has increased. It reportedly began in 1966 but amplified strongly in the 1970s as Western nuclear cooperation with Pakistan became increasingly restricted. Little is known about the early Pakistani technical agreements with China. They could have involved elements of civilian nuclear cooperation, but they have been shrouded in a broader language of scientific and technical cooperation.[8] In September 1986, however, Pakistan and the People's Republic of China signed a formal accord for peaceful nuclear cooperation. Given the importance of this PRC-Pakistan nuclear relationship, it is separately discussed following the next section.

Major Pakistani Nuclear Import Relationships

The primary foreign suppliers for Pakistan's development of nuclear technology are listed, in conjunction with areas of supply, in table 11–3. The United States originally was the main supplier for Pakistan's nuclear research program, including the swimming-pool reactor at Islamabad and its enriched uranium fuel.[9] The United Kingdom also assisted Pakistan with nuclear research. For example, the United Kingdom considered offering design and technical support to Pakistan on laboratory-scale plutonium separation and research. But Belgium and France finally became the sources for New Labs, a "hot cell" facility, at Pakistan's Institute for Nuclear Science and Technology (PINSTECH), the applied nuclear research laboratory in Islamabad.[10]

Table 11–3
Principal Pakistani Nuclear Import Relationships

	Reactors			Materials				Sensitive Facilities		Other Facilities	
Supplier	Research	Power	Advanced	Low Enriched Uranium	High Enriched Uranium	Plutonium	Heavy Water	Reprocess	Enrichment	Fuel Fabr.	Heavy Water
Canada	X	X					X			X	
Belgium	X							X			?
France	X	O						X/O			
Japan		X									
Libya					natural uranium*						
Niger					natural uranium*						
U.K.	X			X							
U.S.A.	X			X		X					
U.S.S.R.		O							?		
China (PRC)							?	?	?		

Key

x actual assistance or cooperation occured

o assistance or cooperation was offered or solicited, but did not occur

? possible but undocumented cooperation.

Sources:
CRS, *Nuclear Proliferation Factbook*, 1977; Graham Chronology; Sinha and Subramanian, *Nuclear Pakistan* (1980).

Canada was Pakistan's principal supplier of nuclear power equipment and related support until 1976, when Canada suspended the relationship. Canada provided the Karachi Nuclear Power Plant (KANUPP) with uranium fuel and heavy water.[11] Pakistan's ability to complete a fuel fabrication facility in 1980 is attributed (as with India earlier) to Canadian technical assistance.[12] Belgium reportedly provided Pakistan with a small heavy-water plant.[13]

In the early 1970s, France became a prospective supplier of nuclear power plants to Pakistan and considered Pakistani requests for assistance in building a reprocessing plant—one large enough to be considered "commercial." France concluded an agreement in 1976 to supply this reprocessing plant to Pakistan under IAEA safeguards, but suspended the agreement in 1978 as a result of French policy changes and new uncertainties about Pakistan's intentions.[14] Since then, Pakistan has invited bids to construct a 900 MW(e) nuclear power plant at Chashma.[15] Although French, West German, and Spanish (a Westinghouse subsidiary) firms have expressed interest in this project, no actual bids have been made. Formal overtures have been inhibited by political, financial, and nonproliferation considerations.

Pakistan turned to Niger—directly, and also perhaps through Libya—for supplies of natural uranium to fuel KANUPP after Canada suspended cooperation.

A now well-known story of Pakistani nuclear program imports concerns the surreptitious acquisition of uranium enrichment technology and equipment.[16] Pakistan sidestepped formal channels by buying components directly from private firms. Some of these firms may have been unaware of Pakistani intentions, but others must have guessed and suppressed their curiosity for the sake of business.[17] The nuclear end uses of Pakistan's procurement of components for enrichment were concealed. Pakistan purchased dual-use components and equipment, whose export, unlike specifically "nuclear" equipment and materials, previously was not strictly controlled.

Pakistan's procurement of reprocessing technology was a different matter. This program originally was embedded in an official agreement with France to supply a reprocessing facility,[18] was subject to IAEA safeguards, and had been approved by the IAEA after Pakistan's acceptance of a safeguards framework agreement. Pakistani imports under the terms of those agreements followed legitimate rules of international cooperation before 1978.

After France suspended the contract, Pakistani procurement was perceived in a different light. Yet, before suspending this contract French agencies and firms apparently had transferred to Pakistan virtually all the technical and design information for the project. Moreover, certain design and construction activities by French firms, and related Pakistani procurement, continued beyond the time the contract was declared suspended. There is evidence that Pakistan thereafter made an independent effort to build reprocessing facilities. These have not been an immediate proliferation concern because of the absence of unsafeguarded spent fuel to reprocess.

Nuclear Cooperation between Pakistan and China

The People's Republic of China has taken an interest in Pakistan's security since the early 1960s. Closer political relations have evolved steadily, leading to Chinese arms supply after the 1965 Indo-Pakistani conflict. Pakistan played an important intermediary role in the high-level U.S.-PRC contacts during the first Nixon administration, paving the way for the normalization of relations between the United States and China. Chinese support for Pakistan's resistance to Soviet pressure has been explicit since the Soviet invasion of Afghanistan. The Karakorum mountain highway now connects Pakistan and China overland.

Some have leaped to the conclusion that Chinese interest in Pakistan is so deep that China must have intentionally and specifically transferred to Pakistan the know-how for manufacturing the atomic bomb.[19] What are the allegations, and how much do they rest on facts? What are the most plausible explanations for those fragments of information that pertain to this relationship? How do they bear on emerging supplier issues?

Consider the following media allegations and their "scholarly echoes," in ascending order of seriousness from a nonproliferation point of view:

> The Pakistani foreign minister, then a former Army general, witnessed a nuclear test at the Chinese test site in 1983.

> Chinese technicians were present for extended periods of time at Kahuta, the site of Pakistan's now acknowledged but off-limits uranium enrichment facility.

> China has helped Pakistan develop sensitive nuclear technology, enrichment, and perhaps reprocessing.

> China provided test facilities in China for a Pakistani nuclear explosive test.

> China provided Pakistan with the "design" of the fourth Chinese nuclear explosive device (a uranium device).

On the first allegation, a Pakistani foreign minister's visit could in fact have coincided with a Chinese nuclear test on at least one occasion. There is no reliable evidence that the minister witnessed the test, but even if he did, what should we infer? Foreign guests have frequently witnessed nuclear tests conducted by Western countries; no one has construed this to mean the observers were getting help to go nuclear.

More serious would be the charge, if it were more than rumor, that China tested or allowed a Pakistani nuclear explosive device to be tested at Lop Nor. This type of action is not necessarily inconceivable, and it is not unprecedented. The United States has permitted the United Kingdom, one of the original nuclear-weapon powers, to test nuclear weapons at U.S. test sites for years. Interestingly, both the first allegation and the fourth originated with Indian sources, the latter being made public by M. K. Rasgotra, then head bureaucrat of India's Ministry of External Affairs.[20]

The most serious allegation is that the government of China knowingly transferred to Pakistan a design based on its fourth nuclear explosive device. There is no solid evidence in the public record for this allegation.[21] When it is probed regarding its meaning and origin, one is led back to Indian sources and to reports in the West that seemed to have some credence because British sources retransmitted them.

Even if not substantiated, are not these allegations plausible? While nothing has been found to suggest that they are more than speculation,[22] the history of sensitive Soviet assistance to China's nuclear program in the 1950s[23] and of sustained high-level French collaboration with the Israeli nuclear weapons program[24] leads one to be cautious. Moreover, it is entirely possible that Chinese individuals gave help to the Pakistanis that was not officially sanctioned or known.

Reports of early Chinese assistance to Pakistan in sensitive technology are also poorly substantiated (see table 11–4). The reports of Chinese technicians being present at Kahuta apparently are well-founded.[25] But what were they about? The most plausible explanation is that the Chinese were curious about the gaseous centrifuge uranium enrichment technology that Pakistan had secreted from Almelo, Holland, and were willing to help Pakistan get it operational. The Chinese knew a lot about uranium enrichment because of their successful experience with gaseous diffusion. But they did not have, and surely would be interested in, the uranium centrifuge technology that Pakistan was assembling at Kahuta.[26] If so, Pakistan may have acted as a conduit for retransfer of knowledge of this technology to China, a peculiar example of emerging supplier activity.

Chinese technical efforts to help make Kahuta operational are commonly perceived in the West as Chinese help for "the Pakistani bomb program." Evidence in the literature on this point is sketchy and inconclusive, but concrete enough to be considered.[27] Even so, it is not self-evident that Chinese leaders should have drawn the conclusion that, because their technicians were present at Kahuta, China was helping Pakistan make

Table 11–4
Pakistani Nuclear Transactions with Third World States

Region/Partner Country	Date of Action	Type of Transaction	Source
Asia People's Republic of China	July 1966 (?)	Agreement on economic and technical cooperation signed in Beijing with Pakistani scientists, including nuclear scientists.	(3)
	May 1976	Bhutto visit to Beijing, some speculate, may have reached agreement on sensitive nuclear cooperation.	(3)
	Jan. 29, 1977	PRC signed agreement in Islamabad on scientific and technical cooperation, probably including help Pakistani nuclear energy program; team of PRC scientists visited Pakistan following March.	(3)
	June 1978	Reports that PRC Vice Premier Keng Piao's visit to Pakistan offered help to build nuclear reprocessing plant in Pakistan.	(3)
	May 1979	Agha Shahi, Foreign Affairs advisor to Pakistan, visited Beijing; some suspect Shahi solicited help from PRC with uranium enrichment process.	(3)
	Fall 1979	Trial run of Kahuta enrichment plant reportedly using UF6 of PRC origin; may have resulted in plant accident.	(2)
	Sept. 1986	PRC-Pakistan signed accord on cooperation in peaceful uses of nuclear energy; reportedly, the accord "is within" the IAEA safeguards and specifically forbids the transfer of nuclear material for military uses.	(5)
Middle East Libya	mid-1970s	Libya reported to be one of loan sources for $100 million in loans to help pay for French-supplied reprocessing plant in Pakistan.	(3)
	Feb. 1974	Qaddhafi agreed at Lahore to help finance Pakistan's nuclear program, with $200 million reportedly delivered in two separate cash shipments in 1975 and 1976.	(2)
Iran	mid-1970s	Loan assistance for nuclear projects from Iran and Arab states, during Bhutto period, reported at over $450 million.	(2)

Table 11–4 continued

	July 1974	Pakistanis sought help from Tehran, and sent a team to study Iran's nuclear program in 1975.	(3)
Islamic Conference Organization (ICO)	Jan. 1987	President Zia-ul-Haq chairs the Islamic Committee for Technology and Sciences of ICO, which expects to promote scientific and technological research, including that in the nuclear field.	(4)
Niger	various	Niger legally sold Pakistan natural uranium under IAEA safeguards (which Pakistan could fabricate into fuel for KANUPP), but there also indications Niger sold to Libya larger quantities of natural uranium that Libya transferred to Pakistan without IAEA safeguards (and which could be the source for Pakistan's enrichment program).	(2)
Saudi Arabia	mid-1970s	Kingdom reportedly would provide loan to cover purchase of French-supplied reprocessing plant, in return for Pakistani training of Saudis in nuclear power techniques.	(2)

Sources:
1. Graham Chronology.
2. Weissman and Krosney, *The Islamic Bomb* (1981).
3. Sinha and Subramanian, *Nuclear Pakistan* (1980).
4. Hamzah, "Interview with President Zia-ul-Haq," in *Al'Anba* (Kuwait), Jan. 25, 1987, FBIS, *Daily Report: South Asia*, Feb. 4, 1987, pp. F1–F6.
5. *The Muslim* (Islamabad), Sept. 20, 1986, p. 4, cited in *Worldwide Reports*, Nov. 3, 1986, pp. 63–64.

atomic bombs. The history of peaceful nuclear cooperation is replete with technical assistance by more advanced to less advanced countries that could arouse suspicion. What has changed are the standards that are applied today. These are still changing, and properly so, but a lag in understanding is different from a violation. China's isolation from the nonproliferation regime before 1984 means that its officials are still absorbing the norms on "sensitive technology" that emerged in the West only in the late 1970s and early 1980s, and then not wholly uniformly.[28]

It is also possible that certain individuals within China's leadership unofficially sympathized with Pakistan's effort to acquire a nuclear weapons capability, insofar as a "threat of proliferation" by Pakistan might deter the "threat of proliferation" by India.[29] But there is no hard evidence in the literature that China intentionally aided nuclear weapons development in Pakistan, or anywhere else in the world. This is not to say that China necessarily has always taken proper precautions (any more than the advanced nuclear suppliers) against the abuse of its nuclear transactions. Nor does it say that top leaders have always known everything that is going on in different corners of their country. But even on these issues, evidence is scarce. In any case, explaining proliferation by Pakistan requires no deus ex machina.

New information may emerge from monitoring exchanges under the PRC-Pakistan nuclear cooperation agreement, which was announced in September 1986. This accord puts their bilateral nuclear cooperation on a public and more transparent footing. Reportedly, it commits the parties to accept IAEA safeguards on nuclear equipment and material that each buys from the other. It could require that any major PRC nuclear exports to Pakistan come under IAEA safeguards. The U.S. interest is that transactions under its terms be conducive to nonproliferation in the South Asian subcontinent. If they are, we can hope to see more balanced discussions of the Pakistan-China nuclear relationship.

Pakistani Nuclear Trade with Third World Countries

If India's actual nuclear exports to Third World countries are minimal (whatever their potential), Pakistan's so far are virtually nonexistent. The items in table 11–4 on Pakistani nuclear transactions with Third World countries show imports, but no income-earning exports. PRC transactions with Pakistan, already touched on, support the point. Several items in table 11–4 seem to link Iran, Saudi Arabia, and Libya in the 1970s as financial backers of Pakistan's nuclear program, particularly of Pakistan's acquisition from France of an IAEA-safeguarded reprocessing plant.[30] The French contract was approved by the IAEA Governing Board, including its U.S. member, as a legitimate project under the earlier ground rules of peaceful nuclear cooperation, and thus was no embarrassment to a financial backer. Pakistan's covert procurement of enrichment technology is in a different class. For this, Pakistan may have received Libyan funds, but there is no hard evidence that any other state knowingly funded Pakistan's enrichment program.[31]

Finally, an intriguing item in table 11–4 is the reference to the Pakistani role in the Organization of the Islamic Conference (OIC), where the late President Zia-ul-Haq chaired the Committee for Technology and Sciences. If Pakistan sought an alternative channel for the kinds of nuclear exports it could offer today—mainly nuclear technical education and training, scientific information exchange, and possibly limited nuclear engineering services—the OIC could provide it. Zia acknowledged in an interview that he was aware of the constituency-building potential of Pakistan's leadership of the Technology and Sciences Committee, and that there was sentiment to have the OIC serve its members as an alternative "club" for nuclear cooperation.[32]

Structure of Pakistani Nuclear Decision Making

The formal structure of institutions and responsibilities that has evolved for nuclear policy in Pakistan is fairly elaborate,[33] but probably misleading on where and how domestic or international policy decisions are actually made. Thus, it tells us less about how commercial nuclear export decisions would be made—if and when Pakistan reaches that point—than one might wish.

The structure of decision making on nuclear issues that prevailed in Pakistan before 1989 had two key features:[34] (1) decisions originated directly and personally with the effective head of government (in Zia's case, the president; under Z.A. Bhutto, whichever office he occupied, first as president, and after 1973 as prime minister), filtering down to the technocrats of the Pakistan Atomic Energy Commission (PAEC) and other relevant agencies; and (2) the atomic energy establishment was bifurcated between civilian power program responsibilities and the military-managed R&D activities of the uranium enrichment program.

The civilian nuclear program, now under the auspices of the Ministry of Science and Technology and the PAEC, began and functioned in the open. It joined the IAEA, benefited from agreements of cooperation, and accrued safeguarded nuclear facilities and material. In the early years, before the first onset of martial law in 1958, Pakistan's atomic energy establishment apparently enjoyed autonomy in scientific affairs, but, unlike its counterpart in India, was not a major force in policy making.[35] This was readily explained by Pakistan's limited financial resources for nuclear research and energy development and the preoccupation of establishing the new nation after independence. The steps involved in organizing the atomic energy program in Pakistan lagged behind those of India by several years. Support was pro forma under the early regime of Ayub Khan, but increased somewhat in the early 1960s as Pakistan watched new developments in India.

Zulfikar Ali Bhutto, then a youthful cabinet minister, first with Fuel and Natural Resources and from 1963 as foreign minister, began to prod for a more active nuclear energy program.[36] The research reactor at PIN-STECH, negotiated in the late 1950s, finally was brought into operation between 1963 and 1965. Otherwise, KANUPP, which was started between 1962 and 1965 and completed in the early 1970s, was the only significant new project nurtured in those years. The Finance Ministry and the Planning Commission appear to have played a joint role in Pakistan in curbing the expansion of the nuclear program, successfully persuading Ayub to overrule Bhutto's earlier proposals for major expenditure on a reprocessing facility.[37]

The real watershed came with Bhutto's assumption of power as head of government in December 1971. Thereafter, for all practical purposes, the program was run from the top. Bhutto took virtually personal control over the nuclear research and energy program. He became the driving force behind plans to acquire sensitive technology—both on the visible track of purchasing reprocessing capability from France and on the covert track of acquiring uranium enrichment technology.

To assert direct control, Bhutto forced I.H. Usmani to resign as PAEC chairperson. A bureaucrat, Usmani lacked technical expertise and reportedly favored a strictly civilian nuclear energy program. He was replaced by the present incumbent, Munir Ahmad Khan, who had held a responsible position in the IAEA (reactor division head) and had been trained in a U.S. university and energy laboratory. Munir Ahmad Khan was more compliant, as well.

Under M.A. Khan's leadership, the PAEC continued to preside formally over the civilian nuclear research at PINSTECH and the elements of a nuclear power program at Karachi, as well as planning for an ambitious nuclear energy construction program.[38] The plan included desalinization of sea water for Karachi,[39] a heavy-water plant, and a spent fuel reprocessing facility.

The bifurcation of the program in Pakistan seems to have been in order to secretly pursue the acquisition of centrifuge technology for a uranium enrichment project. In any case, this project was segregated bureaucratically from the PAEC and other elements of the civilian program and placed under the defense authorities.[40]

The enrichment project, or at least the centrifuge operation at Kahuta, was set up under the technical guidance of Abdul Qadir Khan. He was made director of the Engineering Research Laboratory (ERL), located near Islamabad airport, but associated with the Kahuta plant 25 miles southeast of Islamabad.[41] The Kahuta plant apparently is the larger of two uranium centrifuge facilities, the other being a pilot centrifuge plant at Sihala, just southwest of Islamabad. A third plant at Golra, also close to Islamabad, was identified recently by reports in the United Kingdom. Another facility associated with the enrichment project is a pilot hexafluoride plant in Dera Ghazi Khan, a more remote district.

Each of these operations appears to be controlled by the Special Works Organization (SWO), a section of the Pakistan Ordnance Department, and run essentially by the Army's corps of engineers. The SWO also has an Electronics Division and an Explosives Division, in charge of development and production of conventional munitions, presumably with expertise applicable to the detonation of nuclear explosives. The covert procurement of materials, components, and equipment for the enrichment program was centered in the SWO and its parent department, coordinating with the diplomatic missions abroad. The head of the SWO apparently reported directly to President Zia-ul-Haq.[42]

There is fragmentary evidence from the 1984 krytron incident, however, that the PAEC is also involved in covert, sensitive nuclear procurement (see table 11–5). Krytrons are high-speed electronic switches whose

Table 11–5A
Foreign Firms in Sensitive Nuclear Supply to Pakistan

Name	Host Country	Transaction Dates	Type of Supply to Pakistan
Reprocessing Projects			
Alcom	Italy (Milan)	1979	special vessels
Aries	France (Paris)	mid-1970s	electronic process control
Belgonucleaire	Belgium	1960s and 1970s	design and engineering
Bignier Schmid-Laurent (BSL)	France (Soissons)	April 1979	special vessels
Saint-Gobain Techniques Nouvelles (SGN)	France	mid-1970s	design and engineering
Robatel	France (Lyons)	mid-1970s	process control
Enrichment Project			
Aluminium-Walzwerke Singhen Gmbh	FRG (Singen)	mid-1970s	centrifuge metal compon.
CES Kalthof, GmbH	FRG (Freiburg)	mid-1970s	fluorine pilot plant
CORA Engineering	Switzerland	mid-1970s	gas solidification
Emerson Electric	U.K.	mid-1970s	inverters
Leifeld Co.	Holland (Ahlen)		centrifuge rotor parts
Leybold Heraeus	FRG (Hanau)	mid-1970s	pumps, vacuum equipment for gas (hexafluoride) purification
Rohstoff/Einfuhr	Switzerland	mid-1970s	high vacuum valves and gas (hexafluoride) handling
Team Industries	FRG (Stuttgart)		
Van Doorne Transmissie BV	Holland (Tilburg)	mid-1970s	special metals and parts
VAT (Vakuum)	Switzerland	mid-1970s	high vacuum valves

Sources:
Sinha and Subramanian, *Nuclear Pakistan* (1980).
Weissman and Krosney, *The Islamic Bomb*

Table 11–5B
Fronts for Covert Pakistani Nuclear Procurement

Name of Firm	Base of Operation	Type of Procurement
Khalid Jassam General Trading	Abu Dhabi	electronic components
Source Reliance International	U.K. (London)	centrifuge project
Tech Equipment	Pakistan	inverters
Weargate Limited	U.K. (Swansea)	inverters

sale is strictly controlled because they can be used for the construction of nuclear weapons. In June 1984, three Pakistani nationals were arrested for attempting to smuggle krytrons out of the United States. Their contact in Pakistan was S.A. Butt, reportedly a director of supply and procurement for the PAEC.[43]

Although it was a civilian prime minister, Bhutto, who first asserted direct control over the atomic energy establishment, General Zia-ul-Haq retained the pattern. With the restoration in 1986 of an elected National Assembly and induction of a cabinet under a politician, Prime Minister Mohammed Khan Junejo, it was possible to wonder then whether there would be any shifts of influence or posture in this sensitive policy area. But until his death in August 1988, General Zia personally remained in charge and issued almost all official declarations on international nuclear policy.[44]

Under Zia, M.A. Khan maintained his position as PAEC chairperson and worked diligently in IAEA circles to combat the international opprobrium that Pakistan suffered. There were indications of PAEC restlessness with the existence under separate lines of authority of the controversial enrichment program. A.Q. Khan's occasional trumpeting of the breakthroughs in his enrichment program probably are officially sanctioned, but his style suggests a possible power struggle behind the scenes.[45] Still, the bifurcation in the program remained.

The historical tension with the economic planners, however, was partly resolved during the Zia regime. The reliability of Pakistan's electric power supply in urban areas had deteriorated noticeably. In part, this was a happy symptom of modernization, indicating rapid growth in consumption and economic demand. But as a problem of prolonged duration, it also retarded industrial output. Thus, it became a useful negotiating point with international lending institutions, which have a stake in the success of capital investment in energy development, including nuclear over the long term. Domestic planners suppressed their skepticism about the relative cost of nuclear solutions, knowing these make a strong case for external concessionary financing.

Norms in Pakistani Policy Relevant to Nuclear Commerce

Pakistan has selectively joined elements of the international nonproliferation regime, but emulated India by staying out of the Nuclear Non-Proliferation Treaty (NPT). Pakistan has also voiced an objection against NPT discrimination, but less stridently then has India. Under Zia, Pakistan claimed readiness to join the NPT, or indeed any safeguards regime, if India would undertake the same obligations.

Pakistan has accepted IAEA safeguards on its research reactor and on KANUPP—safeguards which were retroactively upgraded by the IAEA in the early 1980s. Under Z.A. Bhutto, Pakistan agreed in 1976 to relatively stringent safeguards on the reprocessing facility and replication of that technology, although the safeguards were not implemented because France suspended the contract.[46] Pakistan has declined to put other facilities, including the enrichment plants and reprocessing capabilities it is building independently, under safeguards.[47]

Pakistan, while not enamoured, is not among those that vehemently castigate the Nuclear Suppliers Group (NSG) or unconditionally condemn the NPT. But Pakistan has been the most celebrated example of circumvention of the NSG's intent and, indeed, the specific stimulus for upgrading the export-control trigger lists to deal with sensitive components and dual-use equipment related to enrichment.

Pakistan's stated position on international nonproliferation norms can be described as equivocal and conditional.[48] Pakistan says that it is willing to subscribe to the same nonproliferation assurances or constraints as India. But its approach to nuclear commerce has been defiant of the nonproliferation reasons for the tightening embargo. Certainly, during Bhutto's tenure and apparently also under Zia, Pakistan's import practices were intended to circumvent the export controls of the major supplier countries. This experience inspires no confidence that Pakistan's own nuclear export policies will be based on internationally accepted nonproliferation ground rules. But neither does it prove that Pakistan will be irresponsible. This remains to be seen. Given Pakistan's tendency to emulate India's nuclear policies, as noted earlier, one could conjecture that whatever nuclear export standards India adopts will also become the model for Pakistan.

Pakistan's nuclear policy norms could undergo change following the consolidation of popularly elected government under Benazir Bhutto. She became prime minister in late 1988, after making campaign statements that declared that her own nuclear policies would be confined to peaceful purposes, thus hinting that Pakistan's efforts to develop nuclear weapons capability will be suspended under her leadership. Changes in Pakistan's operating norms could also be facilitated by bilateral developments. When

Indian Prime Minister Rajiv Gandhi visited Pakistan for the first time in the last week of December 1988, he formalized with B. Bhutto the previously oral agreement of 1985 with Zia in which Pakistan and India pledged not to attack each other's nuclear facilities.

The formal agreement covers sensitive facilities, such as the once-secret enrichment facility at Kahuta in Pakistan, and obligates each side to notify the other annually on the exact location of their nuclear facilities.[49] It creates an incentive not to have secret facilities, because undeclared facilities, logically, are not covered by the agreement.

Thus this no-attack pledge covering nuclear facilities is a major step toward increased nuclear program transparency, in India as well as Pakistan. It is an important bilateral confidence-building measure, and it could be an important precedent for further nonproliferation developments in South Asia. Together with the IAEA safeguards requirement in the Pakistan-China agreement for peaceful nuclear cooperation, it is conceivable that the basis is emerging for norms in Pakistan that would favor responsible nuclear export policies and practices.

Capabilities

To undertake a major nuclear supply role in the international market, a state must at a minimum have: (1) demonstrated success in building and operating nuclear energy facilities, particularly power plants; (2) technical ability to provide fuel, fuel cycle services, and engineering and other operational services to another nuclear program; and (3) the credibility of commitments or contracts entered into.[50] The third point has two dimensions, one being sufficient industrial capacity to produce nuclear equipment or fuel for export and the second being a reputation for reliability in performing on commitments.

Pakistan barely begins to meet the first of these criteria. Indeed, Pakistan's general industrial infrastructure is so much less developed than India's, for example, that offering to sell major equipment to another country for its nuclear power program today is fanciful. The metallurgical industries in Pakistan are nascent at best. A Soviet-supplied steel plant, Pakistan's first, has only been in operation for about two years. Its record remains to be evaluated, and the chain of downstream users has yet to emerge.

On a more modest level, niches for possible Pakistani nuclear exports may come to exist. They probably would not be commercially profitable, but could arise in the context of political or security ties. They could arise with countries that find it difficult, perhaps because of poor nonproliferation credentials, to import nuclear equipment and services from the major suppliers.

Niches of interest could form in the areas of nuclear research and information on sensitive technology—particularly reprocessing and enrichment. Although Pakistan lacks the infrastructure to build and export nuclear power reactors or major generating components, it does have a modern scientific and engineering establishment. This Pakistani establishment is small in comparison to India's or those of Western countries, but is substantial when compared to that of most developing countries. It operates with Western languages, primarily English, but also French, German, and others. Thus it is capable of transmitting scientific knowledge and training. It can also provide nuclear engineering and design services, at least to the exent that Pakistan has domestic experience with the construction of facilities and equipment for fuel fabrication, spent-fuel handling, reprocessing, and enrichment.

These capabilities will become more substantial as Pakistan develops domestic metal-producing and metallurgical industries, or, if it is successful in attracting suppliers, it is able to proceed with the installation of nuclear power plants. They will grow through experience with existing facilities, such as the hot cell laboratory-scale reprocessing facility in New Labs (associated with PINSTECH), or with success in completing and operating the undeclared reprocessing facility. Pakistan evidently has operational enrichment experience at Sihala and Kahuta, although the dimensions and technical effectiveness of these operations remain obscure.

There is no record at this point, however, of significant nuclear export activity by Pakistan, or even of any major marketing initiatives designed to develop a potential customer base. Scientific information exchange and research cooperation between Pakistan and several other countries could, of course, eventually lead in that direction.

The induction of China into the IAEA system, and acceptance by Western supplier governments of peaceful nuclear cooperation agreements with China, are steps that create opportunities to discourage China from contemplating dubious nuclear export activities. It is not clear whether the PRC-Pakistan nuclear cooperation channel will be active enough to influence Pakistani incentives in favor of adopting responsible nuclear export policies for the future. But urging China to condition its nuclear cooperation with Pakistan on nonproliferation and safe export policy criteria is a matter that Western powers should continue to encourage.

Concluding Observations

This review of Pakistani nuclear transactions deals primarily with the import side of the picture, because Pakistan remains a recipient rather than a supplier. The commercial nuclear export potential for Pakistan today is meager and probably will remain so for a long time. There is reason for concern, however, in that Pakistan has acquired sensitive nuclear technology and appears to be determined to develop the technical capability for nuclear weapons. This could lead Pakistan into troublesome nuclear transactions or relationships with countries that are both more capable in nuclear affairs, such as China, and less capable, such as Iran and the Gulf states.

Such transactions could arise on the demand side from some of these other countries, or be initiated by Pakistan. Their logic might have less to do with legitimate development of the peaceful uses of nuclear energy than with a catering to locally embedded political and security interests, in which case they could easily be corrosive to the nonproliferation and nuclear export control regimes.

Pakistan illustrates even more clearly than India the core dilemma of peaceful nuclear cooperation with developing countries that are outside the Western security system. Past efforts to apply sanctions—intended, and properly so, to put the brakes on proliferation activities—can leave the target country with no way to obtain legitimate nuclear technology and services, such as for electric generation, than to go outside legitimate channels. This reinforces these countries' incentives to assemble future capabilities in a manner that attempts to immunize them from external pressure. This in turn may lead them not only to stay out of an international control system, but to attack it as inimical.

The dilemma becomes even more acute if the country that goes outside normal channels for nuclear imports finds that it also has strong incentives to remain outside normal channels when it explores possible nuclear cooperation or export options available to itself. In that case, the market opportunities it is likely to encounter may be relatively few and far between, but nonetheless include dangerous and temptingly lucrative offers.

Pakistani leaders are less likely than Indian ones to press within the United Nations or other diplomatic forums for wholly different international control concepts or mechanisms. Pakistanis have been more preoccupied with consolidating their future as a nation and have less room for grandiose schemes. Thus, Pakistan is unlikely to challenge NPT or nuclear export regime norms frontally. Its circumvention of Western nuclear export controls has been pragmatic rather than ideological. Pakistan's sub rosa procurement activities are therefore not necessarily a good basis for predicting its behavior as a nuclear exporter with a stake in a system of international control.

But there will be no quick solution to the nuclear export dilemma in this part of the world. Now that the Soviet Union seems to be firmly committed to withdrawing from Afghanistan, all South Asian nuclear issues are contingent on the outcomes of Indo-Pakistani relations and whether these will lead toward nonproliferation or further proliferation. If India and

Pakistan could be persuaded to agree to a standstill without weapons, such as a bilateral agreement to refrain from testing nuclear explosives, it may be possible to work toward a gradual normalization of nuclear commercial behavior under safeguards. The formalized Indo-Pakistani no-attack pledge of late 1988 could be a step in this direction. Statements by Rajiv Gandhi on the occasion of his December 1988 trip to China could inspire useful further steps.[51] In the context of such improvements, one objective should be to find a way to gradually engage Pakistan in more comprehensive supplier arrangements, with stakes that limit its incentives for second-tier supplier activities. An overall solution is going to require that more be done to improve the security not only of Pakistan but of the entire surrounding region.

Notes

1. See my companion case study of India, ch. 8 in this book.

2. Agreements for nuclear cooperation with international organizations, such as the IAEA, are not counted here. These agreements often relate to safeguards, but the IAEA is also a conduit for smaller nuclear transactions from individual supplier countries, as well as a source of nuclear technical assistance in its own right.

3. I am indebted to Tom Graham for the opportunity to use the compilation of Pakistani agreements for cooperation in his chronology. See Thomas W. Graham "South Asian Nuclear Proliferation and National Security Chronology," 10 January 1986 (unpublished).

4. See Roberta Wohlstetter, *"The Buddha Smiles": Absent-Minded Peaceful Aid and the Indian Bomb,* Report to the U.S. Energy Research and Development Administration, (Los Angeles: Pan Heuristics, April 30, 1977), p. 61ff.

5. See table 2 in my companion piece, ch. 8 in this book.

6. See table 4 on Pakistani nuclear transactions with Third World states, with related discussion.

7. This is an example of Randy Rydell's interesting concept of "archipelagoes," or diverse structures of nuclear cooperation in outlying regions that contrast with mainstream norms and practices. See his "Navigating the Archipelago," in Rodney W. Jones, Cesare Merlini, Joseph F. Pilat, and William C. Potter, eds., *The Nuclear Suppliers and Nonproliferation: International Policy Choices* (Lexington, Mass.: Lexington Books, 1985), ch. 12.

8. See table 4 for specific dates and reports speculating on the nature of PRC-Pakistani nuclear cooperation.

9. The U.S.-supplied 5 MW(t) "swimming pool" type research reactor was set up at PINSTECH in 1963 under IAEA safeguards and was put into operation in December 1965. Nuclear Pakistan: Atomic Threat to South Asia, New Delhi: Vision Books, 1980, p. 33. Sinha and Subramanian, *Nuclear Pakistan* (1980), p. 33. France reportedly upgraded this research reactor to 8 or 10 MW(t). See Steve

Weissman and Herbert Krosney, *The Islamic Bomb*, New York: NY Times Books, (1981), p. 77.

10. New Labs pilot reprocessing facility, planned to be completed in 1982, was reported by one source to have the capacity to extract 10 to 15 kilograms of plutonium a year. British Nuclear Fuels, Ltd., designed a much smaller operation for Pakistan in about 1970, but dropped the project when Pakistan asked for a larger-facility design. The project apparently was inherited by Belgonucleaire and the French SGN nuclear engineering firm. See Weissman and Krosney, *The Islamic Bomb* pp. 80–82, 214–15.

11. Designed for a capacity of 137 MW(e), KANUPP was to be a major source of electric power for the city of Karachi. It is based on CANDU technology, i.e., a heavy-water moderated, natural uranium fueled, pressurized reactor. To date, it is Pakistan's only power reactor.

12. Sinha and Subramanian, *Nuclear Pakistan*, p. 43.

13. Belgonucleaire won the contract to build a heavy-water plant of about 13 tons annual production capacity in Multan, with a planned completion date of 1980. See Brij Mohan Kaushik and O.N. Mehrotra, *Pakistan's Nuclear Bomb*, New Delhi: Sopan Publishing House, (1980), p. 54.

14. See Weissman and Krosney, *The Islamic Bomb* pp. 161–172 for extensive discussion of French activities and policy changes in this context.

15. Originally, Chashma was to be a 600 MW(e) plant. The decision to upgrade the plan probably reflected the trend toward larger reactors among Western vendors of light-water reactors. Construction of a light-water reactor, which uses low-enriched uranium fuel, would have provided a programmatic justification for Pakistan's acquisition of uranium enrichment capability.

16. Weissman and Krosney provide a detailed early account in *The Islamic Bomb* chps. 11–13; see also Jones (1981), and Spector (1984).

17. See table 5 for a list of Western firms and host countries reported to be suppliers of items used by Pakistan in its enrichment program.

18. Ibid.

19. See ch. 12 by Michael Brenner in this book.

20. Also interestingly, India's best-known nuclear weapons advocate, K. Subrahmanyam, used Swedish seismic data to show that no test in China in the time frame in question had characteristics resembling the sort of device Pakistan might manufacture or, for that matter, a device based on China's design for its fourth test. India's handling of this incident appeared to be a sophisticated public diplomacy exercise.

21. The clearest and most credible U.S. journalistic source on this issue when it arose was Leslie Gelb. See the successive *New York Times* articles, "Pakistan Links Peril U.S.-China Nuclear Pact," 22 June 1984; and "Peking Said to Balk at Nuclear Pledges," 23 June 1984. Gelb attributed to official U.S. official sources a firm finding that a Chinese presence had been established in Pakistan at Kahuta, the site of Pakistan's enrichment facility. But Gelb treats the allegation that China transferred nuclear weapons design information to Pakistan quite differently. He avoids giving it credence as a firm finding by U.S. officials and merely acknowledges it as a report from overseas that had aroused concern. Since then, the allegation that China gave a nuclear weapon design to Pakistan has been recycled in

the media and other publications, giving it a life of its own, but it has not been substantiated. If there was ever a sound basis to this charge, it seems most unlikely that the U.S. administration would have concluded an agreement for peaceful nuclear cooperation with China in 1984, and most unlikely that the U.S. Congress would have consented, even with the conditions attached by the Senate.

22. For an early discussion of this issue, see my "Nuclear Supply Policy and South Asia," in Jones et al., *The Nuclear Suppliers*, pp. 167–68.

23. See John W. Lewis and Xue Litai, *China Builds the Bomb* (Stanford: Stanford United Press, 1988).

24. See, for example, Pierre Pean, *Les Deux Bombes*, Fayard (U.S. Library of Congress translation, 1986).

25. See Gelb articles in the *New York Times*, op. cit. Information available leaves it unclear what such technicians were present for or what they were doing.

26. See Jones, "Nuclear Supply Policy and South Asia," pp. 167–68 for conclusions drawn when these reports surfaced; subsequent information has done nothing to change these conclusions.

27. In table 4, I have included reports that hint at sensitive PRC assistance to Pakistan's power program (cf., notes on January 1977 agreement). For instance, the reported June 1978 visit of the PRC vice premier to Pakistan alludes to possible help with construction of the reprocessing plant in Pakistan, while the reported exchanges of 1979 indicate possible PRC assistance to Pakistan in its sensitive uranium enrichment effort, including help with uranium conversion to hexafluoride gas for the centrifuge operation. These should be treated with caution unless proved.

28. See Rodney W. Jones, "China and the Non-Proliferation Regime: Renegade or Communicant?" in *PPNN Occasional Paper No. 3* Southampton, U.K.: University of Southampton, (forthcoming).

29. For additional contextual material on regional power relationships and implications for proliferation, see my "Pakistan's Nuclear Options," in Hafeez Malik, ed., *Soviet-American Relations with Pakistan, Iran and Afghanistan*, New York: St. Martins, (1987), pp. 199–216; "Nuclear Technology Transfers to Asia: The View from India and Pakistan," *Journal of Northeast Asian Studies* 5 (Winter 1986): 22–34; and "Strategic Consequences of Proliferation in South Asia: Outlook from the United States," in Neil Joeck, ed., *Strategic Consequences of Nuclear Proliferation in South Asia* (London: Frank Cass) (1986), pp. 28–39.

30. Maulana Kausar Niazi, information minister in Prime Minister Bhutto's cabinet and subsequently a member of the Senate in Pakistan, published an Urdu book in 1987 entitled *Lai-in Kat-gayah* ("The Line Was Cut"—alluding to the surprise military takeover of July 1977). His highly interesting, even characteristically sensational, remarks on Bhutto's nuclear decisions have been excerpted, translated into English, and published in India as a pamphlet: *The Pakistan 'Islamic Bomb'—Revelations by Maulana Kausar Niazi* (New Delhi: Ministry of Information, n.d.), hereafter cited as *Niazi Revelations*. This source should be treated with extreme care since information ministers are known for skills in "disinformation," and Niazi, though ostensibly a religious leader, is regarded by Pakistanis as something other than a paragon of veracity.

Niazi claims he was personally involved as an emissary to the Saudi Kingdom at the highest level in Pakistan's $300 million fundraising effort for the reprocessing plant, and that the effort "received positive response . . . particularly from Libya, Saudi Arabia, UAE, Kuwait and Iraq." See Ibid., p. 2. Niazi's most interesting claim is that Bhutto, once he recognized what A.Q. Khan could do with "enrichment," became disenchanted with the reprocessing deal, but continued negotiations on reprocessing with France to camouflage Pakistan's covert enrichment project. Niazi goes so far as to say that Bhutto also tried to induce the United States to put pressure on France to cancel the reprocessing deal unilaterally, enabling Pakistan to escape penalties in the French contract. Although Bhutto's penchant for histrionics makes this story plausible, it could be a rationalization of the way things did turn out after Bhutto was deposed. It does not signify that Pakistan has given up its interest in developing reprocessing, only that Pakistan no longer counts on French help.

31. Negative evidence, of course, is hardly proof, but in this case could indicate that the Middle East states mentioned, Libya apart, distinguish in their own assistance policies between IAEA-approved projects and projects that do not have that stamp.

32. See Yahya Hamzah, "Interview with President Zia-ul-Haq," in *Al'Anba* (Kuwait), 25 January 1987, in Foreign Broadcast Information Service (FBIS), *Daily Report: South Asia*, 4 February 1987, pp. F1–F6. Hamzah notes Zia's promise of "Pakistan's readiness to provide the Islamic states with Pakistan's experience in the field of using the atom for peaceful purposes." Asked about the work of this committee, Zia said (among other things): "we have determined the various states who have an interest in this [nuclear] field. We have proposed the establishment of something like a club for scientific and technological researches" [p.F2].

33. One source identifies the principal agencies of nuclear policy formulation, execution, and administration as: (1) the Ministry of Science and Technology, the executing and implementing authority for government policy and decisions; (2) the chief scientific advisor to the prime minister (or, when appropriate, to the president), who sifts advice and makes recommendations; (3) the Pakistan Academy of Sciences, the consultative and advisory organ on all scientific and technical matters; (4) the Planning Commission and the National Economic Council, which share the role of setting priorities for development, authorizing projects, and allocating resources for projects; and (5) the National Science Council and the Pakistan Science Foundation, which help draft policy and distribute funds. See Shirin Tahir-Kheli, "Pakistan," in James E. Katz and Onkar S. Marwah, *Nuclear Power in Developing Countries* Lexington, Mass.: Lexington Books (1982), pp. 257–62.

The National Economic Council has been the key agency in foreign procurement for civilian nuclear projects, such as KANUPP. The principal functions of the Pakistan Atomic Energy Commission have been in (1) planning the nuclear energy program,; (2) supervising the administration of power operations, safety, and nuclear facility construction projects; and (3) liaison with international technical institutions such as the IAEA. Other agencies of the government that could have played important roles historically are the Ministries of Finance, Industries, and Economic Affairs.

34. The decision-making pattern may change due to the eventual impact of significant events that occurred just before this chapter was revised for the press.

President Zia-ul-Haq was killed in an air crash in August 1988, and Benazir Bhutto, daughter of the former Prime Minister, Zulfikar Ali Bhutto, became the prime minister following parliamentary elections in November 1988. As of this writing in January 1989, however, it is too early to know whether changes in the decision-making structure will occur.

35. The Pakistan Atomic Energy Commission (PAEC) was created in March 1956 at the recommendation of a twelve-member Atomic Energy Committee of scientists formed in 1955 and given the task to prepare a comprehensive nuclear energy scheme. It had antecedents in the Pakistan Council of Scientific and Industrial Research (PCSIR), formed in 1953. The structure created in March 1956 actually was an Atomic Energy Council, with three elements: (1) a "governing body," which included two ministers and two secretaries of the central government, together with the chairperson of the Atomic Energy Commission; (2) the commission itself, with a scientist as chair and six other scientists as members; and (3) an Advisory Committee, consisting of about thirty members drawn from among scientists, industrialists, medical doctors, and academicians. The Atomic Energy Council had authority not only to plan for nuclear energy, but was also entrusted with "negotiations for cooperation in the nuclear field with international atomic energy bodies." Sinha and Subramanian, *Nuclear Pakistan*, p. 30. See also Akhtar Ali, *Pakistan's Nuclear Dilemma: Energy and Security Dimensions*, Karachi: Economist Research Unit, 1984, pp. 275–76; and Tahir-Kheli's chapter on "Pakistan", in Katz & Marwah.

36. Munir Ahmad Khan, the PAEC chairperson, in 1976 described Bhutto as the real architect of the program, the expediter providing impetus, from the time he entered government in 1958. See Sinha and Subramanian, *Nuclear Pakistan*, p. 32.

37. See Sinha and Subramanian's discussion of the opposition to the Ayub government's and Bhutto's plans for nuclear technology by Mohammed Shoaib, finance minister, and Said Hasan, deputy chairperson of the Planning Commission. Ibid., p. 34. A similar adversarial relationship existed in India, but there, especially in the same period, the Department of Atomic Energy was more successful in pressing its plans and winning a significant share of resources.

38. A comprehensive nuclear energy plan issued by the PAEC in 1974–75 envisaged commissioning twenty nuclear power reactors, with a total generating capacity of 9,600 MW, by the year 2000. Ibid., p. 13.

39. The two planned dual-purpose desalination/power plants were to be built on the Arabian Sea near Karachi and in Baluchistan. The one for Karachi, to be built between 1977 and 1982, was to generate 400 MW(e) and produce 100 million gallons of fresh water daily to cater to Pakistan's biggest city. The proposed plant in Baluchistan was to generate 300 to 500 MW(e) and produce 60 million gallons of fresh water every day. After this, the PAEC envisaged a series of agro-industrial complexes powered by nuclear energy along the Mekran coast in the mid-1980s. Sinha and Subramanian, *Nuclear Pakistan* p. 38.

40. Niazi claims that he pushed for bifurcation to give Abdul Qadir Khan, the enrichment track proponent, a freer hand. *Niazi Revelations*, pp. 4–8. Putting his program under the cover of a defense organization also protected its secrecy against close legislative scrutiny.

41. After the enrichment program became public knowledge and A.Q. Khan gained notoriety, President Zia had the laboratories renamed the Abdul Qadir Khan Engineering Research Laboratories.

42. See, for general background, Sinha and Subramanian, *Nuclear Pakistan*, pp. 65–66, 112–18; and, for certain reported details on the pilot hexafluoride plant, Weissman and Krosney, *The Islamic Bomb*, p. 219.

43. For a brief account, see Leonard S. Spector, *Going Nuclear* Cambridge, Mass.: Ballinger (1987), p. 105.

44. This impression was nearly universal among a wide variety of sources during my visit to Pakistan in September 1987.

45. See *Niazi Revelations* for remarks on this bureaucratic infighting, in which Niazi champions A.Q. Khan over M.A. Khan.

46. This is in contrast to India, which has unsafeguarded reprocessing facilities (except that they are subject to inspection when they are processing safeguarded spent fuel).

47. Note, however, that India currently is on record as developing its own enrichment capability, has a pilot plant completed and is building a larger plant. Neither is under safeguards. India will claim these are "indigenous," and no doubt in part they will be. But where is the dividing line? India almost certainly will import some of the components. If it can do so openly (or quietly), is this because it subscribes to a different norm than Pakistan, or because its suppliers apply their norms differently to India and Pakistan?

48. On one important NPT-related norm, however, namely acknowledgment that so-called "peaceful nuclear explosions" are really misnomers for weapons tests, Pakistan is much closer to the nonproliferation regime than is India.

49. See the Associated Press report in *The Washington Post*, 1 January 1989, p. A31.

50. This is quite apart from factors of economic demand, or political considerations in international relations, which may affect whether a nuclear export capability can be exercised.

51. See Rodney W. Jones and Harald Müller, "Who Wants a Nuclear Sarajevo? Nonproliferation in the Middle East and South Asia," *Arms Control Today* (January/February 1989) pp. 15–22.

12

The People's Republic of China

Michael Brenner

Concern about the proliferation of nuclear weapons has undergone a perceptible shift in focus. As the contributions to this book attest, we are placing more emphasis on the multiplication of sources for weapons-related materials and technology, the growth of sophisticated industrial and engineering capabilities in threshold states, and the condition of latent—or potential—proliferation they can create. A cardinal feature of this picture is the role played by new suppliers in the nuclear marketplace who offer a variety of materials, equipment, and services that cover an impressive span of the fuel cycle.[1]

Most prominent among them is the People's Republic of China. China is in the forefront of our attention for several notable reasons. It is, for one thing, a weapons state possessing a significant nuclear force comprising hundreds of warheads and a formidable array of delivery systems (including ballistic missiles and nuclear submarines). The size and composition of its forces bespeaks a sophisticated set of resource, engineering, and manufacturing capabilities covering uranium processing and enrichment, heavy water, fuel fabrication, warhead design, plutonium reprocessing, and nuclear waste management. This formidable military program, dating back to the 1950s, has endowed the PRC with extensive experience in nearly all facets of nuclear operations and management.

China is also committed to an ambitious civilian program that aims at self-reliance in the design, manufacture, construction and running of nuclear-fueled electricity-generating plants. To further this objective, it has sought out foreign technology while expanding domestic programs. Energy holds a key to Chinese economic development, and nuclear energy has been

In the preparation of this paper, I have had the benefit of valuable comments and criticism from Harry Harding, John Lewis, David Mozingo, and Yangmin Wong.

accorded an important place in the PRC's comprehensive energy strategy. Removing the energy bottlenecks that threaten to stifle the modernization process is a priority of China's leadership. Yet, chronic shortages of foreign exchange constrain the purchases of critical energy technologies abroad and, thereby, hamper development plans. Hence, incentives are present for earning badly needed hard currency through exports—including nuclear items—and for obtaining technology and know-how through exchange agreements.

The PRC has been the center of proliferation concern because of its past nuclear activities. In the early 1980s, it engaged in dealings with threshold states that increased the risks of weapons proliferation while contravening the norms of international nuclear commerce expounded by traditional suppliers. China's technical assistance to Pakistan in bringing on line the Kahuta enrichment plant (and allegedly in bomb design as well) is the most egregious expression of an uninhibited nuclear export policy in the early 1980s, which also entailed the supply of sensitive materials to Argentina and South Africa.[2]

The PRC's reversion from these earlier policies to a position close to that of major supplier states represents a noteworthy diplomatic achievement in the cause of nonproliferation. How and why this single accomplishment was made are questions deserving close examination. So too is the associated issue of whether the transformation is complete and permanent.

There is a strategic dimension to China's position as a nuclear exporter. The PRC is a major power whose actions have a significant impact on world affairs. Yet, it has emerged only recently from a prolonged period of self-imposed isolation during which it was largely out of touch with the collective effort at building a nonproliferation regime. Its tardiness in coming to terms with the proliferation issue, and the lingering doubts as to how far the process of consciousness-raising has proceeded, underscore the need to refine our understanding of Chinese interests and purposes in its external nuclear relations. Finally, China has a vital security stake in Asia that conditions its relations with neighboring states, including Pakistan and India, whose nuclear status has been affected by Chinese export policies and whose nuclear future will impinge directly on the PRC's interests. Its proximity to the most immediate of proliferation flashpoints highlights the question of where nuclear policies figure in the larger picture of Chinese strategic thinking.

China's size, resources, and strategic importance set it apart from other new suppliers. Yet, in certain respects, the PRC exemplifies the indefinite status of the emergent nuclear power that has made it so worrisome a factor in the proliferation equation. The PRC's undeniable strengths and capabilities are matched by equally evident weaknesses and dependencies. Economic progress, for one, has been strikingly uneven. China has the ability to design and to construct complex, demanding nuclear facilities (for example, a uranium enrichment plant and nuclear-powered submarines), but stands in need of foreign assistance to exploit the energy potential so crucial to its economic future. It has embarked on a dramatically innovative program of industrialization that could vault China into the front ranks of newly industrialized nations, yet is frustrated by the constraints imposed by the acute shortage of foreign exchange.

The PRC's security situation exhibits similar contradictions and incongruities. Despite its nuclear arsenal, it feels vulnerable to Soviet power and sees in the expansion of Soviet political presence in Asia a constant threat to its own would-be status as a dominant regional power. An overriding interest in checking the Soviet Union's ambitions implicitly could devalue concern for the risks attendant upon a nuclear arms race between Pakistan and India. The cultivation of ties with the United States, inspired by the same set of strategic interests, must be balanced against the opportunity costs of tarnished credentials as a leader of progressive Third World forces.[3]

These foreign policy dilemmas have their rough counterparts elsewhere among the emergent new players in the proliferation game. In China's case, they are accentuated, and given heightened meaning, by a more fundamental ambivalence as to its aspirations and expectations as a world power preoccupied with its own affairs. Its international role is inexorably bound up with the as yet unresolved struggle to consolidate internal political reforms and to establish a durable line of policy for the PRC's economic development.

How do we make sense of these intersecting policy spheres and extract their meaning for China's external nuclear relations?

To understand the PRC's nuclear policies we must take account of both the background factors that condition official attitudes and those more immediate motives and purposes that underlie a particular action. Determining how they come together, in China's case, is complicated by three features of the PRC: (1) the inaccessibility of decision making; (2) a political system that has been in a state of flux; and (3) a distinctive political culture where conventional touchstones of analysis do not always apply.

In order to compose the diverse elements of the policy environment into a coherent picture, I shall use concrete instances of Chinese nuclear exports as the analytical point of departure.

For our purposes, there are two readily definable sets of policies around which to organize our analysis. The first embraces China's active nuclear dealings in the period from roughly 1980–83. Most prominent, and important, is the assistance extended to Pakistan. Nuclear exports to other states is denoted as a secondary reference point. The second is the PRC's remarkable shift in declaratory policy, and conduct, since 1984. It is represented by repeated official disavowals of any encouragement or support to threshold (or would-be) weapons states; entry into the International Atomic Energy Agency (IAEA); acceptance of most international rules governing nuclear exports, including the requirement of IAEA safeguards on all nuclear exports; and apparent discontinuation of its controversial nuclear assistance programs.

I shall first seek to explain and interpret these events. Then I shall draw on the conclusions reached to appraise the PRC's current outlook on nuclear matters and to speculate about its future conduct.

Strategic Outlook and Nuclear Weapons

China and the Bomb

Preserving its political independence and geographic integrity have been the overriding goals of the PRC's foreign policy since the Communist party took power in 1949. Affirming China's standing in the world has been the contrapuntal theme woven into its geostrategic concerns.

First the United States and then the Soviet Union was seen as posing a manifest threat to China's security. Nuclear weapons figured in the PRC's strategic field of vision from the outset. They were the most dramatic—if not necessarily the most important—evidence of power disparity between the PRC and its antagonists. China's response was a weapons program of its own, which reached the milestone of a successful nuclear explosion in 1964. While seeking the bomb, the PRC's leadership consistently denigrated its significance. One of the puzzles that confronts an analyst of Chinese nuclear policy is the genuineness of this conviction, and whether it is undifferentiated in terms of location and circumstance.

The officially stated view clearly has downplayed the value of nuclear arms and denied their uniqueness. Their revolutionary impact on conventional military doctrine and on the utility of force, generally acknowledged elsewhere, was rejected. At times, in the past, China's leadership has been brazen in disparaging the danger they pose. Declaratory policy, and to some unknowable degree attitudes as well, have undergone marked shifts in recent years toward restraint and reasonableness. On the basis of the record of past statements and acts, there remains reason to ponder how complete the transformation of the PRC's outlook on nuclear proliferation and the risks attendant upon it has been.

During the Mao era, in the late 1950s and 1960s, China's approach toward weapons of mass destruction seemed a cavalier one. The official line, at least, was that these weapons in no way altered the historically determined logic of an inevitable Communist victor in its struggle with capitalist imperialism (as revealed by Marxist-Leninist doctrine and refined by Mao). The PRC's success in repelling the American assault on North

Korea was cited as evidence in support of this contention. Moreover, the inherent moral and physical strength of the Chinese nation, as mobilized and led by the Communist party, was seen as an unbeatable force that could not be obviated by any technological marvel of the battlefield. The singular resilience of the PRC—its destiny to survive and flourish—became the dominant theme in the wake of Beijing's split with Moscow and the Soviet Union's reclassification as an enemy of the Chinese people.[4]

The PRC's attitude toward the Nuclear Non-Proliferation Treaty (NPT) was apiece with stated views about nuclear weapons generally. It expressed the same combination of ideological conceit and calculating Chinese self-interest. The public stance was one of unalloyed hostility. China opposed any efforts to control proliferation as a "show of arrogance" by the superpowers. A statement expressing official policy in 1963 contained the following provocative passage:

> Whether or not nuclear weapons help peace depends on who possesses them. It is detrimental to peace if they are in the hands of imperialist countries; it helps peace if they are in the hands of socialist countries. It must not be said indiscriminately that the danger of nuclear war increases along with the increase in nuclear powers. Nuclear weapons in the possession of a socialist country are always a means of defense against nuclear blackmail and nuclear war. So long as the imperialists refuse to ban nuclear weapons, the greater the number of socialist countries possessing them, the better the guarantees of world peace.[5]

In 1966, two years after China acquired nuclear weapons, Zhoi-En Lai characterized the draft Nuclear Non-Proliferation Treaty as "a great conspiracy against all peace-loving countries and people" designed to perpetuate the superpower monopoly.[6] As late as 1978, Foreign Minister Huang Nua was declaring that non–nuclear-weapons states should not be compelled "to abandon their right of possessing nuclear strength for self-defense."[7]

Doubtless, there was more than a touch of hyperbole to these declarations. This was the period of revolutionary activism and the Cultural Revolution, dominated by Mao's insular, xenophobic view of the world. Hostility toward the superpowers was complemented by a vigorous effort to portray the PRC as an advocate of Third World causes.

Indulging in rhetorical excess can be seen as an exercise in confidence-building for a vulnerable state, as well as a mark of revolutionary zeal. It can be taken as a defiant gesture directed alike at external foes and ideological backsliders at home. Whatever the precise mix of motives, the PRC's persistent opposition to the "discriminatory" NPT, coupled with its blanket condemnation of arms control, made China an obstacle to universalizing nonproliferation norms.

Current Strategic Perspective

Perceptible modification of China's self-defined role as the enfant terrible of international politics began to appear shortly after the diplomatic break-through with Washington in the early 1970s. The PRC's reemergence onto the main stage of world affairs has been accompanied by a tempering of Chinese public statements concerning the control of nuclear weapons and their spread to other states. Private exchanges have been more revealing of a progressively more "realistic" attitude about the dangers of nuclear war and the need to restrain the nuclear arms race.

Much of this new enlightenment in Chinese thinking is explainable by reference to the PRC's security interests. China has a self-evident stake in slowing the pace of an arms competition that threatens to degrade her own nuclear force. Similarly, Beijing would like to engage others in an effort to constrain Soviet power. Above all, the PRC has a vital interest in cultivating ties to the United States as a counter to the Soviet Union—both in the USSR's strategic calculations and to block Soviet expansionism. Toward these ends, China's post-Maoist leadership has taken a markedly more pragmatic approach to nuclear weapons, as well as to its external relations generally.

The Recent Record on Proliferation

In the 1980s, the PRC's nuclear export activities got star billing on the stage of proliferation diplomacy. Coming at a time when China itself was negotiating for reactor technology from established suppliers, they underscored the uncertainty about the degree of convergence between the PRC's attitude toward spreading weapons capabilities and that of most other nuclear-capable states. The negotiation of a bilateral nuclear cooperation agreement with the United States became the occasion, and the setting, for China to confront the issue of proliferation.

The protracted discussions with the United States were punctuated by revelations of the PRC's nuclear dealings with a number of threshold states. Controversial actions fall into two categories: (1) the extensive, prolonged program of nuclear cooperation with Pakistan that is generally believed to have entailed technical aid in building the Kahuta centrifuge enrichment facility, assistance in acquiring the ability to handle uranium fuels, and, perhaps, provision of information on warhead design; and (2) the probable sale of heavy water and high enriched uranium to Argentina, and allegedly of both items to South Africa as well.

The Pakistani transactions have been the most disturbing. The extent of China's contribution to a nuclear program clearly aimed at developing weapons supports the judgment that it was the most direct act of proliferation by a nuclear state in more than two decades (or since the USSR terminated its nuclear cooperation program with the PRC in the 1950s). The further prospect of a nuclear arms race with India on the politically troubled subcontinent added to the consternation.

Unsettling reports of the Pakistani connection began to circulate as early as 1981. (The program is believed to have begun in 1979 or 1980.) Intelligence sources soon confirmed suspicions that the Chinese had provided Islamabad with valuable help in bringing on line the unsafeguarded Kahuta plant—the facility that would provide the high-enriched uranium needed for an atomic bomb. Later reports that Beijing had gone a significant step further in making available sensitive information about the engineering of a nuclear explosive circulated a couple of years later; they are credited by Western intelligence services, although they were never proven. Whether the PRC extended so critical a boost to the Pakistani effort or not, the aid that was given poses a question of motivation that must be addressed in order to make sense of China's current policies on nuclear exports.[8]

An answer to the question of motivation would also have to account for the other nuclear export activities, reports of which were surfacing about the same time.

Item: The PRC reportedly shipped heavy water to Argentina (used as a moderating element in certain types of reactors, including some capable of producing weapons-grade plutonium) and high-enriched (20 percent) uranium (a critical start-up fuel that also has potential weapons applications) for use in research reactors.[9]

Item: The PRC allegedly sold heavy water to South Africa, as well, in addition to supplying low-enriched (30 percent) uranium that may have allowed the Pretoria government to triple production of weapons-grade uranium at its Valindaba enrichment plant.[10]

Evidence was accumulating that the PRC was acting directly counter to nonproliferation norms. A pattern began to emerge of a major supplier state so insensitive to the proliferation danger as to trade freely in sensitive commodities to countries with presumed nuclear ambitions.

The PRC's initial response to these charges was guarded and evasive. When confronted by the U.S. delegation in the talks on a bilateral nuclear cooperation agreement in 1984, Chinese negotiators denied them outright. No explanations, no apologies. Exchanges were portrayed simply as the continuation of a cooperative program dating from the mid-1970s (although little prior publicity had been given it). The entire affair was represented as innocent in intent and of little moment. The defensive posture taken by the PRC's leadership evinced no sense of embarrassment about being caught in reckless acts. Rather, it conveyed dismay that Washington (and other capitals) should place so much importance on proliferation and on steps that might contribute to it.

As conviction hardened that the PRC indeed had flagrantly violated nonproliferation norms, Washington felt it had no choice but to suspend further consideration of the nuclear cooperation agreement until satisfied that Beijing had ceased all assistance to the Pakistanis.

Reappraisal

The negotiation with the United States of a nuclear cooperation agreement proved to be the vehicle through which the PRC came to terms with the wider implications of its growing, and seemingly unrestrained, program of nuclear commerce. China had to move up a steep learning curve on proliferation matters. For Washington, to rappel China up that slope became the prime incentive in continuing talks with Beijing. The ensuing adjustment of Chinese thinking can be understood as the PRC's accommodation to yet another slice of global political life it had been free to disregard during its period of self-imposed isolation.

The adjustment was not entirely smooth. In April 1984, the U.S./PRC bilateral accord was initiated in a much-heralded cermony in Beijing by President Reagan and Chinese leaders. The nuclear pact was the highlight of the president's visit.[11] It had become a visible symbol of friendly cooperation between the United States and China. Yet within weeks of the signing ceremony, it was jeopardized by renewed reports of Chinese assistance to Pakistan. Chinese technicians were again present at the Kahuta enrichment plant, according to intelligence reports. In response, the American administration had no choice but to suspend further action on the agreement.

The process of reassurance by Beijing continued. Senior Chinese officials confided to the United States that all nuclear cooperation with Pakistan of a sensitive nature would cease. This time, they clearly were embarrassed at having been caught with their fingers in the cookie jar. They had been burnt diplomatically, and they were eager to remove doubts about their commitment to a responsible nonproliferation position.

Through a series of public statements and informal communications, Beijing made known its readiness to become part of the collective, institutionalized effort to contain the spread of nuclear weapons. The PRC, at a turning point in post-Mao foreign policy, applied for membership in the International Atomic Energy Agency. China was admitted in October 1983 and assumed its place in the organization on 1 January 1984. Henceforth, the PRC would require safeguards on all of their nuclear exports (Table 12–1 shows the status and form of China's several nuclear cooperation agreements).

Accession to the IAEA was a step of no small symbolic importance. It

Table 12–1
PRC'S Nuclear Cooperation Agreements

Region/Country	Date of Origin	Type of Cooperation
Asia		
Indonesia	1985	Technical assistance training
Japan	1985	Comprehensive
Pakistan	1986	Comprehensive
Middle East		
Iran	1985	Reactors and reactor sites
Europe and North America		
Finland	1987	Comprehensive
France	1984	Comprehensive
West Germany	1984	Comprehensive
Italy	1984	Comprehensive
Romania	1984	Comprehensive
Spain	1985	Comprehensive
United Kingdom	1985	Comprehensive
United States	1985	Comprehensive
Yugoslavia	1985	Technical assistance; materials and equipment
South America		
Argentina	1985	"All aspects" of nuclear fuel cycle research and development
Brazil	1983	Aerospace: fuel technology and guidance systems
	1984	Nuclear materials and equipment

represented an about-face from the earlier Chinese position of condemning multilateral arms control measures. Moreover, Beijing was now a participating member of a body whose raison d'être was to promote civilian nuclear cooperation under regulation by an international organization whose staff was empowered to conduct on-site inspection of facilities under safeguards.

On May 15, Premier Zhao Ziyang made the first public statement of China's new thinking on proliferation for a Chinese audience. In his report to the Second Session on the Sixth National People's Congress, Zhao formally repeated his declaration that:

> China is critical of the discriminatory Treaty on the Non-Proliferation of Nuclear Weapons and has declined to accede to it. But we by no means favour nuclear proliferation, nor do we engage in such proliferation by helping other countries to development of nuclear weapons.

On 18 January 1985, Vice Premier Li Peng stated in an interview with China's official Xinhua News Agency:

> I wish to reiterate that China has no intention, either at the present or in the future, to help non-nuclear countries develop nuclear weapons. . . .

China's nuclear cooperation with other countries, either at present or in the future, is confined to peaceful purposes alone.

In June 1985, the PRC voluntarily offered to accept IAEA safeguards for some of its indigenous facilities. It was a move not required by treaty, but it emulated symbolic actions taken by the United States and the Soviet Union to minimize differences in treatment of weapons and nonweapons states under the Non-Proliferation Treaty. An agreement between the IAEA and PRC for the application of agency safeguards to some civilian nuclear power facilities was signed in late 1988.[12]

Nuclear Attitudes: Past and Present

How does one read the PRC's record on nuclear exports and what does it auger for the future? One issue above all others must be clarified in order to make an assessment. Non-proliferation officials and analysts have puzzled over the key question from the recent past: What calculation of national security could have prompted the PRC to judge favorably Pakistan's advent as a nuclear power, with its potential for sparking a regional nuclear arms race on its borders? From today's perspective, I believe an explanation can be found both in the PRC's view of its strategic interests and in the meaning of nuclear weapons for its leadership.

It is easy for outsiders to undervalue the PRC's connection with Pakistan. Regionally, Pakistan has acted as a counterweight to India, the USSR's ally and China's foe. Pakistan has proven its usefulness to the PRC in other concrete respects as well. Long China's window on the Third World (and a convenient access point), the Pakistanis played a crucial intermediary role in the historic opening to the United States. The Islamabad government is associated, in Chinese eyes, with the radical reworking of the PRC's external relations thereby inaugurated.

Pakistan, as friend to both the United States and the PRC, is an integral part of this arrangement, as viewed from the Chinese standpoint. For both powers, Islamabad's role in Asian geopolitics became more central with the Soviet invasion of Afghanistan in late 1979. In serving as refugee and supply base for the mujaheedin, Pakistan has made itself indispensable to the common effort of preventing the consolidation of Soviet control. Its value to the PRC and the United States thereby has been enhanced.

In this context, it becomes easier to understand China's positive response to a request from Islamabad, as a longstanding ally, to cooperate in a development project for centrifuge enrichment (a technology of value to the Chinese for its potential contribution to military and civilian needs alike). To deny the request—one presented, no doubt, as an extension of the ongoing nuclear technical assistance program, whose civilian and military components probably were not clearly differentiated—might antagonize a prized ally. To cooperate would augment an important diplomatic asset. Moreover, it is not inconceivable that Beijing saw Pakistan as so deeply committed to securing the bomb, no matter what, that China thought it might as well garner the dividends of cooperation.

But did these gains overshadow the potential risks, in the form of an accelerated Indian nuclear weapons program? Apparently in Chinese eyes they did.

There is a reasonable basis on which Beijing could have weighed the benefits and costs so as to judge the prospect of two rival nuclear weapons states on its borders as an acceptable outcome. Above all, a Pakistani nuclear program acts as a counterweight to India. The PRC's continuing alliance with the former has created a serious, potential danger for Beijing, accentuated by India's growing military strength. It threatens Pakistan and also threatens to pose an acute dilemma for China. In the event of another Indo-Pakistan war, it is likely that superior Indian forces would gain the upper hand. A Pakistani call for assistance from its ally would put the PRC in a ticklish situation: to respond would create the risk of an unwanted military confrontation with India; failure to respond would result in a loss of credibility and face. By contrast, a nuclear-armed Pakistan might be in a position to stalemate the Indians—that is, mutual deterrence would militate against hostilities of any magnitude or constrain the combatants were war to break out nonetheless.

There is a plausability to this line of analysis. But questions remain about the unavoidable risks that attach to a nuclearized political environment. Are they outweighed by the strategic benefits? Or are they less troubling to China than we may think? Historical and cultural factors suggest that the PRC leadership might view the emergence of nuclear forces on the sub-continent as a less-than-dire development. It may well be that senior officials in Beijing downplayed the dangers posed by spreading nuclear capabilities (at least by comparison to official views held in other major nuclear states). This is not to say that they remain attached to the cavalier outlook of an earlier period. One need not presume the survival of Mao's recklessly radical ideas about the insignificance of the military atom to take seriously a hypothesis that the PRC's views about proliferation risks, however modified, are still influenced by distinctive Chinese beliefs and outlook.

A powerful sense of China's capacity to survive is a central political and cultural fact that may engender a less-than-apocalyptic view of nuclear weapons generally. A lingering residue from a policy that offered principled support for the right of other states to take up the nuclear option if they deemed it in their national interest can lower inhibitions on doing things that might encourage them down that path. So can the hard-headed view of strategic interests sketched above.

In sum, the evidence suggests an explanation of the PRC's assistance to Pakistan's nuclear weapons program that identifies a proximate cause—China's fears about a Pakistan military weakness vis à vis India—and three enabling factors: a perceived geostrategic interest in a strong, friendly Pakistan; an ongoing program of nuclear cooperation; and, perhaps, a *relatively* tolerant attitude toward nuclear weapons spread in general. A further contributing consideration would have been the chance to give access to centrifuge enrichment technology.

Other Sensitive Export Activities

The PRC's other controversial nuclear transactions, with Argentina and South Africa, do not raise the same kind of tangible security issues.[13] However, there may have been an indirect connection between these more or less contemporaneous activities. If we are correct in ascribing to the PRC a relatively relaxed attitude toward spreading weapons capabilities, it would indicate both little inhibition about engaging in sensitive nuclear commerce generally and the lack of restrictive export rules. Given this broad disposition, there is no reason for Beijing to be troubled by the incremental progress of threshold countries on the other side of the globe.

The PRC's thinking about atomic arms may be taken as the necessary factor that made possible these sales of sensitive nuclear materials; so too, as we shall see, may be the inadequacy of coordinating mechanisms in the PRC's decision-making system. What, though, of the sufficient cause? The place to look for plausible incentives and motivations is China's civilian nuclear energy program and the energy demands of its economic development plans. Here, as with security matters, an analysis of what underlay past behavior will aid us in assessing present and future policies.

The Domestic Nuclear Program

Background

China is experiencing an energy crisis of major proportions. The Seventh Five-Year Plan (1986–90) set ambitious energy goals. Even if met, though, economic activity is likely to be constrained by chronic shortages. Projected growth rates of the gross value of industrial and agricultural output (GVIAO) and gross energy production point to an energy/GNP coefficient of .46—that is, the target of doubled energy production can match the demand of a quadruple GVIAO only if we assume a .46 ratio between now and the end of the century. There is no precedent for this in either the present economies of today's industrializing countries or in the historical experience of the industrialized world.[14]

The problem is not one of inadequate resources, but rather of geographic maldistribution and the heavy capital costs of their exploitation. The regional imbalance of supply and demand is pronounced. Most of China's coal reserves lie in the less populated and underdeveloped northern provinces, far from the heavy energy demands of the south and east.[15] Similarly, almost three-quarters of China's hydropower potential is found in the southwest, which has less than 20 percent of the population and less than 10 percent of the GVIAO.[16]

In the light of these exigent energy needs, and given the country's substantial capabilities in the nuclear field (developed mainly for military purposes), it was only logical that the PRC should look to nuclear power to fill the gap in its energy inventory. Nuclear power offered the promise of economical electricity generation close to main centers of industry. Moreover, nuclear technology offered a symbol of the new China to arise from the chaos of the Cultural Revolution. Posters extolling the four modernizations—of agriculture, industry, defense, and science and technology—showed either a nucleus with its circulating electrons or a nuclear power station.

The most salient features of the civilian nuclear program's current status can be summarized in the following points:

1. Nuclear energy has been earmarked to make a significant contribution to meeting China's rapidly growing energy needs. The current goal of 10.5 megawatts by the end of the century represents only a modest portion of projected energy consumption;, it is, though, a significant share of estimated *electricity* production—the most critical, and inadequately developed, component of the nation's energy mix. Moreover, the country's energy shortage is most acute in the industrial zones of the southeast, where expanded electric power capacity is most needed.[17]

2. The PRC's overall energy program calls for a doubling of the country's energy supply by the end of the century. Attaining that goal is crucial to China's plan of quadrupling the GVIAO—using 1980 as the baseline.[18]

3. In the early 1980s, the PRC promulgated a plan for rapid development of an extensive nuclear power program built around imported technology and hardware.[19] The stated goal was ten 900 MW reactors in operation by the end of the century, at a non-Chinese procurement cost in the order of $7–10 billion (U.S.). That plan has now been shelved. Only two reactors have been purchased abroad, from France's Framatome, to be located at Daya Bay in Guandong province opposite Hong Kong (whose electric utility, China Power and Light, holds a 25 percent share in the project). A third plant, in Sunan, near Shanghai, had been projected and

discussions held with possible bidders, for example, Framatome and the Kraftwerk Union (KWU). But that project is now on hold indefinitely.

The new watchword is self-reliance. China's avowed "indigenization program" is designed to fill gaps in the country's repertoire of engineering, industrial, and managerial skills; to obtain from foreign sources only that technology and hardware now unavailable in the PRC; to maximize the use of components of Chinese manufacture in projects under the direction of foreign contractors (for example, at Daya Bay); to minimize the importation of foreign components for indigenous projects (for example, the Chinese designed Quinshan reactor and its successors); to use Quinshan as a testing ground for Chinese technology; and to accentuate the crossover of capabilities from the nation's military program to its civilian programs.[20]

4. Severe foreign exchange shortages have been the main factor in the earlier plans for the purchase of technology abroad and for the telescoping of stages in the indigenization program. It is the lack of hard cash that forced Chinese officials to reshape their nuclear program so as to buy only strategic foreign assistance instead of whole plants from abroad.

5. The heavy foreign exchange demands of the earlier nuclear plan created incentives to earn hard currency via export sales. Lowering the priority given imported technology, and the scaling-back of nuclear power targets generally, has eased the pressure to generate hard currency from exports to cover partially the costs of technology and equipment from abroad, even if that incentive is not removed entirely.

Organization and Structure

Like other nuclear powers, China's nuclear industry was initially set up to develop a weapons capability. In the early days, this was done under the auspices of a defense, scientific, and technical agreement with the Soviet Union. But when the Soviets abruptly pulled out in 1959, the Chinese had to go it alone. Their success in building an atomic bomb, first exploded in 1964, and their H-bomb two and a half years later, is testimony to the Chinese scientific engineering and industrial abilities.[21] By the 1980s, the PRC had an impressive nuclear infrastructure: a gaseous diffusion enrichment plant, some seventeen plutonium production reactors of Russian design, a small reprocessing facility, a number of research reactors including a zero energy fast reactor, an embryo nuclear submarine program, and a large number of highly trained nuclear engineers and technologists.[22]

The program promulgated in the early 1980s foresaw the letting of contracts to foreign vendors, beginning with the Daya Bay project. The intense bidding for the Daya Bay sale concluded in January 1985 with the signing of a contract with Framatome to supply the two 900-megawatt reactors for the Daya Bay project. Britain's General Electric Company will provide the turbines and related convential power-generating equipment for the plants.[23]

Formal signing of the contracts was delayed more than a year in the absence of final authorization from Beijing. The year 1985 was one of agonizing reappraisal for China's nuclear planners. All economic projects entailing heavy expenditures on purchases from abroad were undergoing critical scrutiny and their future placed in jeopardy. The nub of the problem was, once again, the PRC'S foreign exchange difficulties. Collapse of world oil prices cost China $6.6 billion (U.S.) in 1985, a significant fraction of its annual export earnings. Moreover, although the PRC is now the world's fifth largest oil producer, the mounting energy demands of its domestic economy are beginning to curtail exports. With the outlook for revenues from petroleum exports bleak, and foreign exchange earnings to cover a surge of imports growing but still insufficient, retrenchment was inevitable.[24]

Nuclear Retrenchment

Major decisions were made by the State Council in the early part of 1986 that completely recast the civil nuclear program. The ultimate goal of self-sufficient manufacture was reiterated and highlighted. Developing internal capabilities would have precedence over the import of complete power stations from abroad. The schedule for the Daya Bay project was slowed considerably and the prospective role of components of Chinese manufacture expanded. (The aforementioned Sunan project was put off to some unspecified future date.)

As the revised plan has evolved, the accent on internal technical resources has been sharpened. The aim is to develop a standardized, indigenous nuclear plant liable to serial production. Qinshan I, due on-line in the early 1990s, is the prototype. The State Council has given approval for the construction of two 600 MW(e) units at Qinshan, building on the experience of the 300 MW(e) unit at the site. Currently, plans are under review for another half-dozen nuclear plants, on Hainán Island, in Fujian province at Harbin, and at other locations in energy-poor regions. All are likely to employ pressurized water reactors—although there is interest in a high-temperature gascooled reactor technology as well.[25] In addition, Sunan may be reviewed as indigenous 2 x 600 MW(e) units. (The range of foreign participation in China's nuclear program is presented in Table 12–2).

There have also been noteworthy organizational changes. In an action of perhaps far-reaching significance, responsibility for nuclear power in 1986 passed from the Ministry of Water Resources and Electric Power (MWREP) to the Ministry of Nuclear Industry (MNI). When Chairman Hua promulgated the nuclear power program in 1978, the two ministries

Table 12–2
Foreign Firms Supplying Nuclear Assistance To the PRC

Name	Host Country	Transaction Dates	Type of Supply
Qinshan 1 **Power Station** (indigenous reactor)			
Mitsubishi (under Westinghouse license)	Japan	1988–89	Pressure vessel
Toshiba, Ishikawajima-Hirama	Japan	1988–89	Technical assistance
KWu	West Germany	1988–89	Nuclear instrumentation
Sulzer	Switzerland, Italy, Sweden	1988–89	Power plant components: valves, turbine controls, fire-resistant cables and pumps
Qinshan 2,3 **Power Stations**			
KWu	West Germany	Pending	Design and architectural engineering
KWu	West Germany	Prospective	Reactor components
Framatome	France	Prospective	Reactor components
Guandong Power Station **(Daya Bay)**			
Framatome	France	1987–92	Nuclear Island: vessels, steam generators, and other components
Spie-Batignettes	France	1987–92	Construction engineering
GEC	United Kingdom	1987–92	Turbines
ESAB	Sweden	1987–92	Nuclear welding facilities
WEIR	United States	Prospective	Pumps
U.S. Nuclear Research Station	United States	Current	Personnel training
Bechtel	United States	Current	Quality-control engineering
Framatome	France	Current	Personnel training
Mitsubishi	Japan	Prospective	"Technical assistance package"
Miscellaneous			
Brown-Boveri, Deutsche Babcock, Mannesman, Strabag	West Germany	Prospective	Development assistance for 100 MW(e) HTG reactor
Framatome	France	1988	PWR simulator
Cogema	France	1990–91	Enriched fuel

Table 12–2 continued

Name	Host Country	Transaction Dates	Type of Supply
Spie-Batignettes	France	1987–92	Construction engineering
GEC	United Kingdom	1987–92	Turbines
ESAB	Sweden	1987–92	Nuclear welding facilities
Weir	United States	Prospective	Pumps
U.S. Nuclear Research Station	United States	Current	Personnel training
Bechtel	United States	Current	Quality-control engineering
Framatome	France	Current	Personnel training
Mitsubishi	Japan	Prospective	"Technical assistance package"

engaged in a classic power struggle for control of the program. The MNI, which had developed wide-ranging nuclear capabilities in directing the military program after the Russian pull-out in 1959, thought itself perfectly able to build the needed nuclear power stations. The MWREP argued the case for taking advantage of the experience and means developed by the industrialized countries.

Each ministry was given a part of the overall responsibility and allowed to follow its own path. MWREP was lead agency for negotiating with foreign vendors for the Daya Bay and abortive Sunan power plants, while MNI retained responsibility for the Qinshan reactor project. The evident friction between the two agencies was widely reported, and it was observed by Western business and governmental visitors who dealt with the Chinese on nuclear matters in the early 1980s. Interministerial competition was exacerbated by the multiplication of nuclear bureaus at the provincial level. The resulting disarray forced a consolidation of policy-making authority. In 1984, the Nuclear Power Leadership Group was created as a committee of the State Council (the PRC's highest governing authority). Vice-Premier, and former MWREP head, Li Peng was appointed chairperson. Li became premier in November 1987, succeeding now Party Chairman Zhou Ziyang.

With Li Peng's as chair, there was the suggestion of a tilt toward an import-based nuclear program. The deepening foreign exchange crisis, however, soon settled the issue on other terms. In late 1985 and early 1986 the PRC moved to consolidate management of its civilian nuclear program. The MNI was given complete responsibility for the civilian program: plant design, construction, and operations, as well as most research and development. The MWREP's domain has been limited to hydro and fossil-fired plants, as well as transmission and distribution for the entire national power grid.[26] Having won the battle to control civil nuclear construction, the MNI became indisputably the main player on all nuclear matters in the PRC. Its domain included both China's military and civil programs. The MNI now devotes approximately 40 percent of its work to civil applications.

In 1988, another organizational reform amalgamated the MNI and the MWREP into an overarching Ministry of Energy that embraces coal and petroleum resources too. The new ministry grew out of the former energy bureau of the State Planning Commission. In its current enhanced status, its main responsibility is to provide "guidance planning" across the energy sector. In particular, the Ministry is mandated to mediate disputes over resource allocation and to rationalize investment decisions. However, the ministry's constituent bureaus continue to enjoy financial autonomy in two respects: (1) they are free to distribute funds among programs and projects within their own domain; and (2) they are permitted to retain earnings from domestic commercial activities and export sales. Although the precise degree of integration that will result is unclear, indications are that the MNI will retain most of its organizational autonomy under the new set-up, loosely overseen by the Ministry of Energy while still reporting to the Nuclear Power Leadership Group on broad, and sensitive, policy matters.

In the military sphere, the Nuclear Industry Bureau shares responsibility with the former Ministry of Machine Building (MMB)—combined in 1986 with the Ministry of the Ordnance Industry to form the State Commission of Machine Industry. The MMB provides sophisticated manufacturing capability in producing conventional components and precision parts for the PRC's nuclear programs. The MNB is also a participant in the nuclear field, contributing fuel fabrication and fine machine tool capability.

Jiang Xinxing, head of the MNI, has become the country's most prominent spokesperson on all nuclear questions since 1986. He has stressed the importance of nuclear exports, which are the responsibility of a subsidiary agency, the China Nuclear Energy Industry Corporation (CNEIC), headed by Liu Shulin.

The CNEIC is in effect a trading company set up "to link the ministry to the civilian economy and, particularly, to facilitate its entry into international trade," following the pattern established for all of the governmental ministries with mixed military and civilian responsibilities.[27] This arrangement has twin goals: to make defense-based technology available to the civilian sector; and for the defense industries to improve their technology through cooperative international civilian projects. In the new organizational arrangement, the CNEIC's corporate status is confirmed and its profit-making orientation underscored.

Liu has been quoted as saying that China's nuclear industry has now matured to the point where it can offer a complete system of nuclear technologies and services. The initial emphasis is on natural uranium, where Liu has set an export goal of 1,000 tons per annum. The CNEIC has moved quickly to engage brokers and to write contracts—with Finland, France, and West Germany, to date. In the longer term, it has been stated that enriched fuel and complete fuel elements will also be available for export along with services and instrumentation. The CNEIC has, as well, entered into an arrangement with a German company, Inter-Nuclear Gmbh, to represent it and to act as the PRC's agent in offering spent fuel management to European utilities.[28] (A more detailed survey of the PRC's past and prospective nuclear exports is provided in tables 12–3 and 12–4).

Reactors too figure in China's prospective export list. The PRC has hopes for developing a version of its Qinshan reactor for sale abroad. The talks with Pakistan on peaceful nuclear exchanges have focused on a 420 MW(e) reactor, two of which might eventually be sold. A reactor type of this size, suitable for the small grids of most newly industralized and developing nations, has no counterpart in the international marketplace. Mainline vendors had never been able to produce a design that is economical to manufacture (although it appears that Framatome may soon offer such a model).[29]

Table 12–3
PRC Export Transactions

Country	Date of Action	Type of Transaction
Argentina	1982–83	Heavy water; 20%-enriched uranium; uranium hexaflouride
Pakistan	1975–present (?)	Technical training re. nuclear engineering and operation
		Technical assistance re. Kahuta centrifuge enrichment plant
		Technical assistance re. bomb design (alleged)
South Africa	1981–82 (?)	HEU; heavy water (alleged)
France (Electricite de France)	1986	Natural uranium
Finland (TVO)	1987	Natural uranium
West Germany (GKN)	1986	Natural uranium
West Germany (KWu)	1987	Natural uranium
United States (Allied Corp.) (Sequoyah Fuel Corp.)	1988	Natural uranium
Nueyco International Corp.★	1988–present	Broker agent

★Nueco: exclusive brokerage trading contract with China Nuclear Energy Industry Corp. as of 1988.

Table 12–4
PRC's Potential Nuclear Export Items

Natural uranium

Enriched uranium

Fabricated fuel assemblies

Heavy water

Research reactors

Power reactors (óf Chinese design)
600 MW
300 MW

Spent fuel services

Reprocessing services

Technical assistance: design/construction

Training: nuclear physics, engineering, operations

Miscellaneous:
Reactor components
Dual-use technology
Metal alloys
Electronic equipment

Nuclear Exports: Decision Making and Licensing

Today, decision-making authority on nuclear questions is somewhat easier to locate. It seemingly is lodged with the former Ministry of Nuclear Industry (recast as an autonomous bureau within the Department of Energy) under the aegis of the State Council. It reports to the newly created Ministry of Energy, but significant oversight is provided by the Council's Nuclear Power Leadership Group. Ultimate authority for sanctioning exports probably resides there as well. However, the degree of latitude enjoyed by the CNEIC is not known. Nor are the formal procedures for granting licenses available to us.

A centralized Ministry of Foreign Trade (MFT), which was in existence until 1982, officially had chief responsibility for foreign trade and, along with the State Planning Commission, the allocation of foreign exchange. In fact, the foreign trade corporations set up under other ministries became semiautomous. In 1982, a partial consolidation took place with the formation of the Ministry of Foreign Economic Relations and Trade (MOFERT). The degree of actual centralization that occurred, though, is unclear. There is reason to believe that decision making on technology transfers follows complicated routes with shifting responsibilities. For example, a regulation promulgated in 1986 charged MOFERT with the task of reviewing and approving contracts for the importation of technology. This authority does not appear to cover exports, though.

All the available evidence supports the conclusion that judgments made at the level of the State Council set the frame of reference for nuclear export decisions, and that individual transactions are made by the CNEIC. Such was probably also the case in the early 1980s when the reported shipments to Argentina and South Africa took place. What remains obscure is the level at which the decisions were made to permit those exports and whether political criteria were brought into play. Given the opaqueness of Chinese decision-making, it is understandable that a number of artful theories should be brought forth that purport to explain these deals in terms of unmonitored initiatives by officials in the MNI or MWREP.

They can be neither proven nor disproven, but these hypotheses lack plausibility on two grounds. First, principal responsibility for exports lay with the CNEIC, whose ministerial link was to the MNI, which had opposed the policy of drawing heavily on foreign technology and equipment. It was the MWREP, though, that might have had to justify its call on scant hard currencies (to meet the hefty cost of imports) by earning foreign exchange on its own. The MNI might have had some interest of its own in exports, since revenues earned by nuclear sales abroad would brighten the funding picture for nuclear programs generally. But the incentive was clearly less compelling for the MNI than for the MWREP.

The other reason for skepticism is that these hypotheses presume a laxness in oversight by political superiors, along with a consonantly wide range of discretionary power at the ministerial level, that is unsubstantiated by the evidence—however cloudy it may be. The importance conventionally attached to nuclear matters suggests that the top state and party leadership could not fail to have addressed issues of nuclear commerce. All the more so given that the PRC was, at the time, embarking on a venturesome new course in launching its own civil nuclear program and inaugurating collaboration in Pakistan's bomb program. Ministers as senior as Li Peng (soon to be promoted to Vice-Premier) and Jiang Xinxing (in charge of the nuclear weapons program) could hardly have been unaware of the issue's significance or of sentiment among the top leadership.

This is not to argue that, of necessity, there had to have been a focused examination of these relatively minor (in parochial Chinese eyes) export transactions. It was still a period of comparative insularity in the PRC's diplomacy. And those best prepared to warn of harmful political consequences—in the Ministry of Foreign Affairs—may not have been actively consulted. Yet, I find it hard to avoid the conclusion that service government officials gave at least tacit sanction to the Argentinian sale.[30]

This assessment does not preclude excessive zeal in a policy context defined by central decisions. Guidelines on nuclear exports perhaps could have been interpreted liberally as allowing (encouraging?) sales of heavy water and enriched uranium on a less-than-selective basis. Earning foreign exchange doubtless is a constant in the calculation of all of China's official traders.

The latter incentives remain; it is high-level policy toward nuclear exports, and their proliferation implications, that have changed. And, with it, the undoubted tightening of oversight on all nuclear transactions.

Prospects

The PRC's attitude toward nuclear exports and weapons proliferation has gone through a process of reevaluation which has a number of identifiable stages. At first, there was a striking insensitivity about proliferation risks and a disregard for the proliferation concerns of other powers that manifested itself in relaxed, if not wholly uninhibited, export practices; this phase extends from the 1960s through the early 1980s, covering nuclear dealings with Pakistan, Argentina, and South Africa. This was followed by the "burning finger" stage: China's controversial actions expressed an inattentiveness to their strategic and political implications, creating a political furor and imposing diplomatic costs.

The learning phase is next in sequence. This was a period of consciousness-raising about how deeply other states take proliferation matters, about the political investments that have been made in a world nonproliferation regime, about the links between civilian nuclear commerce and military programs, and about the potential costs to one's own security from a wider dissemination of nuclear arms. For the PRC, this learning process was compressed into the short span of time between 1982–85—although in some respects it continues today. This phase also sees the crystallization of a coalition within the government in support of more restrictive export policies and a tougher stance on proliferation. The key is a shift in thinking at the top: presumably, in the PRC's case, in the Nuclear Power Leadership Group of the State Council. The watershed decisions were China's application to the IAEA and its acceptance of the terms for a bilateral agreement with the United States.

The last stage is typified by the building-up of effective export control mechanisms. Effective enforcement is a matter of will and capabilities. For a country with few true private enterprises (none in the nuclear field), an elaborate control system is less imperative than in free-market economies. Direction from the top should ensure that no items identified as nuclear-sensitive are exported without proper approval and conditions. The outstanding issue, for China and traditional suppliers alike, is identifying dual-use and marginal commodities that could have value to the enterprising would-be proliferator.[31]

The PRC's commitment to the IAEA's safeguards regime and to more prudent export policies seems to be irreversible. The evolution we have seen in Chinese policy is grounded in a realistic appraisal of its national interests. As a practical matter, Beijing must take due account of the importance attached to nonproliferation by the United States and other nations. Strategically there is no alternative to the United States as an offset to Soviet power. Whatever the prospects for Sino-Soviet relations, cordial ties with Washington will remain a foundation-stone of China's security arrangements.

Less clear is how the Chinese understand their relationship to areas of the world that lie outside their range of strategic concern. China has yet to define fully its new position in global affairs since its emergence from its Maoist era cocoon. While it certainly has acquired a finer-grained picture of its external environment and has cultivated a more flexible and sensitive diplomacy, some residue of past isolation endures.

Consonantly, it is likely to remain comparatively insensitive to the conflicts that trouble regions beyond its ken. The generalized commitment to responsible nuclear export policies can be expected to prevent the reckless acts of the past. But it is legitimate to ask whether it is a sufficient guarantee that items of trade of marginal sensitivity (and on the margins of whatever control systems are in place) will not be exported.

The concern is of course not specific to China. It is noteworthy, though, that as the PRC extends its already impressive capabilities in civil—and military—nuclear power, Chinese export potential grows. And especially so in those gray area items that are eluding even the administrative grasp of some traditional suppliers. The stress placed on exports to earn the hard currency desperately needed to pay for China's heavy import requirements implies an active search for marketable products.

The potential and disposition to export must be balanced against Chinese progress up the learning curve on proliferation. It is easy to understate achievement to date. The full meaning of the PRC's participation in collective institutions, and its subscription to their rules of conduct, is more impressive when we keep in mind how far Beijing has come. The Chinese have accepted the principles of U.S. consent rights on retransfers and reprocessing, and of verification. They have accepted the obligations of IAEA membership, with the qualification of national prerogative they imply. In so doing, the PRC has allowed its international conduct to be judged by other parties. It is a concession that has no parallel in modern Chinese history.

These changes can properly be viewed as accurate signposts of progress in the maturation of the PRC's international outlook generally.

Notes

1. I outline these issues in my paper, *Spreading Nuclear Capabilities: New Trends*, Center for International and Strategic Affairs, U.C.L.A., Research Note no. 17 (Los Angeles, June 1986).

2. Chinese nuclear export and technical assistance programs are examined in detail in Leonard D. Spector, *Nuclear Proliferation Today: The Spread of Nuclear Weapons 1984* (New York: Vintage, 1984).

3. The PRC's security dilemmas are appraised in A. Doak Barnett, *The Making of Foreign Policy in China* (Boulder, Colo.: Westview Press, 1985). See also the report of the Atlantic Council, *China Policy for the Next Decade* (Washington, D.C.: 1983).

4. The extremity of Maoist views on nuclear arms was revealed in a couple of memorable diplomatic encounters. In January 1955, in remarks welcoming the Finnish Ambassador on presenting his credentials, Mao declared:

> The Chinese people are not to be cowed by U.S. atomic blackmail. Our country has a population of 600 million and an area of 9,600,000 square kilometers. The United States cannot annihilate the Chinese nation with its small stack of atom bombs. Even if the U.S. atom bombs were so powerful that, when dropped on China, they would make a hole right through the earth, or even blow as a whole, though it might be a major event for the solar system.

5. *Peking Review*, 16 August 1963.

6. Cited in statement of Senator William Proxmire to the Senate Committee on Foreign Relations, 9 October 1985.

7. Cited in statement of Senator John Glenn, 9 December 1985, *Congressional Record*, 99th Cong., 1st sess., p. S17147.

8. The PRC's nuclear collaboration with Pakistan is discussed at length in two reports by Leslie Gelb, *New York Times*, 22, 23 June 1984.

9. The nuclear commerce with Argentina, broadly accepted as established in Washington and other capitals, was—for all intents and purposes—confirmed by then Chinese Prime Minister while on a visit to Buenos Aires. Asked if China had sold or would sell the nuclear materials to Argentina, Zhao said he did not know the details, but China "probably had in the past." *Journal of Commerce*, 12 November 1985, p. 17.

Argentinian interest in obtaining HEU from China continue, but now under safeguarded conditions on normal commercial terms. See *Nuclear News* (July 1988).

10. The evidence is assayed by Spector, *Nuclear Proliferation Today*, chapter 5.

11. *New York Times*, 6 June 1982.

12. Subsequent Chinese nuclear export behavior generally conforms to the principle enunciated by the PRC's leadership. Some suspicion remains about continuing collaboration with Pakistan on sensitive projects despite the two countries having signed a nuclear cooperation agreement in September 1986 that promises to place under IAEA safeguards all materials and equipment exchange. However, there are no indications of questionable export practice to other parties. Moreover, senior

government officials avail themselves of every opportunity to reaffirm their adherence to nonproliferation norms.

14. These issues are analyzed in Hunghuei Chou, *The Chinese Communists' Energy Problems*, Studies of Chinese Communism (Taipei: May 1986). See also the revealingly candid appraisal in *Renmin Ribao* [Points and Criticisms], June 1986. The best overall description of the Chinese energy bureaucracy and the energy policymaking process is the excellent study of Kenneth Lieberthal and Michael Oksenberg, *Bureaucratic Politics and Chinese Energy Development* (Washington, D.C.: International Trade Administration. U.S. Department of Commerce, 1986).

15. *Chou, Chinese Communists' Energy Problems*, Chs. 1, 2.

16. For coal, see Ji Shubao, "Energy Resources and Coal Reduction in China," *Energy Systems and Policy* 10, no. 2. For hydroelectric, see *China Power Industry* 5 (May 1986).

17. There is considerable literature on China's energy program, its interest in foreign technology, and the place accorded nuclear power. Among the more informative general works are: *Energy Technology Transfer to China: A Technical Memorandum* (Washington, D.C.: Office of Technology Assessment, September 1985); U.S. Congress, House of Representatives, *China's Economic Development and U.S. Trade Interests*, Report of the Special Subcommittee on U.S. Trade with China of the Committee on Energy and Commerce, May 1985, pp. 15–17, 31–38 (on nuclear development); and David Denny, "Electric Power and the Chinese Economy," *China Business Review* (July/August 1985): 14–17.

18. These targets are stated in the comprehensive energy strategy prepared jointly by the State Energy Commission and State Planning Commission and approved by the National People's Congress in April 1986 (*Renmin Ribao* (14 May 1985)); *The Seventh Five-Year-Plan* (Beijing: The People's Press, 1986). See also the report of Lu Jingting, Minister Counselor for Science and Technology, Embassy of PRC (Washington, D.C.), *China's Energy Development*, November 1986.

19. The dimensions of the PRC's nuclear program as it took shape in the early- and mid-1980s are considered by: Matthew J. Matthews, "Nuclear Power Shapes Up," *China Business Review* (July/August 1985): 23–27; U.S. Congress, House Committee on Energy and Commerce, Hearing before the Special Subcommittee on U.S. Trade with China of the Committee on Energy and Commerce, 98th Cong., 2d sess., 22 February 1984, pp. 11–16, 33–44 (nuclear); Martin Weil, "China's Power Industry," *China Business Review* (July/August 1985): 17–22; and "China's Nuclear Industry Comes of Age," *Nuclear Engineering* (June 1986). The status of China's revised and scaled-down nuclear program is outlined in *Nuclear News* (March 1988) and *Nuclear Engineering, International* (June 1988).

20. *Financial Times*, 6 March 1986; *Nuclear News* (April 1986).

21. The PRC's weapons program is recounted in detail by John Lewis and Citai Xue, *China Builds the Bomb* (Stanford: Stanford University Press, 1988).

22. *Nuclear Engineering* (June 1986).

23. *China Reconstructs* (March 1987).

24. The foreign exchange constraint on the PRC's economic development is discussed in The World Bank, *China: Long-Term Development Issues and Options* (Washington, D.C.: The Johns Hopkins University Press, 1986). See also Wolfgang

Kenner and Kurt Wiesegart, *The Chinese Economy: Structure and Reform in the Domestic Economy and Foreign Trade* (New Brunswick, N.J.: Transaction Books, 1985). The outlook for oil exports is reviewed in the New *York Times*, 16 May 1988.

25. *China Reconstructs* (April 1986).

26. *Nuclear News* (August 1986).

27. U.S. Congress, Office of Technology Assessment, *Technology Transfer To China*, June 1987, p. 43. Logically, as former minister of the MWREP Li Peng might have been expected to bring to the Leadership Group the ministry's traditional interest in imports, yet Li himself has often endorsed a protectionist philosophy and has been relatively outspoken in his support of the principle that China should rely, to the greatest degree possible, on indigenous equipment.

28. *Nuclear News* (August 1986).

29. *Nuclear Engineering* (June 1988).

30. Furthermore, it should be noted that the period 1979–82 was one of comparatively tight central control over the economic ministries (and provinces). The decentralization of responsibilities for economic development did not come into play until 1983–84.

31. A retrospective look at the PRC's conduct on nuclear exports suggests that its actions can best be understood as an amalgam of motivations and circumstances. One sees a pattern composed of several elements. There were important strategic considerations in the PRC's aid to Pakistan and the perception of nuclear materials and technology as useful diplomatic assets. China's broader export program was also a function of economic conditions: the availability of excess enrichment capacity and heavy-water production created incentives for sales abroad (Rydell's "supply push" hypothesis); the interest of buyers was strong and apparent (the "demand pull" hypothesis); and the need to acquire foreign exchange was a constant background factor. In its role as nuclear supplier, the PRC sold and bartered in both economic and political currencies, in a manner that underlies the fungibility of prized technological assets.

13
South Africa:
As a Nuclear Supplier

David Fischer

Transactions

Motives for Entering the International Nuclear Market

South Africa's main reason for entering the international nuclear market is, and always has been, to sell its uranium abroad. From 1939–45 South Africa took part in the war against Nazi Germany, and the South African government of the time sought to help the Allied war effort in all ways that were practical. Later, during the Cold War, it tried to help build up the West's nuclear arsenal.

In 1944, the British government secretly asked General Smuts—prime minister of South Africa since 1939 and a member of Churchill's War Cabinet—to survey South Africa's deposits of uranium. The survey, carried out with U.S. and British help, showed that the deposits were large, generally low-grade, but, in most cases, associated with gold and therefore could be profitably mined. In 1951, South Africa became a significant producer, with lucrative contracts for the sale of all its output to the U.S.-U.K.-Canada Joint Development Agency and one of the three main suppliers to the U.S. nuclear weapons program. In time, government controls eased and uranium production and marketing became a purely commercial operation. The mining "houses" of Johannesburg mined and processed the ore and marketed it to customers abroad through their jointly operated Nuclear Fuels Corporation, NUFCOR. In the 1960s the Rio Tinto Corporation began to develop the giant Roessing mine in Namibia. Rio Tinto sells the output direct to customers abroad.[1]

South Africa's motives for enriching uranium were also initially commercial: to increase the value of its exports by selling the enriched product instead of selling uranium concentrates (U_3O_8 or yellowcake). However, enrichment, unlike mining and processing of yellowcake, is in the hands of a state-owned corporation, Uranium [Enrichment] Corporation of South Africa (UCOR).

The South African government sought but was unable to secure French or West German investment to build a plant large enough to enrich all its exports. In the late 1970s, faced with a cutoff of U.S. supplies of enriched uranium, the South African government decided to build a "semicommercial" plant near the pilot facility where it had tested its enrichment process. This semicommercial plant was due to begin production before the end of 1988 (a year behind schedule). It is large enough to meet the fuel needs of three large (ca. 1,000 MW) reactors (300,000 SWUs p/a). Two power reactors of 921 MW each are in operation in South Africa, and UCOR is now offering its spare SWUs for sale abroad.[2]

South Africa has also offered to sell its enrichment technology to "friendly" countries, but such countries as may merit this appellation have shown no interest in recent years. South Africa is also technically able to manufacture plants for mining and processing uranium ore, as well as a limited range of nuclear equipment that it has been unable to obtain from abroad and has recently manufactured to meet its own requirements (probably "hot cells," fuel fabrication plants, and certain research reactor components). There are also unconfirmed reports of some tritium production. There are no reports that it has exported any of these items.

Market Disincentives

Falling world demand and prices for uranium or of contracts and the impact of sanctions or of contracts discontinued for political reasons have induced South African producers to cut back prospecting and development of new reserves and to close down or mothball certain mines and cut back production in others. The West's surplus of enrichment capacity has eroded South Africa's interest in expanding its own beyond its limited domestic needs.

Major Nuclear Transactions Since 1980

For many years the South African government has seen the country in a state of siege. The UN Security Council's embargo in 1977 on the export of arms to South Africa and the fall of the Shah of Iran, which cut off the last remaining official source of oil from abroad, reinforced the siege mentality, which has been further strengthened by recent events. As a result, the shroud of official secrecy that surrounds the more sensitive areas of South African external trade has become difficult to penetrate. The South African

Nuclear Energy Act of 1982 makes it a criminal offense to disclose, without official permission, any information about uranium reserves, output or potential output, or terms and conditions of sale. Despite these draconian provisions a surprising amount of information is readily available in the form of official statistics on reserves (if not on exports) and from the mining corporations and NUFCOR.

A study of known transactions since 1980, reported in trade and technical journals, reveals a clear pattern:

1. Almost all South African and Namibian uranium is marketed under long-term contracts and, until now, all has been exported in the form of yellowcake.

2. All exports since 1980 have gone to the United States (now embargoed),[3] Western Europe (chiefly EEC countries), Japan, and Taiwan. The main importers in Western Europe have been West Germany, the United Kingdom, France, Spain, and Belgium. Until 1984 the main customer for Namibian (Roessing) uranium was the United Kingdom; it has since been replaced by Japan and France. Among the customers, Taiwan, and in a different sense, Spain and Japan, might be viewed as "emerging suppliers."

3. The only known cases of "exotic" exports were, in the early 1960s, the sale of 10 tons of yellowcake to Israel and the proposed sale, in 1983, of 1,400 tons of yellowcake to Iran.[4] Apparently, despite the rupture of relations between South Africa (where the Shah spent several years during World War II) and Iran after the Ayatollah seized power, Iran continues to press for fulfillment of a contract under which South Africa would deliver 1,400 tons of yellowcake to Iran. As late as September 1987 NUFCOR decided not to go ahead with the delivery in view of the impact that it might have had on already strained U.S.-South African relations.

4. Another potentially exotic export was the sale in 1987 of 2,000 tons of yellowcake to Romania. It lapsed, according to NUFCOR, because the Romanian authorities were reluctant to provide satisfactory information about the safeguards to be applied to the material.[5] Perhaps the Romanians were reluctant to be too explicit about the source of the material.

This pattern seems to be a continuation of that described in the 1980 United Nations report on "South Africa's Plan and Capability in the Nuclear Field."[6] The experts who wrote the report remarked (in paragraph 13) that West Germany obtained 27.2 percent of its uranium from South Africa during the period 1965 to 1977 and was expected to obtain 50 percent from South Africa and Namibia during the period 1977 to 1986. In 1977, France had signed a contract for the supply of 900 tons of uranium for ten years (at $27 per pound). The United Kingdom would buy 1,300 tons a year (or about 65 percent of its total needs) from the Roessing mine in Namibia until 1982. Taiwan had signed a contract to buy 4,000 tons from South Africa between 1984 and 1990. South Africa was said to be the second most important supplier of uranium to the EEC (Canada was the first).

Transshipment through South Africa

There has been no serious indication of a transshipment through South Africa of any nuclear related items. In 1983 an unlikely report appeared in the South African press that a Cape Town firm had acted as intermediary for shipping a U.S. computer via Cape Town (and Sweden?) to the USSR!

Safeguards Required by South Africa for Export Purposes

On 31 January 1987, the South African Atomic Energy Corporation (SAAEC) released a statement that it had assured the U.S. government that it would conduct and administer its nuclear affairs in a manner which is in line with the spirit, principles and goals of the Non-Proliferation Treaty and the Nuclear Suppliers Group Guidelines. The statement referred to concern that South Africa's progress in uranium enrichment had led to allegations that South Africa might become a supplier of nuclear technology, materials and equipment outside the NonProliferation Treaty regime.

This assurance, it was explained, would mean in practice that South Africa would require IAEA or IAEA-Euratom safeguards on any exports of uranium to non–nuclear-weapons states (NNWS) and would require such safeguards if it made available "sensitive technology" to any other country. It would also require such safeguards on sales of enriched uranium or of nuclear equipment, though (presumably) only in the case of exports to NNWS. This differentiation is not clear from the text of the statement.

Acceptance of the Nuclear Suppliers' Guidelines also means that South Africa has thereby engaged itself to "exercise restraint" in the export of sensitive material or sensitive technology, such as highly-enriched uranium and enrichment technology. What the guidelines mean by "restraint" has not been defined.

It is implicit in the statement that South Africa will *not* insist on full-scope safeguards in the importing country nor will it require safeguards on exports to nuclear weapons states (NWS) except, possibly, safeguards on exports of "sensitive" technology. On both these points South Africa's policy is thus less stringent than those of the United States, Australia, and Canada, though probably similar to the policies of Niger and Gabon, which export chiefly to France. This somewhat less stringent policy may give South African exports of uranium a political and commercial advantage in sales to NWS and to non-NPT NNWS. In the past, as noted, the United Kingdom has been a major customer, and France is still a significant one. Whether in the long term this "safeguards advantage" would outweigh the political costs of buying heavily from South Africa remains to be seen. The only non-NPT client of South Africa seems to have been Israel, and that was in the late 1950s or early 1960s (assuming that Taiwan may be regarded as party to the NPT).

Revenues from South Africa's Nuclear Exports

Given official secrecy, one can make only rough estimates about the value of South African nuclear exports. The following estimates include exports from Namibia (except where otherwise indicated), but cover only exports of uranium (yellowcake) and not of other nuclear materials or plant, which would amount to a very small proportion of total nuclear exports.

According to the reports of IAEA/NEA, the total uranium production of South Africa and Namibia varied between 8,637 tons per year and 10,188 tons per year in the period 1979 to 1983.[7] Various reports in *Nuclear Fuel* indicate that South Africa's unexported stockpile was growing at the rate of about 1,000 tons per year during that period (it amounted to 6,000 to 7,000 tons in 1983).[8] The price paid by Japan for shipments to be made in 1987 was between $30.50 and $32 per pound.[9] Assuming an average price of $30 per pound for long-terms contracts, and that exports were about 8,000 tons per year, the total revenue earned from sales abroad would be of the order of $480 million per year.

The total value of South African exports in 1985 was $16,400 million.[10] Uranium would then have represented about 2.4 to 3 percent of the total value of South African and Namibian exports. Interestingly, this is about the same amount as a recent estimate of the direct costs to South Africa of the anti-apartheid sanctions imposed by the U.S. Congress.[11]

However long-term prices of uranium have since fallen as low as $22–$25 per pound (spot prices as low as $12.50 per pound). Moreover, in October 1988 the head of NUFCOR forecast that, partly as a result of sanctions, there would be a dramatic drop in South African uranium production—to about 82 million pounds or about 4,000 tons per year over the next ten years. These two factors would imply that annual revenue from uranium sales would drop as low as $200 million per year. Assuming that aggregate South African exports remain near the 1985 level, uranium would then account for as little as 1.2 percent of the total. Namibian independence seems a prospect in 1989, and Namibian production will then no longer be accounted for as part of the South African total.[12]

Since the U.S. imposed its embargo in 1986, several other leading customers have reduced their dependence on South African's uranium. The Japanese government has directed Japanese utilities not to renew any contracts with South Africa and Namibia when the existing contracts expire. Taiwan is actively seeking to diversify its sources of supply.[13] In Western Europe, Spain is apparently following the Japanese lead. Britain ceased imports from Southern Africa some years ago. Only West Germany and, to a lesser extent, France remain important customers.

South Africa's political isolation has thus tangibly reinforced the impact of market forces. And, as the ring closes, what is left becomes increasingly uncertain. Namibia's independence may make it respectable to buy its uranium again, rather than that of South Africa. The advent of a Social-Democratic government in West Germany might imply the loss of the last major customer.

However, South Africa may be able to retain or even recover some of its markets if it accedes to the NPT. This question will be examined under the section on "Changes in South Africa's Export Practices."

Sales and Approaches That South Africa Has Declined

In the early postwar years, South Africa, bound by its commitments to the U.S.-U.K.-Canada Joint Development Agency, turned down a request by France for the sale of uranium. In 1977, South Africa reportedly turned down a request by Pakistan, but it is difficult to believe that Pakistan would have defied Third World opinion by making such a purchase when it could get yellowcake with little difficulty from Niger, and had already once done so.[14] Reports of unrequited approaches by Iran and Romania have already been mentioned.

Instances of Illegal Activities

No explicitly illegal activities—in the sense of breach of obligations under a treaty or international agreement—have come to light. The sale of 10 tons of yellowcake to Israel in the early 1960s may have helped Israel toward the bomb, but it was in no way illegal at the time. The U.S. technicians and engineers who, it has been reported, are or were working at the Koeberg power plant, may have been breaking U.S. laws, but they do not, of course, apply in South Africa.[15]

Assessment of South Africa's Nuclear Export Policy

With the exception of the sale to Israel, South Africa's nuclear export policy has been prudent. Since that sale it appears that all exports to NNWS have been made under IAEA or IAEA-Euratom safeguards. All of South Africa's NNWS customers since the mid-1960s have become parties to the NPT. So far, South Africa has not exported its enrichment technology, but this may be due to the absence of customers rather than restraints.

Changes in South Africa's Export Practices

On the whole, South Africa has followed the lead of its main Western European clients, and, like them, it has become more restrictive and stringent with the passage of time. In the late 1950s, and until the London

Nuclear Suppliers Group (NSG) was formed, South Africa usually took part in the informal meetings of supplier nations in London and Vienna. With the exception already noted, there is no record of any unsafeguarded South African export to a NNWS.

South Africa had little to lose by formally declaring in January 1984 that it would adhere to the NSG guidelines. It may have hoped that this would help to ensure the goodwill of its main customers, all of which, except Taiwan, had accepted the guidelines. The declaration also helped South Africa to resolve a problem in its relations with the U.S. Department of Energy, which was charging the South African Electricity Supply Commission (ESCOM) for the enrichment of fuel for the KOEBERG reactors despite the fact that the U.S. Nuclear Non-Proliferation Act of 1978 made it impossible to grant an export license for the fuel.[16]

The declaration nevertheless represented a formal (though unilateral) international undertaking to apply the guidelines and the requirements of Article III-2 of the NPT and was in this sense a tightening up of export policy. The extent to which it was due to U.S. pressure—or, at least, to a desire to give assurances to the United States—as well as to keep in step with South Africa's main trading partners in Western Europe is clearly reflected in the language of the declaration.

Pressure to deprive South Africa of its rights and privileges as a member of the IAEA came to a head at the meetings of the IAEA's Board of Governors in mid-1977. Coupled with Western pressure, it probably led to President P.W. Botha's statement on 21 September 1977 that he hoped that South Africa would "soon be able to sign the NPT." This pronouncement was sufficient to enable the three NPT depositary governments—the United States, the Soviet Union, and the United Kingdom—to deflect a motion for South Africa's suspension that had already been tabled at the September 1987 IAEA General Conference.

In August 1988, a delegation that included the South African ministers for foreign affairs and mineral and energy resources went to Vienna to discuss the questions of NPT accession with the representatives of the United States, the Soviet Union, and United Kingdom, and subsequently with representatives of twenty-two other governments. On 16 September, in a letter to IAEA Director General Blix, South Africa affirmed its "objective and desire" to joint the NPT if certain concerns were met. The main specific concern put forward was whether, in the event of accession, South Africa would have "the ability to market its [uranium] commercially like all other producers, subject only to Agency or equivalent safeguards." Subsequently, on 21 September the three depositary governments issued a statement that they were "resolved to press South Africa further to accede to the NPT," noting that the issue "remains under consideration in Pretoria."[17]

This was sufficient to gain a further year's stay of execution at the 1988 General Conference.

At the time of this writing (June 1989), there is no clear indication of what action the South African government will eventually take. If it fails to accede, or at least to make an unambiguous move toward accession, before September 1989, it is possible that the General Conference will proceed with South Africa's suspension—in effect, expel South Africa from the IAEA but another year's stay of execution is also possible if the September 1989 elections put a relatively "moderate" president in office in South Africa.

What would the effect of expulsion be on South Africa's nuclear export policies (and on the agreements under which the IAEA now applies safeguards on all reactors in South Africa)? There can be no certainty, but the commercial interests at stake are probably too important to be put at risk by any rash action, particularly by a reaction that would antagonize South Africa's remaining customers and put them under pressure to embargo imports from South Africa. Renouncing the NSG guidelines or denouncing the safeguards agreements would be such a rash action. Moreover, South Africa has little incentive to engage in small under-the-counter deals that might jeopardize its Western European market or to seek customers in the restricted, perhaps nonexistent, markets outside its traditional clients. It seems likely, therefore, that even in the worst case Pretoria would wish to abide by the guidelines and safeguards agreements.

However, there are other dangers for South Africa if it fails to ratify the NPT and is therefore deprived of its rights in the IAEA. It will then run the risk of becoming a nuclear outcast: out of the IAEA; out of the NPT for good, since its "defenders," having had their hopes falsely raised, would probably abandon any further effort to persuade Pretoria to ratify; out of the international nuclear community. Under these circumstances, the doubts that already exist about South Africa as a dependable long-term supplier of uranium might become even stronger, and South Africa's remaining customers might turn to other sources.[18] Moreover, it might become difficult for conservative Western leaders like Prime Minister Thatcher and Chancellor Kohl to resist such pressure as may arise to ban all uranium imports from a nuclear outcast. Certain gold mines, moreover, might become less profitable without their uranium by-product. The loss of the uranium market might thus have a serious knock-on effect. Finally, South Africa's failure to ratify the NPT under these circumstances would be seen by many as confirmation of their suspicions that South Africa has a secret nuclear arsenal.

The nonproliferation regime would also be the loser. Denied legitimate markets abroad, what was left of South African nuclear exports might well go underground; there would be little to lose.

Structure of South Africa's Nuclear Program

Export Licensing

Authority over the entire nuclear program of South Africa is largely concentrated in the Atomic Energy Corporation of South Africa. However, "the right to prospect and mine for source material does not vest in the state."[19]

NUFCOR negotiates long-term contracts on behalf of the mining houses. Usually the head of NUFCOR negotiates directly with the purchasing utility or, occasionally, the purchasing governmental organization. It is left to the mining company to meet its contractual obligations with the individual utility abroad.

The procedure for obtaining official sanction for the export is as follows.

1. After negotiation with the purchasing utility, NUFCOR (headquarters in Johannesburg) applies to the SAAEC (in Pretoria) for an export permit. The application must indicate: the amount of material to be exported; the expected timetable (schedule) of exports; the price to be paid by the utility; and the safeguards that will be applied in the importing country.

2. On behalf of the Minister for Mineral Energy and Resources the SAAEC approves/disapproves the export. In the event of approval (the normal case), NUFCOR may proceed with the contractual arrangement but must apply for an individual export license at the time of shipment (or times of shipments).

3. Each year NUFCOR submits a consolidated application to the Department of Customs and Excise, again specifying for the following year the amounts of material to be exported, the destinations, timing, price, and the safeguards to be applied.

4. If the export license is granted, the Department of Customs and Excise issues a stamp of approval when the actual shipment takes place. The export permits are subsequently returned to the SAAEC for its records.

5. The only problems that have arisen in recent years have been with Romania (in obtaining clarification about the safeguards to be applied in that country) and with Iran. As a result, although the first shipment to Romania under the 2,000-ton order was ready for dispatch, NUFCOR decided to withdraw from the deal. When Romania renewed inquiries, NUFCOR referred the inquiry to the Canadian marketing agency, inviting the latter "to be my guest." In the Iranian case, the shipment was ready for loading at Durban but was cancelled, chiefly out of concern that it would further exacerbate relations with the United States if South Africa shipped uranium to Iran at that time.[20]

It may be noted that the SAAEC includes representatives of the Ministry of Foreign Affairs as well as the Ministry for Mineral and Energy Resources—that is, it has political as well as commercial and technical inputs.

This description of marketing procedures is in line with the broad outline given in the 1980 United Nations report, "South Africa's Plan and Capability in the Nuclear Field" (see footnote 6), viz:

> All uranium mined in South Africa itself is processed into U_3O_8, or yellowcake, and then marketed by the Nuclear Fuels Corporation of South Africa. The Corporation is a private service company owned by those gold mining companies which produce uranium and by a set of seven major mining-finance companies. Uranium from processing in Namibia is marketed through the British-based transnational Rio Tinto Zinc Corporation.

As noted, Rio Tinto Zinc also owns the Palabora copper mine in South Africa and markets the copper produced as a by-product.

It is not clear which entity would market enriched uranium or enrichment technology if and when South Africa has surplus SWUs (enrichment capacity) for sale. UCOR owns both the technology and the SWUs and, unlike NUFCOR, is state-owned. However, NUFCOR is a well-developed and experienced marketing organization. There has also been talk of "privatizing" UCOR.

The Weight of Different Actors

As indicated, individual decisions to sell uranium are commercial, taken by the mining and finance companies on the basis of negotiations conducted by NUFCOR and subject to final approval by the SAAEC and vetted by the Department of Customs and Excise. In normal circumstances, the approval of the SAAEC would be automatic; noncommercial considerations would only enter into exceptional, "exotic" cases, such as those already mentioned concerning Iran and Romania.

Safeguards are a different matter. The chief actors are the SAAEC—normally the head of the SAAEC, currently Wynand de Villiers, acting also on behalf of the Minister for Mineral and Energy Resources—and the Ministry for Foreign Affairs. Safeguards negotiations with the IAEA involve both the SAAEC and foreign affairs. The Minister for Mineral and Energy Resources has been personally involved in certain recent discussions, including those in Vienna in August 1988. On quasitechnical issues, such as the acceptance of IAEA safeguards on the sensitive semicommercial enrichment plant, the SAAEC and the Minister for Mineral and Energy Resources would probably have the final word.[21]

On major issues, such as acceptance of the NPT, it is obvious that the state president would make the final decision, probably in the framework of the State Security Council—a powerful statutory committee on which key ministries, such as Defense, foreign affairs, and finance, and the civil service heads of key departments are represented. The former state president, P.W. Botha, "graduated" from the Ministry of Defense, and his successor in the post of Minister, Magnus Malan, is regarded as one of the most powerful members of the State Security Council. It is understood that the members of the cabinet responsible for foreign affairs and for economic matters would need little persuasion to accept the NPT, but that opposition would come from defense (and perhaps, for somewhat personal reasons, from the head of the SAAEC).[22] In other words, the cabinet and its advisers are divided.

With respect to the private sector, it is clear that the only actors of importance are the mining and finance companies and their agents. The major financing companies include Anglo-American, Anglo Vaal, Charter Consolidated, Consolidated Goldfields, Federale Mynbou, General Corporation (Gencor), Goldfields of South Africa, Johannesburg Consolidated, Rand Mines, and Rio Tinto. In almost every case the principal South African interest of the multinational corporation concerned, such as Anglo-American, is in gold mining (or copper, as in the case of Rio Tinto).

The political parties, parliament, the unions, and the media play virtually no role in decisions about nuclear exports or export policy.

The Norms

Declaratory Policies

South Africa's declaratory policy regarding nuclear exports was described previously in the section on "Safeguards Required by South Africa for Export Purposes." Long before its declaration of 31 January 1984, South Africa had stated that it would not allow its uranium sales to be a means for increasing the number of nuclear weapons states.[23]

From the beginning, South Africa's attitude toward the NPT has been ambivalent, perhaps because of conflicting counsels in the administration. Unlike India, Argentina, or Brazil, South Africa has no objection in principle to the NPT. In 1968 it voted for the resolution of the UN General Assembly that "commended" the treaty. The South African representative took an active part in the discussions at the IAEA on the standard NPT safeguards agreement. Unlike India, Pakistan, or Israel, South Africa has virtually no military incentive to construct a nuclear arsenal. The threat to white rule comes from within, not from beyond the border.

In 1977, the willingness of the U.S. administration to make a "significant concession," chiefly in the form of a commitment to supply fuel for the KOEBERG power reactors and the SAFARI research reactor, nearly brought South Africa into the NPT. South Africa backed away from the incipient agreement when its legal advisors came to the conclusion that the U.S. Congress would not permit the administration to carry out its part of the bargain.

In 1985 the Ministry of Foreign Affairs again reviewed the situation. In 1986, during negotiations with the IAEA, it was indicated that the conclusion of a safeguards agreement covering the new semicommercial enrichment plant would be seen in Pretoria "as a first step [*sic*]" in its consideration of acceding to the NPT. The negotiation of that safeguards agreement was suspended after Pretoria put forward two proposals that the IAEA could not accept.

These uncertain movements have now been overtaken by the events of 1987 and 1988.

How Far Are Prevailing Views Shared?

The smaller of the two opposition parties, the Progressive Federal Party,[24] regularly raises the question in Parliament of why South Africa has not ratified the NPT, and it regularly receives the bland reply that the matter is "under consideration." Apart from such gentle pressure, until recently there was no criticism of the government's policy on the NPT and virtually no discussion of it in the media. However, the possibility that South Africa might be expelled from the IAEA, President Botha's September 1987 statement about joining the NPT, and subsequent events have finally drawn some media attention to the issue. The English-language media, most of which express opposition views, welcomed the positive parts of the president's statement and urged him to go ahead and ratify the NPT as soon as possible. The only Afrikaans-language newspaper that I have seen welcomed the reservations that it read into the president's statement.

What Explains the Prevailing Views?

Clearly, the situation is at present in flux and the outcome is uncertain. Until recently the South African government saw little advantage in joining the NPT and thought that its ambiguous stance might be a useful factor in its relations with Washington. Obviously South Africa was technically capable of carrying out a nuclear test; if it did so African states might begin to desert the NPT and cause it to start unravelling at a particularly awkward time. South Africa's nuclear capability, unfettered by a treaty prohibition, might thus be seen as a hedge against a U.S. (or British or French) decision to abandon the country to mandatory UN Security Council sanctions. But now the costs of rejecting the NPT are becoming obvious, and Pretoria may perceive that its interests lie in ratifying it.

Government and Public Attitudes and Their Changes with Time

There is little public discussion of any nuclear issues—whether nuclear power, nuclear proliferation, or, until President Botha's 1987 announcement, whether South Africa should ratify the NPT. Among academic circles in Cape Town there has been some sporadic and ineffectual concern about the safety of the KOEBERG nuclear power plant, visible on a fine day across Table Bay, but all the political parties declare that they support nuclear power. The erosion since 1977 of South Africa's position in the IAEA has been reported in the media, as were the decisions by the United States to cut off nuclear fuel supplies and, in 1986, to embargo uranium imports from South Africa. These were all seen as part of the international campaign against South Africa, or at least against its present system and, accordingly, were either deplored or welcomed. But other matters stand much higher on the national agenda.

Until recently the Electricity Supply Commission planned to build a second nuclear power plant on the coast of the Western Cape. The demand for power has, however, grown more slowly than ESCOM expected, and it is unlikely that South Africa will be in the market for a new plant during this decade.[25]

The government is obviously aware of the fact that it will be unable to import additional nuclear plants unless it ratifies the NPT.[26] However, while nuclear power might offer the better economic solution for generating electricity in the Cape, which is about 1,500 kilometers or more distant from South Africa's coal fields, the country's coal reserves are very large (about 10 percent of the world's reserves, or fourth largest) and cheaply mined. However, South Africa may find it difficult to maintain its present substantial coal exports. Moreover, if stability returns in Mozambique, South Africa will again be able to draw on 2,000 MW from the Cahora Bossa dam on the Zambia River, or 4,000 MW if extra turbines are installed. In a recent and unexpected about-face, the South African government has restored its relations with the government of Mozambique and is helping the latter defend the Cahora Bossa dam and its high-tension power line to the Transvaal.

In the 1950s and early 1960s, uranium production and processing were seen as a source of export revenues and of fuel for power generation. In the 1970s, the construction of the pilot enrichment plant at Valindaba opened the way to nuclear weapons, if the government chose to take it. As South

Africa's isolation increased and as its frontiers seemed to become insecure with the collapse of the Portuguese empire, the arrival of Cubans in Angola, its own abortive strike into that country, and the collapse of "White Rhodesia," the weapon option may have become interesting. In 1977, Soviet satellites spotted and U.S. satellites confirmed apparent preparations for a nuclear test in the Kalahari desert. South African politicians and senior military staff were given to making bellicose but ambiguous references to the country's ability to defend itself by nuclear means, if need be.

Since then, such statements have become less frequent, although in August 1988 Foreign Minister "Pik" Botha again referred to South Africa's ability to make the bomb, and de Villiers, the head of the SAAEC, added that "whether we are going to manufacture nuclear warheads is another matter. This is still to be decided.")[27] There are, in fact, no clear indications that a nuclear arsenal is in the making.[28] Since 1985, violent unrest in black townships has again underlined the fact that nuclear weapons are irrelevant to the forces that challenge the regime. The restoration of amicable relations with Mozambique and the Anglo-Namibia settlements, provided they endure, should make it even less plausible to argue that South Africa is under any military threat from beyond its frontiers. If there is a threat, it emanates outward from South Africa and not from its neighbors.

But in a situation as exposed as South Africa's there will continue to be voices in the establishment that favor keeping open the nuclear option. They might refer to South Africa's demonstrated inability to impose a military solution on Angola, to the toll that the Angolan campaign took on South Africa's still largely irreplaceable aircraft, and to the imminent "loss" of Namibia to argue that South Africa's military vulnerability is growing, and that now is no time to renounce nuclear weapons.

Leaving aside any speculative military use, South Africa's uranium resources are today of some value as a minor source of electric power, and of diminishing economic and political importance in a world where uranium is in surplus and where South Africa's share of the market is shrinking.

Capabilities

Present and Planned Ability of South Africa to Export Nuclear-Related Items

South Africa produces or is capable of producing the following nuclear-related items that appear on the Emerging Nuclear Suppliers Database list (* denotes a significant producer; ** denotes a major producer):

Natural uranium★★

Enriched uranium★

Zirconium★ (15 percent of WOCA output)

1015 Hafnium (Free of zirconium for cladding

1018 Research Reactors (?))

1036 Uranium Enrichment★ (Aerodynamic–stationary walled centrifuge)

1047 Special purpose high explosives

Miscellaneous (UF_6)

South Africa probably also has the capability to produce several reactor components and electronic components on the database list. However, the production of reactor components and other fuel cycle plants and equipment would be for domestic use in most cases, often "one-off" single items to substitute for those no longer obtainable from abroad. Enrichment cascades would, presumably, be an exception, being produced in relatively large numbers. For practical purposes, one need only regard South Africa today as an actual but declining exporter of natural uranium, enriched uranium, zirconium, and "Helikon" enrichment technology.

If the semicommercial 300,000 SWUs per year enrichment plant is now in operation, South Africa will soon be able to export one-third of its output, either in the form of enriched South African uranium or toll enrichment of another country's uranium. The plant finally started operation in 1988. The head of the SAAEC, Wynand de Villiers, indicated that the SWUs would be available from 1988 but there may have been some slippage since then.[29] De Villiers also said that some of the surplus SWUs would be available in the form of UF_6.

Efforts to Expand Exports

In 1986, the official international forecast was that primary exploration for uranium would probably "remain in a depressed state at least until the early part of the next decade," but that the high level of gold exploration in the Witwtersrand Basin "will continue to add to South Africa's uranium resources."[30]

There are no known plans further to expand South African enrichment capacity. The U.S. decision not to enrich South African uranium either for its own utilities or for reexport might serve as a stimulus to expand South Africa's capacity, but this seems unlikely. There is surplus capacity in

Western Europe, and Eurodif or Urenco would probably be happy to take over from the United States.[31]

South Africa's decision to build its first two nuclear power reactors was not in any way related to its much earlier decision to mine and export uranium. However, Pretoria's decision in 1977 to build a semicommercial enrichment plant was probably prompted by Washington's decision to cancel the fuel supply contracts for the KOEBERG nuclear power plant and by the difficulties that South Africa encountered in finding a replacement for those contracts. Indirectly, therefore, the decision to cut off nuclear fuel supplies to South Africa may lead to a situation in which South Africa itself will enter the enriched uranium market on a limited scale.

South Africa as a Nuclear Importer

In the early postwar years, some of the machinery for producing yellowcake was imported, but it is probable that South Africa is self-sufficient in this regard today. In the 1960s and early 1970s, there were numerous reports about the role that the West Germany firm, STEAG, and several other German institutions and laboratories had played in helping South Africa to turn the "Helikon" enrichment concept into an engineering reality at the Valindaba pilot plant.[32] It was also reported that South Africa received help for this project from Britain (a UF_6 production plant, or at least its major components), the United States, France, and Belgium. However, it was also reported in the late 1970s that South Africa sought but failed to obtain very large compressors and computational facilities from abroad, and particularly from the United States, and that its failure was a major factor in the decision to abandon plans for a large enrichment plant that would have been able to enrich all of South Africa's uranium exports.[33]

One may speculate that South Africa has obtained from abroad at least some components for the plants that fabricate fuel for the SAFARI research reactor and that it will do so for the KOEBERG reactors. These would, however, consist largely of high-precision but not specifically nuclear metal-working machinery. If, against expectations, South Africa were to try to expand its own enrichment capacity, it would probably have to turn abroad for some of the main machinery needed, such as large computational facilities and large corrosion-resistant compressors. At this stage, however, this is no more than speculation; there is no evidence in the technical press.

In the past there have been reports that South Africa purchased enriched uranium or other nuclear technology from China,[34] that it was about to buy a heavy water production plant from Switzerland,[35] and that it "bid against" Iraq for the purchase of 12 kilograms of plutonium in an auction in a hangar at Khartoum airport.[36] The first two reports were denied by the governments concerned, and the third appears to have been the product of somewhat gullible reporting by two technically innocent BBC reporters. While South Africa would have use for substantial quantities of low-enriched uranium for the KOEBERG plant, the story of how it obtained the first loadings for KOEBERG is well known and documented in considerable detail.[37] It also seems unlikely that China would knowingly run the political risk of supplying South Africa with a strategic commodity (conceivably supplies could have been arranged through an intermediary without China being aware of their final destination). A Swiss (or any other) heavy water production plant would have no place in the South African fuel cycle.

There has been no indication of South African interest in acquiring reprocessing technology at this time. The agreement with France for the supply of the two KOEBERG reactors stipulates that the spent fuel from the reactors will not be reprocessed in South Africa and that plutonium recovered from the spent fuel will not be stored in South Africa. At present the only other possible source of spent fuel (for reprocessing) would be the SAFARI research reactor, but it is understood that, at least while the reactor is using fuel enriched in the United States, the spent fuel of South African originals, which replaced the original American supplies, will remain under IAEA safeguards whatever its destination.

Conclusion

The uncertainties that cloud South Africa's prospects also envelop all aspects of its nuclear future: whether it will accede to the NPT; or whether it will advance further along the path to nuclear weapons; whether it can retain the market for its nuclear exports; and whether it will eventually be able to expand its nuclear power capacity and thus again become an importer of nuclear technology. The answer to the latter three questions depends considerably on the decision that the government of South Africa makes about the first.

Notes

1. All Namibian output comes from the Roessing mine. Rio Tinto also operates a large mine, the Palabora, in the Transvaal (South Africa), which produces uranium as a by-product of its main output, copper. This uranium, too, is marketed by Rio Tinto and not by NUFCOR.

2. There are conflicting reports about South Africa's own nuclear power

290 · International Nuclear Trade and Nonproliferation

plans. Until fairly recently the South African Electricity Supply Commission (ES-COM) had tentative plans for building a second nuclear power plant (with a third power reactor) somewhere along the coast of the Cape Province (the first nuclear power plant is located at Koeberg, on the coast near Cape Town), and there were reports in 1986 and early 1987 that the South Africans had made informal approaches to French and Germany reactor manufacturers. It appears, however, that the growth in demand for electricity is a good deal lower than was earlier estimated and that plans for a third power reactor have been postponed. In any case, no country will agree to supply South Africa with another nuclear power plant unless it accepts the NPT (and there is no assurance at present that South African adhesion to the NPT would open the way to such a purchase). South Africa has other energy options: it has the fourth-largest coal reserves in the world.

3. It is understood that the U.S. administration has interpreted the ban as applying to all South African uranium concentrates (U_3O_8) that are sent to the United States, but not to uranium hexaflouride (UF_6, the gas that is used as the feedstock for enrichment). Presumably the logic for this differentiation is that concentrates are sent direct from South Africa to the United States and are identifiably South African, while UF_6, possibly containing uranium from a variety of sources, is processed in Europe or the Far East and then sent to the United States for enrichment.

4. The sale of the 10 tons of yellowcake to Israel was reported to the IAEA, but the shipment was not placed under IAEA safeguards. The proposed export to Iran—which would have been under safeguards because Iran is a party to the NPT—was likewise reported to the IAEA in 1984, but Pretoria later informed the IAEA that the shipment had been cancelled because the Gulf had become unsafe for shipping. In 1987 the Iranians again pressed NUFCOR to dispatch the shipment; NUFCOR demurred.

5. Discussion with the General Manager of NUFCOR in October 1977.

6. United Nations document A/35/402 of 9 September 1980.

7. Namibian exports are still de facto controlled by South Africa. Presumably the South African declaration of 31 December 1984 about the safeguards it will require on its own exports will also apply to Namibian exports until Namibia gains its independence.

8. *Nuclear Fuel*, 19 December 1983.

9. *Nuclear Fuel*, 21 April 1986.

10. Barclays Bank *ABECOR* report, November 1986.

11. "For South Africa a Golden Cushion," *International Herald Tribune*, 4 November 1987. The cost to South Africa of U.S. sanctions was estimated at 2 to 3 percent of its exports of about $15 billion.

12. *Nuclear Fuel*, 17 October 1988, 28 November 1988.

13. *Nuclear Fuel*, 12 January 1987 reported that Taipower was looking to Australia and Canada to replace South Africa, despite the fact that South Africa "recognizes" the Republic of China and Australia and Canada do not. From personal knowledge, I can confirm that Australian producers are in contact with Taiwan. *Nuclear Fuel*, 10 February 1986 reported that Taipower had already made a deal with COGEMA (France) so as not "to depend so heavily on South Africa."

14. Steve Weissman and Herbert Krosney, *The Islamic Bomb* (New York, 1981) p. 186.

15. "Waxom Comments on US Workers at Nuclear Plant," *Worldwide Report* JPRS-TND-85-004, 26 February 1985.

16. *Nuclear Fuel*, 18 July 1983, 27 February 1984.

17. *Nuclear Fuel*, 3 October 1988.

18. In January 1987, the head of NUKEM in West Germany had already declared that West German nuclear power plants would be little affected by a total embargo on South African uranium.

19. See the official summary of South Africa's Nuclear Energy Act of 16 June 1982.

20. The information on procedures is based on notes made after discussions at NUFCOR in October 1987. The description of the procedures to be followed in seeking export permits and licenses may not be accurate in every detail but the general description is correct. NUFCOR handles only the export of uranium and not of other listed materials. I was unable to obtain information about the procedures followed when zirconium is exported, but suppose that they follow the same pattern. Some echo of the aborted Iranian transaction may be found in an extraordinary report in the London *Observer*, 17 May 1987, which reported that "Namibia uranium may fuel Iran's A-bomb." The news report is exceptionally full of errors.

21. The export policy declaration of 31 January 1984, declaring South Africa's acceptance of the NSG guidelines, was issued by the SAAEC in the form of a press release by its chairperson, but its explicit purpose—to set at rest the fears of the United States—implied an act of foreign policy. The declaration bears the marks of an interdepartmental hybrid.

22. Dr. de Villier's experiences with the IAEA have not always been fortunate. When, for the first time, he led a South African delegation to the IAEA's General Conference (New Delhi, 1979) the delegation's credentials were (illegally) rejected and the delegation was expelled. Dr. de Villier's efforts to negotiate a safeguards agreement for the semicommercial enrichment plan and to have Dr. Blix visit South Africa for that purpose were not successful.

23. George Quester, *The Politics of Nuclear Proliferation* (Baltimore: The Johns Hopkins University Press, 1973), p. 200; cited in UN Document A/35/402.

24. Until the elections in 1987, the Progressive Federal Party was the official opposition in Parliament. As a result of those elections it was displaced by the Conservative Party, a right-wing group that had broken away from the governing National Party several years before hand, fearing that the latter's policies would lead to the end of white rule. The views of the Conservative Party about the NPT are not known but one may surmise that they are negative. The Conservative Party is likely to gain many further seats in the September 1989 elections.

25. See note 2.

26. All countries manufacturing nuclear power plants today are bound by the NSG guidelines to insist, at a minimum, that the plant they export is placed under IAEA safeguards. But the IAEA Board of Governors would not, at present, approve a safeguards agreement with South Africa that applied only to a nuclear power plant; the board would insist on fullscope safeguards, i.e., the NPT.

27. The South Africa (Afrikaans) newspaper) "Die Beeld" quoted in "Focus on South Africa" an official monthly newsletter of the South African Department of Foreign Affairs, September 1988.

28. Except for the "double flash" over the South Atlantic apparently observed in 1979 by a U.S. Vela satellite.

29. *Nuclear Engineering International* (April 1986).

30. *Uranium Resources, Production and Demand,* (IAEA: 1986). Published by IAEA and NEA of OECD. This is a biennial survey compiled on the basis of official national reports.

31. Such, at least, was the opinion in summer 1987, of a senior official at the London Uranium Institute.

32. Leonard Spector *Nuclear Proliferation Today: The Spread of Nuclear Weapons 1984* (New York, October 1984) 1984, pp. 284–87. Spector lists the countries and the companies that supplied components and facilities for the unsafeguarded Valindaba pilot plant. He points out, however, that these supplies were delivered before the NSG guidelines existed and, in many cases, before the NPT came into force. Many of the items could not be supplied today unless the plant for which they were destined was under IAEA safeguards. The main supply made after the NPT came into force was, in Spector's words, that of "the most powerful industrial-process computers available," manufactured by the U.S. Foxboro Corp. and licensed for export in 1973. Spector's 1985 and 1986 annual surveys of proliferation also list, in the footnotes to their chapter on South Africa, the names of the presumed suppliers to the Valindaba plant.

33. Informal discussions in the late 1970s with the late Ampie Roux, former head of the South African Atomic Energy Board. This seems to be somewhat at odds with Leonard Spector's statement about the computers supplied by the Foxboro Corp. (note 32).

34. See, for example, *The Financial Times,* 25 November 1985, carrying the Chinese foreign ministry's denial of Senator Cranston's charges that the PRC had assisted South Africa in the development of nuclear weapons.

35. See, for example, *Nucleonics Week,* 30 July 1984. The South African denial was reported in the East London *Daily Dispatch,* 27 July 1984.

36. Tim Cornwell, "Plutonium for Sale: The Buyers and Sellers in the World's Deadliest Market", *The Listener* (London), 5 November 1987, pp. 4–5.

37. Most of the 100 tons of fuel had originally been bought by the Swiss utility, which wished to build a nuclear power plant at Kaiseraugst near Basel. Because of environmentalist opposition the start of construction had been delayed for several years (in fact, the project is probably defunct). The utility therefore decided to sell the fuel and put it in storage at Eurodif in France. It was bought and resold to ESCOM in South Africa, apparently at a premium price. The remainder of the 100 tons was similarly obtained from Belgium through another U.S. broker—"SWUCO," of Rockville, Maryland. According to one of the South African papers that carried the story (the *Star* of Johannesburg, 14 April 1982), this was the uranium that had previously been alleged to have come from China.

14
South Korea

Peter Hayes

South Korea aspires to become a major nuclear supplier in the world nuclear market. There is no doubt that South Korea has great potential to fulfill these aspirations. South Korea is well positioned in terms of competitiveness, market relationships, institutional capability, ability to deliver, and commitment to nonproliferation values. As a mercantilist state, South Korea hopes to capitalize on its close relationships with transnational nuclear corporations in this endeavor. It hopes to participate in two- or three-way joint ventures—especially with the American firms that have traditionally predominated in the South Korean domestic nuclear business—to market their nuclear wares abroad.

South Koreans view themselves as a bridge for American nuclear vendors between the West and Asia, most notably to China. In the event that the Chinese market draws on its domestic nuclear industry rather than on external nuclear suppliers, South Korea hopes to penetrate nuclear markets in the advanced countries. Many South Korean nuclear proponents view the revival of these markets as inevitable in light of the ineluctable demise of world oil supplies.

Other South Koreans, particularly those outside the nuclear bureaucracy, are skeptical of the feasibility of this strategy. For them today, nuclear exports look like a mirage on an ever-receding horizon. These skeptics are also often the strongest elite critics of the pace and size of the domestic nuclear power program. Ironically, the more they prevail in slowing the growth of the domestic nuclear sector, the faster surplus nuclear construction and manufacturing capacity may emerge. At that time, political-economic imperatives may supplement the mercantilist and bureaucratic imperatives that currently underlie the South Korean nuclear export orientation.

This chapter is divided into four parts. The first section describes South Korea's intent to become a nuclear supplier in the 1990s. It delineates the networks of prior transactions and relationships that South Korea may use to penetrate export markets. The second section reviews South Korea's nuclear export potential, particularly its technological acquisitions from the domestic nuclear program. These capabilities will determine the rate at which South Korea can enter specific nuclear markets. The third section describes the institutional framework in South Korea for the review and approval of nuclear exports.

The last section expands on South Korea's commitment to nuclear nonproliferation. It shows that this commitment, though strengthened since the 1970s, is still ambiguous. It concludes that nuclear weapon aspirations still lurk in the subterranean strata of Korean politics.

South Korea's Nuclear Trade Relationships

By 1987, South Korea was building no fewer than ten nuclear power reactors, with two more on order. As a result of South Korea's pragmatic import substitution strategy, this program placed South Korea at the center of a web of contractor relationships (see table 14–1).

Table 14–1
Foreign Nuclear Firms or Agencies Active in South Korea

AUSTRALIA
   Energy Resources of Australia—uranium yellowcake
BELGIUM
   Belgatom—planning and engineering training for KNE
CANADA
   Atomic Energy of Canada—CANDU reactor components, heavy water, natural uranium; attempted transfer of "technology in the reprocessing field" in 1984; proposed joint venture to supply a CANDU to Turkey.

   Canatom—architect–engineer for KNU 3.

   General Electric Co—fuel fabrication services for KNU 3.
EUROPE
   Eurodif—enrichment supplier for 2 Framatome units.

   Cogema—agent for Eurodif supplies; also for fuel fabrication joint venture with Korea and Government of Gabon for uranium exploration.

   Societe Franco-Belge Fabrication de Combustibles—fuel fabrication, assembly for KNU 9 and 10.
FRANCE
   Framatome—LWR reactor components, licensing, fuel supply, training; architect-engineering, turbine-generator for KNU 9 and 10.

   Societe Generale pour les Techniques Nouvelles (and related companies) for pilot HWR/PWR fuel fabrication plant, yellowcake refinery, and pilot CANDU fuel UO_2 conversion plant; post-irradiation examination facility, radwaste treatment pilot plant.
GERMANY
   Kraftwerk Union—design, engineering, manufacture and in-core management of PWR fuel assemblies for KNFC 200 tonne fuel fabrication plant.

   Reaktor-Brennelement Union—supplying technology for KWU fuel fabrication plant.

Table 14–1 continued

Urangesellschaft—exploring for uranium with Daewoo Co in Canada's Northwest Territories.

JAPAN

Mitsubishi Heavy Industries—invited by KEPCO to bid on KNU 11 and 12, reportedly for political reasons. Unknown if tendered bid.

Watch Japanese firms for involvement in nuclear deals between South Korea and China.

UNITED KINGDOM

GBH/NEI, Parsons—turbine-generator supplier for KNU 3.

UNITED STATES

Nutech—engineering and consulting services.

Combustion Engineering—reactor vessels, licence and technical assistance, training, heavy component technology, especially for steam generators.

General Atomics—Triga II (1962) and III (1972) research reactors.

Aerojet General Nucleonics—research reactor (1978)

Seargent and Lundy—subcontractor for architect-engineering for KNU 11 and 12.

Corner and Lada—design of pipe supports and hangars for KNU 5 and 6.

Anschutz Corporation, joint venture with KEPCO and Taiwan Power Co to explore for uranium in Paraguay.

Bechtel International—architect-engineering services, construction (for KNU 5,6,7,8), quality assurance, technology transfer, bid evaluation consultant to KEPCO.

Continental Oil—supplier of yellowcake.

U.S. Steel—supplier of yellowcake.

Ebasco Overseas Corporation-Korea—engineering and construction (for KNU 9 and 10), consulting and financing advice, power plant operations.

General Electric Co—components, technology transfer, turbine-generators, licensing.

Westinghouse Nuclear Korea—NSSS components, technology transfer, site technical support, construction (KNU 1 and 2 only), interface with architect-engineer, joint ventures with Korean firms and licensing, fuel fabrication for first core and early reloads for KNU 1 and 2 (through 1989), for 5 and 6 (through 1988), 7 and 8 (through 1986); turbine-generator for KNU 7 and 8.

Allied Chemical Co—agent for yellowcake and supplier of uranium hexafluoride.

Separate Work Unit Corporation—brokerage of enriched uranium.

U.S. Department of Energy—enrichment contracts.

Kaiser Engineers and Construction Inc—planning and feasibility studies for MOST.

Source: Nuclear Assurance Corporation, *Nuclear Fuel Cycle, Materials, Services, and Sources*, report to U.S. ACDA, September 1983, pp. 173–4; Nuclear Assurance Corporation, *Nuclear Materials and Fuel Cycle Services, Sources, Inventories, and Stockpiles*, report to U.S. ACDA, September 1979, p. 111–239; O. Smith, "Emerging Nuclear Suppliers Research," (mimeo) Anco Engineers Co, Los Angeles, June 15, 1986; *Nuclear Engineering International*, "Korea to Get KWU Fuel Technology," December 1985, p. 4; E.W. Kim *et al*, *The Electric Future of Korea*, Report RM-83-8, Resource Systems Institute, Honolulu, 1983, p. 202 and 212; *Nucleonics Week*, November 14, 1985, p. 7 and December 19, 1985, p. 11; J. Goldblat, *Non-Proliferation: The Why and The Wherefore*, Taylor and Francis, London, 1985, p. 330; Kaiser Engineers and Construction Inc, *Long Range Nuclear Power Program Study*, report to Ministry of Science and Technology, December 1974.

Note: Includes past contracts which may have expired.

These transactions do not only involve suppliers of nuclear equipment and services. They also commit South Korea financially to official and private bankers. By mid-1980, South Korea had acquired about $2.4 billion of direct loans and financial guarantees for nuclear imports.[1] This financial dependence links South Korea's proliferation behavior to its desire to continue receiving external development financing.

South Korean Export Potential

As we shall see, South Korea has not yet fulfilled its nuclear export potential. The scale and rate at which South Korea will become a significant supplier depends on five factors. First, nuclear manufacturing and services capabilities must exceed domestic demand. Second, consumers must perceive the South Korean nuclear industry as an experienced and reliable supplier of nuclear services and equipment. Third, South Korea's nuclear industry must build a solid reputation for manufacturing, building, and operating nuclear plants that are safe and efficient. Fourth, South Korea's nuclear industry must have access to export financing and markets. Finally, its products and services must be competitive—and, of course, a market must exist.

According to these criteria, South Korea will not emerge as a major supplier of services for some time. South Korea is short of experience and skilled nuclear personnel. Its crash program of nuclear construction has stretched thin the available personnel for architect-engineering, construction, and design. Export of manufactured items, however, is another matter. The Changwon industrial complex is vastly underused. Should orders be placed, South Korea would have little difficulty fulfilling them. For big-ticket items, however, South Korea lacks the muscular export financing required to shoulder its way into nuclear markets. South Korea has already established a track record for meeting construction schedules. It remains to be seen whether this achievement has rested on the sacrifice of quality controls that will later afflict operating capacity factors. Of course, it would take only one catastrophic failure like Three Mile Island or Chernobyl to reverse all the gains. South Korea already suffers from a reputation for reckless success in industrial construction. This perceived trait may be a severe liability on the world nuclear market.[2]

At this stage, South Korea has yet to export nuclear equipment or services. The potential for exports is obviously a function of the scale of the domestic nuclear power program. With ten nuclear reactors online or under construction, more than 25,000 people are now engaged in nuclear activities in South Korea.[3] Whether still more reactors will be built depends on decisions yet to be made in South Korea's energy bureaucracy.

The bureaucratic lineup is complex. The Economic Planning Board, the planning bureau of the electric utility KEPCO, and the Korean Oil Company are all known to favor coal over further nuclear plants. The Ministry of Energy and the electricity bureau and senior management of KEPCO are pronuclear.

In 1987, a furious bureaucratic battle between these factions and their allies surfaced in public, a rare treat for the South Korean public. The conservatives launched a campaign to slow growth, principally by criticizing the planning assumptions used by KEPCO in studies published by the Korean Development Institute.[4] Pronuclear advocates immediately fired back a salvo calling for accelerating nuclear growth rates.[5] The fierce struggle was reflected in the restructuring of the Atomic Energy Commission (AEC). Formerly, the AEC had been headed by the chairman of the Ministry of Science and Technology (MOST). The politics of the AEC until then had reflected the tension between the goals of MOST (maximize safety) and the those of Ministry of Energy and Resources (maximize nuclear growth). That chairman was replaced by the deputy prime minister, who is concurrently the chairman of the Economic Planning Board (which maximizes economic rationality).

In a related power play, the status of KEPCO was also reduced in the aftermath of a scuffle between the parastatal Korea Heavy Industries Corporation and the private Hyundai Company for contracts on reactor units 11 and 12. Unlike his predecessor, the new head of KEPCO no longer has intimate ties with the presidential Blue House, making KEPCO more susceptible to the guidance of the Economic Planning Board. KEPCO is also being privatized, further diluting its political power.[6]

In spite of these machinations and maneuvers, however, major policy decisions appear to be made at the highest level and probably reflect political and security considerations more than technocratic advice or bureaucratic warfare. But to date, South Korea has spared no effort in acquiring its own nuclear fuel cycle while maximally substituting for nuclear imports for reactors.

The South Korean approach contrasts with that of emerging suppliers such as India or Argentina. Instead of seeking autarky, South Korea has proceeded by acquiring patent licenses and technical assistance agreements from established nuclear vendors as the most practical path to a commercial nuclear industry. As long ago as 1981, American reactor vendors scrambled to offer their fabrication capabilities for boiling-water reactor (BWR) and pressurized-water reactor (PWR) components, breeder reactor components, and turbine and fossil fuel plant components.[7]

South Korea first used local labor for nonspecialized tasks such as the civil works. Next, they introduced local construction firms to design and to engineer the civil works, initially as subcontractors to foreign firms and later as primary contractors subcontracting to foreign firms. Local manufacture of noncritical parts and, later, nuclear-certified items followed. Concurrently, they developed a nuclear architect-engineering firm, first for the auxiliary and balance of plant portions of the reactor and more recently for the Nuclear Steam Supply System (NSSS) itself.[8] The electric utility now controls two subsidiaries devoted to the engineering and manufacturing tasks (KOPEC and KHIC, respectively).

Table 14–2
Development Country X Independent Manufacturing Capability Time Requirements (Years)

Area	Small System Basic Ind.	Adv. Ind.	Medium System Basic Ind.	Adv. Ind.
Uranium[1]	5–10		5–10	
Conversion	3–5		3–5	
Enrichment (sub-critical centrifuge)	uncertain		uncertain	
Construction[2]	20		20	
Nuclear Regulatory	0–5		0–5	
Nuclear Manufacturing[3]	27	13	27	13
Specialty Steel	impractical		impractical	
Heavy Water	15		15	
Nuclear Systems Eng.	7–9		7–9	
Plant Operations[4]	6		6	
Fuel Fabrication[5]	11		11	
Zirconium[6]	2–5		2–5	
Reprocessing[7]	See note	4–5	See note	4–5
MOX[8]	6–7		6–7	
Waste Disposal[9]	none		none	

Source: L. Droutman, *International Deployment of Commercial Capability in Nuclear Fuel Cycle and Nuclear Power Plant Design, Manufacture and Construction for Developing Countries*, Westinghouse Electric Corporation report to Oak Ridge National Laboratory, ORNL/Sub-7494/4, October 1979, p. 10–9.
Notes:
1. Assumes uranium exists. Includes exploration, mining and milling.
2. Includes construction and plant design.
3. On basis technical assistance. Includes procedures, NSSS components, tubing, steam turbine, process instrumentation and control and nuclear controls. Electrical systems and plant computer are bought on open market.
4. Includes plant operators, utility headquarter engineering staff, training center and services center.
5. Includes fabrication and design.
6. On basis technical assistance; otherwise, 7–10 years.
7. Excludes any front-end regulatory licensing time. Basic industry must first progress to advanced basic industry.
8. Assumes UO_2 fuel fabrication capability and excludes regulatory licensing time.
9. Assumes storage in reactor spent fuel pool using high density storage racks.

Table 14–3
Phased Schedule for Nuclear Components Facility

	Calendar Year Completion of First Component	
	Basic Industry	Advanced Basic Industry
Plant Commercial Operation	0	0
Accumulator	3	2
Pressurizer	3	2
Heat Exchanger	4	2
Steam Generator	6	4
Pressure Vessel	8	6
Control Rod Drive Mechanisms	10	7
Core Internals	15	8
Reactor Coolant Pumps	15	8
Valves	7	3
Steam Turbine (Stationary)	5	3
Steam Turbine (Rotating)	15	8

Source: L. Droutman, *International Deployment of Commercial Capability in Nuclear Fuel Cycle and Nuclear Power Plant Design, Manfuacture and Construction for Developing Countries*, Westinghouse Electric Corporation report to Oak Ridge National Laboratory, ORNL/Sub-7494/4, October 1979, p. 6–122.

South Korea aspires to rapid localization of nuclear supply. The planned rate seems highly unrealistic, as it took Japan twenty-one years to reach 90 percent domestic nuclear content.[9] Westinghouse estimates that it takes eight to fifteen years to develop a nuclear cadre capable of nuclear construction, nuclear engineering/design, and nuclear manufacturing[10] (see tables 14–2) and 14–3). How does South Korea measure up against these baseline schedules?

Manufacture of Nuclear Reactor Equipment

KEPCO decided to gain design experience from foreign firms before beginning to manufacture hardware. To this end, KEPCO dispatched engineers to foreign producers to learn the basic design of components and the NSSS. Initially, they focused on auxiliary systems such as the boron recycling system, the residual heat removal system, and chemical or volume control systems. At the same time that they were studying the design, they participated in actual design work. They intend to attain full localization in NSSS design by the end of the 1980s, excepting key parts of the NSSS such as the control rod drive mechanism, the internal core, the reactor coolant pump, the pressurizer heating elements, and the reactivity controls.

Also beyond South Korean capabilities for the foreseeable future are parts of the nuclear turbine-generator, such as the rotating parts, forged blades, and so forth.[11]

The nuclear establishment in Seoul is divided into realists and optimists regarding the rate of localization. In 1980, for example, the Ministry of Commerce and Industry held that South Korean firms should produce 35 percent of the components for units 5 and 6. The Ministry of Energy and Resources managed to limit the goal to about 10 percent.[12]

A cursory glance at table 14–4 shows that the Korean Advanced Energy Research Institute (KAERI) did not match capability with requirements to construct the schedule. Only three years later, KEPCO published localization targets that showed that the utility had already collided with reality. Instead of aiming, for example, at KAERI's target for 1983 of 90 percent domestic production of reactor pressure vessels, KEPCO reduced its goal to 26 percent by 1988.[13]

By 1985, Korean manufacturers actually produced 28 percent of the NSSS for units 9 and 10, instead of KAERI's target of 83 percent of the NSSS for the same year.[14] Although adopting a "Korean standard design"

Table 14–4
Schedule for the Development of Domestic Capability to Manufacture Nuclear Power Plant Components

Item	Weighing Factors By Cost %[1]	Year				
		1979	1981	1983	1985	1987
Mechanical Equipment						
Reactor vessel	4.06	5	40	90		
Reactor internal	2.47	5	30	70	95	
Control rod drive mechanism	1.96	5	20	40	60	80
Steam generator	7.14	5	20	50	80	
Reactor coolant pump	3.26	0	0	20	50	75
Pressurizer	0.88	30	50	80		
Heat exchanger	4.14	47	80	100		
Vessel	1.19	83	100			
Pump	4.29	16	30	70	95	
Valve	5.71	8	30	70	95	
Turbine HP LP.	10.06	5	10	30	50	65
Main condenser	3.40	10	40	80		
Material handling equipment	1.66	40	70	90		
Water & waste treatment equipment	1.32	40	60	85		
Fire protection equipment	0.42	20	50	90		
HVAC equipment	1.68	30	50	90		

Table 14–4 continued

Item	Weighing Factors By Cost %[1]	1979	1981	1983	1985	1987
Boiler	0.12	100				
Turbine (feed pump)	0.58	10	30	80		
Air compressor	0.10	100				
Machine tool	0.28	100				
subtotal	54.72	8.3	18.1	34.6	43.3	46.0
Instrumentation and Control (I&C)						
I&C system	3.00	10	21	50	80	
I&C component	3.81	2	23	46	60	
Radiation monitoring instrument	0.25	10	44	65		
subtotal	7.06	0.4	1.6	3.4	4.8	4.8
Electrical Equipment						
Motor	—	30	50	95		
Main generator & Diesel generator	6.66	7	14	36	54	77
Transformer	1.92	41	71	95		
Circuit breaker & switch	1.71	30	70	95		
Distribution board and panel	1.81	100				
Rectifier & inverter	0.08	60	80	95		
Battery & charger	0.08	100				
Electrical equipment	0.82	59	80	90		
Communication equipment	0.18	100				
Lighting device	0.14	100				
subtotal	12.17	3.9	5.8	8.3	9.5	11.0
Material						
Raw material	—	30	70	90		
Structural steel	8.78	49	91	100		
Reactor coolant pipe	0.26	30	100			
Pipe & fitting	6.93	20	44	100		
Cable & wire	3.94	45	69	97		
Large cast & forged steel	—	0	40	100		
Pipe support	0.60	50	70	100		
Filter	0.03	40	100			
Insulation	1.19	60	100			
Civil work material	3.72	100				
subtotal	25.45	12.3	19.3	25.3	25.3	25.3
TOTAL	100	24.9	44.8	71.6	82.9	87.1

Source: A.D. Little, *U.S./Republic of Korea Energy Assessment: Electric Sector* Evaluation, report to Argonne National Laboratory, Cambridge, Massachusetts, May 1980, pp. 7–17, 18.
Note: [1]Weighted by cost of each component of total cost of plant.

on the Italian model may speed up localization, South Korea cannot avoid importing materials required for local nuclear manufacture. Materials amount to 50 percent of the cost of major nuclear items, such as the reactor vessel.[15] The local content ratio of materials for units 9 and 10, for example, was only 13 percent overall—7 percent for the nuclear island and 37 percent for the conventional island.[16]

Nonetheless, by 1986 South Korean firms were producing key components of reactor pressure vessels, emergency diesel generators, steam generators, pressurizers, and control rod drive mechanisms at KHIC's Changwon complex. The South Koreans also passed an important test of the international market in 1985, when they obtained ratings from the American Society of Mechanical Engineers that qualified their nuclear products to be of acceptable quality.[17]

KEPCO hopes to achieve full transfer of NSSS technology, including core design, from the vendor for units 11 and 12. By 1986, a three-way bureaucratic division of labor had reportedly been struck in Seoul. KAERI will receive the software from a foreign vendor (presumably Combustion Engineering, the NSSS supplier for units 11 and 12). KHIC will receive manufacturing expertise. KOPEC will receive engineering expertise. And KEPCO will manage the whole system.[18] In 1987, Westinghouse was selected to supply these units. Said one American vendor: "We told them if they want the store, they can have it, because light water reactors are not part of America's future. So they bought the store."[19]

In reality, however, the South Korean nuclear industry has a long way to go before full localization will be achieved.[20] In 1985, the Ministry of Science and Technology (MOST) admitted that high-technology parts required for nuclear safety are beyond local capability. "Thus, for the time being," MOST stated, "foreign countries such as the United States, England and France will remain the major supply sources for main parts of Nuclear Island, turbine generators and other components."[21] A foreign engineer working on South Korean nuclear projects reportedly said in 1985: "They are lot less further along on localization than I thought they would be." Reaffirming that South Korea intends to export nuclear items, an energy official also admitted that lack of technology and financing are "problems which won't be solved soon."[22]

Little is known about South Korea's intentions to manufacture heavy water or CANDU Canadian Deuterium Uranium reactors. A World Bank consultant mentioned discussions on this matter in 1979.[23] In 1984, Canada reportedly offered to transfer complete CANDU technology to South Korea. The offer included the authority to export CANDU technology. Canadian newspapers quoted a draft technical cooperation agreement that would "provide the means for transferring the complete Candu 600 NSP [600 MW(e) Nuclear Steam Plant] design and engineering technology and the maintenance and support services necessary." The Canadian deal would have allowed Korea Power Engineering Company to use CANDU technology "in an ongoing program in Korea, Canada and third countries." Canadian officials said that the proposed deal was a sweetener to induce South Korea to build another CANDU reactor at Wolsung. It was a necessary part of the offer in 1983 for South Korea to participate under license in constructing a CANDU reactor in Turkey.[24] It is not known if the 1984 CANDU offer was related to another deal that year halted by the U.S. State Department. If it was, it reveals how, from the American perspective, South Korea could skirt the edge of transgressing its nonproliferation commitments in nuclear exports.

At the time, (Atomic Energy of Canada Ltd) (AECL) reportedly proposed—and the United States stopped—recycling of spent fuel from a U.S. light-water reactor (LWR) in South Korea into mixed oxide (MOX) fuel for the CANDU at Wolsung.[25] The U.S. Department of Energy stated that the United States pressured "Canada to back away from the Canadian proposal to transfer technology in the reprocessing field."[26] According to South Korean officials, the technology they sought from Canada was for making MOX fuels.[27] They also claim that the relationship was merely the innocent pursuit of pure research, not an effort to build a MOX plant. They were irritated and resentful of what they regarded as unjustified American intervention in their affairs.[28]

Services

Architect-Enqineering/Construction. Korea Nuclear Engineering Services Inc. (KNE) was organized in 1975 as a joint venture between Korea Atomic and Burns and Roe. KNE was to undertake architect-engineering services for Korean nuclear projects. In 1976, Burns and Roe relinquished all of its shares to KAERI, which assumed full ownership. KNE was reorganized in 1977, and KECO and eleven major industrial firms in Korea became stockholders. KAERI retained more than 50 percent of the shares. Later that year, KECO (now KEPCO) acquired a controlling interest in KNE. In 1980, KECO had 95 percent of the shares, KAERI 4 percent, and eleven industrial firms a mere 1 percent.[29]

In September 1980, the Daewoo engineering and construction firm tried to elbow out foreign contractors altogether. The U.S. Embassy reported that month that Daewoo had secured President Chun Doo Hwan's approval to combine all aspects of the power industry—manufacturing, construction, and engineering—within Daewoo.[30] Kaiser Engineering and Bechtel representatives met with the Commercial Section to seek the U.S. Embassy's aid in reversing the decision, which would have allowed Daewoo

Table 14–5
KNE Participation Program, 1982

Unit No.	KNE Participation	Remarks
Nuclear #2	• Design for site facilities	
Nuclear #3	• Participation in construction management	
Nuclear # 5 & 6	• Participation in Off-shore engineering : 8.5% • Participation in On-shore services : Preliminary estimation is 30.4%	17 KNE engineers are resident in Norwalk, Ca. as of Dec. 1981 (Bechtel)
Nuclear # 7 & 8	• Participation in Off-shore engineering : 15% . • Participation in On-shore services : preliminary estimation is 32.0%	43 KNE engineers are resident in Norwalk, Ca. as of Dec. 1981
Nuclear # 9 & 10	• Participation in Off-Shore engineering : 16.5% • Participation in On-shore services : Under discussion	11 KNE engineers are resident in Paris, France. Total of 30 KNE engineers are to be dispatched.

Source: S. Levy, *Update Review of Safety Aspects of Nuclear Power Program in Republic of Korea*, report to World Bank and United Nations Development Program, Bascom California, June 1982, p. 58.
Note: KNE is now called KOPEC

to secure internally the equipment on projects for which it was also construction manager.[31]

Evidently, the decision was reversed (it probably contravened Eximbank, Asian Development Bank, and World Bank regulations too). Not long afterward, Bechtel was selected as KNE's partner from the five architect-engineers long associated with the South Korean thermal power program. KNE was thereby established as the sole South Korean architect-engineer as well as the consulting firm responsible for technical agreements with foreign engineering companies.[32]

In 1979, KNE had technical cooperation agreements with eight engineering firms[33] (see table 14–5). In 1982, for example, KNE had sixty engineers working with Bechtel in California and eleven in France.[34]

In July 1982, KNE was renamed KOPEC after a proposal to set up a joint venture with Bechtel had been considered and rejected.[35] Industry insiders say that the Bechtel joint venture was aborted because of strong opposition from nationalist South Korean engineering firms such as Taihan Corporation. KOPEC will be the primary contractor for architect-engineering for units 11 and 12. As of 1985, KOPEC could offer a wide variety of services.[36]

Research and Development.

Fuel Cycle Research and Development. The national center for nuclear fuel cycle R&D is the Daeduk Engineering Center at the Korea Advanced Energy Research Institute. The center was established in February 1975 as the Daeduk Branch of the old Korea Atomic Energy Research Institute. In December 1976, it separated from KAERI to become an independent outfit called the Korea Nuclear Fuel Development Institute (KNFDI). In 1978, it moved from Seoul to the Daeduk Science Town. In December 1980, it was consolidated with the old KAERI and became the Daeduk Engineering Center of the new KAERI.[37] (KAERI was set up in 1959 and reorganized in 1981.) "We intend," said a KAERI official in September 1986, "to make KAERI into the Westinghouse of Korea."[38]

The Daeduk Center conducts R&D on nuclear fuel cycle technology, including test and evaluation of nuclear fuels and components. If realized, its goals in the following fields could enable South Korea to export R&D practices to other states:

1. Develop nuclear fuel fabrication technology and other front-end nuclear fuel cycle technologies, excluding enrichment.
2. Develop postirradiation examination (PIE) capability to evaluate fuel performance. This facility was completed with French assistance in November 1985.[39]
3. Develop low- and medium-level radioactive waste technology.[40] In 1982, the Center planned to complete a 5,000 m³ per year medium-level liquid waste treatment facility with the capability to treat medium-level solid wastes.

Nuclear Reactor Technology Research and Development. The primary center for such activity is at KAERI's Nuclear Engineering Test and Evaluation Center which was to have been activated in 1982.[41] In February 1986, the Ministry of Science and Technology announced that KAERI would also construct a 30 MW(t) research reactor by 1990, supplementing the three research reactors supplied by American firms. (A Canadian report stated, however, that the multipurpose research reactor will be a "sister of the Canadian MAPLE," implying some Canadian involvement.[42]) Although the government stated that the new reactor would be built indigenously, sources in Seoul reportedly admit that foreign help will be needed for key portions, including basic design and essential components.[43]

Such a reactor would require about 800 to 1,200 metric tons of nuclear-grade graphite (that is, graphite with a density greater than 1.5 grams per cubic centimeter and a boron content of less than 5 parts per million).[44] South Korea is a major producer of natural graphite and a primary aluminum producer—two prerequisites for taking the easy route to production of nuclear-grade graphite.[45] Nuclear-grade graphite is controlled under the NSG guidelines and the Zangger trigger list. If South Korea establishes a domestic source for this material, it may become a supplier of this material before 1990.

Fuel Cycle Trade

Uranium. South Korea has contracts with suppliers in at least eight countries.[46] South Korea has developed the capability to explore for and develop uranium resources in the overseas joint ventures and in domestic R&D (see above).

Uranium Enrichment. In 1983, the Nuclear Assurance Corporation estimated South Korea's uranium enrichment requirements from 1983 to 2000 as about 19,039 metric tons of separative work units.[47] At that time, 69 percent of this figure had already been contracted for from the United States and France.[48] It seems unlikely, therefore, that South Korea will attempt to enrich its own uranium, short of a radical technological breakthrough. South Korean export capabilities in this area appear minimal.

Fuel Fabrication. In the late 1970s, the KNFDI (as noted earlier, then a separate activity spun off from the old KAERI) set up small pilot plants for fuel pellet fabrication and testing.[49] In 1982 (after KNFDI's remerger with KAERI and further reshuffling of KAERI), KEPCO and KAERI jointly established the Korea Nuclear Fuel Company Ltd. (KNFC) to localize the fabrication of nuclear fuels.[50] In December 1985, KNFC contracted with the German Kwaftwerk Union for technical know-how and equipment to construct and operate a 200 metric tons per year PWR fuel fabrication plant at KAERI's Daeduk complex at Taejon, 150 km south of Seoul.[51] It seems entirely possible, therefore, that South Korea could enter the market for fabricated fuel and fuel fabrication plants in the early 1990s. A decision to expand the capacity beyond the domestic demand would be a good indicator of this potential.

Spent Fuel Storage. So far, South Korea has relied on expanding storage at each reactor's spent-fuel pool by increasing the racking density—a solution that American and Korean officials had seen as adequate through the year 2000.[52] More recently, however, it has become apparent that on-site storage will reach its limits by 1990.[53] There is talk in Seoul of constructing a centralized spent-fuel retrievable storage site on the Korean mainland. In

1986, the South Korean National Security Council reportedly requested that nuclear scientists analyze the vulnerability of such a site to a North Korean air raid.[54] South Korea could export spent-fuel storage services in the future.

Reprocessing. As noted earlier, South Korea continued to try to acquire reprocessing technology. This effort was made at virtually the same time that South Koreans were authoring a report on the economics of reprocessing, as part of a U.S.–South Korean study on long-term spent-fuel storage alternatives for KEPCO. The report, one of a series conducted under the auspices of the Joint Standing Committee on Nuclear and Other Energy Technologies, was completed in 1983. It reportedly concluded that the high uncertainty regarding the, at best, marginal economics of reprocessing precludes its adoption by South Korea.[55]

There is little doubt that South Korea still aspires to acquire reprocessing technology. South Korea remains committed to introduction of the fast breeder reactor (FBR). The Ministry of Science and Technology states that FBR core design, safety analysis, and sodium handling techniques are being studied "to prepare for the commercial operation of FBRs in [the] future."[56] The South Koreans regard the plutonium as too valuable to think of disposing of it. They reportedly ignored Swedish offers to see Swedish disposal services for a South Korean disposal site.[57] At the thirty-first General Conference of the IAEA in 1987, the South Korean minister of science and technology proposed that the IAEA devise an international mechanism to manage the recycling of spent fuel to extract its energy potential.

American officials are confident that South Korea will not acquire plutonium reprocessing technology. They view the successful blocking of the French-Belgian reprocessing deals due to heavy American pressure as evidence that the United States can stop any new reprocessing proposal by South Korea. They believe that the security alliance endows the United States with sufficient leverage to achieve this end. This position, however, is questionable for two reasons.

First, the South Korean military is far less dependent on the American military than it was in 1976. It has become largely self-reliant in deterring and defending against a hypothetical North Korean attack. American forces are appreciated more for their symbolic value and nuclear connotations than for their war-fighting capabilities. A South Korean near-nuclear option might suffice in South Korean eyes to substitute for the U.S. nuclear threat against North Korea. South Korea also wants to match Japanese capabilities in a technological area with such power potential, although more for political prestige than for military reasons.[58]

Second, South Korea is likely to acquire reprocessing capability in the early 1990s, whatever the United States thinks or does, if it perceives that North Korea is obtaining that capability. The North Korean indigenous 30 MW reactor will startup around 1990. Shortly thereafter, it will have spent fuel to deal with. Although the Soviets are likely to be very prudent in this area, China is a possible wild-card supplier of reprocessing technology to the North Koreans. Because of its deteriorating military position relative to South Korea (and its anxiety about American nuclear weapons), North Korea may have high motivations of its own to obtain reprocessing technology. It is unknown if and doubtful that the North Koreans are wise enough to recognize the likely impact of their behavior in this sensitive area on South Korea. Nor can it be said with certainty that China would resist North Korean requests in this area.[59]

What is clear is that the South Koreans take a dim view of North Korean intentions in this area. They believe that reprocessing cannot be justified on economic grounds for a program of fewer than ten power plants. As North Korea has yet to start building even one power plant, the South Koreans would conclude that North Korean reprocessing of spent fuel from the research reactor would have military motivations. South Korean perceptions of North Korean activity in this area also may be distorted. "It is the Northern Puppet [North Korea]," declared the South Korean Ministry of Defense in September 1987, "that has been mentioned as one of those countries which are capable of manufacturing nuclear weapons."[60]

Against this hard-line view is that of other South Korean officials, who note that like France, India, and China, North Korea found the NPT to be discriminatory. They are reassured by the Soviet's role in convincing the North Koreans to sign the NPT in December 1985. They look gleefully toward the day when IAEA inspectors will swarm over North Korea as they do South Korea. They believe that a North Korean bomb would undermine its security. Whether this liberal view is more widespread in the South Korean state than that of the hard-liners—or as influential in decision making in the locus of political power in South Korea, the army headquarters—is unknown. North Korea's nuclear program set off alarm bells in Washington D.C. in 1989 when U.S. spy satellites photographed a nuclear facility that could be a reprocessing plant. This discovery has led to great consternation in Seoul, confirming the worst fears of hard line anti-communitists as to North Korean intentions.

Waste Disposal. In 1986, a special committee chaired by the president of KAERI was set up to construct a nuclear waste disposal facility by 1991.[61] KAERI studies and discussions about waste technologies are continuing with overseas firms.[62] It appears that KNFC, part-owned by KAERI, has been charged with managing spent-fuel and radioactive waste handling.[63]

South Korea could therefore become active in supplying waste management services.

Prospects for South Korean Nuclear Exports

Intentions and Motivations. By the early 1990s, the South Korean nuclear industry will be capable of exporting technologies across the entire fuel cycle, excepting enrichment, heavy water, and reprocessing technology, and some materials (such as specialty steels) and advanced nuclear components for LWR and CANDU reactors. In those areas that it has tackled, it will become capable virtually on schedule according to Westinghouse's experience (see table 14–2) for a country with a medium-sized power system and a relatively advanced industry—albeit at a much lesser rate than that earlier advertised by South Korea.[64] Table 14–6 lists South Korean nuclear firms which might be involved in nuclear exports.

South Korean officials have advertised their intent to break into the nuclear market since the mid-1970s.[65] Beforehand, no consensus had been reached among technocrats regarding the eventual scale of the domestic nuclear industry. Some South Korean officials aver that they will export construction techniques before they will sell equipment abroad. Services, they say, will be followed by component exports and architect-engineering services. In fact, the reverse may be the case, as construction capabilities are stretched to the limit while manufacturing capabilities are underutilized. What is undeniable is that immediate export prospects are poor. Said one South Korean official in December 1987: "There are no markets in sight."[66]

South Koreans believe that they are ideally placed to act as a bridge between American firms and the Chinese nuclear market. But they also recognize that diplomatic obstacles block that path so long as relations with North Korea—a Chinese ally—remain hostile. Indeed, in spite of the political difficulties, a South Korean businessman reportedly made overtures to the Chinese in 1984 to build jointly a nuclear power plant in Pakistan.[67] South Korean officials also refer to Indonesia and Malaysia as possible buyers.[68] But they believe that traditional suppliers such as the Dutch would compete intensely in such markets.[69] Furthermore, the Asian nuclear market is likely to be sluggish for many years.[70]

The first evidence that South Korea might be a serious nuclear export contender, however, was the report of proposed participation in a CANDU export to Turkey in 1983. The deal reportedly foundered because of a lack of financing. South Korea was also not impressed with the small volume of business offered by Canada—reportedly on $50 million of subcontracting.[71] In August 1985, KEPCO signed a technical cooperation agreement with

Table 14–6
South Korean Nuclear Firms

Dong Ah Construction Industrial Co—power plant construction, civil engineering and architecture, steel fabrication, heat exchangers. (on KNU 9, 10)

Daewoo-ITT Engineered Products Ltd.—shop fabricated piping for power plants, hangars and supports.

Daewoo Heavy Industries Ltd.—diesel engines, machine tools, compressors, generators, construction equipment.

Daelim Industrial Co., Ltd.—power plant construction, civil engineering, architectural work.

Gold Star Co.—wire and cable, heavy industrial equipment, electrical and electronic equipment, process equipment. Subsidiaries include Gold Star Cable Co, Gold Star Instrument and Electric Co.

Hankook Jungsoo Industries Co.—water treatment systems.

Hyosung Heavy Industries, Ltd.—electrical equipment for power plants, switchgear, disconnects, electric motors, fans and blowers, circuit breakers. Licensee of Westinghouse, Hitachi, Toshiba, and several German companies.

Hyundai Engineering and Construction Co—major construction projects in Korea and abroad, construct power plants, civil works, marine and offshore facilities such as oil rigs (worked on KNU 5,6,7,8), produces steam generators, boilers, reactor coolant systems including heat exchangers, piping, stainless steel tanks (KNU 5,6) at Changwon complex, licensed by Westinghouse and Combustion Engineering for NSSS production, and GE Co (UK) for nuclear/conventional turbine-generators.

Hankuk Inspection and Development Co. Ltd—Non-destructive testing and inspection.

Honam Engineering Co. Ltd—Non-destructive testing and inspection.

Korea Advanced Energy Research Institute (KABNI)—inspection, non-destructive testing of components, qualification testing, establishment of a national quality assurance program, regulatory review and licensing.

Korea Electric Power Co. (KEPCO)—utility management, development of electric power resources, generation, transmission, and distribution and electricity, investment in electrical business.

Korea Electric Power Group consists of KEPCO and subsidiaries including:

Korea Heavy Industries and Construction Co (KHIC)—production of power generating equipment including turbine-generator, boiler, reactor vessel.

Korea Electric Power Operating Service Co (KEPOS)

Korea Power Engineering Co (KOPEC)—architect-engineering of power plant

Korea Nuclear Fuel Co (KNFC)—design, fabrication and processing of nuclear fuel, research and development of nuclear fuel.

Korea Electrotechnology and Telecommunication Research Institute (KETRI)—tests, research and examination related to electricity business, development of electric equipment performance tests and type approval tests for appliances.

Korea Gas Corp. (KGC)—production and supply of natural gas.

Korea Electrical Security Corp (KESCO)—safety examination and survey of electric facilities, consulting services for use of electricity.

Il Jin Electric and Machinery Co. Ltd.—electrical equipment and fittings.

Pusan Steel Pipe Industrial Co.—steel pipe fabrication.

Shin Han Scientific Instrumentation Co. Ltd.—trading company providing nuclear instrumentation and analytical instruments.

Table 14–6 continued

Sambu Construction Co. Ltd.—civil engineering, power plant construction, transmission lines, structural steel erection.

Sangjie Commercial Co. Ltd.—trading company specializing in power plant equipment and nuclear fuel supply such as uranium, enrichment services, shipment.

Sam Yong Inspection Engineering Co. Ltd.—non-destructive testing and inspection.

Sammi Steel Co. Ltd.—stainless steel tubes, specialty steels, seamless tubing and pipes.

Taihan Electric Wire Co. Ltd.—attempted and failed at joint venture architecture-engineering firm with Bechtel, electrical cables, nuclear power plant cables, high voltage conductors.

Tong Heung Electric Co. Ltd.—chillers, air conditioners, heat exchangers, fans and blowers.

Yu Hang Atomic Industrial Co. Ltd.—non-destructive testing and inspection.

Source: KEPCO literature: C. Smith, "Emerging Nuclear Suppliers Research," (mimeo) Anco Engineers, Los Angeles, June 15, 1986.

Egypt's two utilities, the Egypt Electricity Authority and the Nuclear Power Plants Authority. (Other similar agreements are listed in tables 14–7 and 14–8). The agreement, reportedly an Egyptian initiative, covers conventional and nuclear power.[72] In 1983, Hyundai Construction Company was said to be talking with Westinghouse about a joint venture to participate in the Egyptian El Dabba nuclear project. Hyundai was eager to be involved, but the South Korean government nixed the deal because of a lack of export financing.[73]

Table 14–7
South Korea's Technical Cooperation Agreements

— Personnel Exchange Program with Taiwan Power Co., the Republic of China

— An Agreement for Cooperation in the Area of Resources and Technology with Taiwan Power Company, the Republic of China

— Personnel Exchange Program with Kyushu Power Co., Japan

— Technical Cooperation Agreement with Commission Nacional de Energia Atomica (CNEA), Argentina.

— Technical Cooperation Agreement with Ontario Hydro, Canada

— Technical Cooperation Agreement with Electric Power Development Company (EPDC), Japan

— Technical Cooperation Agreement with Belgium Utilities

— Technical Cooperation Agreement with Egypt Electricity Authority and Nuclear Power Plants Authority (of Egypt)

Source: Nack Chung Sung, "The Nuclear Power Industry Future in Korea," paper to Conference, Nuclear-Electric Power in the Asia-Pacific Region, Resource Systems Institute, Honolulu, Hawaii, January 24–28, 1983, p. 28; *Engineering News Record*, "Koreans Map Nuclear Future," August 22, 1983, p. 33.

Note: Other agreements may have been signed after 1983.

Table 14–8
South Korean List of Nuclear International Agreements

Nations and Organizations	Type of Cooperation
IAEA & Other UN Agencies	• Technical cooperation through IAEA including regular technical assistance and other technical and financial assistance programmes funded by UNDP, FAO and other organizations since 1957.
	• The Agreement between the Government of the ROK and IAEA for the Application of Safeguards in connection with the Treaty on the Non-Proliferation of Nuclear Weapons, has been in effect since 1975.
	• The Regional Cooperative Agreement (RCA) between the Government of the ROK and the IAEA for research, development and training related to nuclear science and technology has been in effect since 1974.
U.S.A.	• The Agreement for Cooperation between the Government of the ROK and the USA concerning Civil Uses of Atomic Energy has been in effect since 1956.
	• The Agreement concerning a Grant by the Government of the USA in the Acquisition of Certain Nuclear Research and Training Equipment and Materials between the ROK and the USA has been in effect since 1973.
	• The Agreement between the US Nuclear Regulatory Commission and the Atomic Energy Bureau of the Ministry of Science and Technology, ROK has been in effect since 1976.
	• Annual meeting of the ROK-US Joint Standing Committee on Nuclear and Other Energy Technology has been held since 1977.
France	• The Agreement for Technical Cooperation in Atomic Energy between the Ministry of Science and Technology of the ROK and the Atomic Energy Commission of the French Republic has been in effect since 1974.
	• The Agreement between the IAEA, the Government of the ROK and the Government of the French Republic for the Application of Safeguards has been in effect since 1975.
	• The Agreement between the Government of the Republic of Korea and the Government of the French Republic for the Peaceful Uses of Nuclear Energy was signed on Apr. 4, 1981.
	• Annual meeting of the ROK-France Joint Co-ordinating Committee on Nuclear Energy has been held since 1982.
	• ROK-French agreeement to cooperate in R&D on PWR fuel rod behavior, between Commissariat de l'Energie Atomique and KTERI.
Canada	• The Agreement between the Government of the ROK and the Government of Canada for Cooperation in the Peaceful Uses of Atomic Energy has been in effect since 1976.
	• Annual meeting of the ROK-Canada Joint Co-ordinating Committee on Nuclear Energy has been held since early 1983.
Australia	• The Agreement between the Government of the ROK and the Government of Australia concerning Co-operation in Peaceful Uses of Nuclear Energy and the Transfer of Nuclear Material has been in effect since 1979.
Spain	• A Complementary Agreement of Cooperation between the Atomic Energy Commission of the ROK and La Junta de Energia Nuclear of

Table 14–8 continued

Nations and Organizations	Type of Cooperation
	Spain for Development & Application of the Peaceful Uses of Atomic Energy has been in effect since 1976.
Belgium	• The Agreement between the Government of the ROK and the Government of Belgium for Cooperation in the Field of the Peaceful Use of Nuclear Energy has been in effect since March, 3, 1981.
Japan	• Annual science and technology ministerial meetings have been held since 1968.

Source: Ministry of Science and Technology, *1985 Atomic Energy Activities in Korea*, Seoul, 1985, pp. 28–30; Nuclear *Fuel*, "French, South Koreans Sign Agreement for Fuel Rod R&D," October 22, 1984, p. 10.
Note: Content of agreement with Germany is not known to author.

Today, South Korean motivations to export are complex. At least four less obvious goals should be added to the obvious ones—achieving economies of scale for the domestic program, obtaining technological spin offs, and saving foreign exchange on energy and technology imports. First, the promise of foreign exchange from nuclear exports may have insulated the domestic nuclear commitment against attacks by skeptics in the Economic Planning Board and the oil industry. Second, South Korea may seek to use nuclear exports to obtain diplomatic advantage over North Korea. Third, South Korea is sensitive to being perceived as subordinate to Japan. South Korea may feel compelled to enter a "prestige race" with Japan by acquiring reprocessing technology to match Tokai Mura.[74] This motivation exists quite apart from South Korea's proliferation propensity. American officials attribute South Korean disinterest in a regional reprocessing site to this concern.[75]

Another element may swim in murky depths that are even more opaque: the propensity of South Korean firms to nibble at the edges of the nonproliferation regime by entering the "gray market."[76] American officials believe that the parastatal and semiofficial nature of most South Korean nuclear firms precludes them from dabbling in dangerous waters.[77] In this view, the strong South Korean state shapes private corporate behavior, in contrast to the looser state-corporate relations in traditional supplier nations.

Against this view, however, is the fact that the South Korean arms industry has reportedly exported arms against American wishes. The South Koreans are furious over the American refusal to allow them to export arms produced under American license.[78] In 1985, for example, the United States knocked back all but $80,000 of the $13 million of exports requested by the South Koreans.[79] Americans feel that the South Koreans have "cheated" by occasionally exporting arms to Iran and Iraq.[80] The South

Korean Government strongly denies that exports of military equipment to Iran or Iraq took place. American protests were so strong, however, that the government admitted that they might not have monitored exports by private firms.[81] Informed Americans assert that it is more accurate to say that the government chose to overlook these sensitive exports, giving de facto approval. Many of the South Korean nuclear contractors are also key defense firms.[82] To export items on the trigger list might be far more damaging to U.S.–South Korean relations than squabbles over exporting slightly modified American tank technology.[83] Nonetheless, South Koreans might try to walk a fine line on nuclear exports. Furthermore, as an American Embassy official said in 1986, "Small companies will do anything for a buck" and may represent the likely route of nuclear leaks out of South Korea.[84] One possible mechanism for clandestine private flows would be via Korean underworld organizations linked to the Yakuza gangs in Japan.[85]

A related consideration is the probable contractual form of future South Korean exports. As explained later, South Korea is likely to make major nuclear exports as part of a consortium of firms. In such cases, the room for side deals will be severely constrained and closely monitored. However, going along for the ride—protected in part by the status of the primary contractor—may stimulate the South Koreans to entertain illusions about "marginal" cases. Firms such as Bechtel reportedly did not hesitate in the 1970s to promise that they would make KHIC the "Bechtel of the Far East."[86] These sweeteners thrown into bids for domestic nuclear contracts may have fueled South Korean illusions as to the potential for South Korean nuclear exports. The fact that bribes were paid to KEPCO officials by American and Canadian nuclear exporters to win nuclear contracts does not necessarily throw any light on South Korean nuclear export behavior in the future.[87] But the underlying dynamic in these cases—intense interstate, intercorporate, and intracorporate competition for nuclear business—sets up a situation in which corruption and extralegal activities are commonplace in Korea.[88] When this pressure is exerted in a state in which fulfilling quotas or meeting schedules is a matter of saving face, officials are often inclined to cut corners. As officials are also endemically underpaid in South Korea, the wonder is that corruption is not more widespread.[89] Nor is corruption limited to lower-level officials. Former South Korean President Chun Doo Hwan's close relatives were implicated in major financial scandals, a major element of popular disaffection with the regime.[90] Westinghouse did not hesitate to use a local "consultant" to influence former Philippines president Ferdinand Marcos's choice of nuclear contractor—reportedly placing $87 million into his Swiss bank account.

Added to external pressures is the possibility that South Korean nuclear manufacturers may find themselves bankrupt if the pace of nuclear development slows in South Korea. After noting that KHIC can construct components for two 900MW PWRs a year, KOPEC's president Kun-Mo Chung warned in 1985: "If the [domestic] market is not there, we will have to go to the export market."[91] The same goes for KOPEC's 1,000 engineers. Chung added that although South Korean firms cannot handle turnkey export nuclear plants, "We can beat Japanese companies on pressure vessels hands down."[92] Even more than in the First World, idle plants and hands could add a powerful imperative to export to all comers.

The Shape of Things to Come. The entry of South Korea into international nuclear trade is unlikely to look like the Indian or Argentinian approach. South Korea has purposely involved foreign firms in all aspects of its nuclear program, both to obtain and to speed technology transfer and to exploit their international marketing contacts in future exports from South Korea. Its likely mode of entry, therefore, will be in a joint venture with one of the many foreign nuclear contractors in South Korea.

In many ways, the orders garnered in East Asia in the late 1970s were the last gasp of the nuclear industry in its traditional multinational garb. Since then, American firms appear to have embraced a new philosophy of coupling American technology with East Asian productive resources. A new form of truly transnational sourcing appears to be on the horizon. With this strategy, American firms would retain design and management functions, while joint ventures in South Korea, Taiwan, or Spain would specialize in many of the labor-intensive and heavy industrial items formerly subcontracted in the United States.

In the event of a nuclear comeback, however, American firms will find that transnational production is likely to be a slide into relative decline. To retool would take American companies four or five years. Even then, it is unlikely that they would be competitive. In 1982, the U.S. Department of Commerce concluded: "[If] a resurgence does not occur until the mid to late 90s, if foreign firms dominate certain segments of the fuel cycle, and if U.S. technological obsolescence occurs, foreign firms could become the preferred source of supply."[93] The South Koreans are banking on exactly this scenario.

South Korea is relatively weak, however, in nuclear research and development. To reduce construction costs and to make localization easier, the South Koreans have adopted a standardized design for the balance-of-plant[94] and may have done so already for the NSSS.[95] This strategy will decrease construction and even operating cost. But it will leave the South Koreans unable to stay abreast of the latest in nuclear high technology and an unlikely source for whole plants.

As a partner in a bilateral or triangular nuclear production cycle, however, the South Koreans could become formidable competitors in the 1990s.

"Realistically," says one South Korean official, "this cannot happen until the late 1990s."[96]

The Institutional Framework

Nuclear Institutions

The South Korean nuclear power program involves four major ministries and numerous governmental and quasi-governmental agencies (see figure 14–1). The Economic Planning Board authoritatively allocates economic resources in South Korea. It is staffed by highly trained technocrats and is supervised by the deputy prime minister, who is also minister of the board and chairperson of the Council of Economics Ministers.[97] The board exercises control over various phases of the nuclear power program by virtue of its investment review of projects with national implications. It is also charged with ensuring that energy and economic planning are integrated at the national level.[98]

The Ministry of Energy and Resources is responsible for the development of overall, long-term energy policy, including the establishment of an electrical infrastructure. This ministry was established in 1978.[99] One of its five bureaus deals with electricity; the rest focus on mining and fossil fuels.[100] This bent, especially toward coal, sometimes pushes the Ministry of Energy and Resources to oppose the further expansion of nuclear power. In this view, it is often joined by the Coal Generation Department at KEPCO, which opposes the pronuclear perspective of the Nuclear Power Generation Department and senior KEPCO management.[101] On the basis of the Electric Business Law, the ministry regulates and supervises KEPCO, the major utility.[102] The Nuclear Power Division within the ministry's Electricity Bureau is responsible for planning the development of nuclear power in South Korea.[103]

The Ministry of Commerce and Industry is principally concerned with developing a local industrial infrastructure. In the nuclear program, it promotes domestic participation.[104]

The Ministry of Science and Technology (MOST) is heavily involved in the nuclear program. MOST was created in 1967 to oversee scientific and technological support for South Korea's second five-year plan. MOST has significant energy-related functions, including the administration of the nuclear program. The Atomic Energy Bureau (AEB) and KAERI are the major affiliated agencies dealing with nuclear energy.[105]

The AEB has four divisions: Nuclear Policy, Nuclear Energy R&D, Nuclear Reactor, and Radiation Safety. These organizations have potential bearing on nuclear export policy and implementation. The Nuclear Energy R&D Division, for example, is responsible for "provision of management

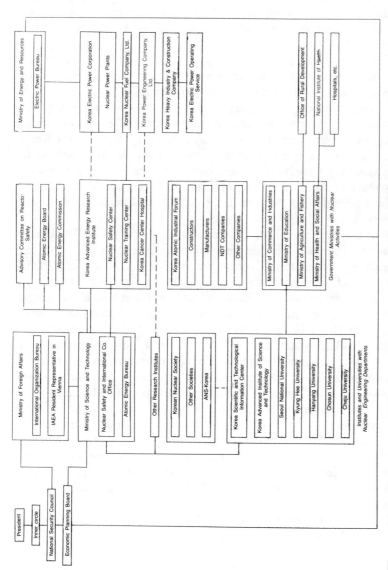

Figure 14–1. Structure of Nuclear Decision-Making in South Korea

Source: Y.S. Ha, *Nuclear Proliferation, World Order and Korea*, J. Chung," Nuclear Power in Korea," Seoul National University Press, 1983, p. 175; *Power Projections*, April 1987, p. 3. Youngnok Koo, "Foreign Policy Decision-Making," in ed. Youngnok Koo and Sung-joo Han. *The Foreign Policy of the Republic of Korea*, Columbia University Press, New York, 1985, p. 25.

for technology development to localize nuclear power plant manufacture [and] the nuclear fuel cycle."[106] The Nuclear Reactor Division is charged with "authorization for acquisition, production, import and export ownership [sic], control and management of nuclear materials and nuclear fuel cycle facilities."[107]

MOST's Atomic Energy Commission is responsible for licensing and regulating the operation of nuclear power reactors.[108] The commission would appear to have little bearing on export activity.

Generic import/export procedures throw little light on how South Korea will proceed to monitor and control nuclear trade. Because of foreign exchange controls, some exports are "export-restricted items." South Korea therefore already has a system that can impose controls. By implication, exports are generally unrestricted unless posted. Under current procedures, all exports must be licensed by the Ministry of Trade and Industry. The items to be exported must first be inspected by a customs house before they are cleared.

In 1982, the South Korean government amended the 1958 Atomic Energy Law.[109] The law legalized previous presidential decrees and expanded regulatory control to many areas not previously covered. In particular, chapter 5 of the law sets out controls on nuclear component manufacturing, construction, architect-engineer, and nondestructive testing firms.[110] Previously, local manufacture of nuclear safety–related items were required by a 29 December 1980 decree to obtain a MOST manufacturing permit. The rationale behind the amendment was to strengthen the legal regime by spelling out requirements in the law instead of by decrees.[111]

According to Article 37 of the new Atomic Energy Act, the requirement to obtain a MOST permit applies to "any person who intends to undertake the manufacturing business for nuclear reactor, the related facilities or the components specified in the Prime Ministerial Ordinance."[112] The same requirement applies to anyone intending to refine, convert, fabricate, or process nuclear fuels.[113] The components covered by the law include the reactor pressure vessel, steam generator, pressurizer, liner plate of the reactor containment vessel, pipes, and other items for pumps, valves, and tanks.[114]

The law does not specify the procedures for import or export of nuclear items. Article 106 states, instead:

> The procedures for import or export of the reactor and related facilities, nuclear fuel materials or radioisotopes shall be determined by the Minister of Science and Technology in consultation with the Ministry of Commerce and Industry.[115]

Nuclear Export Procedures

As of December 1987, the Atomic Energy Law designated only the export of nuclear fuel elements a controlled item. Exports of dual-use items, such as pumps or graphite, require the buyer to state their use. If the use is nuclear, then MOST must approve the export.[116]

South Korean officials say that it is still premature for South Korea to establish a full-blown export control system until nuclear exports are realized. "As yet," Moon You-Hyun, director of the Nuclear Cooperation Division of MOST told a U.S. nuclear export control team in September 1987, "Korea has not dealt in [nuclear] exports. Additionally, we don't expect there will be any possibility to export such nuclear items in the foreseeable future."[117]

The South Koreans informed the Americans that when exports occur, South Korea will develop its own system of export controls. "We fully recognize," added Moon, "the necessity of a nuclear export control system in Korea."[118] Furthermore, South Korea intends to export only to NPT signatories, each of which would need an agreement with Seoul to buy nuclear goods. Stated Moon:

> Presently, we feel that the nuclear exports will be maintained in the future with condition that the counterparts will be restricted to NPT signatory countries. In addition, such exported items will be used only for IAEA safeguards inspections systems.[119]

It is evident, therefore, that South Korea has already established the legal framework and administrative apparatus to control nuclear exports, even if the specific procedures remain to be spelled out.

The South Korean Commitment to Nonproliferation

South Korea remains ambiguously committed to the values and expectations that form the core of the nonproliferation regime. The commitment remains enigmatic because South Korean rhetoric and actions remain contradictory.

South Korea's Nuclear Safeguards System

South Korea became affiliated with the IAEA as a non-member-state in 1957. In 1984, the government sponsored research into the safeguards system. Most of the recommendations relate to improvement of measurements and reporting procedures.[120] Up to 1985, South Korea had signed bi- or trilateral safeguards agreements with the IAEA, the U.S., France, Canada, Germany, and Australia. (See Appendix 14A) South Korea also ratified the Non-Proliferation Treaty in 1975.

South Korea has established and maintains a national state system of accounting and control (SSAC) to ensure that nuclear and other materials subject to NPT safeguards are monitored under the IAEA full-scope safeguards activity on all nuclear facilities in South Korea.[121] (see figure 14–2). The Nuclear Policy Division within MOST's Atomic Energy Bureau is responsible for safeguards and international cooperation.[122]

The U.S. Nuclear Regulatory Commission and the Department of Energy have reportedly provided technical assistance in SSAC technology. Also, U.S. State Department officials say that they once had "reason to raise the level of South Korean awareness about future exports."[123]

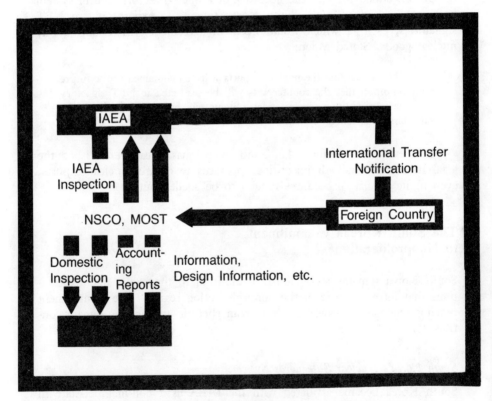

Figure 14–2: South Korea's Safeguard System

Source: Ministry of Science and Technology, *1985 Atomic Energy Activities in Korea*, Seoul 1985, p. 27.

Indicators of Ambiguity

South Korean leaders still refer occasionally to nuclear deterrence as a valued option and express doubt about the reliability of American extended deterrence. In 1981, for example, then-president Chun Doo Hwan threatened to reduce North Korea "to ashes" if provoked by the North, adding: "We have the means to do it."[124] His statement promptly revived speculation that South Korea may have secret nuclear weapons capabilities. Some South Korean actions are equivocal because the activity is inherently "dual-capable." In October 1978, the South prominently paraded modified American Honest John and Nike Hercules missiles. *Military Review* noted that these missiles "could also be used as platforms for nuclear warheads."[125] South Korea continued development of indigenous missile technology until at least 1980, when the program finally collided with economic reality.[126]

Undoubtedly, more people now adhere to nonproliferation values in South Korea than in 1971—the year that South Korea decided to build its own nuclear weapons. The true believers in nuclear power—the South Korean scientists and technologists who steered the program into its current prominence—are generally strong supporters of nonproliferation for South Korea.

The Ministry of Science and Technology shares these sentiments:

> The Government of the Republic of Korea attaches great importance to the prevention of nuclear weapon proliferation through universal adherence to the IAEA safeguards system and the Non-Proliferation Treaty. The strict observance of the Treaty and IAEA Safeguards will further promote international activities for peaceful uses of nuclear energy such as the supply of nuclear reactors, exchange of technologies related to nuclear fuel, information exchange and personnel training. Korea will therefore try to maintain its close relationship with IAEA and friendly nations to promote the peaceful uses of atomic energy.[127]

Apart from the "ambiguous" indicators noted earlier, South Korea has so far supported the four major pillars of the nonproliferation system.[128] First, South Korea allows full-scope safeguards on its nuclear facilities—although it is said to be a little taken aback by the level of inspection, especially for the CANDU.[129] Second, South Korea maintains tight security over its domestic nuclear fuel cycle. Third, to date it has not exported any nuclear materials that would contravene the nonproliferation regime. South Korea, however, is not among the twenty-three countries that have advised the secretary-general of the IAEA that they will observe the authoritative interpretation of Articles II and III of the NPT, spelled out in the Zangger trigger list.[130] In December 1987, senior South Korean officials seemed unaware of this procedure.[131]

Fourth, as a non–nuclear weapons state party to the NPT, South Korea is committed by virtue of Article II not to receive, control, or manufacture nuclear weapons or devices and "not to seek or receive any assistance in their manufacture."[132] That South Korea was engaged in a clandestine nuclear weapons program at the very time it was ratifying the NPT—and its subsequent behavior—leaves a residual uncertainty as to the depth of this commitment. Indeed, South Korea's delegate to the IAEA General Conference in 1976 called, on the one hand, for improving the IAEA safeguards system and asserted, on the other, that "non-proliferation of nuclear weapons should not interfere with the peaceful application of nuclear energy."[133] South Korea has not taken a high profile at the IAEA. It did not address the 1985 or 1986 General Conferences, although it did speak in 1987.[134] Nor did it make a statement at the 1985 NPT Review Conference, sending only a Geneva-based South Korean diplomat rather than a full-fledged delegation.

On the other hand, South Korea has hosted two IAEA training courses in Seoul, has sent its scientists to Vienna, and has been active in the IAEA's Regional Cooperative Agreement for Research, Development and Training Related to Nuclear Science and Technology.[135] South Korea may also soon allow the IAEA to set up an IAEA inspectors' office in Seoul.

Such behavior may be consistent with not being recognized as a legitimate state at the United Nations—that is, a desire to be seen but not heard at the IAEA. Nonetheless, the fact remains that South Korea is not a prominent international exponent of nonproliferation diplomacy.

The bilateral agreements for technical cooperation and nuclear supply also lock South Korea into nonproliferation commitments. The U.S.–South Korean agreement, for example, gives the United States intrusive rights of inspection.[136] The Australian–South Korean agreement specifically reserves the Australian government's consent to South Korean reprocessing of nuclear materials derived from Australian uranium.[137]

The first test of the strength of the bilateral agreements occurred in 1984. South Korea failed to inform the United States about the loss of twenty-four tons of heavy water at the Wolsung CANDU plant on 15 November 1984. "We were deeply disappointed," said U.S. Ambassador-at-Large Richard Kennedy, "that we were not adequately informed of the accident."[138]

Conclusion

If international nuclear trade revives, South Korea is likely to be a highly motivated and competitive supplier, especially in a joint venture in which Korean productivity is linked with the partner's political-diplomatic muscle and supplier financing (that is, with American firms backed by the U.S. government).

South Korea's behavior in these hypothetical markets remains to be seen. Certainly, South Korea's export activities in analogous sectors, such as arms exports, leaves much to be desired. Supply-push factors could motivate South Korean suppliers to enter gray markets—most likely, in dual-capable items with ambiguous proliferation potential. If and when South Korea should become a major supplier, sufficient time will have elapsed for major changes in the international nuclear market itself and in U.S.–South Korean security relationships. The more that nonproliferation values are diffused in the existing international nuclear market and beyond the Suppliers' Club, the more likely it will be that South Korea—a passive supporter of the nonproliferation regime—will internalize these norms as a nuclear supplier.

Conversely, most security analysts concur that American leverage stemming from the security relationship has drastically fallen in Seoul. Trade conflicts and intra-alliance stresses induced by the domestic process of democratization, combined with the likely effects of U.S. consolidation of its overseas military commitments in the 1990s, may reduce still further the United States' ability to affect South Korean behavior. The geopolitical trends in Northeast Asia currently favor South Korea and would suggest that Seoul will not find it in South Korea's interest to break its nonproliferation commitments. Should South Koreans perceive North Korea to be acquiring the bomb, however, their nonproliferation commitments would be severely stressed. Although this development would move up the security stakes for all parties in the Korean conflict, it would not necessarily mean that South Korea would become an irresponsible nuclear exporter. Indeed, at such a time, South Korea would likely be trying to curry favor with Washington in order to keep American icing on its nuclear cake.

Notes

1. Eximbank, "Authorization for Nuclear Power Plants and Training Center, From Inception Through March 31, 1980, Computer printout (Washington, D.C., 1981).

2. Interviews with American corporate officials.

3. Ministry of Science and Technology (MOST), *1985 Atomic Energy Activities in Korea* (Seoul, 1985), p. 31.

4. "Overinvestment in Power Generating Projects Bared by KDI," *Chosun Ilbo*, 29 November 1987.

5. "Korea Needs 8 N-Plants by 2010: KEEI," *Korea Times*, 6 September 1987, p. 6.

6. Interviews in Seoul, December 1987.

7. "GE and C-E Team Up to Meet Westinghouse License Offer in Korea," *Nucleonics Week*, 27 August 1981, p. 1.

8. R. Lester, "The Nuclear Power Plant Industry in the Asia-Pacific Region," Paper presented at Resource Systems Institute Conference, Hawaii, 1983.

9. T. Kimura et al., *The Electric Future of Japan*, Report RM837 (Honolulu: Resource Systems Institute, 1983).

10. L. Droutman, *International Deployment of Commercial Capability in Nuclear Fuel Cycle and Nuclear Power Plant Design, Manufacture and Construction for Developing Countries*, Westinghouse Electric Corporation report to Union Carbide Corporation Division, Oak Ridge National Laboratory report ORNL/Sub-7494/4 (October 1979).

11. E.W. Kim et al., *The Electric Future of Korea*, Report RM 838, (Honolulu: Resource Systems Institute, 1983), pp. 213–214.

12. "South Korea Reassesses Nuclear Program in Face of Various Pressures," *Nucleonics Week*, 8 May 1980, p. 9.

13. Kim, et al., *The Electric Future*, p. 215.

14. "Koreans Strive for Self-Reliance in Nuclear Plant Construction," *Nucleonics Week*, 19 December 1985, pp. 9-10.

15. Droutman, *International Deployment*, p. 6–39.

16. *Nucleonics Week*, 19 December 1985, p. 10.

17. MOST, *1985 Atomic Energy Activities*, p. 40; "KOPEC Acquires N-Certificate from ASME", *Business Korea*, (August 1984): 21.

18. Ibid. and interviews in Seoul, September 1986.

19. As related by a U.S. Embassy official, Seoul, December 1987.

20. It will be important to know if localization indices are adjusted for subcontracting to foreign subcontractors by South Korean primary contractors for items produced for units 11 and 12. If not, the localization figures will be inflated.

21. MOST, *1985 Atomic Energy Activities*, p. 15.

22. Cited in *Engineering News Record*, 22 August 1985, p. 33.

23. J. Bolduc, "A Review of the Power Sector in Korea," Annex 4 to World Bank, *UNDP/IBRD Korea Energy Study Mission*, Vol. 2, 1 June 1979, p. 21.

24. "Canada Is Offering South Korea Complete CANDU Technology," *Nucleonics Week*, 9 February 1984, p. 11.

25. P. Taylor, "Ottawa Denies U.S. Killed A-Deal," *Globe and Mail* (Toronto), 16 October 1984, p.5.

26. U.S. Department of Energy, briefing paper on U.S./R.O.K. Joint Standing Committee on Nuclear and Other Energy Technologies, 26 February 1986, p. 1.

27. Interview with South Korean official, Seoul, September 1986.

28. Interviews in Seoul, December 1987.

29. Arthur D. Little, *U.S./Republic of Korea Energy Assessment: Electric Sector Evaluation*, Report prepared for Argonne National Laboratory, Argonne, Illinois, May 1980, pp. 7–13.

30. U.S. Embassy, "Consolidation of Power Plant Engineering under Daewoo," Cable to U.S. Secretary of State No. 0150913Z, September 1980, partly declassified under a Freedom of Information Act request.

31. Ibid.

32. Ibid., pp. 7–12; Arthur D. Little, *U.S./Republic of Korea*.

33. Kyung Ho Hyun, "Nuclear Power and R&D Activities in Korea," in *Proceedings of the Symposium on Nuclear Energy* (KAERI and Korea Nuclear Society, 12 April 1979), p. 91.

34. S. Levy, *Update Review of Safety Aspects of Nuclear Power Program in Republic of Korea*, Report for World Bank and UN Development Program (Bascom California, June 1982), p. 59.

35. Kim et al., *The Electric Future*, p. 196.

36. These services include feasibility studies, planning and conceptual engineering, detailed engineering and design, procurement services, construction management and supervision, quality assurance and consulting services, plant test and start-up operations, engineer and operator training, information and data processing. MOST *1985 Atomic Energy Activities*, p. 39.

37. Levy, *Update Review*, p. 67; MOST, *1985 Atomic Energy Activities*, pp. 42–43.

38. Interview in Seoul, September 1986.

39. MOST, *1985 Atomic Energy Activities*, p. 12.

40. Levy, *Update Review*, pp. 67–70.

41. Arthur D. Little, *U.S./Republic of Korea*, p. 7–12.

42. Atomic Energy of Canada Ltd, "Nuclear Power in Korea," *Power Projections* (April 1987): 3.

43. Shin Ho-Chul, "South Korea Will Construct a 30-MW Research Reactor by 1990," *Nucleonics Week*, 6 February 1986, pp. 11–12.

44. B. Keisch, *Export Controls on Nuclear-Grade Graphite*, Brookhaven National Laboratory Report No. BNL-31433, report to U.S. Department of Energy, May 1982, declassified under a Freedom of Information Act request, p. 6.

45. Ibid., pp. 16–17.

46. Australia, Canada, France, Gabon, Morocco, Paraguay, South Africa, United States.

47. Nuclear Assurance Corporation, *Nuclear Fuel Cycle Materials, Services and Sources*, Report to U.S. Arms Control and Disarmament Agency (ACDA), 1983, p. 176.

48. Even this figure may overestimate enrichment requirements, as MOST published estimates of annual and cumulative enrichment requirements in 1985 for the mid-1990s that were about 25 percent lower than the 1983 estimate cited in this text. MOST, *1985 Atomic Energy Activities*, 1985, p. 12.

49. Arthur D. Little, *U.S./Republic of Korea*, pp. 7–6.

50. MOST, *1985 Atomic Energy Activities*, p. 41.

51. "Korea to Get KWU Fuel Technology," *Nuclear Engineering International*, December 1985, p. 4.

52. Interviews in Washington, D.C., June 1987; Seoul, October 1986.

53. Interviews in Seoul, December 1987.

54. Interviews in Seoul, September 1986.

55. Interviews in Washington, D.C., May 1987; Nuclear Assurance Corporation, *Nuclear Fuel Cycle*, p. 173.

56. MOST, *1985 Atomic Energy Activities*, p. 21.

57. Interview in Seoul, September 1987.

58. In 1980, the South Koreans were said to be stalling the renegotiation of the U.S.–South Korean agreement to supply enriched uranium, according to a congressional staffer, "because they want to see what we renegotiate with Japan. They don't want to give us *a priori* rights on reprocessing if our agreement with

Japan doesn't contain it." Cited in N. Serafino, "South Korean SWU Shortfall Predicted; Congress Shortly to Consider Remedy," *Nuclear Fuel*, 17 March 1980, p. 3.

59. On China's ambiguous nonproliferation stance, see J.R. Subramanian, "Second-Tier Nuclear Suppliers: Threat to the NPT Regime?" in R. Jones et al., eds., *The Nuclear Suppliers and Nonproliferation*, Lexington Mass: Lexington Books, 1985), pp. 98–100.

60. Ministry of Defense, reply to Open Questions on nuclear weapons in Korea, submitted by three citizen organizations on 8 September 1987 in Hangul (originals and translation available from author).

61. "South Korea Will Construct a 30-MW Research Reactor by 1990," *Nucleonics Week*, 6 February 1986, p. 12.

62. "Koreans Strive for Self-Reliance in Nuclear Plant Construction," *Nucleonics Week*, 19 December 1985, p. 11.

63. MOST, *1985 Atomic Energy Activities*, p. 42.

64. In Droutman, *International Deployment*, Advanced is defined as having the following technological capabilities: rebar steel and concrete locally available, basic fabrication, wiring from schematics, capability to manufacture and to assemble electronics components, manufacturing of agricultural implements, precision casting and forging capability, capability to read engineering drawings to perform the above, plus ability to interpret, adapt, and plan from drawings; precision machining/fabrication to thousandths of an inch; capability to produce conventional electrical components such as motors, transformers, and so forth (p. 1-16).

65. G. Murray, "Moving to Nuclear Power—At Home and For Export," *Christian Science Monitor*, 5 November 1982.

66. Interviews in Seoul, December 1987.

67. "Koreans Map Nuclear Future," *Enqineering News Record*, 22 August 1985, p. 33.

68. Interview with KAERI officials, September 1986.

69. Interview with South Korean officials, September 1986.

70. See, for example, "Economy Slows Nuclear Growth in Pacific Basin Countries," *Nuclear Industry* (October 1983): pp. 14-16.

71. Interview with South Korean official, Seoul, September 1986.

72. "Koreans Map Nuclear Future," *Engineering News Record*, 22 August 1985, p. 33.

73. Ibid.

74. On Tokai Mura, see Nuclear Assurance Corporation, *Nuclear Fuel and Reprocessing and Mixed-Oxide Fabrication Services*, Report to U.S. ACDA, September 1983, pp. 202–14.

75. Interviews in Washington, D.C., June 1987.

76. For more information on the gray market, see L. Spector, "Nuclear Smugglers," *Bulletin of the Atomic Scientists* (June–July 1986): 34–36.

77. Interview at American Embassy, September 1986.

78. See Chung-in Moon, "South Korea: Between Security and Vulnerability," in J. Katz, ed., *The Implications of Third World Military Industrialization* (Lexington, Mass.: 1986), Lexington Books, pp. 242–61.

79. South Korean source, December 1986. Approvals ranged from 3 percent in 1981–82, to 8 percent in 1983, to 3 percent in 1984. See Ibid., p. 260. It is

possible that the low approval rate may be the result of American policy to chastise persistent offenders by refusing approval for further exports. See "A Hello to Arms: Military Exports Soaring for South Korean Firms," *Asian Wall Street Journal*, 6 January 1978, p. 7.

80. Moon, *South Korea*, p. 261; R. Atkinson, "U.S. Promises S. Korea It Will Get Better Arms," *Washington Post*, 10 May 1984, p. A21.

81. Moon, *South Korea*, p. 261.

82. J. Nolan, "South Korea: An Ambitious Client of the United States," in M. Bzroska and T. Ohlson, *Arms Production in the Third World* (London: Taylor and Francis, 1986), p. 221.

83. M. Duffy, "Tank Talks: Can Koreans Export U.S. Technology," *Defense Week*, 22 April 1985, pp. 1, 16.

84. Interview with American official, Seoul, September 1987.

85. On Koreans in the Yakuza, the Japanese equivalent of the mafia, see D. Kaplan and A. Dubron, *Yakuza*, (Reading, Mass.: Addison-Wesley, 1986), pp. 190–92. Koreans in the Yakuza reportedly have close links with Mindan, the progovernment South Korean residents' association, and with the KCIA—now the Defense Security Command. They are alleged to have supported the kidnapping of Korean dissident Kim Dae Jung in 1973. The Yakuza are heavily involved in South Korean drug running into Japan, the off-base PX black market, and prostitution, albeit (unlike Japan or the United States) with state sponsorship or state sanction.

86. Interview with former Bechtel procurement officer for KNU 6 and 7, May 1984.

87. For a documented case of Bechtel's bribery of KEPCO officials, see M. Dowie et al., "Bechtel, A Tale of Corruption," *Multinational Monitor*, 5, no. 5 (May 1984): 10–16. For the Canadian activity, see Standing Committee on Public Accounts, "Payment to Agents-Korea," *First Report (The Atomic Energy of Canada Limited Report)*, House of Commons, Toronto, 27 February 1978, pp 26-46.

88. Interviews with former Bechtel officials, August 1983 and May 1984. By intracorporate competition, I mean the dynamic setup by top-level management setting growth targets that are the basis of corporate promotion and individual survival. Those who achieve go up; those who fail are sacrificed. This competition generates corrupt practices even as edicts against it are issued by top-level management.

89. Interviews with former Bechtel officials, August 1983 and May 1984, and with American officials, U.S. Embassy, September 1986.

90. S. Harrison, "Is South Korea Going to Be the Next Philippines?" *Washington Post*, 25 January 1987, p. B1.

91. "Koreans Strive for Self-Reliance in Nuclear Plant Construction," *Nucleonics Week*, 19 December 1985, p. 11.

92. Ibid., p. 11.

93. U.S. Department of Commerce, "U.S. Nuclear Industry Survey," Mimeo (Washington, D.C.: Office of Major Projects, December 1982).

94. "South Korea is Likely to Again Postpone Plans for Its Next Two Nuclear Units," *Nucleonics Week*, 22 September 1983, pp. 2–3.

95. Koreans strive for Self-Reliance in Nuclear Plant Construction," *Nucleonics Week*, 19 December 1985, p. 9.

96. Interview in Seoul, September 1986.

97. Kim et al., *The Electric Future*, p. 275.

98. Ibid, p. 274.

99. Ibid.

100. Ibid.

101. Interview with South Korean official, Seoul, September 1987.

102. Ibid.

103. Kim et al., *The Electric Future*, p. 274.

104. Nack Chung Sung, "The Nuclear Power Industry Future in Korea," Paper presented at Conference on Nuclear-Electric Power in the Asia-Pacific Region, Resource Systems Institute, Honolulu, Hawaii, 24–30 January 1983, p 11.

105. Kim et al., *The Electric Future*, p. 274.

106. MOST, *1985 Atomic Energy Activities*, p. 35.

107. Ibid., p. 35.

108. Kim et al., *The Electric Future*, p. 274.

109. Levy, *Update Review*, p. 11.

110. Ibid.

111. Ibid., pp. 40, 49.

112. MOST, *Atomic Energy Laws of the Republic of Korea, 1985* (Seoul: MOST/KAERI, 1985), p. 30 (in English).

113. Ibid., pp. 32–33.

114. Ibid., p. 292.

115. Ibid., p. 58.

116. Interviews in Seoul, December 1987.

117. Moon You-Hyun, Director, Nuclear Cooperation Division, MOST, Address to U.S. Nuclear Export Control Team (mimeo) (Seoul, 2 September 1987), p. 1.

118. Ibid.

119. Ibid., p. 2.

120. MOST, *Atomic Energy Laws*, p. 26.

121. MOST, *1985 Atomic Energy Activities*, p. 26.

122. Levy, *Update Review*, p. 41.

123. Interview in Washington, D.C., June 1987.

124. UPI, "South Korean Chief Threatens to Reduce the North to Ashes," *Washington Star*, 27 June 1981, p. 9.

125. "Republic of Korea, Artillery Rocket," *Military Review* (August 1979): 82.

126. Interview with former U.S. Ambassador to South Korea, May 1987. This source stated that the missile program continued into the early 1980s after Park Chung Hee was assassinated in October 1979.

127. MOST, *1985 Atomic Energy Activities*, p. 2.

128. L. Dunn, "The Emerging Nuclear Suppliers: Some Dimensions of the Problem," in Jones et al., *The Nuclear Suppliers*, p. 123.

129. Interview with American official, U.S. Embassy, Seoul, September 1986.

130. Interview with State Department official, June 1987; for the text of the Zangger trigger list and background, see D. Fischer and P. Szasz, *Safeguarding The Atom* (London: Taylor and Francis, 1985), p. 219.

131. Interviews in Seoul, December 1987.

132. See J. Davidow, *Comparative Study of European Nuclear Export Regulations*, Vol. 1, Report by lawfirm Mudge Rose Guthrie Alexander and Ferdon to Lawrence Livermore Laboratory, Livermore, California and New York, August 1985, p. 13.

133. "Statement of Dr. Hyung Sup Choi, Minister of Science and Technology and Head of Delegation of the Republic of Korea, to the 21st General Conference of the IAEA," Mimeo, 1976, p. 3.

134. According to the files of U.S. DOE officials.

135. Hidetake Kakihana, "International Cooperation in the Field of Atomic Energy and the Role of the International Atomic Energy Agency," in *Proceedings of the Symposium on Nuclear Energy*, KAERI/Korea Nuclear Society, 12 April 1979, Seoul, p. 17.

136. The U.S. agreement (1972, amended in 1974), for example, gives the United States the right to review reactor designs and other equipment relevant to safeguards applications and to inspect places and data relevant to safeguards implementation on source and special nuclear materials. See "Agreement for Cooperation Between the Government of the United States of America and the Government of the Republic of Korea Concerning Civil Uses of Atomic Energy," *U.S. Treaties and Other International Agreements*, 24 UST, 24 November 1972, pp. 785–786.

137. Department of Foreign Affairs, *Agreement between the Government of Australia and the Government of the Republic of Korea concerning Cooperation in Peaceful uses of Nuclear Energy and the Transfer of Nuclear Material*, Treaty Series 1979, No. 5, 2 May 1979, p. 5.

138. "South Korea's Failure to Inform the U.S. About the Event at Wolsung," *Nucleonics Week*, 13 June 1985, p. 11.

15
Spain:
An Emerging Nuclear Supplier

Ciro Elliott Zoppo

The Context

Nuclear export activities in Spain, as elsewhere, occur in a political, economic, and technological context. The factors operating the process are not always explicitly related in the public and the private sectors, nor between these sectors, by the relevant decisionmakers. A redefinition of Spain's policies in the nuclear sector has been going on since at least 1984, when a new energy plan was legislated by the newly elected Socialist government. It would be accurate to suggest that this process remains dynamic and not fully completed for policy purposes.

This condition has resulted from the fact that Spain underwent a crucial political regime change from dictatorship to parliamentary democracy about a decade ago, with the transition to democracy only recently consolidated. Moreover, no policy in regard to nuclear nonproliferation existed during the Franco regime. Instead, Spain's official position was to maintain the right to preserve a nuclear option for national defense. However, this option was not developed into a concerted program to develop a nuclear military capability. There is some evidence, beyond the public statements by individual officials of the Franco regime, that activities were pursued in the nuclear sector that could have provided Spain with capabilities useful in creating a military option. But it is debatable whether these activities reveal an actual policy intention to create a military option.[1]

Although there was an interest in the military atom early in the Franco regime on the part of some influential military officials, like Admiral Carrero Blanco and General Juan Vigon, the first significant development relevant to the possible creation of a military option occurred in 1955, when the United States gave Spain a three hundred fifty thousand dollar

I should like to acknowledge, with appreciation, the invaluable comments of Don Jose Mario Armero and the research assistance provided for this chapter by Carmen Perez, of CISA, and Katlyn Saba and Luis Pascual, of INCI.

credit to develop civilian nuclear production under the "Atoms for Peace" program. This money catalyzed an intensive period of development that led, among other results, to the installation of the first research reactor using enriched uranium (a know-how relevant to military purposes) and the unsuccessful attempt, pursued by Admiral Carrero Blanco, to purchase a nuclear power plant from France, running on plutonium (another technology also relevant to a military program).[2]

Reportedly, U.S. and Soviet pressures led France to substitute a graphite-gas system at the installation. During the 1960s, Spain constructed the Vandellos I, a natural uranium reactor, critical in 1971, from which plutonium of potential military utility could be obtained when combined with the experimental "Coral" reprocessing plant. Vandellos was under only French discretionary safeguards, without IAEA safeguards. In 1971, the Centro Superior de Estudios de la Defensa Nacional [governmental Center for the Study of National Defense] produced a study that allegedly concluded that Spain could implement a military nuclear option. The present government has admitted that theoretical studies on the use of tactical nuclear weapons had been conducted in the Ministry of Defense. However, no reliable information has come to light, since the demise of the Franco regime, to suggest that the Spanish government ever decided, in fact, to move toward implementing an option to go militarily nuclear.[3]

A Spanish nonproliferation policy is just emerging, concomitantly with publicly debated legislation to guide and manage the civilian use of nuclear power. At the onset of the democratic regime, both the Union Centro Democratico [the Union of the Democratic Center] and the Partido Socialista Obrero Espanol (PSOE) [Socialist Party] equivocated in regard to Spanish accesion to the Nuclear Non-Proliferation Treaty (NPT). In addition to the politically sensitive issues of sovereignty and national independence, perceived by the parties across the political spectrum, there were other constituencies negatively disposed toward the NPT. The traditionalists among the military have taken the position, explicitly, that Spain should not adhere to the NPT, nor to any agreement whose "generalized safeguards" would abort a future option to acquire nuclear weapons for defensive use in Spain's particular circumstances. The Spanish Navy has been especially concerned about foreclosing technological developments permitting it to develop nuclear propulsion—a position even endorsed, in 1983, by the Socialist government in a public declaration by Fernando Moran, then foreign minister. Another argument advanced to maintain a military nuclear option—with appeal to the political Left, as well—suggests that if Spain decided to choose neutrality in foreign policy, it would need nuclear weapons to maintain it. The nuclear industry, as an interest group, has also been in opposition.[4]

A resolution of this policy issue has taken place with Spain's decision to opt for a policy of nonproliferation. In March 1987, Spain's Council of Ministers approved the adherence of Spain to the NPT, and the Spanish government ratified it before the years' end. Spain was already a signatory of the Limited Test Ban Treaty. Consequently, it is now clear that with the advent of the Socialist government, a nuclear military option has been removed from Spain's security and foreign policies. But it should be emphasized that this was primarily a political decision, the consequence of two important changes in Spanish domestic politics: the military's seeming acceptance of the legitimacy of civilian authority, and the Socialists' outright majority in the Cortes, first gained in the 1982 elections and reaffirmed in 1986. The policy context was provided by the Spanish government's redefinition of defense policy, presented for parliamentary debate in October 1984.[5]

A public and official statement of the Ministry of Defense has clarified that "the Spanish armed forces do not train in the battlefield use of nuclear weapons because Spain has renounced their manufacture and use." Moreover, the Spanish government, having been admitted to membership in the European Economic Community (EEC), was under pressure from the other members of Euratom to regularize its status, which had to be peculiarly defined so long as Spain remained aloof from the NPT. The strong antinuclear swell in Spanish public opinion, regarding the stationing of U.S. nuclear weapons on Spanish soil, that surfaced in the debate on the government's referendum on NATO membership, was also a consideration in the decision.[6]

Also relevant to an examination of Spain as an emergent nuclear supplier are the major revisions that have taken place in the foreign policy of Spain. In the wake of the regime change, Spain has joined the North Atlantic Treaty Organization (NATO) and has been admitted to membership in the European Community.

Membership in the alliance has incorporated Spain formally into the security of Western Europe and provided it with a NATO shield for its national defense. This augments the bilateral security relationship with the United States, established in 1954 and now being renegotiated. Among most Spanish military, the bilateral agreements with the United States are viewed as important and not easily replaced. However, in both the nationalist right and the modernizing center of the military there are those who believe that the bilateral relationship with the United States needs substantial revisions. So does the Socialist government, while believing that the Atlantic alliance is a necessary complement to the national defense.[7] Membership in the alliance is also viewed by some influential members of the Spanish government as in some ways supplanting the U.S.-Spanish relationship, as well.[8]

Two themes have developed in the reform of Spanish defense policy.

The first reaches for greater autonomy from the United States and national independence in national policy. The second promotes the development of a Spanish defense industry more capable of developing its own armaments, or at least manufacturing them on national territory. This Socialist approach to national defense is well grounded in the government, and generally shared with the military.[9]

Spain's insistence that no U.S. nuclear weapons be stationed on Spanish soil, which arose in connection with U.S. military bases, was a harbinger of Spain's changing nuclear policies.[10] In regard to the Spanish military, Spain's membership in NATO also weakens or eliminates tendencies toward preserving a nuclear option. Nevertheless, the military of the General Directorate for Defense Policy, in the Ministry of Defense, were extremely reluctant to support Spain's adherence to the NPT, on the grounds that security in the Mediterranean region is too unstable to eliminate a future nuclear option for Spain, and that by not acceding to the NPT Spain would maintain an implied deterrence against possible aggression not otherwise available.[11]

Although the decision to join the nonproliferation regime clearly establishes a Spanish policy not to seek the military atom for national defense, it does not necessarily directly impact on nuclear technology transfer for commercial purposes. Accession to the NPT has not been a crucial policy issue either in the government or in public debate.[12] What happens in regard to the civilian atom is more a function of attempts to promote industrial development in Spain and to ameliorate the balance of trade problem. It is also related to the impact on the nuclear industry of Spain's participation in the European Common Market, and membership in Euratom in particular. For example, in its negotiations with Euratom the Spanish government has had as a major concern the adaptation of its bilateral nuclear agreement with the United States, which expires in the year 2001, to the Euratom system.[13]

Public concern about the safety of nuclear reactors is the most trenchant attitude in the electorate. Together with the insistence that no U.S. nuclear weapons are to be stationed on Spanish soil, these are the only broadly based popular attitudes of political significance regarding nuclear matters. There are no specifically antiproliferation movements worthy of note.[14]

Partnership in the European Community has brought Spain into a range of significant economic and political relations with major consequences for the Spanish economy and Spanish politics, both internal and foreign. The future of the nuclear industry in Spain is being affected by membership in Euratom and by the commercial avenues provided by transactions in the Common Market.[15]

There is already some evidence to suggest that both in the definition of the next national energy plan and nuclear safety, Spain's participation in the European Community is beginning to impact on Spanish decisionmaking. The government's focus on civilian nuclear activities has intensified in all aspects, but particularly those connected with the growth and management of the national energetic capacity, including the generation of electricity through nuclear technology and nuclear safety.[16]

Policy focus on the use of nuclear power for producing electricity has been tasked through the definition of the national energy plan, bureaucratically lodged in the Ministry of Industry and Energy. Nuclear safety has been the responsibility of the Consejo de Seguridad Nuclear [Council for Nuclear Safety]. This agency has been very active in its efforts to pursue agreements and collaboration with international and other nations' nuclear safety organizations, like the Nuclear Regulatory Commission (USNRC), the Organization for Economic Cooperation and Development's (OECD) National Energy Agency (NEA), and the International Atomic Energy Agency (IAEA). For example, Spain has negotiated agreements for the exchange of information regarding nuclear safety with the United States, France, Mexico, Portugal, and Italy, and has been actively pursuing means to implement collaborative efforts in this field with appropriate Euratom organizations.[17]

A moratorium on the completion and the construction of nuclear power plants has centrally focused the Socialist government's efforts to reexamine the national situation in the nuclear sector and to explicitly develop long-term and detailed policies to guide Spain's nuclear industry. The moratorium was in force for over four years. Since it expired legally in January 1987, the public debate on the future of nuclear energy in Spain has intensified. A major actor in the debate has been the Ministry of Industry, charged with the projection of the nation's electric power requirements to 1992.[18] According to the Instituto Nacional de Fomento de la Exportacion [National Institute to Promote Export], there were, as of 1986, eight nuclear power units in commercial operation, representing somewhat over 22 percent of national electric production.

This debate should not be viewed in isolation from developments connected with the PSOE's original plan for economic and social progress.[19] With the establishment and the legitimization of parliamentary democracy in Spain came the necessity to complete the reform of the economic model that had been created during the Franco dictatorship, and incipiently reformed after the 1970 agreements with the Common Market countries, to fully adapt the model to the new political system.

It is sufficient to merely illustrate the organization of the Spanish economy under Franco, which prevailed unmodified for the first twenty years of his regime, 1939 to 1959, to appreciate the magnitude of changes required. This notwithstanding, the Stabilization Plan, which first went into effect starting with the decade of the 1960s, followed by the 1964, 1968, and 1972 development plans, began to gradually liberalize the economy.[20]

Franco's corporate state had led to the creation of vertical syndicates in the different sectors of economic activity. Employers and employees came under the same institutional mandate, primarily in order to control workers. The law for the regulation and the defense of the national industry made all industrial development subject to governmental authorization. The government also controlled prices and wages. Foreign investment could not exceed 25 percent of the assets of any Spanish enterprise. This regulation went hand in hand with restrictions against international trade.[21] Severe exchange controls, high tariffs, and a multiple exchange rate system were imposed. Moreover, in 1941, INI, the Instituto Nacional de Industria [National Institute for Industry], was established to strengthen defense industries and to promote self-sufficiency in areas where private sector resources were insufficient.[22] In a word, autarchic self-sufficiency was the national goal, with industrialization based on import substitution.

After the signing of the 1970 trade agreement with the European Community, Spain continued its progress toward a liberal economy. Nevertheless, an emphasis on indicative planning perpetuated for the state a strong role in guiding industrial development.[23] This has especially been the case with the nuclear industry. The Franco regime had set up, in 1948, a Comite de Estudios Nucleares [Committee for Nuclear Studies] to perform nuclear research and development. This committee engendered the creation, in 1951, of the Junta de Energia Nuclear [National Agency for Nuclear Energy].

By 1958, two private companies, CENUSA and NUCLENOR, effectively subsidized by the Spanish government, were established with the aim of developing nuclear power for electricity production. The private sector contributed 40 percent of their cost. By 1968, the first commercial power plant, the Jose Cabrera, went into operation, followed by another, the Garona, in 1971, and Vandellos I the following year, to complete the first generation of Spanish nuclear power plants. These fulfilled the requirements of the National Electricity Plan of 1969, the first ever projected during the Franco regime.[24]

Since the end of the Franco dictatorship, Spain has had to implement not only the transition to democratic institutions and to cope with a continuing economic crisis—in the second half of 1986 unemployment was at 20.6 percent and inflation at 8.6 percent—but also to deal with ideological pressures on economic policy. The economic crisis, which had already developed during the final years of the previous regime, affects all important sectors of the economy, including the nuclear, in both internal and international aspects.[25] With the coming to power of the Socialists, the economic reforms had to countenance also, initially at least, the values of Socialist ideology related to the economy and to the nuclear sector.[26]

These ideological premises, focused on the responsibilities of the state in economic terms, have been reshaped, in turn, by the responsibility of governing. The PSOE's socialism has become unorthodox and pragmatic, much to the discomfort of its ideologues. The government's economic plans do not pivot on nationalizations. To the contrary, they have been characterized by attempts to privatize some public sector companies.[27]

The transition to a new model of the economy is yet to be fully achieved, including within the nuclear sector. Although it may be true that a changing model of the national economy may have no immediate impact on nuclear export motivations, it will have a direct impact on industrial nuclear capabilities and eventually on patterns of trade.

The Transactions

In the early years of the development of civilian nuclear energy, the United States played the pioneering role in nuclear technology transfer. Beginning with the "Atoms for Peace" program, launched in 1953, the United States' principal international objective became the promotion of civilian nuclear technology under safeguards. The U.S. Atomic Energy Commission (later replaced by the Nuclear Regulatory Commission) promoted civilian uses of nuclear energy through the dissemination of information, the training of technicians, export of research equipment, distribution of enriched fuels, and prospecting for natural uranium.[28]

Eventually, the advocacy of civilian applications of nuclear energy was emulated by other industrial countries and enshrined in the International Atomic Energy Agency (IAEA). Expectedly, this led to the creation of vested interests in nuclear technology that stimulated commercial aspirations and international status politics in developing and advanced countries alike. These early promotional policies by the United States and European countries capable in nuclear technology helped to shape an image of the atom as the midwife of economic progress and energy independence in developing countries.[29]

Taking established, primary nuclear suppliers as a norm, incentives for transferring nuclear technology abroad include national prestige and diplomatic leverage considerations, the promise of economic profit for the national nuclear industry, and the expectable animus of technologists involved in the nuclear sector. Certainly, this has been the case in the United States, Britain, France, Canada, and West Germany. The fact that the Soviet Union does not have a private economic sector will qualify the case of the Soviet Union. But in regard to nuclear technology transfer, the need to project an image of technological sophistication has substituted for the profit motive.

These incentives for nuclear technology transfer have also been among the rationales impelling Spain, during the final years of the previous dictatorial regime and since the advent of the democratic system.[30] Before the 1980s, the shortfalls in Spanish national capabilities inhibited significant activities in export. Creating a national nuclear sector can be rationalized by considerations of national prestige connected with the image of the nation as an industrial or modernizing country and by concrete requirements for energy independence. Both of these factors have existed and continue to operate in Spain.[31]

In Spain, considerations of image and prestige are related to other foreign policy considerations that manifest themselves in terms of the Spanish political, economic, and foreign policy elites' definitions of priority areas for the projection of national policies. These are Europe, Latin America, and the Arab world.[32] This is to be expected in regard to Europe because of Spain's colocation with other European nations geographically and historically. But it is also the product of particular circumstance. For over a decade Spain had been increasingly drawn into the European economy,[33] and since the end of the Franco regime into the shared political values of European parliamentary regimes as well.

In regard to Latin America, this has been the case because, regardless of political regimes, Spain has pursued a policy of special relations with the region, rationalized by its former status as the ruling country. The diplomatic posture toward the Arab Mideast and the Maghreb has also been defined as special.[34] In the eyes of Spanish foreign policymakers, these areas have special historical affinities due to the centuries of Islamic ascendancy in Spain. Nevertheless, it should be pointed out that Spain's special outlook toward Latin America and the Arab world does not necessarily result in greater commerce for Spain, including that connected with nuclear export, when compared with Europe.

It is a fact that in the export of capital goods, 45 percent of Spain's foreign sales have been to the EEC countries, while 20 percent have been to Latin America and 13 percent to the Arab world. Still, the percentages of exports to Latin America and the Arab countries are substantially ahead of those to other regions. The rest of the Third World combined has accounted for only 7 percent, with an equal amount for the United States and Canada together.[35] Moreover, Spain has had a somewhat greater margin of success, and more opportunity to reach agreements, autonomously, in the nuclear sector in Latin America. It is not clear in what degree this outcome is due to cultural affinities and to what degree it has resulted from Spain's deliberate selling point that its own experience, and success, in developing a significant level of nuclear capability in a little over a decade is uniquely useful to developing countries.

The international status of Spain, and its foreign policy posture toward the developing world, can also make it an attractive partner in the nuclear field. These considerations are viewed by some of the pertinent decisionmakers as providing Spain with future opportunities in Asian and African developing countries.[36] Such views are fostered in government policies by the private sector. This dovetails, in policy, with the priorities assigned to Latin America and the Muslim world.

In 1980, SENER was awarded a consulting contract by Pakistan's Atomic Energy Commission for plant design criteria, updating main component specifications, basic engineering, systems design, quality assurance, and costs for the Chashma nuclear power light-water 900 MW plant. An important aspect of the project was a technology transfer program whose object was to create a capability for the design and construction of nuclear power plants in Pakistan.[37] In addition, SENER has carried out joint services abroad, in the nuclear sector, with Asea-Atom (Sweden), Fertimex and Comision Federal de Electricidad (Mexico), Astra Evangelista, S.A. (Argentina), Comision Chilena de Energia Nuclear (Chile), and CERN (Switzerland), among others. The project for Fertimex was for a plant producing yellowcake from phosphoric acid, using a basic process developed by Spain (JEN). In Argentina, SENER provided quality assurance for the heavy water pilot plant in Atucha. For CERN, Geneva, it provided the basic design, procurement, and construction management for the "Muon chamber."[38]

The symbiotic relationship between the development of a domestic nuclear industry, supported and facilitated by the national government, and the potential benefits from technology transfer for the balance of payments is illustrated by reference to the fact that today between 20 and 40 percent of the production of Spanish construction companies involved in nuclear technology transfer has come from work abroad, to a great degree in developing countries (see table 15–1). The creation of an overseas market has been viewed by those involved in nuclear technology as a contribution to the Spanish economy. Spanish companies have been poised for the propitious moment to enter the nuclear markets in India and China.[39]

Concisely, Spain is using its own past experience as an importer of nuclear know-how and technology as the basis for its strategy in nuclear exports. It is recognized, nevertheless, that developing countries in general face financial and debt crises that do not allow them to easily tackle investment programs of the magnitude required by nuclear projects.[40] This, together with factors like profitability, might become a disincentive for export.

Another potential disincentive—a speculation on my part, not a fact—may be the relatively high failure rate of projects for nuclear technology transfer with which Spain has been involved. One characteristic of the

Table 15–1
Nuclear Transactions between Spain and Other Countries

Region/Recipient Country	Date of Action	Type of Transaction	Source
Latin America			
Mexico	1982	Westinghouse sources reveal that they are working with several Spanish firms to manufacture fuel-cycle technology, uranium enrichment, and smaller equipment and technology for export. Mexican nuclear technicians have been trained in Spain.	(1)
	Mid-1980s	Joint project between SENER, Fertimex, and Comision Federal de Electricidad for a plant producing yellowcake from phosphoric acid, using Spanish technology (JEN).	(2)
	Mid-1980s	ENUSA offers and presumably provides fuel fabrication services to Mexico in connection with the U.S. firms DOE and Technabexport.	(3)
	1985	ENSA exports a weld of main circulation piping and steam piping to Comision Federal de Electricidad of Mexico for its Laguna Verde nuclear plant.	(4)
Chile	1970–77	Agreement reached for a research reactor and fuel to be sited near Santiago. The reactor in financially supported with Spanish government funds to 50% of con.	(5)
Argentina	1980	SENER provides quality assurance for the heavy-water pilot plant in Atucha II.	(6)
	1984–86	Spanish participation in the international cooperation project to supply the reactor pressure vessel and its internals for the heavy-water pilot plant in Atucha II. Spain is represented by ENSA, which is providing the heavy water reactor head.	(7)
Ecuador	1984–85	Intergovernmental agreement for the supply of a complete nuclear research center, including the reactor, fuel, and "hot laboratories."	(8)
Colombia	February 1985	President Betancur signs into law	(9)

Table 15–1 continued

Region/Recipient Country	Date of Action	Type of Transaction	Source
		a nuclear cooperation agreement with Spain, which is concluded in December 1980.	
Middle East			
Egypt	Mid-1980s (in process)	Westinghouse, leading a multinational consortium, bids for the Al-Dab'qh plant in Egypt. Egypt has decided to press ahead with its nuclear program, but it has been questioned in government circles whether Egypt can afford to proceed with such an expensive project.	(10)
	Mid-1980s	ENUSA is involved in negotiations regarding a nuclear power plant to be built in Egypt, to supply the first core and several refuelings for the PWR reactor. This participation includes design, manufacturing, and staff training.	(11)
	December 1984	ACOM-ATAC bids on the Al-Dab'qh nuclear power plant in Egypt, Westinghouse consortium.	(12)
Israel	Mid-1980s	Plan to create a site and to install a nuclear reactor together with Westinghouse. Despite Israeli and Spanish government agreement on a deal, U.S. government opposition through Westinghouse aborts the contract.	(13)
Iraq	1980s	Spanish involvement through an obscure ad hoc engineering group in the Iraqi efforts to rebuild the processing plant destroyed by an Israeli air strike.	(14)
Iran	1986	Negotiations held jointly between Spanish and Argentinian firms with the Iranian Atom Commission to complete the work required at the Busher nuclear power installation, suspended in 1979 during the revolution.	(15)
Turkey	October 1983	Both Westinghouse and General Electric of the U.S. are competing by using reference to Spanish plants for Turkey's nuclear power project.	(16)

Table 15–1 continued

Region/Recipient Country	Date of Action	Type of Transaction	Source
West Asia			
Pakistan	1980	SENER is awarded a consulting contract by Pakistan's Atomic Energy Commission for the Chasma nuclear power light-water 900 MW plant. The project includes technology transfer to create a capability for the design and construction of nuclear power plants in Pakistan. In December 1984 SENER says it will extend its open-ended contract for two more years.	(17)
	Mid-1980s	Transaction involving cooperation between Spanish firms and Westinghouse aborted through indirect intervention of the U.S. government.	(18)
East Asia			
Japan	March 1985	Japan's Central Research Institute of Electric Power Industry begins to exchange information with European countries via the Unipede significant event reporting system (USERS). Spain is member of USERS since its founding.	(19)
People's Republic of China	October 1985	Spain and the PRC are to sign a nuclear cooperation agreement during the Third International Conference on nuclear technology transfer, held in Madrid in October 1985.	(20)
North Africa			
Morocco	Late-1980s	Spanish initiative in good competitive position that has not been consummated yet because of possible lack of funds on the Moroccan side.	(21)
Europe			
France	1986	The French Commisariat a l'Energie Atomique signs an agreement with the Spanish JEN and the Spanish waste management company ENRESA on radioactive waste management. The agreement covers exchange of information and various services to be rendered by JEN and ENRESA.	(22)
Switzerland	Mid-1980	Joint service carried between SENER and CERN that provided the basic design,	(23)

Table 15–1 continued

Region/Recipient Country	Date of Action	Type of Transaction	Source
		procurement, and construction management for the "Muon Chamber."	
Portugal	Mid-1980s (in process)	Initially favorable prospects to build a joint Spanish-Portuguese nuclear plant on their common border, later reviewed by Portugal. The nuclear plant will now be sited in Portugal only, and the technology will no longer be primarily Spanish because the bidding has been opened to others.	(24)
West Germany	1982	ENSA supplies KWU to West Germany, with miscellaneous repair parts for reactors, and in 1985 and 1986 provides pressurizers to KWU's ISAR-2 and GKN-2.	(25)
	Late-1980s	ACOM-ATAC bids on the ISAR II nuclear power plant in West Germany.	(26)
Yugoslavia	1985	INITEC and Spanish Westinghouse, in a consortium also involving companies from the U.S., Switzerland, and Finland, are reportedly participating in negotiations for the construction of a nuclear power plant to be sited at Prevlaku.	(27)
United Kingdom	1983	ENSA supplies the United Kingdom's atomic energy authority mock-ups.	(28)
North America United States	1984	Spain has become the tenth participant in the Loss-of-Fluid-Test (LOFT) project located in the U.S. Idaho National Engineering Laboratory.	(30)
	June 1986	Spain and the United States sign two memoranda of understanding concerning energy research and development. The pacts are over nuclear energy rad waste management and may include joint projects and exchanges of personnel, testing samples, and information.	(29)

1. *Nucleonics Week*, 28 January 1982, p. 2.
2. Secretaria de Estado de Comercio, Forum Atomico Español, *La Industria Nuclear Española* (Madrid, June 1986), p. 39.

Table 15–1 continued

Region/Recipient Country	Date of Action	Type of Transaction	Source

3. "Spain Joins the World's Light Water Reactors Fuel Vendors," *Nuclear Engineering International* (June 1986).
4. EQUIPOS NUCLEARES S.A., Reference List of Nuclear Production.
5. Interviews with pertinent Spanish government officials and selected managers of the Spanish nuclear industry, March, June, and September 1987.
6. Industria Nuclear Espanola, p. 39.
7. "Spain Joins the World's Light Water Reactors," p. 15.
8. *Luz y Fuerza* (January–February 1985).
9. "Agreement with Spain," *Worldwide Report*, 1 April 1986.
10. Interviews, 1987; and *Worldwide Report*, 26 March 1986, p. 46.
11. *Industria Nuclear Española*, pp. 157–62.
12. Ibid., pp. 129–34.
13. *Flash Atomico*, no. 89, 20 March 1985.
14. Interviews, 1987.
15. London *Times*, 9 March 1987; *Le Monde* (Paris), 10 March 1987; and *Nucleonics Week*, 30 October 1986, pp. 4–5.
16. *Nucleonics Week*, 6 October 1983, p. 83.
17. SENER "Energy," Las Arenas (Vizcaya), January 1984, pp. 2, 3, 8; and *Nucleonics Week*, 6 December 1984, pp. 9–19.
18. Interviews, 1987; and *Flash Atomico*, no. 89, 20 March 1985.
19. *Nuclear Engineering* (April 1985): 8.
20. *Nuclear News*, (November 1985): 103–106.
21. Interviews, 1987; and *Flash Atomico*, no. 89, 20 March 1985.
22. *Nuclear News* (September 1986): 74–75.
23. *Industria Nuclear Española*, p. 39.
24. Ibid.
25. Equipos Nucleares.
26. *Industria Nuclear Española*, pp. 129–34.
27. *Flash Nuclear*, no. 88, 28 February 1985.
28. Equipos Nucleares.
29. *Nuclear News* (June 1984). 70.
30. Ibid. (November 84): 176.

Spanish nuclear export industry involved in major export projects is that it must usually join with companies from advanced nuclear countries to be effective competitively. This aspect must be emphasized, because it is the basic Spanish approach to nuclear export, making Spain's transactions instrumentally related to the policy decisions in the governmental and private sectors of primary nuclear suppliers.[41]

During the 1980s almost all such ventures have not borne fruit, notwithstanding Spanish government subsidies in the form of guaranteeing companies outlays through loans at reduced interest, as low as 2 percent, and long-term conditions of up to fifty years. An illustration of the commitment of the Spanish government in supporting a nascent Spanish export capability, shown in the past, are the subsidies given to JEN in connection with an agreement with Chile for a research reactor and fuel to be sited near Santiago, in the 1970s. The reactor, which started operation in 1977, was financially supported with Spanish government funds to 50 percent of costs.[42]

Seven major projects are in question, involving Egypt, Iraq, Israel, Mexico, Morocco, Pakistan, and Portugal. Some of these agreements were successfully negotiated, like the one with Egypt, but could not begin implementation because of lack of funds in the recipient country. Spain is involved through a group from INI, contributing engineering services and equipment worth about $400 million. The transaction also involves Westinghouse (United States), Framatome (France), Kraftwerk Union (West Germany), and Japan, and was set to begin the building of the nuclear reactor site this year. Another transaction, in Mexico, is also a joint venture, but involves many competitors, including two Spanish industrial groups bidding against each other; it has not been successful, again, seemingly, because of financial shortfalls in the recipient country. Others, like the transactions with Pakistan and Israel, were on the way to success. In Israel, the plan was to create a site and to install a nuclear reactor together with Westinghouse. Former Prime Minister Peres and the Israeli government were keen to conclude a deal, as was the PSOE Spanish government. But U.S. government opposition, leveraged through Westinghouse, aborted the contract. Another transaction with Pakistan, also involving cooperation with Westinghouse, was similarly aborted through the intervention of the United States.[43]

In Morocco, a Spanish initiative has been in a good competitive position, but no Moroccan decision has been made, again possibly for lack of funds. The Spaniards have also been involved, through an obscure ad hoc engineering group, in the Iraqi efforts to rebuild the processing plant originally built by the Italians and subsequently destroyed by an Israeli air strike. It is not clear where matters stand. Finally, although originally prospects looked quite good for building a joint Spanish-Portuguese nuclear plant on their common border, Portugal decided to review the decision to site at the border, using primarily Spanish technology. The nuclear plant will now be sited in Portugal only, and the bidding has been opened to includes others, especially the British.[44]

Additionally, three transactions are worthy of notice. During the past several years, an intergovernmental agreement was reached with Ecuador for the supply of a complete nuclear research center, including the reactor, fuel, and "hot" laboratories. The financial assistance from the Spanish government, though less than 50 percent, was to be substantial. A nuclear cooperation agreement was signed between Spain and Colombia in 1986, and in 1985 two Spanish companies (in a consortium also involving companies from the United States, Switzerland, and Finland) were reportedly participating in negotiations for the construction of a nuclear power plant to be sited at Prevlaku, Yugoslavia. Spain is represented by INITEC and Spanish Westinghouse. T. former would provide engineering services, the latter the reactors. More recently, in 1987, there were reports that Spanish and Argentine firms were jointly negotiating with the Iranian Atomic Energy Commission to complete the work required at the Busher nuclear power installation, suspended in 1979 during the revolution. The point nuclear technology would be provided by Kraftwerk Union through ENACE, an Argentine company in which it owns 25 percent of the stock—the remaining 75 percent belongs to the Argentine Atomic Energy Commission.[45]

Interpolating from the various sources utilized, the following summary points may be tentatively made.

Spanish uranium exploration, mining, and extraction technology is exportable to developing countries, in particular to Latin America, because of the competitive advantage possessed by Spain in regard to language and historical ties. The fact that the Spanish government, instead of private industry, manages the uranium industry makes this export more attractive to the governments of developing countries. This sector has been strengthened by recent policy decisions. Empresa Nacional del Uranio (ENUSA) has announced an investment program of $63 million for the next five years to enlarge domestic uranium production. Concurrently, investment plans have also been announced for Empresa Nacional de Residuos (ENRESA), Spain's nuclear waste management organization.[46]

In the area of nuclear fuel conversion and enrichment, Spain was until recently poorly postured for export. Until the 1980s, there was no domestic program, although ENUSA owned 11.11 percent of the uranium enrichment consortia Eurodif, which enabled it to participate in the enrichment production of the Tricastin plant in France. Nevertheless, because of a relatively large and not totally usable stockpile of enriched uranium, ENUSA has attempted to sell enriched uranium abroad—to the United States, Sweden, and Mexico, for example. Such transfers would be subject to the retransfer conditions imposed by DOE (United States), Techsnabexport (Soviet Union), and Eurodif (France).[47]

With the start-up of the Juzbado fuel fabrication plant in June 1985 and the completion of three batches of fuel, fuel fabrication is a technology now available in Spain. ENUSA now joins the ranks of the world's LWR fuel vendors. This is an example of how a technology recipient country becomes a vendor country, itself transferring nuclear technology. The current capability was spawned, in December 1972, when ENUSA entered into technical assistance contracts and patent licenses with Westinghouse and General Electric for the design and manufacture of nuclear fuel and core components. The licenses impose no limitations on export, so that ENUSA has offered, and presumably provided, fuel fabrication services to Mexico. However, the bids were in conjunction with the U.S. companies mentioned.[48]

Regarding the export of equipment for commercial nuclear power plants, most export sales relate to the primary nuclear circuit and ancillary equipment for fuel-loading purposes. Because of long-standing experience, Spanish companies can be competitive in required, but not specifically nuclear, goods such as pressure vessels, valves, and their installation. Grosso modo, Spain can neither provide all the essential components required nor be sufficiently competitive cost-wise without government subsidy; nor can it provide sufficient design capability for a full fuel cycle, in competition with American and French competitors and often with British and German vendors.[49]

As of May 1986, there were eight nuclear power units in commercial operation in Spain (for a quick comparison: there are three in Italy, eight in Belgium, five in Switzerland, and forty-nine in France). Two additional ones are under moratorium. On these ten sites, seven Westinghouse PWR reactors, four General Electric BWR reactors, two Kraftwerk Union PWR reactors, and one Framatome graphite-gas reactor have been installed. There is no capability, therefore, to manufacture nuclear reactors in Spain. It should be pointed out in this context, however, that practically 100 percent of the engineering design, procurement, construction management, preoperational testing, and start-up of nuclear power plants being built in Spain can be done by Spanish firms, using local resources and capabilities. This can be, and has been, variously translated into export potential.[50]

What Spain can surely provide, principally through the JUNTA de ENERGIA NUCLEAR, is assistance in the establishment of research laboratories, research reactors, hot-cell facilities, research reactors fuel fabrication, and research reactors reprocessing facilities. Developing countries represent practically the only market for such exports. Spain has targeted, consequently, Latin American countries particularly for its export efforts in these areas. For developing countries in general, Spain is also competitive in infrastructure engineering and consultant services. These services include plant engineering and design, applied mechanics and structural dynamics, procurement and construction management, plant operational testing and start-up, and quality assurance.[51] Again, there is a direct correlation between domestic nuclear industry capacity and technology transfer as a nuclear supplier. Spain is now in the position of being able to transfer technology to Third World countries that are in a situation similar to that of Spain at the beginning of its nuclear program.

The Structures

The relationship between formal decisionmaking procedures and the actual decisionmaking process operates, in the first instance, in shared values. Shared values leaven the unspoken assumptions that set the parameters for the actual negotiations to reach decisions on specific transactions that occur between regulating officials and private entrepreneurs. This is particularly so in the nuclear sector in Spain, where government participation through the public sector has been substantial for years and could increase under a Socialist government.

In Spain, what are the assumptions and normative values about nuclear commerce that are shared by political decisionmakers and private entrepreneurs? To begin with, the Spanish government has been, all along, a strong supporter of the export of nuclear technology. Diplomatic channels have been used to promote export, with officials in the Ministry of Trade and in the Foreign Office taking an active role in support of exporting companies. Through JEN and INI, the government itself has been directly and indirectly involved in commerce involving Spanish nuclear technology transfer.[52]

The Spanish government has also played, during the 1970s and 1980s, an instrumental role in nuclear exports by providing financial support, including at times outright subsidies—as was done in the transaction that provided Chile with a research reactor in the 1970s. At times this support has taken the form of facilitating loans from the state to be combined with those from private banks. These loans continue to be obtainable at interest rates as low as 2 percent and for periods of up to fifty years for repayment.[53] An illustrative example is the research technology transfer to Mexico. Another example of traditional governmental attitudes toward nuclear exports is the strong support given SENER when this private-sector company was entering into an agreement for quality assurance services for a heavy-water plant in Argentina. Upon the request of the Argentine government, the Spanish Ministry of Trade officially assured Argentina that the Spanish government would not curtail the activities of SENER. Allegedly, similar attitudes would prevail if Third World countries, like Pakistan, requested assistance in areas such as reprocessing.[54]

Spanish private-sector managers and entrepreneurs remain convinced that the key to success in international agreements dealing with nuclear technology transfer is sufficient flexibility to permit both the transmitters and the recipients a continuous adaptation to the circumstances of each recipient country. They see the ultimate objective of the technology transfer to be the creation of local capabilities in the several industrial sectors that participate in a nuclear project. In fact, they believe the greatest success in the technology transfer process to be epitomized when a country that has been, and continues to be in some respects, a recipient of nuclear technology transfer, eventually becomes itself a technology transmitter. Spain is cited as an example. Some government role is seen as necessary, but primarily to ensure reasonable reference terms and to avoid the squandering of economic resources. Such views are found in both public and private sectors. In regard to technology transfer, Spanish decisionmakers in the private sector believe that technology is best transferred through know-how and technical assistance arrangements, usually without patent licenses.[55]

There is little question that after many years of intimate relationships between the public and private sectors in nuclear development, it is difficult to draw a clearly distinguishable line between formal decisionmaking procedures and the intrinsic relationship between the bureaucracy and the nuclear export sector. This is made all the more difficult by the fact that the government is itself involved in nuclear commerce because of public-sector ownership, through INI, for example.

INI's public ownership represents the most important Spanish business group, with a total turnover of 1.500 million pesetas and one hundred seventy thousand employees. It is one of the most important European industrial groups. The activity of INI unfolds in the strategic economic sectors, as well as in the high technology and industrial service sectors. Highly significant in the national economy, INI works in close collaboration with the private sector and finds foreign partners for joint projects, as well. In this respect, the significant collaboration of INI with important international technological projects like EUREKA, ESPRIT, EFA, and AIRBUS, among others, is illustrative.[56]

Nevertheless, how does the relationship between the public and private sectors in nuclear energy actually function? And how does government decisionmaking affect it? At the outset, it should be made clear that because Spain has not yet fully elaborated a well-defined nuclear export policy, the effective mandate of individual decisionmaking entities—and the actual relationships among them—continue to be in flux.[57]

A nexus exists, prima facie, between the nuclear export sector and the Ministry of External Affairs. One pertinent department within the ministry, the Directorate for Technical International Cooperation, has been charged by the government to coordinate the negotiations with Euratom and the IAEA. However, nuclear export decisions are jointly discussed between the Ministry of Commerce and the Ministry of Industry and Energy, and only occasionally with the Foreign Ministry, and then on a case-by-case basis. The Ministry of Industry and Energy has been by far the most important actor, crucially involved in the drafting of the numerous bilateral agreements Spain has throughout the world.[58] Because of the intimate relationship between the energy sector and the nuclear sector, and energy and the economy, this is understandable.

Other entities relevant to nuclear technology export are the Secretaria de Estado de Comercio [State Agency for Trade], the Instituto Nacional de Fomento de la Exportacion [National Institute for the Promotion of Exports], the parliamentary Comision de Industria, Obras Publicas y Energia [Committee on Industry, Public Works and Energy], and the Foreign Ministry's Directorate for Security and Disarmament.[59]

It is also undeniable that the Spanish nuclear industry has acquired notable weight in policymaking, most visible in the Ministry of Industry and Energy. One reason for the growth in this influence has been the increased financial participation of the industry in the construction of nuclear power plants for generating electricity. In the second generation of nuclear power units, Spanish industry invested in the range of 80 to 85 percent.[60] Another reason has been the growth in the number of public and private sector firms involved in nuclear export activities during the recent decade.[61]

The symbiotic relationship between the public and private sectors of the Spanish nuclear industry, with its implications for export and nuclear technology transfer, must be framed within an ambitious National Development Plan for Electronics and Informatics, launched by the government in 1984. Its basic objective is to propel Spain to technological equivalence with the rest of Europe. One feature of the plan is to create high-volume export-oriented sectors. It calls for changes in the laws on public entity purchases and on technology development, as well as modifying the government structure to handle these sectors. Among the instruments to be used to accomplish these goals are investment loans, export credits, and R&D subsidies.[62] The Spanish nuclear export sector has been benefiting from similar government assistance. Concurrently, also in 1984, a reformulated national energy plan was launched.

It may be too early to assess what impact the energy plan and the other legislation noted above will ultimately have on the Spanish nuclear export sector. However, it must be pointed out that there exists an intimate relationship between what happens in the government subsidy and in private-sector profits and national energy requirements, and the capacities for export in the Spanish nuclear sector. Retrenchment in government subsidy, consequent reduction in R&D, and investment or financial problems in the private sector can directly impact on nuclear export capabilities.

Several developments are worth noting in this connection: curtailment in the future growth of nuclear plants in Spain; the consequent retrenchment in regard to nuclear-related manufactures and activities; the effects of the financial crisis in the energy sector of Catalonia on financing in the private sector of energy; and the decline in the manufacture of nuclear equipment by some major Spanish firms.

In 1986, nuclear production of electric energy achieved second place, ahead of electricity generated hydroelectrically, for the first time ever, providing 29.1 percent of national consumption. Net consumption of electricity increased in the same period 2.4 percent. Nevertheless, energy demand fell below the 3.7 percent average for the preceding decade, and it is unlikely that the moratorium on the construction or completion of the five nuclear power plants previously projected will be lifted.[63] The only possible exception may be the Vandellos 2 plant.

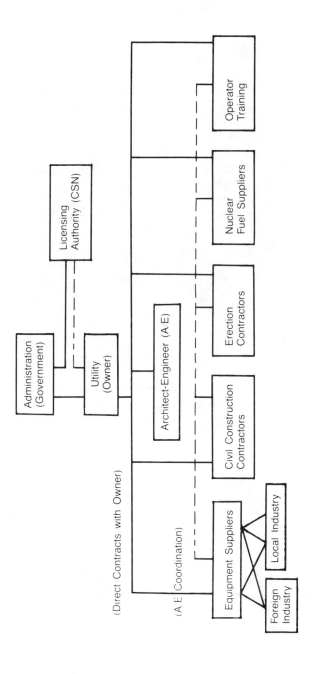

Figure 15–1. Decisional Flowchart of the Interface between Public and Private Sectors in Spain's Nuclear Industry

Source: Secreteria de Estado de Comercio, Forum Atomico Español, *La Industria Nuclear Española* (Madrid, June 1986), p. 9.

Moreover, the severe financial crisis that hit Fuerzas Electricas de Cataluña (FECSA) during the second half of 1987 has had quite an impact on the electric energy utilities, negatively affecting the nuclear sector. Constructora del Pirineo S.A. (COPISA) has left the nuclear business, another major company, CENEMESA, is retooling from nuclear equipment to military hardware (helicopters), and so is General Electric Español. Because the government will no longer subsidize Grandes Bienes de Equipo, the production of nuclear equipment is also in jeopardy.[64]

Although the decisional flowchart in figure 15–1 relates to domestic operations, it does expose the basic relationships between the government and the public and private sectors in the construction of the infrastucture and the installation of a nuclear power complex.

It is apparent that the Spanish government continues to be a strong supporter of the export of nuclear technology, in order to both help the domestic industry and to improve its international diplomacy in the Third World. The guidelines generally governing the export of nuclear technology are the acceptance of IAEA safeguards regulations and the London Nuclear Supplier Group guidelines. Spain's own domestic nuclear operations have been under direct and explicit IAEA safeguards since 1981. The export of sensitive nuclear equipment requires special licenses by the ministries of commerce and industry. The Foreign Office is consulted when nuclear exports may have diplomatic repercussions. CSN, the licensing authority, may also be consulted, but under circumstances not yet fully clear.[65]

Safeguards became more stringent on all Spanish nuclear operations as the result of the negotiations for Spain's membership in the European Community, specifically Euratom—although, paradoxically, Spain's legal right to a military option was recognized. Practically, however, because Spain had not set aside any nuclear facilities, the acceptance of both IAEA and Euratom inspection of all Spanish nuclear facilities makes an eventual clandestine military operation highly unlikely.

Spain's particular relationship and safeguard obligations in Euratom took about three years to clarify. Spain encountered, during the negotiations required to join Euratom, several complications and difficulties created by the positions assumed by the Netherlands and Denmark. Both countries would vote against Spanish membership as long as Spain was not a signatory to the NPT. Difficulties were also posed by Australia, an important supplier of nuclear raw materials to the EEC, which insisted that only countries belonging to the NPT could be provisioned. One of the means by which these objections could be met was for Spain to accept more safeguards, which it did—not only on Spanish territory, but wherever Spain conducted nuclear activities.[66]

The Norms

During the Franco regime, the Spanish government steadfastly refused to accede to the NPT. During the transitional phase to the parliamentary regime, under the UCD government, the position remained unchanged. The only dissenting voice regarding the NPT was that of the PSOE.[67]

Once elected and firmly in power, however, the Socialist government too returned, in 1984, to the traditional Spanish position on the NPT.[68] Yet on 24 February 1987, the Spanish government officially announced accession to the Nuclear Non-Proliferation Treaty, and later in the year ratified it.

To ferret out the determinants that finally induced the Spanish government to join the NPT, is to clarify its significance for Spanish nuclear technology transfer. Two factors played a crucial role in the decision. The first, strongly focused in domestic politics, may be labeled "the denuclearization of Spain." The second, which could be labeled "the adaptation to membership in the European Community," derives from Spain's recent normalization in Western international politics. Together they organized the pressures that led to the changes in the official Spanish attitude toward nuclear proliferation, returning the PSOE to its original position.

Concern about the role of the atom in Spanish society arose first in a military context, and exclusively in regard to U.S. nuclear weapons stationed in Spain. This concern was catalyzed by the "Palomares incident," in the 1960s, when a U.S. bomber mistakenly released a nuclear bomb in flight, which landed in the sea off the town of Palomares. Thereafter, public fears, combined with nationalism, forced the Spanish government, through the means afforded by the negotiations required to renew the use of U.S. military facilities on Spanish territory, to require all U.S. nuclear weapons stationed in Spain to be withdrawn.

Antinuclear attitudes in Spain remained focused on concern with American military operations in a nationalist mold until the transitional Sotelo government launched an ambitious nuclear energy program at the beginning of the 1980s. Thereafter, Leftist parties, spearheaded by the PSOE, focused Spanish antinuclear attitudes on the nuclear energy program—in terms not primarily of Spain going militarily nuclear, but of a national economy going nuclear in the energy field, with the attendant fears concerning nuclear safety. It was the latter that agitated, and continues to agitate, the public most in domestic politics.[69]

It should be underscored, however, that concern with the potential harmful effects of the civilian atom centers on safety, the environment, and economic and political aspects at home. The nuclear debate is very politicized in regard to the autonomies in Cataluna and the Basque country, where it becomes involved with the issue of separatist terrorism. There is practically no attention given to the international proliferation aspects. Looking ahead, it is doubtful that nonproliferation will become a significant issue relating to the transfer of nuclear technology in the political debate. There is no influential interest group to mobilize the issue. The "denuclearization of Spain" remains focused on the homeland. Its future depends more on the state of the economy, particularly as it defines itself in energy requirements and technological progress, and on the mix of public and market economics shaped by the policies of the Socialist government, in general and in the nuclear sector.[70]

Participation in the European Community seems to have had a more significant impact on Spanish nuclear technology transfer policies than domestic political unrest about nuclear matters. The political acculturation of the Spanish foreign policy elites and of government and industrial technocrats, which has been occurring during recent years in connection with negotiations for Spain's participation in the European Community and Euratom, suggests that Spain is adopting assumptions and attitudes closely resembling those of other West European countries. A considered judgment would place Spain closest to the French model of participation—an approach that combines a strong political commitment to national independence with notable commercial pragmatism.

I should like to acknowledge, with appreciation, the invaluable comments of Don Jose Mario Armero and the research assistance provided for this chapter by Carmen Perez, of CISA, and Katlyn Saba and Luis Pascual, of INCI.

Notes

1. Antonio Sanchez-Gijon, "España Potencia Atomica," *El Pais*, (Madrid) 25 June 1976; "La Bomba Atomica Que Nos Legò el Franquismo," *Actual*, (Madrid) 20 April 1982, pp. 33–41; Antonio Brotons, "España y el Tratado de No Proliferacion Nuclear," *Sistema 66*, Madrid (May 1985) [all published in Madrid]; and Angel Viñas, *Non-Proliferation: The Why and Wherefore* (Stockholm: SIPRI, 1986).

2. "España y el Fantasma de la Bomba Atomica," *Blanco y Negro* (Madrid, March 1980).

3. "La tentaciòn de la bomba," *El Pais, (Madrid) Sunday ed., 1 February 1987; "España posee estudios precisos para fabricar armas nucleares," El Pais*, 1 February 1987; "Serra admite que hacen estudios teorico sobre el uso de armas atomicas," *El Pais*, 2 February 1987.

4. The position of the traditionalist military is explained in General Eduardo Munilla Gomez, *Introduccion a La Estrategia Militar Espanola* (Madrid: Publicaciones del EME, 1984), p. 202. General Munilla was, at the time of this publication, retiring as the head of the Defense Policy Section of the Ministry of Defense.

See also: Otero Madrigal [vice-president of the Council of Europe], "Espana nunca debe firmarlo el TNP," *El Pais*, 30 April 1982. The neutralist argument is in *Diario 16* (Madrid) 26 June 1983.

5. "Decalogue" presented by Prime Minister Gonzales to the Cortes in parliamentary debate on Spanish defense. Spanish Congress, Foreign Policy Committee, "Sesion Informativa," 18 February 1983, and *El Pais*, 23 October 1983.

6. *El Pais*, 29 January 1987' "El Pais", Madrid; and *ABC* (Madrid), 11 April 1987. A detailed analysis of the Spanish government's decision to accede to the Non-Proliferation Treaty is in: Katlyn Saba *Spain and the Non-Proliferation Treaty* (Madrid: INCI, July 1987).

7. "La politica de defensa espanola y la Otan," *Ideas*, no. 1 (1984): 355; Jose L. Buhigas *et als.*, *Bases y Reducciones: La Negociaciones EE. UU.* (Madrid: INCI, 1987). For a discussion of how Spain arrived at its decision to join NATO, see: Javier Ruperez, *Espana En La Otan; Relato Parcial* (Barcelona: Plaza & Janes, 1986).

8. *Interviews* with military officers of the Spanish Defense Ministry, selected officials of the Spanish Foreign Office, and officials of the PSOE charged with defense matters, November and December 1986 and June and September 1987.

9. Ibid.; and *El Pais*, 19 November 1986.

10. The definitive works on Spanish defense during the Franco era are: Angel Vinas, *Los Pactos Secretos de Franco con Estados Unidos* (Barcelona: Ediciones Grijalbo, 1981); and Antonio Marquina, *Espana En La Politica de Seguridad Occidental 1939–1986*, EME, (Madrid: Coleccion "Ediciones Ejercito", 1986). As the latter's title suggests, Marquina also covers the period of the present democratic regime. For a debate on the pros and cons of Spain's participation in NATO, see: Instituto de Cuestiones Internacionales, *Espana Dentro de la Alianza Atlantica* (Madrid, 1986). A complete narrative of the reorganization of Spanish defense in the democratic regime is in: Ministerio de Defensa, *Memoria: Legislatura 1982–86* (Madrid, 1986).

11. *Interviews*, note 8; and Katlyn Saba, *Spain and the Non-Proliferation Treaty*, p. 9.

12. Saba, *ibid.*, p. 7.

13. See, for example: Forum Atomico Espanol, *Espana en la Cee: Experiencia de la Explotacion Nuclear en la Comunidad Europea* (Madrid, November 1985); and *Interview* with a Foreign Ministry official, September 1987.

14. *Interviews*, note 8; and Saba, *Spain and the Non-Proliferation Treaty*, p. 10

15. Estado Espanol, Consejo de Seguridad Nuclear, *Informe al Congreso de Los Diputados y al Senado*, Madrid, 31 December 1985 and 30 June 1986.

16. *Luz y Fuerza* (Madrid, January–February 1985): pp. 21–24, and "El Ministerio de Industria estudia poner fin a la moratoria nuclear," *El Pais*, 20 April 1987.

17. Federación de la Energia UGT-ICCF, Apendice, *La Crisis Nuclear: Una Alternativa Socialista para Espana*, (Madrid: Ediciones Blune, 1981) and Government of Spain, Congress "Informe al Congreso de Diputados y al Senado," 15 October 1986, pp. 136–137.

18. *ABC*, 9 July 1987; *El Pais*, 9 July 1987; and *Luz y Fuerza*, March–April and May–June 1987.

19. The political and philosophical framework is explained in: Felipe Gonzales, *Socialismo y Libertad* (Barcelona: Galba, 1978).

20. Alison Wright, *The Spanish Economy, 1959–1976* (London: Macmillan, 1977), pp. 26–48.

21. *Ibid.*

22. *Ibid.*

23. L. Tsoukalis, *The European Community and its Enlargement* (London: George Allen & Unwin, 1981), p. 80; and Victor Perez Diaz, "Politicas economicas y pautas sociales en la Espana de la transicion: la doble cara del neocorporatismo," in Juan Linz, ed., *Espana: Un Presente Para el Futuro* (Madrid: Instituto de Estudios Economicos, 1984), pp. 33–48.

24. Secreteria de Estado de Comercio, Forum Atomico Espanol, *La Industria Nuclear Espanola* (Madrid, June 1986), pp. 2–3.

25. Avelino Garcia Villarejo, *Espana Ante la Actual Crisis Economica* (Barcelona: Editorial Labor, 1977), pp. 152–72, 184–94.

26. Eladio Garcia Castro, *La Crisis Economica: Alternativa Democratica al Pacto de Moncloa* (Madrid: Manifiesto Editorial, 1978).

27. *Nations Business*, (December 1987): 64.

28. An examination anticipating nuclear technology transfer as a proliferation problem is in: Ciro E. Zoppo, "Toward a US Policy on Nuclear Technology Transfer to Developing Countries," California Seminar on Arms Control and Foreign Policy, Santa Monica, July 1972.

29. Ibid.

30. *Interviews* with pertinent Spanish government officials and selected managers of the Spanish nuclear industry, March, June, and September 1987.

31. Ibid.

32. Ibid. For the Franco period, see: Jose Mario Armero, *La Politica Exterior de Franco* (Barcelona: Editorial Planeta, 1978), pp.183–99; 233–39. For the period of the democratic regime, especially regarding the Socialist outlook, see: Fernando Moran, *Una Politica Exterior Para Espana* (Barcelona: Editorial Planeta, 1980), pgs. 289–404.

33. J.B. Donges, "La insuficiencia de la productividad en la economia española," in Juan Linz, ed., *España: Un Presente Para el Futuro* (Madrid: Instituto de Estudios Economicos, 1984), pp. 99–124, and 127.

34. *Interviews*, note 8; and Moran, *Una Politica Exterior Para España*.

35. "Sercobe," in Forum Atomico Español, *Industria Nuclear Española*, p. 120.

36. *Interviews*, note 8.

37. SENER, "Energy," Las Arenas (Vizcaya), January 1984, pp. 2, 3, 8.

38. Forum Atomico Español, *Industria Nuclear Española*, p. 39.

39. Industria Nuclear Española, and *Interviews*, pp. 67–69.

40. Ibid., p. 66.

41. *Interviews*, note 8.

42. Ibid.

43. *Interviews*, note 8; and *Flash Atomico*, no. 89, 20 March 1985.

44. Ibid.

45. *Luz y Fuerza* (January–February 1985); "Agreement with Spain," *Worldwide Report*, 1 April 1986; *Flash Nuclear*, no. 88, 28 February 1985, p. 87–G;

London Times, 9 March 1987; and *Le Monde* (Paris), 10 March 1987.

46. "Investing in U and Waste Management," *Nuclear News* (April 1986): 86

47. "Empresa Nacional del Uranio," in *Industria Nuclear Espanola*, p. 159.

48. "Spain Joins the World's Light Water Reactor Fuel Vendors," *Nuclear Engineering International* (June 1986).

49. *Interviews*, note 8; and *Industria Nuclear Española*, pp. 3–5.

50. "Ciencia y Futuro," *ABC* (Madrid), 13 May 1987.

51. *Interviews*, note 8; and *Industria Nuclear Española*, p. 39.

52. *Interviews*, note 8.

53. Ibid.

54. Ibid.

55. "Seminario Internacional sobre la Transferencia de la Tecnologia en la Fabricación Nuclear," Sesiones Plenarias, *Nuclear España* (December 1985): p. 81.

56. *Nations Business* (December 1987): 68.

57. *Interviews*, note 8.

58. Ibid.

59. Ibid.

60. SENER, "Energy," Las Arenas (Vizcaya), January 1984, pp. 2, 3, 8.

61. An idea of the size and makeup of the sector relevant to nuclear technology is in: *Industria Nuclear Española*, pp. 15–162. Interviews with selected members of the business community sustained this information.

62. "Spain Outlines Ambitious Plan for Its High-Tech Industries," *Business America*, 9 July 1984, pp. 27 ff.; *Industria Nuclear Española*, pp. 1–7.

63. *El Pais* (June 1985); *Expansion* (Madrid), 26 May 1987; *Cinco Dias*, 15 May 1987; and *ABC* (Madrid), 9 July 1987.

64. *Interviews*, note 8; and *Expansion*, 5-13 May 1987.

65. *Interviews*, note 8.

66. *El Pais*, 15 October 1984 and 11 February 1987.

67. "España y el Fantasma de la Bomba Atómica," *Blanco y Negro* (Madrid, March 1980).

68. Ibid.

69. *Interviews*, note 8.

70. Ibid.

16
Taiwan

George H. Quester

T his is an attempt to analyze what the Republic of China (ROC) and its domain on Taiwan will be like as a nuclear supplier in the future. Because of the advanced state of its nuclear industrial activities, and because of its threatened position—ousted from the United Nations and treated as a "pariah state," with the Communist People's Republic of China on the mainland never totally renouncing the military option for seizing control over Taiwan—the Taipei regime has long been a source of concern as to whether it would seek to acquire nuclear weapons for itself.[1] Strong U.S. government interventions have several times been required after reports that research was under way in Taiwan laboratories on the reprocessing of plutonium and on other prerequisites to the production of a nuclear weapon.

But the focus here will be on a different question, less on whether the Republic of China would seek to acquire nuclear weapons for itself and more on whether it will be a cooperative or noncooperative partner in the 1990s and beyond, as we seek to head off other states that might be trying to acquire nuclear weapons for themselves. If some state in the future were to imitate Pakistan's behavior, shopping around the globe for the separate components of what could be put together as a nuclear weapons program, thus acquiring enriched uranium or plutonium at a weapons-grade level and then completing the necessary steps for bomb assembly, would Taipei be a good or bad place for it to shop?[2] Will the Republic of China and the facilities it controls on Taiwan be difficult or easy to enlist and control and coordinate, in what we have come to think of as a nonproliferation "regime"?

Transactions

The Republic of China has not yet really emerged as a supplier in the international market for nuclear materials and services, and I am thus largely speculating about the future here. Consistent with what has been the pattern on Taiwan's nuclear imports, the dominant motive on nuclear planning in general has been economic and is likely to continue to be economic, with "prestige" considerations being a product of, rather than an alternative to, such considerations as economic effectiveness and profit. The nuclear power program has played an important role in supporting the general economic prosperity of the island, and this prosperity has, in turn, been a major means for protecting the Republic of China against the worst of what could be viewed as a "pariah state" situation (see table 16–1).

Motives

In the 1970s, it was suspected that Taiwan's nuclear imports had been solely or mainly motivated by a desire to acquire nuclear weapons, or at least the option of nuclear weapons.[3] Such apprehensions arose at a time when most nations, including the United States, were terminating formal diplomatic relations with the Taipei regime, and when the prospect loomed that the world would simply close its eyes to the future of the island. The vitality of the ROC economy since then has proven a powerful antidote to such "pariahtude," with the nuclear factor thus being politically effective more because of its economic than because of its military configuration.

To dwell briefly on the concerns about the military uses the Republic of China might have made of nuclear technology for itself, it is one of the few places in the world where reactors have ever been built and gone into

Table 16–1
Taiwan's Nuclear Cooperation Agreements

Country	Dates of Origin	Type of Cooperation
Canada	1960s	Research reactor
United States	1950s	Training
	1970s	Power reactors
	1960s	Natural uranium
	1970s	Uranium enrichment
South Africa	1960s	Natural uranium
France	1970s	Uranium enrichment

Sources: Jon Payne, "Taiwan: Counting on Nuclear Energy," *Nuclear News* (September 1985): 74–78; Janine Holc, "Taiwan's Nuclear Energy Program," in *Country Notes* (Washington, D.C.: Center for Development Policy, August 1982); Leland Collins, *Korea and Taiwan: Security and the Nuclear Option* (International Energy Forum, 1984); and *Nuclear Fuel Cycle Materials, Services, and Sources* (Washington, D.C.: U.S. Arms Control and Disarmament Agency, 1979), pp. 209–16.

operation on schedule. Amid worldwide skepticism in the 1970s about whether "nuclear power production" was being used as a dual-purpose euphemism in nations seeking to acquire nuclear weapons options, the pace of such activity on Taiwan naturally enough caused concern.

Anyone making the case in the United States that nuclear weapons would emerge as a spinoff from what purportedly was intended for peaceful purposes—or from what actually was intended for peaceful purposes—thus could put Taiwan on his or her worry list, along with Brazil and Argentina, and West Germany earlier. If the nuclear investments involved were optimal for the domestic economic needs of the territory involved, there would still be reasons for concern about whether weapons production could assuredly be headed off. If the investments involved seemed at all premature, more-over, in light of reasonable predictions on economics and technological development, all the more worries would emerge about whether weapons were what was actually being sought. And having reactors go into operation on schedule might thus be simply an underlining of such worries.

When the OPEC oil price increases of the mid-1970s greatly increased the economic burdens of those states that were not self-sufficient in petro-leum, however, some of the skepticism had to abate. Taiwan is now second in the world in the percentage of its electricity produced by nuclear means, behind only France, hovering (along with Belgium) at close to 50 percent of its power coming from its six operating power reactors.[4] Electric power produced by nuclear reactors has proven to be cost-effective on Taiwan—costing perhaps half as much as electricity produced from fossil fuel—and is also much less of a draw on foreign exchange.

Work was under way in the middle 1970s at the Institute of Nuclear Energy Research on aspects of nuclear technology that would have been much more specifically useful to weapons production, and hardly so plausi-ble for civilian purposes, but this was halted when the U.S. government conveyed its strong objections to the Taipei regime.[5] Similar work was reportedly also detected in the spring of 1988, with the U.S. government again protesting and the ROC government again giving in.[6]

Transactions to Date

Although there have been periodic announcements by officials in the nu-clear development program that the Republic of China looked forward to exports in this field and wanted to be able to share its technological expertise as a way of earning foreign exchange, such announcements have been more generic and premature than detailed. In 1986, J.H. Chen, presi-dent of the Taiwan Power Company, granted an interview in which he commented that the company would be happy to work with Third World countries in the field of nuclear energy.[7] Apparently a team of advisors had gone to Thailand some years earlier to assist in that country's general planning for nuclear possibilities, and more recent discussions had been carried on with a utility in the Philippines; yet absence of diplomatic relations was generally a barrier, along with the narrowness of the actual experience on Taiwan, to any active pursuit of such projects.

The basic disincentives to a major entry by Taiwan into the international nuclear supplier market are thus twofold. First, Taiwan has not developed much of an indigenous capability in nuclear technology and services. Second, it is under a diplomatic cloud, since it is accorded formal diplomatic recognition by only a very few countries in the world. As will be discussed, the latter factor may become double-edged at some later time, perhaps causing the world's nonproliferation regime new concerns once the Republic of China indeed has important services or materials or equipment to export.

One kind of clandestine transaction that is normally worrisome for the nonproliferation regime is not likely to involve Taiwan—that of transshipments, where the Republic of China would itself be used as a go-between. Such transactions generally involve using some *nonsuspect* state as a euphemistic cover or intermediary, freeing the seller of any imputation of guilt if the sale is discovered, as the further delivery of the sensitive materials to their destination was allegedly something that could not have been suspected. Because of the Republic of China's status as an international pariah, (that is, as a regime with which very few nations have normal diplomatic relations) however, it would not work out as such a go-between state: it would not offer an excuse, to whoever was doing the selling, that nothing sinister was intended in the sale.

Since there are at present no formal diplomatic dealings involving the ROC regime at international bodies, there have been no occasions for formal elaborations of policy on safeguards over exports. The Taipei regime does not get invited to Nuclear Non-Proliferation Treaty (NPT) Review Conferences and the like. The fact that Taiwan is not yet in a position to export items on anyone's trigger list also precludes explication of a policy on safeguards.

The Republic of China has to date obtained no significant revenues from nuclear exports. Much more important to foreign exchange earnings have been all those ordinary exports that are facilitated by the cheaper electric power produced in nuclear reactors imported to the island, fueled by follow-on imports from abroad. The regime in Taipei has to be continually concerned about future flows of income and foreign exchange, even though its economy is presently doing well, and it may thus be considering the possibility of nuclear exports—but such exports are largely over the horizon.

The most significant overseas nuclear venture of the Republic of China hardly amounts to an export—namely, investments in uranium mining operations in the United States and other locations, so as to assure future fuel supplies for the reactors on Taiwan. The Republic of China has significant reserves of hard currency and thus can be of assistance to any such ventures that are short of capital. In 1985, it was announced that the Taiwan Power Company and the Rocky Mountain Energy Company in the United States had agreed on a joint venture in uranium exploration and development.[8] Earlier, there had been a venture, without positive results, in prospecting for uranium in Paraguay jointly with the U.S. Anschutz Mineral Company, and there were also signs of interest in a joint venture with French companies in Gabon.

Like any country operating power reactors, the Republic of China has had to be concerned about assuring its sources of uranium and its fuel fabrication services. About 70 percent of its uranium has come from South Africa, with the fuel being fabricated in the United States.[9] Interest has been shown (with a substantial concern for revenue by suppliers seeking Taiwan as a customer) in other linkages on uranium and on fuel supplier and enrichment services. Yet a number of such countries—for example, Australia—have been embarrassed by the difficulties imposed by the absence of diplomatic relations.[10]

Changes Over Time

It has to be noted that some earlier concerns about Taiwan as a nuclear recipient—that is, as a state that takes in nuclear imports and uses them for the production of nuclear explosive weapons—have also included speculations about Taiwan as an exporter. Worries emerged quite early about "pariah internationales" and "nuclear gray-markets," whereby regimes like the Republic of China and Israel and South Africa and South Korea (all somewhat under a cloud in the world diplomatic community and all also threatened militarily by hostile neighbors) might have been cooperating on the production of nuclear weapons: Each state would hold a piece of the puzzle, in its trained personnel or the nuclear operations it already had under way, and the consortium might then together sort out the process of producing nuclear warheads.[11]

Given the secrecy that all such states have had to adopt in the face of the hostility of neighbors and the world community, it has been inherently impossible to test and verify the rumors that have emerged. Many of these rumors have stemmed from sources as tainted as East Germany or the Soviet Union. Most of the allegations have pertained to possible cooperation between Israel and South Africa, with Taiwan and South Korea being brought into these supposed conspiracies somewhat less often.

There is one form of possible sensitive nuclear "export" that every regime engaged in nuclear power production would be willing to deliver if there were any "importers" willing to handle it—nuclear wastes and spent fuel. For the moment, the worldwide array of ecology movements has erected a general barrier to most such movements of these dangerous materials—materials that might also lend themselves to the production of weapons. West Germany and France and other operators of power reactors have encountered a larger problem in this regard; the United States, which once offered itself as the place to which such materials could be returned, has largely backed out of such a role.

For the moment, the ROC government intends to store its nuclear wastes on Orchid Island, 42 miles off the coast of Taiwan, and thus expects to be able to handle this problem for a considerable time into the future, at least to the year 2050.[12] Some spent fuel from a research reactor was agreed to be returned to Savannah River in 1985 (interestingly, this was fuel not of U.S. origin, but originally supplied by Canada).[13]

Ironically, the one regime in the world that has offered to be a recipient of such nuclear waste materials is the People's Republic of China, amid worries expressed in the West that this would lead to the augmentation of Beijing's nuclear weapons stockpile. It is quite difficult (but perhaps not impossible) to imagine a process whereby spent fuel and nuclear wastes from Taiwan would wind up being shipped, through intermediaries, to be transformed into fissionable nuclear weapons material in the People's Republic of China.

In a world where Taiwan would not have to respond to outside influences, the idea of selling nuclear wastes to another country that wished to convert such materials into a form usable for nuclear weapons might have seemed inherently appealing. The Republic of China would be rid of a hazard to its own health and ecology, and it would be paid in cash for having assisted nuclear proliferation. As long as the ultimate recipient was not a regime hostile to the Republic of China, like the Communist People's Republic of China, what would be the harm, for example, in selling to Argentina?

This kind of analysis probably underrates the extent to which the Taipei regime is aware of the hazards, to itself, in any uncontrolled and continuing spread of nuclear weapons around the world. And it certainly would underrate the extent to which the U.S. government continues to monitor what happens to spent fuels and nuclear waste materials on Taiwan. Although largely unwilling to accept custody of such materials for disposal or storage on its own territory, the U.S. government has certainly not washed its hands of a concern as to where these materials are moved.

Taiwan is a small part of the world economy and of the world political system. As such, it cannot ignore outside pressures. Much of the analytical problem here thus comes in gauging the nature and the relative weight of such pressures. What the United States thinks, and is happy about, will have to count for a great deal on Taiwan for a long time into the future. Yet what the United States thinks, and is happy about, has also had to count for a great deal in West Germany, and the results of nuclear supply decisions were nonetheless on several occasions less than optimal.

While U.S. inclinations will remain important, there may be other foreign governments that also have influence on the Republic of China. Will all their leverage work in the same direction? Because the reactors on Taiwan require a source of fuel, South Africa may be another foreign state to which the Taipei regime at least has to listen. Any foreign country capable of supplying nuclear fuel enrichment services, or capable of handling the disposal and storage of dangerous nuclear waste materials, might similarly find itself being listened to in Taipei.

At the times when the Saudi Arabian government disposes of large reserves of funds (times that have arisen in the past and could arise again), the inclinations and wishes of this government, which, along with South Africa and South Korea, is the principal foreign state still extending formal diplomatic recognition to the Republic of China, might also be influential.

But it would certainly be a mistake to make too much of the simple issue of formal diplomatic recognition. The United States, which officially does not recognize the Republic of China, is definitely more important to the Taipei regime and transacts more real diplomatic business with it than the Republic of Korea or South Africa or Saudi Arabia.

The mere size of the U.S. economic market, along with the U.S. commitment to assist the Republic of China with its defense needs, still works in the direction of giving Washington paramount influence. The fact that Taiwan has a tremendous positive trade balance with the United States offers Washington leverage, even while it also amounts to an additional irritant between Washington and Taipei. If there was ever a need for retaliation against the Republic of China—because it had made nuclear weapons, or because it had too lightly agreed to sell crucial and sensitive nuclear components to another country—it would be possible for the United States to erect barriers against imports from Taiwan, hurting American consumers but hurting the entire economy on Taiwan much more.

But if the United States makes too much use of its leverage as a nuclear fuel supplier in the future, or too much (or too little) use of its role as a handler of waste materials and spent fuels, it may drive the ROC government to be much more subservient to the wishes and needs of some other supplier of such services. Taiwan's special needs for continuing nuclear services are thus always a somewhat double-edged factor, giving Washington a fair amount of leverage, but a leverage that might break down one day if South African or French or other services at some critical point were to replace those of the United States.

As in other forms of embargoes and trade cutoffs, the United States will seek to persuade the Taipei political entity that it is better off going along with its wishes—but in such a way as to not drive that political entity into finding other sources of the economic inputs it needs, the very inputs that gave the United States any leverage in the first place.

Structure

Nuclear matters have been closely controlled and centrally managed by the Taipei regime. There is hardly any educated person on Taiwan, or on this globe, who does not understand that nuclear technology has to be much more sensitive than other forms of energy production, because of the safety risks that go along with the operation of reactors and because of the overlap between peaceful and military uses of nuclear materials.

Because the Taipei regime is more authoritarian, and less democratic, there is no likelihood of anything like the "regulatory meltdown" that some commentators have observed in the regulation and central management of the U.S. nuclear industry. Taiwan is a geographically small area, and the population involved is only some 19 million. While the Republic of China claims to have something of a federal structure, the Taiwan province is basically the only province that Taipei governs, so that the distractions of a far-flung realm could not be the reason for things slipping out of control.

Taiwan remains a small and fairly closed political community. The press and business and labor organizations have not been in the practice of getting into discussions of nuclear matters, with a single very important exception in the recent emergence of concerns about environment and nuclear safety. It has generally been impossible for the press to speculate about nuclear weapons options for Taiwan itself, or about collaboration with any other state in the acquisition of such weapons.

Individual business firms, of course, are everywhere interested in profits, and would be tempted, as in other countries, to lobby for authorization for a sale in a marginal case where someone else might oppose such a sale. This holds equally in the cases where the firms involved, such as the Taiwan Power Company, are owned by the state, for the individual firm manager will still have a personal interest in showing a profit as part of maintaining his professional reputation, whereas someone else might attach higher priority to cooperating with the outside world in restraining the emergence of another Pakistan.

Because the Taiwan nuclear industry has not made heavy investments in new technologies and thus does not have a need to recover the sunk costs of research and development, there is less evidence of any such open division and conflict of interests here, but this kind of conflict could become more serious in the future, comparable to what we have seen in Belgium and Italy and West Germany.

Because much of foreign trade has also had to be under-the-counter (in particular trade with the People's Republic of China and other Communist countries), the entire business community and public at large have also been inclined to go along with less public discussion of the issues involved. The opposition parties in the ROC Legislative Yuan have similarly not challenged the general policy of not discussing nuclear policy, on weapons, options, or on foreign trade.[14]

The diagram in figure 16–1 shows the approximate outlines of the organization and decision processes for nuclear matters on Taiwan.

As an indicator of how centralized, and still how limited, nuclear activities are in the Republic of China, the annual worldwide listing of hundreds of nuclear firms published by *Nuclear Engineering International* contains only one listing for Taiwan, the Taiwan Power Company. Virtually everything that amounts to active participation in nuclear industry in the Republic of China involves Taipower.

One shift toward a possible fragmentation in this unity of nuclear activities on Taiwan has less to do with the flow of technology and more with the more mundane financial considerations that are always important to the individuals involved. In 1982, the fear was expressed that qualified engineers would not be available to Taipower if it was limited to offering the salary rates set by government personnel regulations. Thus it was suggested that a separate organization be established within the company, but outside the official civil service government roster, so that higher salaries could be offered.[15]

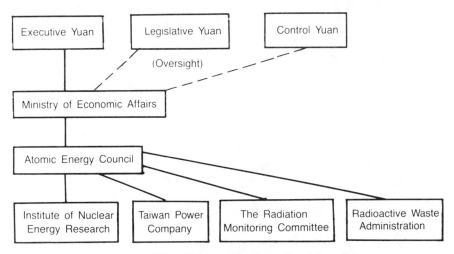

Figure 16–1. The Taiwan Nuclear Decision Process

This Nuclear Energy Group was established in 1984, but with relatively limited prerogatives on salaries, and still fully a part of the Taiwan Power Company. In light of the de-emphasis on nuclear power expansion after 1986, the Nuclear Energy Group was again disestablished as a separate entity.[16]

Two universities on Taiwan have been involved in advanced nuclear research—National Tsinghua University in Shinzu and the Chungshan Institute of Science—but research reactor operations are actually still under the direct control of the Institute of Nuclear Energy Research.[17]

The Bechtel Corporation has an affiliate in Taiwan, Pacific Engineers and Constructors, Ltd. (PECL), which has done planning and design work on the physical installation of reactors purchased from abroad.[18]

Chem-Nuclear Systems similarly formed a Taiwan subsidiary, called Chem-Nuclear Systems Inc.-Taiwan (CNSI-T), with 70 percent ownership by Chem-Nuclear Systems and 30 percent by Taiwan interests, to offer to deal with the disposal of nuclear wastes.[19]

The actual transportation of nuclear wastes by sea to Orchid Island has been handled by a government-owned company, the Retired Servicemen's Engineering Agency (RSEA), which has thus far underbid offers from any foreign firms for the movement of this kind of material.

Other government-owned enterprises on Taiwan that U.S. nuclear parts and components suppliers have mentioned as possible partners for future joint ventures are the China Shipbuilding Corporation, the Tang Eng Iron Works, and the Taiwan Machinery Manufacturing Corporation. As indicated by their corporate titles, these would all be somewhat on the periphery of the nuclear field, but could nonetheless still be important.[20]

The most important center of dissent on the nuclear program on Taiwan has thus arisen in the Legislative Yuan, where a mixed bloc of opposition and Kuomintang legislators has persisted in asking questions about the cost-effectiveness and the safety of investments in nuclear electric power production. Similar challenges to the sensibleness of ROC nuclear policy have emerged in the Control Yuan, a sort of ombudsman and watchdog agency deputized by the Legislative Yuan. While the issue of the possible spin-offs into nuclear weapons production (and of the desirability or undesirability of such a spin-off for Taiwan—one could have imagined critical legislators attacking the government from either direction on this issue) has remained taboo and has not been discussed, the truly civilian issues of cost and safety have been more open to criticism and discussion.

Not drawing the same discussion, however, again because the issues are too premature, has been whatever policy the Taipei regime will eventually impose on exports of sensitive materials.

One relatively solitary critic of the ROC investment in nuclear power, Professor Lin Jun-yi of the Tunghai University Department of Biology, has been voicing his fears of safety hazards and cost-overruns ever since the 1970s. His critical commentary fits the general pattern, by which no reference is made to the possible weapons proliferation side effects of nuclear energy programs.[21] Until the accidents at Maanshan and Chernobyl, moreover, his comments tended not to capture much attention on Taiwan; but the objections of the ecology movement have definitely been more pronounced since then, with an echo in the legislature.

Norms

The Republic of China was deprived of its seat at the United Nations in 1971 and of its seat at the International Atomic Energy Agency (IAEA) in 1972. The Communist People's Republic of China assumed the IAEA seat only in 1984, after for a time paradoxically objecting to the continuation of IAEA safeguards over the reactors on Taiwan.

Because of the vehemence of the Communist objections to the according of any international status to the Taipei regime, it has been impossible for the Republic of China to take part in any NPT Review Conferences or IAEA General Conferences or to be involved in any direct way with the policies put forward by the London Nuclear Suppliers Group (NSG).

We thus encounter an absence of formal declarations about nuclear supply policy from Taipei, in part because there are still so few items that the island could export, and in just as large a part because any formal declarations by the ROC regime amount to an embarrassment for other governments, in the face of the likely irritation of and offense to the PRC. If Taiwan were to export something to another state and wished to have it placed under IAEA safeguards, it would, as things stand, be embarrassingly difficult for the Vienna Agency to negotiate a safeguards agreement.

Barriers to Supplier Coordination

The fact that the Republic of China is exploiting a significant nuclear power program has required that it itself be involved in IAEA safeguards (see Table 16–2). When the Republic of China lost its seat at the United Nations, and then at the IAEA, fears were expressed as to whether the existing safeguards agreements could be made to work in a continuing relationship. Pragmatic and businesslike approaches, on the part of both the Republic of China and the IAEA, have indeed made things go much more smoothly than anyone would have anticipated, but worries remain as to whether such a relationship can be continued—for example, if Taiwan invests in new power reactors of a design and arrangement significantly different from the reactors that are already in place. The two sides have

Table 16–2
Principal Taiwan Nuclear Import Relationships

	Reactors			Materials			
Supplier	Research	Power	Advanced	Low Enriched Uranium	High Enriched Uranium	Plutonium	Heavy Water
Canada	X		X				
United States		X		X	X		X
France				X			
South Africa			X				

basically been operating with existing facility agreements; there is no easy way to negotiate and ratify new agreements, given that the IAEA does not recognize the existence of an entity called the "Republic of China." But a new physical plant might be so different that not even the most level-headed and commonsensical inference from the existing agreements for the first six plants could be made workable. As is true with many other countries as well, the delay in further construction and inauguration of nuclear power plants on Taiwan thus has probably been greeted with a sigh of relief by the inspectorate of the IAEA.

The IAEA's relations with the Taiwan Power Company have been quite businesslike, as noted; but the kinds of cooperative linkages that elsewhere might blossom and grow, with useful spin-offs for future joint efforts on the regulation of supplier activities, is basically constrained by the legal confusion surrounding the entire status of Taiwan.

Apart from such strains in its relationship with the IAEA, the outcast status of the Republic of China also adds problems for future dealings with foreign governments and other international organizations. The absence of embassies and normal diplomatic procedures only slightly complicates relations for any foreign government intent on *buying* something from Taiwan; the economic realities here have often surmounted the political anomalies. But it will, by comparison, be much harder for any foreign government to compare notes with the Taipei regime on *preventing sales*, for such a regulatory task involves much more coordination and more formal acknowledgement of the opposing side's existence than the mere consummation of a sale.

We are basically asking, throughout this chapter, whether Taiwan can be enlisted for the governmentally imposed and governmentally coordinated restraints of something like the NSG, but the nonstatus of the Republic of China will, again and again, be a burden to the kinds of coordination that are needed here.[22]

The Business Drive

One general observation about the nature of the situation on Taiwan, and its impact on the nonproliferation effort, might now be brought forward here. The Republic of China has been serious, not frivolous, about the peaceful application of nuclear technology to the production of electric power—that is, it has been strongly interested in profits and economic returns. Rather than purchasing "dedicated" nuclear facilities—facilities that would be primarily or entirely of use for a military program—the Taipei regime has presided over the purchase and installation of systems that make a lot of economic sense.

Wherever such a priority has been given to civilian applications of nuclear techniques, the outside world has indeed derived *some* assurance against the development of weapons programs. Countries concerned about electricity and economic returns will be more cooperative with the foreign suppliers of nuclear fuel and spare parts and engineering services, and they will not be much in the mood to defy the outside world in any brazen pursuit of nuclear weapons.

Yet this same concern for real economic returns, amounting to reassurance against nuclear weapons acquisition for Taiwan itself, may be just the opposite with regard to any deliberate or inadvertent ROC cooperation with some other country's pursuit of nuclear weapons. The same pattern may emerge as in West Germany, where Bonn has effectively reassured the outside world that it is not trying to acquire nuclear weapons for itself, but has at times seemed quite irresponsible concerning sales to countries like Brazil. A concern for money precludes weapons for one's self, but it does not preclude, and indeed it may facilitate, weapons for others.

"If some distant country wishes to waste portions of its gross national product on a nuclear weapons potential, it is not any of our business to try to overrule this," would be the rationalization that emerged often enough. "If we do not sell the components in question, someone else will sell them," is another version. Concern for continued profits and for extended sales abroad would reinforce such rationalizations, as the most businesslike nation would become an accessory to (someone else's) nuclear weapons programs, even while being businesslike about forswearing such programs for itself.

Habits of Subterfuge

The clouded diplomatic status of the Republic of China has forced the Taipei regime to develop special skills and to cultivate special habits to avert becoming a nonentity. Yet these are skills and habits that may also generate important additional difficulties when we try to enlist the Republic of China into a suppliers' cooperation for the prevention of nuclear weapons proliferation.

For the trading needs of the ROC, and for its political survival as well, much has been accomplished by an application of a Chinese subtlety to these subjects: the de facto ROC Embassy in Washington is named the North American Coordinating Council, the de facto U.S. embassy in Taipei is called the American Institute in Taiwan, and the de facto embassies in other countries are listed as "trading missions." Yet such clever phraseology, however much it helps us get around the sensitivities of the Communist People's Republic of China, also amount to possible sources of miscommunication and confusion in the future. Someone trained to call an embassy a trading mission may get too much into the habit of indulging in other kinds of euphemism and indirection, with the result that messages asking for particular kinds of restraint or cooperation are inadvertently or deliberately misunderstood. One has already seen too many examples of West German or Italian or Dutch nuclear suppliers "misunderstanding" the United States when Washington was asking that something not be sold. The risks of this in the ROC case may be at least as great.

A great deal of secret trade has for some time been underway between the Republic of China and the mainland Communist People's Republic of China, despite the fact that the laws of both regimes expressly forbid this. Goods are sold on each side to intermediaries in Hong Kong or Singapore, with officials winking at the fact that the ultimate destination is known to be "the other China."

Large numbers of people living in Taiwan have for years been arranging to visit their relatives and their birthplaces on the mainland, again by getting permission to visit Hong Kong and then getting permission from the PRC to go further into the mainland of China. Retired soldiers of the Kuomintang have been discovering that their Taiwanese hard currency pension can very handsomely pay their expenses on the mainland, as they return to Taiwan every six months or so to collect their next pension installment.

All of this may seem constructive and necessary for getting around the attitudes of the Chinese (and of the world), attitudes by which there is still a "civil war" under way and by which the nations of the outside world are not free to recognize the existence of more than one Chinese political unit. Yet all of this also cultivates something of a cynicism about rules, as regulations are made to be circumvented, as euphemisms get polished, as laws are respected no more literally than speed limits in the United States. If transshipment has thus become so much of a way of life for Taiwan's trade with the People's Republic of China, will there not be an inclination toward this kind of laundering by transshipment in the future? Can state controls be rigid and fastidiously strict on the substance of the issue, while being cooperatively relaxed and perhaps corrupt on the surface symptoms?

What might actually be getting sold even now by Taiwanese suppliers, against the intentions of the Taipei regime? Optimists about the integration and organization of the ROC government contend that the behind-the-scenes controls must be so good that nothing of any military value is getting to the mainland, or to any other enemy of the Republic of China. This would be to conclude that the Taipei regime has good control over when its rules are being broken and when they are not.

Yet we surely already have the same difficulty with many nonnuclear items that we will encounter on our nuclear-proliferation issue, the phenomenon of dual-use, whereby something that is genuinely valuable for civilian purposes turns out to offer also an enhancement of some government's ability to make war. Computers, or components of computers, or electronic components in general, are commodities on which the Taiwanese economy can expect to be an effective competitor in the future, but where the People's Republic of China might very much need anything it can buy to enhance its own conventional fighting power.

The United States directs most of its vigilance to preventing the purchase of militarily relevant technology not by the People's Republic of China, but by the USSR, and it mounts a parallel effort to keep a state like Pakistan from buying a capacity to produce nuclear weapons.[23] If Washington has thus not yet had much occasion to argue with the ROC regime about export controls, this may be more because the relevant commodities have not yet come into question, rather than because the two governments have their processes for export control so perfectly honed and aligned.

If the Taipei regime can really be sure that its electronics industry is in no way being used to upgrade the conventional warfare systems of the Beijing regime, this would translate into good news for the future management of nuclear technological exports. If the Republic of China has instead been taking its chances here, concluding that the gains of earnings from exports outweigh any marginal losses of control, there would be more reason for concern. By the very nature of the complicated games of dissimulation and indirection that are in play here, it may be impossible for the U.S. government, or at least the American public, to tell which is closer to the actual case.

Analogous problems with other nuclear suppliers (such as Italy) have arisen precisely when the prospective "nth" nuclear weapons state was no immediate threat or enemy to these suppliers.[24] But these at least were not regimes that had continually tolerated secret trade by their merchants. If the ROC regime cared as little as the Italian government has sometimes seemed to care about the uses put to nuclear sales, it might be even less able to do something about such sales.

Future Peaceful Nuclear Growth on Taiwan

While the Republic of China has indeed made an impressive commitment to the use of nuclear energy, there is some reason to question how much this commitment will grow in the future. The experience of the Soviet reactor accident at Chernobyl in 1986 attracted considerable attention on Taiwan, as something considerably worse than the already worrisome U.S. Three Mile Island accident of 1979. Anyone visiting Taiwan cannot escape noticing the density of the population and the proximity of the first two reactors installed on the island to the capital city at Taipei. An ecology movement has surfaced on Taiwan, strongly opposed to all the forms of pollution that have affected the island and all the risks that might be hovering close.

As noted, the operations and safety record of the ROC nuclear operation has been very good, but not perfect, with an accident at Maanshan in July of 1985 thus aggravating local concerns that a reliance on nuclear electrical power may pose too many hazards for Taiwan.

One consequence of all of this has been the postponement of plans for the seventh and eighth nuclear power reactors scheduled to go into operation in Taiwan.[25] Another consequence has been the development of a considerably more open discussion and debate about nuclear matters in the Republic of China. Some topics (as noted, the possibilities of a diversion of nuclear materials into any weapons program) are still basically off-limits to the press and public in Taiwan. But issues of nuclear safety in the reactors and the handling of waste materials and related concerns about ecological impact are now more open, in a way that is likely to slow the further development of nuclear projects on Taiwan.

Capabilities

Returning to our concerns about Taiwan being a source of the kinds of nuclear exports that would facilitate some other state in the pursuit of nuclear weapons options, it is worth repeating that much of this is still over the horizon. Representatives of the nuclear industry on Taiwan show surprise, and even seem flattered, at the suggestion that they might be so much courted and sought after in the foreseeable future. Much of what exists on Taiwan, however well managed and efficiently operated, has still been toward the "turnkey" end of the spectrum, with all the advanced nuclear equipment and technology being imported from the United States. While, as noted, the percentage of the electricity produced by nuclear means on Taiwan is quite high, the absolute total is not so high, because the population governed by the Republic of China is still only some 19 million. The economies of scale that have emerged elsewhere in much larger operations, which by now would have called for the production of indigenously designed reactors, simply have not arisen on Taiwan.[26]

But this is hardly to suggest that no one in the Republic of China has considered the possibilities of a future nuclear export market. Like all the small countries enmeshed in the world economy, the Republic of China has to be continually concerned about finding and maintaining a market niche, staking out the slices of clientele tomorrow to generate overseas credits to continue what is being earned today.

And it is hardly to suggest that Taiwan's sales could never be of value to someone seeking to produce atomic bombs. The essence of our nuclear weapons proliferation worry, as illustrated all too handily by the Pakistani example, is that the component portions of such a move toward sensitive nuclear technology may be disaggregated in a relatively complicated way, such that even small portions of the total jigsaw puzzle can make a critical difference and that the trigger list of sensitive nuclear equipment and ancillary equipment may have to be very carefully drafted and continually expanded.

If foreign trade specialists in Taipei must thus be contemplating some possible nuclear supplier roles that the Republic of China might find tempting in the future, where would one expect to find such sales possibilities?

One thing that Taipei will generally have to offer is experience, for there is nothing, when someone somewhere wants to break into this field, quite like having once worked through the problems of constructing and installing and starting up a nuclear power plant. Experience with the techniques of building the physical plant into which the reactors are to be installed, and of satisfying the safety standards and other critical tolerance considerations, may thus be something in which the ROC government senses an earlier opportunity to win contracts and earn foreign exchange.

Such "human capital"—that is, the experience that rests in people's heads, an experience that inspires confidence elsewhere because the mistakes of the novice can somehow be avoided—is of course the kind of export that has been worrisome in the past. It is much more difficult for a foreign agency or a foreign government to keep track of where engineers are traveling to than it is to monitor the disposal of sensitive nuclear materials. Taiwan is producing more educated people than it can fully employ in all areas of engineering and science and in the social sciences. Being an education-minded society, like all the portions of the world inhabited by Chinese, the Republic of China may be tempted to let its people go to work abroad, because it is good for the economy of Taiwan and because it is good for the morale of the individuals involved.

Turning to the more material forms of nuclear exports, one can imagine cases over time where the Republic of China would earn foreign exchange (and specific foreign friendships) by the sales of the following kinds of items: the high-quality machine tools needed for nuclear industry; computers and certain kinds of computer software; tank and liner plates, pumps and motors and cooling equipment; valves; hangers; nozzles, piping, and pipehandlers; wire and cable, structured steel; switches and electric control and monitoring equipment; cranes, control consoles, motors, gears, and circuit breakers; and finally, the general buildings and physical plant for any reactor or other nuclear facility.[27]

All of these items are somewhat peripheral to nuclear operations, and at the same time can be of great value, because mistakes ordinarily made by novices in the field become less likely when someone with a good record of experience in the handling of nuclear facilities is given the production contract. All of these are also less suspicion-provoking and more "dual use" (dual use in two senses, for they may apply to nonnuclear activities as well as to nuclear, and they of course support peaceful projects as well as potentially facilitating nuclear weapons production).

By contrast, in the next two decades there are less likely to be rumors of sales of anything as big as a reactor from Taiwan to any other regime, or rumors of sales by Taiwan of plutonium or enriched uranium or heavy water. To repeat, Taiwan sees itself as a competent novice in the general nuclear field, an assessment with which engineers around the world would be likely to agree. The economies of scale of nuclear operations in the Republic of China have not been such as to push it up to the cutting edge of nuclear technology, or to burden it with a pressing need to recover development costs.

Conclusions

The larger questions of the future of the ROC regime on Taiwan relate to nuclear technology in several ways. To the extent that the threats to the island are seen as mainly political and military, one worries more again about the Republic of China's own possible interest in a bomb.[28] To the extent that these threats have been addressed and rebuffed by Taiwan's economic strengths, much of the picture has changed. Nuclear production of electrical power has played an important role in Taiwan's economy and has basically disposed the Republic of China to cooperate with the IAEA and the United States.

Translating this economic vitality into future cooperation, or noncooperation, with the global efforts to head off nuclear proliferation then becomes a somewhat more subtle and complicated problem of analysis. It may be businesslike to give up the bomb at home, but it could prove remunerative and businesslike to assist a bomb project abroad, or at least to pretend to be unaware that anything like this was underway in some "nth country." Here we have a great number of unanswered questions, and of problems that have not yet definitely been addressed.

At the least, we have more time, in the ROC case, until Taiwan becomes a plausible source of what is critically needed for someone else's weapons project. Yet the ingenuity of a continuing nonproliferation regime in the Republic of China may continually have to be matched against the ingenuity of another would-be Pakistan.

Notes

1. For a discussion of earlier worries about Taiwan getting nuclear weapons for itself, see Joseph Yager, *Nonproliferation and U.S. Foreign Policy* (Washington, D.C.: The Brookings Institution, 1980).

2. The Pakistani example is discussed in Leonard Spector, *Going Nuclear* (Cambridge, Mass.: Ballinger, 1987).

3. For my earlier statement of such concerns, see George H. Quester, "Taiwan and Nuclear Proliferation," *Orbis* 18, no. 1 (Spring 1974): 140–50.

4. A comprehensive overview of Taiwan's nuclear industry can be found in Jon Payne, "Taiwan: Counting on Nuclear Energy," *Nuclear News* (September 1985): 74–78.

5. See *Washington Post*, 29 August 1976, p. A1; and *New York Times*, 30 August 1976, p. 1.

6. Stephen Engelberg and Michael R. Gordon, "Taiwan Halts Work on Secret Plant to Make Nuclear Bomb Ingredient," *New York Times*, 23 March 1988, p. 1; R. Jeffrey Smith and Don Oberdorfer, "Taiwan To Close Nuclear Reactor," *Washington Post*, 24 March 1988, p. A32.

7. Chen interview cited in Donald Shapiro, "Taipower's Chen Looks to New Construction after Maanshan-1 Restart," *Nucleonics Week*, 6 February 1986, pp. 13–14.

8. Charles Thurston and Donald Shapiro, "Taipower and Rocky Mountain Energy to Sign Uranium Joint Venture Soon," *Nuclear Fuel*, 4 November 1985, p. 12.

9. On Taiwan's hunting for sources of nuclear fuel, see *Nuclear News* (April 1985): 68.

10. Expressions of interest by Australian firms in offering nuclear services to Taiwan are noted in Sheila Haydon and Donald Shapiro, "BP Said to Have Asked Government About Uranium Sales to Taiwan," *Nuclear Fuel*, 3 November 1986, p. 21. On some similar embarrassment about a parallel move by Urenco, see *Nuclear Europe* (February 1983): 14.

11. For example, see J. Miller, "Nuclear Contacts Quietly Widened by Israel, Taiwan and South Africa," *New York Times*, 28 June 1981, p. 10. See also Lewis A. Dunn, *Controlling the Bomb* (New Haven: Yale University Press, 1982), pp. 37–39.

12. On the storing of nuclear waste materials at Orchid Island, see *Nucleonics Week*, 14 February 1985, p. 12.

13. The acceptance of fuel of Canadian origin at Savannah River is discussed in Michael Knapik, "NAC Coordinating Shipment of Spent Fuel from Taiwan to Savannah River," *Nuclear Fuel*, 21 October 1985, p. 12.

14. The interventions and noninterventions of the Legislative Yuan are noted in Donald Shapiro, "Taipower Confronting Unexpected Opposition to Plans for Two More Units," *Nucleonics Week*, 18 April 1985, p. 9. See also *Nucleonics Week*, 25 April 1985, p. 19.

15. Donald Shapiro, "State-Owned Taiwan Power is Preparing to Establish an Autonomous Division," *Nucleonics Week*, 11 March 1982, pp. 7–8.

16. See Donald Shapiro, "Taiwan Power Company is Seeking More Autonomy From the Government," *Nucleonics Week*, 21 February 1985, p. 9; and Donald Shapiro, "Taipower's Chen Looks to New Construction after Maanshan-1 Restart," *Nucleonics Week*, 6 February 1986), pp. 13–14.

17. On the participation of Chinese universities in nuclear research, see Jon Payne, "Taiwan: Counting on Nuclear Energy," *Nuclear News* (September 1985): 77.

18. *Nucleonics Week*, 22 May 1986, pp. 9–10.

19. *Nucleonics Week*, 17 September 1981, p. 10.

20. The firms in which interest has been expressed are listed in "U.S. Nuclear Parts and Components Suppliers are Looking at Taiwan," *Nucleonics Week*, 16 July 1981, pp. 10–11.

21. On the critique of the Taiwan nuclear effort by Dr. Lin, see Rob Laufer, "Lone Voice Raised in Opposition to Taiwan Nuclear Plans," *Nucleonics Week*, 1 May 1980, pp. 3–4. See also Maria Shao, "Taiwan Maps Ambitious Nuclear Plans, But Critics Question Expense and Safety," *The Wall Street Journal*, 13 March 1985, p. 39.

22. The operations of the "London Club" (NSG) and its successor intergovernmental coordination arrangements are outlined in Joseph A. Yager, *International Cooperation in Nuclear Energy* (Washington, D.C.: The Brookings Institution, 1981).

23. The general nature of U.S. efforts to restrict sensitive trade to the USSR is discussed in Henry R. Nau, "International Technology Transfer," *The Washington Quarterly*, 8, no. 1 (Winter 1985): 1–9.

24. On the seeming irresponsibility of some other supplier states, see Albert Wohlstetter, *Swords From Plowshares* (Chicago: University of Chicago Press, 1979).

25. Carl Goldstein, "Taiwan's Delayed Reaction," *Far East Economic Review*, 10 January 1985), pp. 74–75.

26. On the general state of nuclear development on Taiwan, see Janine Holc, "Taiwan's Nuclear Energy Program," *Country Notes* (Washington, D.C.: Center for Development Policy, August 1982).

27. On the listing of items that could be produced on Taiwan, see "U.S. Nuclear Parts and Components Suppliers are Looking at Taiwan," *Nucleonics Week*, 16 July 1981, pp. 10–11.

28. On Taiwan's general future political prospects, see C.T. Cross, "Taipei's Identity Crisis," *Foreign Policy* (Summer 1983): 47–63.

III
Management Strategies

17
Soviet–American Cooperation in Dealing with the Nonproliferation of Nuclear Weapons

Anatoly Belov

The position of the Soviet Union in matters of nonproliferation of nuclear weapons is well known. Conducting a consistent and decisive program toward rallying international efforts for the nonproliferation of nuclear weapons, the USSR believes that preventing the spread of nuclear weapons is destined to become not only one of the elements of an all-encompassing international security system, but also an essential prerequisite for a nuclear-free, nonviolent world.

The foundation of the Soviet Union's approach to the problem of nonproliferation is the desire and readiness to transform the concept that the atom is only peaceful into a universal norm for international relations, as well as to greatly strengthen the existing international nonproliferation regime. Of great potential in this area is cooperation between the Soviet Union and the United States. The political climate in the world, including the development of events regarding nonproliferation, depends first and foremost on the actions of these two nations.

There has been a long history of contact in nonproliferation matters between the Soviet Union and the United States. Thanks largely to these contacts, the Charter of the International Atomic Energy Agency (IAEA) and its verification system, the Nuclear Non-proliferation Treaty (NPT), and the London Agreement on Guidelines for the Regulation of Nuclear Export were developed.

Cooperation between the USSR and the United States in the field of nonproliferation relies on the mutual interest of both countries to prevent additional governments from obtaining nuclear weapons. The positions of the USSR and the United States in matters related to strengthening nonproliferation coincide to a large extent, although the actions of the United States in this regard are not always consistent. In particular, with regard to the export of nuclear materials and technology, the United States sometimes takes measures that can only be viewed as tolerating the nuclear ambitions of countries such as Egypt, Israel, and Pakistan.

Although periodic talks between the Soviet Union and the United States on questions of nonproliferation took place in earlier years, since 1982 there has been a mechanism for regular intergovernmental talks in which a broad range of problems related to ensuring the nonproliferation of nuclear arms are examined. We consider these talks useful. To date, there have been ten rounds of talks, the most recent having taken place in Washington at the beginning of 1988.

In a joint Soviet-American statement of 21 November 1985 on the results of a high-level meeting, both sides affirmed their adherence to the Nuclear Non-Proliferation Treaty and their interest in strengthening, together with other countries, the nonproliferation regime and in further increasing the effectiveness of the NPT by increasing the number of adherents. They also endorsed the policy of conducting regular, constructive Soviet-U.S. talks on problems of nuclear nonproliferation. The Soviet Union emphasized that a practical affirmation of the commitment of both parties to nonproliferation entails concrete and continuing efforts to limit and reduce the number of nuclear weapons, as well as action by both parties to achieve a complete ban on the testing of nuclear weapons. The results of the Third Review Conference of the Nuclear Non-Proliferation Treaty and of the United Nations Conference for International Assistance in the Area of Peaceful Utilization of Nuclear Energy have shown that it is not possible to strengthen nonproliferation without linking it to the issues of the limitation and elimination of nuclear weapons and the complete ban on their testing.

During the course of the bilateral consultations, additional specific measures directed at preventing further nonproliferation are regularly adopted. They include measures aimed at widening the circle of adherents to the NPT, with particular emphasis on the "near-nuclear" nations. Questions regarding the development and application of measures for strengthening the control of the export of nuclear material, technology, and equipment are an important part of the Soviet-U.S. consultations. The Soviet Union favors the observation of strict norms by all nuclear suppliers (including those not party to the NPT) and the closing of any loopholes that allow the spread of nuclear weapons.

During the Soviet-U.S. talks, the problem of raising the effectiveness of the system of IAEA safeguards are analyzed at length. The Soviet side believes in the necessity of taking further practical steps toward increasing compliance with IAEA safeguards in countries not party to the NPT and toward development of provisions for a long-term program to strengthen the IAEA's material and technical base.

The NPT member states have a special responsibility to adhere to the nonproliferation regime. From this stems the need for joint U.S. and Soviet efforts directed at increasing the role and prestige of the Nuclear Non-Proliferation Treaty.

At the special session of the IAEA in 1986, the USSR proposed the development of a reliable set of measures with which to deal with nuclear terrorism in all of its manifestations. Of great concern to specialists is the possibility of deliberate damage to nuclear facilities and the theft of highly-enriched nuclear material. Ensuring the protection of nuclear material and plants is necessitated not only by the increased danger they pose, but by the possibility of their utilization for blackmail and other terrorist acts.

The convention developed by the IAEA for physical security concerns international transport, and it is a good starting point. It is now necessary to think about supplementing it with legal norms to protect nuclear material and facilities within each country. At the special session of the General Conference of the IAEA, the USSR proposed a program for safe development of nuclear energy that calls for development of a reliable set of measures to prevent attacks on nuclear facilities. The importance of resolving this problem goes without saying, as the catastrophic consequences of attacks on nuclear facilities can only be compared with massive use of nuclear arms. It is necessary to conclude an international convention by which all governments would forswear attacks on nuclear facilities. Such guarantees by international law would, at first, encompass all nuclear facilities under IAEA safeguards. It should subsequently be possible to extend this agreement to nuclear plants outside of the IAEA safeguards system, provided that they are utilized for peaceful purposes.

The questions of strengthening the nonproliferation regime and, in particular, controlling nuclear exports, are at the center of the attention of many multilateral forums both within the IAEA as well as outside of it. A problem that is becoming more acute is the application of export controls to new nuclear suppliers. These supplier countries—China, India, Argentina, and Brazil—are already independently taking measures in this direction, and one may assume that they would be ready for a broader exchange of views with other nations, including the "traditional suppliers." Under these conditions it is necessary to find a generally applicable framework in which it is possible to accommodate the exchange of views among all nuclear suppliers. The Committee for the Assurance of Supplies of the IAEA could be such an organization. Unfortunately, it has not yet been possible to reach an agreement on a system of assured nuclear supplies with proper regard for the requirements for nuclear nonproliferation.

Some non-nuclear countries are not ready to accept their nonproliferation responsibilities, which are of an obligatory nature and are based on existing multilateral agreements. Unilateral nonproliferation, in accordance with established international principles, by governments not party to the NPT can be viewed by all governments as an important step in the direction of strengthening the treaty. However, such unilateral actions are not a substitute for participation by these nations in the NPT and other nonproliferation agreements.

The IAEA plays an important role in strengthening the nonproliferation regime. It has now become a unique mechanism that effectively exercises control in one of the most important aspects of the battle to limit nuclear weapons—in the area of nonproliferation and the creation of nuclear-free zones. As was noted in the joint Soviet-U.S. announcement at the high-level meeting of 21 November 1985, the Soviet Union and the United States henceforth intend to facilitate strengthening of the IAEA and to support it by carrying out its provisions and working toward the peaceful utilization of nuclear energy.

It is obvious that the development of cooperation by these nations in the IAEA can further increase the international authority of the agency and its role as a guarantor for the nonproliferation of nuclear weapons. The Soviet Union, by means of practical measures, demonstrates its adherence to the IAEA and provides constructive support for its work.

In conclusion, there is much work to be done in strengthening the nuclear nonproliferation regime. The Soviet Union is ready, together with other nations, including the United States, to apply new thinking to undertake constructive and resolute steps directed at preventing the spread of nuclear arms over the planet. It is necessary to remove the threat of nuclear disaster forever. It is necessary to create a world without nuclear weapons, a world with a suitable climate for trust between governments.

18
Managing Nuclear Supplier Risks: A Comprehensive Approach

Bennett Ramberg

With the appearance of such third-tier suppliers as Argentina, Brazil, South Korea, Taiwan, China, and others capable of producing nuclear components and sensitive nuclear materials, assurance that importers are using nuclear energy benignly and safely may become more uncertain. It is therefore important to integrate emerging exporters and importers into a regime of norms designed to minimize nuclear risks. The experience of the London Nuclear Suppliers Group (NSG) to arrive at a code of conduct is encouraging. Placed in the context of the larger evolving nuclear energy regime that seeks to address nuclear safety, proliferation, terrorism, and military attacks on reactors, the international community has made substantial progress. Still, there is much that remains to be done. To provide a point of departure, it is first worth looking at how far we have come.

The Nuclear Energy Regime: The Past as Prologue

It is well to recall that the nuclear regime in place today emerged from over four decades of difficult pulling and hauling. With the 1949 Soviet and 1952 British detonations, the challenge became how to limit nuclear proliferation in a world where knowledge about the atom could not be contained. With Eisenhower's 1953 advancement of what became the International Atomic Energy Agency (IAEA), there emerged a vehicle. Although designed to be a promotional body, the IAEA acquired a monitory function to verify that nations were not diverting sensitive materials for atomic weapons. The achievement, however, was not easy. In the early years, the Soviet Union, its bloc allies, and some developing nations strongly opposed regulatory functions.[1] However, the United States and its allies persisted.

By the time the IAEA became operational, the United States had some forty bilateral cooperative agreements for nuclear research reactors. Each agreement allowed U.S. inspection to assure peaceful use of U.S. nuclear supplies. However, many importers did not wish to accede indefinitely to scrutiny by the United States. With the burden inspections placed on resources, U.S. officials increasingly looked favorably upon the IAEA as an enforcement vehicle. This added impetus to the creation of an agency inspectorate. Although resistant at first, by 1959 the Soviet Union had reevaluated its own position, spurred by China's development of nuclear weapons—which Moscow supported until it recognized the threat to itself. The Soviets then became both supporters and innovators of nuclear safeguards: they limited exports to light-water reactors that did not use weapons-grade material; they required all spent fuel to be returned, to minimize the danger of plutonium diversion by importers; and they forbade East European recipients to build indigenous enrichment and plutonium reprocessing installations.

The tightening Soviet export criteria did not initially include a role for the IAEA. But Soviet opposition ended, as did that of Western nations, which were concerned about industrial intelligence. This allowed the agency to expand its safeguards to reactors of all sizes in 1964 and to reprocessing and fuel fabrication plants in 1966 and 1968. With the adoption of the Nuclear Non-Proliferation Treaty (NPT) in 1970, safeguards became more extensive.[2] Today, 134 nations are parties to the treaty. (Notable absentees are Israel, South Africa, India, Pakistan, Brazil, and Argentina.)

With its new responsibilities, the IAEA expanded its enforcement staff from three inspectors in 1961 to almost two hundred today. The agency now devotes over one-third of its budget to more than 2,000 inspections conducted each year, a far cry from the less than 4 percent of total expenditures devoted to safeguards in 1962. In addition, the IAEA has developed a number of other nuclear programs: the agency offers technical training on nuclear safety; advice on the use of radiation in food preservation; and it promotes the use of radiation in health sciences, physical sciences, agriculture, and industry.

Although the international nuclear regime of norms and standards has made notable progress, it has also been subject to increasing stress; so far, it has withstood the strains and frequently has used tension to strengthen itself against greater tests. In 1974, India, with the unintentional assistance of traditional suppliers, detonated a "peaceful nuclear device." The plutonium was produced in a Canadian-supplied reactor using heavy water from the United States and fueled with Indian uranium. India's action was disruptive, but it did not prove as damaging as some feared. India was not a member of the nonproliferation treaty, so the NPT was not violated. Since then, New Delhi has not detonated another nuclear device. The Indian test had both negative and positive consequences: It spurred Pakistan's effort to try to develop a bomb, but it also gave nuclear suppliers reasons to convene talks on export guidelines.

India's test marked the first of several nuclear proliferation brushfires in the 1970s and early 1980s. The United States acted as the principal proponent of efforts to diminish the spread of sensitive nuclear technologies and materials, although Canada, particularly after the Indian detonation, played an important role as well. When Pakistan and Korea tried to acquire reprocessing plants from France, the United States prevented consummation. In the process, Washington stimulated European sensitivity to nuclear trade, resulting in the formulation of voluntary nuclear supplier guidelines limiting the export of sensitive technology and material. Soviet-U.S. cooperation manifested itself in 1979 when, upon being informed by Moscow's intelligence that South Africa was prepared to detonate a nuclear device, Washington pressured Pretoria to desist. As a new decade began, the NPT was tested when the 1980 review conference was unable to reach a formal consensus of support.

The most dramatic effort to prevent nuclear proliferation occurred in June 1981 when Israel destroyed Iraq's Osirak reactor, which Israel suspected was an Iraqi guise for developing nuclear weapons. The Israeli action stimulated concern for the vulnerability of nuclear plants to military bombardment. The UN-sponsored Committee on Disarmament considered the implications more intensely, but has been unable to consummate a convention prohibiting such acts. The bombing also had political consequences; in 1982, IAEA members voted to withdraw recognition of Israel's credentials to attend the agency's annual General Conference. As a result, the United States walked out of the meeting and suspended its support for the agency. Although the matter of Israeli participation in the IAEA was resolved within a matter of months, along with U.S. reconfirmation of its commitment, the affair, coupled with efforts to expel South Africa, marked the increased politicization of an institution that was created to provide the international community with a technical service.[3] This is not to say that the IAEA was ever above politics. From its inception it was mired in it, as the United States initially opposed the admission of China, Hungary, North Korea, and East Germany, while the Soviets opposed agency assistance to South Korea, Taiwan, South Vietnam, and Israel. But recent events, taken in light of progress toward universalized membership, augur for more difficult times ahead.

While the nuclear nonproliferation component of the nuclear regime was challenged, a jolt of a different sort occurred in 1979 at Three Mile Island. No lives were lost, and as a result of the accident only 15 curies of radiation were released (compared to 50 million at Chernobyl), but the event highlighted the risks of nuclear facilities. In the United States and elsewhere, Three Mile Island increased doubts about nuclear power's value.

With unfavorable capital markets, slow growth in electricity demand, and a lack of public confidence, utilities cancelled numerous plants. Chernobyl, seven years later, raised even more serious concerns about nuclear safety.

The nuclear regime was buffeted, but efforts to reinforce it continued. By the mid-1980s, IAEA efforts begun in 1974 to establish international safety guidelines, albeit voluntary, bore fruit in the form of five codes of practice and fifty-five safety guidelines. National regulatory institutions around the world are slowly but steadily applying the recommendations. In 1980, the agency created the Committee on Assurances of Supply—an offspring of the 1977–80 International Nuclear Fuel Cycle Evaluation (INFCE) that considered alternatives to plutonium-based fuels—to grapple with such matters as the insulation of consumers from supply interruptions and the sanctity of contracts. In 1983, it established the Incident Reporting System to analyze and record mishaps, followed in 1984 by formation of radiation protection advisory teams (RAPAT) to advise countries about radiation protection and the International Nuclear Advisory Group (INSAG) to evaluate nuclear safety and provide countries with advice.

Throughout the 1970s and 1980s the IAEA steadily expanded the number of safeguard agreements with NPT signatories. In 1975, the agency's director general inaugurated a Standing Advisory Group on Safeguards Implementation—a group of technical experts to study and evaluate the organization's performance. In 1977, it submitted the first Safeguards Implementation Report, providing aggregate statistics and summaries to member states. Application of safeguards has not been without controversy. A former agency employee, Roger Richter, uttered the strongest critique, following the Israeli attack on Iraq's Osirak research reactor. In congressional testimony, Richter alleged that IAEA inspectors ignore irregularities for political reasons.[4] Others have raised concerns about the competence of inspectors and their ability to perform their obligations with limited access and their inability to publicize findings.[5] Still, to the agency's credit, it has made the determination in several cases that it was unable to verify that diversion had not taken place, thereby providing the membership with timely warning to address the challenge.

On another front, the Convention on the Physical Protection of Nuclear Material, which opened for signature in 1979 and recently went into force along with INFCIRC/225/Rev.1, which the IAEA promulgated in 1975 and revised in 1977, provided guidelines for the physical protection of nuclear material, security of nuclear substances in transit, and for cooperation among parties in the recovery and return of stolen nuclear material, as well as sanctions against perpetrators. Although some questions have been raised about the standards and applications, these documents provide a useful foundation that can be built upon in the future.[6]

In 1982, the IAEA announced formation of the Operational Safety

Review Team (OSART). Five inspectors became available to provide any country an independent expert assessment of its plants. OSART was originally intended to address the needs of developing nations, but after Chernobyl the United States, Germany, and the Soviet Union requested visits. Because of the high interest level, the inspectorate is expanding. In 1986, the agency established still another program, dubbed ASSET, or Analysis of Significant Safety Event Teams, to assess important plant operational irregularities.

Complementing the IAEA's nuclear safety efforts are bilateral, regional, and multilateral ventures. The United States has nuclear safety cooperation agreements with twenty-two countries. It also works with the Organization for Economic Cooperation and Development's (OECD) Nuclear Energy Agency to share safety information. Argentina and Brazil recently entered into an agreement whereby each will warn the other of mishaps; they also have discussed measures to minimize nuclear proliferation, thereby helping to reinforce efforts to keep nuclear weapons out of Latin America. Euratom continues to verify the peaceful and safe development of the atom in Europe. Finally, in 1985, parties to the NPT held their third review conference. As opposed to 1980, they reached consensus in support of the nonproliferation regime.

In sum, at present the international nuclear energy regime is battered but still viable. In the 1950s few thought it would get off the ground; in the 1960s, few believed that safeguards could be implemented in a world of sovereign nations. Yet the regime has made remarkable progress despite the strain in recent years. Chernobyl provides the impetus to reinforce the regime based on common interest. No nation wants a nuclear accident. Beyond accidents, no nation wants nuclear weapons used on its territory; no nation wants sabotage or military destruction of its plants. Nuclear exports, from whatever corner, have implications for each of these risks. Improperly manufactured, installed, or maintained facilities pose threats to safety. Ill-protected sensitive nuclear exports—for example, plutonium or highly-enriched uranium—can be stolen by terrorists or nations. Finally, the export of such materials may be grounds for countries to attack atomic plants. Thus the challenge we confront today is how to minimize nuclear risks through greater national responsibility and international accountability.

Reinforcing the Nuclear Energy Regime

Even before Chernobyl, there were a number of proposals to improve the international nuclear energy regime. Attention focused on minimizing the dangers of nuclear weapons proliferation. The literature is peppered with suggestions for multilateral fuel banks and reprocessing and spent fuel storage facilities. Some suggest ways to discourage states from acquiring nuclear weapons through conventional arms sales, strengthening alliances, and creating nuclear-free zones. Calls are also heard for the development of a new generation of inherently safer reactors, which could come on line in a decade. At the same time, others put forward bolder multilateral approaches.

Michael Brenner called for the creation of an organization akin to the London Nuclear Suppliers Group (NSG) but broader in representation, including emerging nuclear suppliers like China as well as major consumers. This group would monitor nuclear traffic and apply sanctions. Joseph Yager, in a Brookings Institution study, suggested formation of an international consultative forum to review nuclear energy challenges and formulate trade rules to be embodied in a treaty. John Simpson proposed an International Nuclear Trading Organization that would bear responsibility for nuclear trade guidelines and the allocating of funds to assist nuclear energy projects, thereby relieving the IAEA of promotional responsibility and allowing it to concentrate on safeguards. More modest were the recommendations of Pierre Lellouche, who advocated consultation among a small group of key nuclear exporters and recipients to provide a political dimension to technical findings bearing on nuclear exports. Less ambitious still were the proposals of a recent European panel of experts who called for a "pragmatic code of conduct" that would apply the NSG guidelines on a case-by-case basis, and the call by David Fisher, past director general for IAEA external relations, for "extreme restraint" in the export of nuclear plants and materials to unstable regions.[7]

Each of these proposals has merit. All clearly advocate greater multilateral cooperation. But none comprehensively defines the performance criteria for multinational efforts. The fact-finding, arbitration, and sanctions in Brenner's argument, the rules of trade in Yager's approach, Simpson's International Nuclear Trading Organization, the "political dimension" in Lellouche's suggestion, the code of conduct offered by the European panelists, and Fisher's restraint need to be fleshed out. There is a pessimistic note running through many of the proposals: Can the international community move forward? The European panelists conclude that in a world of sovereign states, we cannot have an international authority capable of enforcing a nuclear energy regime. The best we can hope for is the ability of outsiders to effect the balance of incentives and disincentives for countries to be more responsive to the purposes of the regime. Before Chernobyl, Brenner and Yager contended that the time to create a more comprehensive body to administer the regime had not yet arrived. Now, in light of the Soviet accident and the contamination of a Brazilian community as the result of the rupture of a canister containing cesium in 1987, we must ask: "If not now, when?" While nations guard their sovereignty jealously, most have made remarkable accommodations by opening their plants to international scrutiny.

However, in the wake of Chernobyl, pessimism seems to dominate. The principal international remedies responding to the incident are two conventions. One requires that states suffering accidents that may result in "an international transboundary release" notify nations which "are or may be physically affected" through the IAEA.[8] The second treaty encourages international assistance.[9] Although valuable, they are in and of themselves inadequate, being akin to closing the barn door after the horse has escaped. These conventions will not prevent future Chernobyls. Bolder suggestions have been made: Chancellor Helmut Kohl called for an international institution to prescribe safety standards and verify implementation, and Hans Blix, director general of the IAEA, suggested binding minimum safety standards.[10]

These last recommendations should be viewed as a point of departure to address nuclear energy risks comprehensively. Antecedents can be found in the most inclusive of all proposals, the Baruch Plan, which advocated an International Atomic Development Authority with "managerial control or ownership of all atomic energy activities."[11] In today's world the IAEA provides a skeleton for this idea. With sufficient new authority, money, expertise, personnel, and responsibility, managed apolitically by a professional technical staff, the most optimistic plan (but all the same, perhaps most unrealistic remedy in the short term, given concerns over sovereignty) would be IAEA licensing of all civil nuclear plants or at least certification of their safety. By being allowed extensive and intensive access to nuclear plants to verify safe operation, inspectors could also assess that facilities were not misused for military purposes and that they were secure against terrorist acts. Thus safety inspection might be a ruse to get a better understanding of other risks posed by plants. And because of its international nature, the agency might be less subject to national commercial pressures that have bent safe operation procedures to get plants on line and keep them operating. This verification would reduce the incentives of countries like Israel to bomb reactors of other nations. Such intrusive licensing inspections could also assure that plutonium and highly-enriched uranium stocks are secure from theft and certify that plant operators are applying rigorous guidelines to prevent sabotage. This would address the risks of misuse of materials supplied by traditional and third-tier suppliers at the recipient's end.

However optimal the foregoing proposal may be, its short-run practicality is another matter. Had the Chernobyl accident resulted in a large number of early fatalities rather than potentially large late fatalities, had it occurred in a country subject to intense press scrutiny, had the nuclear industry acknowledged that the factors that contributed to the accident were not, sui generis, perhaps there would have been an impetus for greater international regulation and scrutiny of other nuclear energy risks. However, we should not be satisfied with the two conventions negotiated thus far, because they represent minimal agreements, albeit ones that required the Chernobyl impetus to consummate (earlier U.S. promotion of such conventions met with strong opposition). And while the Soviet Union displayed remarkable willingness to expose itself to international review and criticism in the IAEA post-accident review conference in August 1986, its openness should be considered only the beginning of a more intense effort to examine more effective modes and methods for managing nuclear energy.

The question remains: How far will countries go to increase national and multilateral scrutiny of nuclear energy? In many nations regulatory resources are strained. A U.S. nuclear engineering professor, after discussions with Korean officials, illustrates the problem: "The regulatory agency staff discussed all the problems, but you could feel the lack of experience. They knew that they had to have a concept of quality assurance and safety, but they didn't have the manpower."[12] Even in the United States, operational and regulatory malfeasance is well documented.[13] There would not be an international problem but for the fact that radiation releases know no boundaries. It is not enough to have adequate controls in one nation and not in its neighbor. Still, given the concern over state sovereignty, it is probably unrealistic to expect foolproof international remedies. Although the nuclear regime in place today represents enormous progress, achievements came incrementally, with certain major accomplishments, notably the nonproliferation treaty.

Assuming that nations share the common goal of minimizing nuclear risks and that concern to prevent future Chernobyls has salience to energize countries to modify behavior and assuming further that incrementalism is more likely, but recognizing all the same that bold measures should be used to test the world's willingness to search for remedies, I propose several multilateral alternatives that I call "International Nuclear Reviews" (INRs). Elaborated elsewhere in detail,[14] each is distinguished by a formal uniform structure and incrementally increasing authority that addresses the whole range of nuclear risks. *The diverse efforts of such a comprehensive approach could mutually reinforce one another to better ensure a benign nuclear energy regime.*

In its most elementary form, INR I, the IAEA would publish a set of guidelines, portions of which would be relevant to exporters, importers, and domestic manufacturers. The checklists, or Nuclear Security Assessment, would encourage exporters (including newly emerging suppliers) of nuclear material, equipment, and important dual-use items to include an international security criteria in export licensing. This would include defining the contemplated nuclear project, its economics, the user's disposition toward nuclear weapons, the facility's vulnerability to sabotage and military attack, safeguards against sensitive nuclear material diversion, and the prospective owner's ability to operate the plant and to manage material safely.

The assessment also would have "action options"—suggested remedies, incentives, and sanctions, including export restraint, that might be applied by IAEA member states should an operator be found out of compliance with INR guidelines. The checklist in this least restrictive INR would not be enforceable, but it would serve as a standard of conduct, just as IAEA guidelines on physical security and nuclear safety already do.

In INR II, the IAEA would expand its responsibility to apply the Nuclear Security Assessment to both export and domestic construction. For this purpose the agency would establish a standing committee of technical experts and social scientists. This committee could be an elaboration of the current Standing Advisory Group on Safeguard Implementation or the International Commission on Nuclear Safety. Access to IAEA inspectorate reports on facilities under construction and in operation would facilitate its task. The standing committee could either circulate Nuclear Security Assessments to safeguard division personnel and/or member states privately. The analysis could also be published, although publication would likely meet with national resistance. These assessments notwithstanding, the agency would have no control over nuclear development other than through the persuasiveness of its impartial findings, pressures interested nations might apply, and, should the reports be published, public opinion.

Because there might be resistance to such an assessment, given its political undertones within the IAEA, INR III would apply the principles of INR I through the suppliers group only, while INR IV would add an expert committee whose conclusions would be advisory, not mandatory. In contrast, INR V would require mandatory application of the Nuclear Security Assessment by suppliers. INR VI would involve emerging suppliers and importers in this mandatory scheme within the rubric of the IAEA. This option would help overcome inevitable importer resentment— particularly among developing states—toward INR III and IV on grounds that they smack of supplier neo-imperialism, cartelism, and the like. Furthermore, INR VI would elaborate IAEA Director of Safety Morris Rosen's call for "development of a clear and universally acceptable approach to safety guided by an international body composed of prominent exporters [that] could alleviate national and international safety concerns, and . . . also positively influence public opinion."[15] In INR VII, the IAEA would license all nuclear facilities, whether imported or domestically produced, using INRs as a foundation. This last approach would comport with former Nuclear Regulatory Commissioner Victor Gilinsky's contention that it "is clear that nuclear technology and unlimited national sovereignty are just not compatible if we want to keep from blowing ourselves up."[16] Table 18-1 presents a comparison of the seven INRs.

Will the INRs work? Desirability and attainability are among the most important criteria for evaluating the INRs. Desirability is measured by relative benefits compared to current protective measures and proposed alternatives. Certainly all of the INRs are more comprehensive, and most are more authoritative, than institutions addressing nuclear risks today.

Table 18-1
International Nuclear Review Summary

INR	Composition	Structure	Authority	Enforcement Options
I	Iaea	Ad hoc committee	Promulgate Nuclear Security Assessment	Informal: self-enforcement and peer pressure
II	Iaea	Standing social science and technical expert group	Monitory application of Nuclear Security Assessment	Informal: self-enforcement and peer pressure
III	Current and emerging nuclear suppliers	Ad hoc committee	Promulgate Nuclear Security Assessment	Informal: self-enforcement and peer pressure
IV	Current and emerging nuclear suppliers	Standing social science and technical expert group	Monitory application of Nuclear Security Assessment	Informal: self-enforcement and peer pressure
V	Current and emerging nuclear suppliers and importers	Nuclear Export Review Board (NERB): standing social science and technical expert group; Board of Governors	Mandatory application of Nuclear Security Assessment	Applies to Inr V, VI, and VII: modify user's behavior via discussions; threaten to withhold nuclear assistance; withhold nuclear assistance; Iaea personnel employed permanently to monitor nuclear facilities; apply permissive action links; limit use of plutonium and highly enriched uranium; return spent fuel to supplier or international repository; limit use of heavy-water reactors; threaten political and economic sanctions; apply economic and political sanctions.
VI	Current and emerging nuclear suppliers	International Nuclear Export Review Board (INERB): standing social science and technical expert group; Board of governors, Secretariat; Director General; General Conference	Mandatory application of Nuclear Security Assessment	
VII	Current and emerging nuclear suppliers and importers	International Licensing board	Mandatory licensing of all nuclear facilities worldwide	

Still, however authoritatively applied, are INRs a good idea, or do they rest on dubious assumptions with inherent flaws?

To accept the work of INRs is to accept the proposition that the problems they treat are worth treating, that proliferation of nuclear weapons in the past has complicated international politics and is likely to do so in the future, that subnational diversion of nuclear materials and sabotage are consistent with terrorist aims and therefore may occur, and that accidents such as Chernobyl are unacceptable. To believe otherwise would, in my opinion, be overly sanguine about the problems posed by nuclear energy and the ability of all states to cope equally, when the application of preventive medicine through the INRs or other authoritative schemes would not exact inordinate costs.

In Chernobyl the most powerful INR, international licensing of all nuclear plants, might have prevented the accident by, at a minimum, requiring installation of quick-starting emergency diesel generators (which are available in other countries), thereby eliminating the rationale for the ill-fated safety test in the first place. Application of the INRs might have prevented or at least slowed nuclear weapons development in Pakistan and could help prevent future Pakistans from acquiring the wherewithal to build nuclear enrichment and other sensitive nuclear facilities. Efforts of this sort are not cost-free. Nations would have to accept greater international scrutiny of their indigenous nuclear programs, as well as exports and imports, but this is a small cost compared to the risks.

Are we likely to see greater material international scrutiny of nuclear programs consistent with the most intrusive INRs? In my view this is unlikely. Lawrence Scheinman put the matter well when he wrote, "what is technically attainable may not be politically feasible."[17] Chernobyl, for reasons discussed earlier, was not sufficiently compelling to prompt material changes in the international regime, although some countries slowed their nuclear program as a result and, in the case of Sweden, one state decided to phase out nuclear energy after the turn of the century entirely. Regrettably, although the nuclear regime has made remarkable progress and the world today is safer as a result, for INRs or other more intrusive and rigorous proposals for international authority to be implemented we are likely to have to await the aftermath of the next Chernobyl or some other major nuclear incident.

Notes

1. Pierre Lellouche, "Internationalization of the International Nuclear Fuel Cycle and Non-Proliferation Strategy: Lesson and Prospects" (SJD diss., Harvard Law School, 1979), pp. 161–62.

2. For elaboration, see Lawrence Scheinman, *The International Atomic Energy Agency and World Order* (Washington, D.C.: Resources for the Future, 1987), chs. 4–5.

3. Ibid., pp. 209–24.

4. U.S. Congress, Senate, Committee on Foreign Relations, *The Israeli Air Strike*, 97th Cong., 1st sess., June 18, 19, and 25, 1981, pp. 12–124.

5. Scheinman, *International Atomic Energy Agency*, pp. 234–35.

6. Gary Milhollin, "The Theft of Nuclear Weapons Material: Four Federal Reports Compared," mimeo, 5 November 1987, available from Bennett Ramberg.

7. Michael J. Brenner, "Renewing the Non-Proliferation Regime: A Multilateral Approach," in Edward C. Luck, *Arms Control: The Multilateral Alternative* (New York: New York University Press, 1983), p. 170; Joseph A. Yager, *International Cooperation in Nuclear Energy* (Washington, D.C.: The Brookings Institution, 1981), p. 140; John Simpson, "The Nuclear Non-Proliferation Problem: Diagnosis and Treatment," in John Simpson and Anthony G. McGrew, *The International Nuclear Non- Proliferation Treaty* (London: Macmillan, 1984), p. 171; Lellouche, "Internationalization, p. 221; Council on Foreign Relations, *Blocking the Spread of Nuclear Weapons*, (New York: Council on Foreign Relations, 1986), p. 63; D.A.V. Fisher, in Paul Leventhal and Yonnah Aleaxander eds., *Nuclear Terrorism: Defining the Threat*, (Washington, D.C.: Pergamon-Brassey, 1986), p. 88.

8. "Convention on Early Notification of a Nuclear Accident," 15 August 1986, mimeo, available from Bennett Ramberg.

9. "Convention on Assistance in the Case of a Nuclear Accident or Radiological Emergency," 15 August 1986, mimeo, available from Bennett Ramberg.

10. *Christian Science Monitor*, 2,3 May 1986, pp. 1, 12.

11. Statement by Bernard Baruch, U.S. representative to the United Nations Atomic Energy Commission, 14 June 1946, in *Documents on Disarmament, 1945–1959*, Vol. 1 (Washington, D.C.: U.S. Arms Control and Disarmament Agency), pp. 7–11.

12. U.S. Congress, House, Committee on Foreign Affairs, *Nuclear Exports: International Safety and Environmental Issues*, 96th Cong., 2d sess., 1980. See also Scheinman's brief discussion of LDC ability to absorb nuclear technology given limited scientific infrastructures. Scheinman, *International Atomic Energy Agency*, p. 255.

13. Daniel Ford, *The Cult of the Atom*, (New York: Simon and Schuster, 1982).

14. Bennett Ramberg, *Global Nuclear Energy Risks: The Search For Preventive Medicine* (Boulder, Colo.: Westview Press, 1986).

15. Morris Rosen, "Establishment of an International Nuclear Safety Body," *International Atomic Energy Agency Bulletin* (September 1983): 3.

16. U.S. Congress, Senate, Committee on Foreign Relations, 97th Cong., 1st sess., 2 December 1981, p. 40.

17. Scheinman, *International Atomic Energy Agency*, p. 231. See also Jack Barkenbus, "Nuclear Power Safety and the Role of International Organization," *International Organization* (Summer 1987): 487.

19

The Emerging Nuclear Suppliers: Some Guidelines for Policy

Lewis A. Dunn

S ince the early 1980s, a growing amount of attention has been paid to a small group of mostly developing countries that have come to be called "the emerging nuclear suppliers." Argentina and Brazil, China and South Korea, India and Pakistan, Spain and Yugoslavia have frequently been mentioned in this category. Their actual and potential nuclear export dealings and policies have been the subject of academic writings and policy papers, of scholarly symposia and exchanges at meetings of the traditional nuclear suppliers.[1] With foundation and other support, UCLA's Center for International and Strategic Affairs has begun a major project to develop a database on the transactions, policies, and export control institutions of the emerging suppliers.[2]

In light of all this activity, it is appropriate to step back and ask: Is there a problem? What do we want from the emerging nuclear suppliers? What do they want from us? What steps should the United States and other established nuclear suppliers take to lessen the risk that the new suppliers will undermine global efforts to prevent the further spread of nuclear weapons? To address these questions, this chapter provides some guidelines for policy toward the emerging nuclear suppliers.

Recognize the Potential Problem—
But Don't Exaggerate

In most discussions of the emerging nuclear suppliers, there is an undercurrent of uneasiness about their potential impact on global nonprolifera-

To appear in William C. Potter, ed., *The Emerging Nuclear Suppliers and Nonproliferation* (Forthcoming). The views expressed in this chapter do not necessarily represent those of SAIC or any of its sponsoring agencies.

tion efforts. On the one hand, that concern rests on a recognition that these new suppliers are potential exporters of the types of equipment, materials, and know-how that have proved troublesome for nonproliferation in the past. On the other hand, many of these countries are not parties to existing nonproliferation treaties and have not accepted the basic nuclear export norms developed by the major nuclear suppliers.

More specifically, though there are important country-by-country variations, on a continuum from a capability to supply some basic "nuclear know-how" to the supply of turn-key nuclear steam supply systems, the emerging nuclear suppliers' export capabilities fall toward the lower end of the spectrum. Nonetheless, as table 19–1 makes clear, some if not many of these countries would be able to export items of potential use for a nuclear explosives program, particularly if exported without International Atomic Energy Agency (IAEA) safeguards. In addition, the majority of these countries, as table 19–2 indicates, are not adherents to the Nuclear Non-Proliferation Treaty (NPT), which would explicitly bind them (under Article III) to require IAEA safeguards on their nuclear exports[3] and implicitly obligate them (under Article I) not to assist other countries to make nuclear explosives.[4] Similarly, the emerging suppliers are not parties to the London Nuclear Suppliers Group (NSG) Guidelines, which regulate nuclear exports by the major suppliers. These guidelines include commitments to require IAEA safeguards on exports, to obtain peaceful-use and other assurances on a government-to-government basis for nuclear exports, and to exercise restraint in the transfer of sensitive reprocessing or enrichment technology or equipment. Indeed, many of these emerging suppliers have publicly criticized the NSG guidelines and called for greater technology transfer between developed and developing countries in this and other areas.

Several other considerations, however, partly temper these more basic concerns. With the notable exception of early Chinese nuclear export practices,[5] the emerging suppliers have so far acted relatively cautiously as nuclear exporters. Moreover, China and Argentina have recently stated that it will become their policy to require IAEA safeguards on exports, although the specific items to be covered remain to be determined and their institutions for export control to be tested fully. In turn, South Africa has stated that it will abide by the NSG guidelines. Further, at the 1987 United Nations Peaceful Uses of Nuclear Energy Conference in Geneva, such emerging suppliers as Argentina and Brazil steered clear of the more extreme rhetorical attacks on the existing nuclear suppliers that found favor with some developing countries.

To strike a balance, there are legitimate reasons for both concern and encouragement about the future nuclear export capabilities and practices of

Table 19–1
Capabilities of the Emerging Nuclear Suppliers

Country	Natural Uranium[a]	Heavy Water	Research Reactors	Low-Enriched Uranium	Enrichment or Reprocessing Aid	Dual-Use Items	Nuclear Explosive Know-How
Argentina	Limited[a]	Future[b]	Yes	Yes	Yes	Yes	No
Brazil	Yes	No	Future	Future	Future	Yes	No
People's Republic of China	Yes	Yes	Yes	Yes	Yes	Yes	Yes
India	Limited	Yes	Yes	Future	Yes	Yes	Yes
Israel	No	No	Future	No	?	Yes	?
Japan	No	No	Yes	Yes	Yes	Yes	No
Pakistan	Limited	No	No	Future	Yes	Yes	?
Romania	No	?[c]	Future	No	No	Yes	No
South Africa	Yes	No	Future	Yes	Yes	Yes	?
South Korea	No	No	Future	No	No	Yes	No
Spain	Limited	No	Future	No	Yes	Yes	No
Taiwan	No	No	Future	No	No	Yes	No
Yugoslavia	Limited	No	Future	No	Limited	Yes	No

[a]Limited: several tons of natural uranium, hundreds of kilograms of heavy water, or small quantities of low-enriched uranium per year.
[b]Future: likely capability to export within three to ten years.
[c]?: Publicly rumored but unconfirmed capability.

Table 19–2
Nonproliferation Commitments and Attitudes of the Emerging Nuclear Suppliers

Country	NPT Party	Waived Tlatelolco into Force	Policy or Treaty Commitment to Safeguards on Exports	Speaks for Supply Restraint in Public Debates
Argentina	No	No	Yes (Policy)	No
Brazil	No	No	No	No
People's Republic of China	No	N/A	Yes (Policy)	No
India	No	N/A	No	No
Israel	No	N/A	No	No
Japan	Yes	N/A	Yes (Treaty)	Yes
Pakistan	No	N/A	No	No
Romania	Yes	N/A	Yes (Treaty)	No
South Africa	No	N/A	Yes (Policy)	Nonparty
South Korea	Yes	N/A	Yes (Treaty)	No
Spain	Yes	N/A	Yes (Treaty)	No
Taiwan	Yes	N/A	Yes (Treaty)	Nonparty
Yugoslavia	Yes	N/A	Yes (Treaty)	No

the emerging nuclear suppliers. Recognition of this duality is the first guideline and starting point for policies of the United States and other existing suppliers toward these new entrants into the nuclear marketplace.

Don't Try to Create a New Set of Global Norms

A closely related guideline for future policy toward the emerging nuclear suppliers is the need to work within existing nuclear supply norms and structures, not to try to replace them with a new set of norms negotiated between the new and the old suppliers.[6] Existing guidelines, norms, and supplier practices are now widely understood, implemented in domestic legislation, and accepted as legitimate by the old suppliers. More importantly, the specific injunctions within the NPT and the London Nuclear Suppliers Guidelines of 1977 have provided a sound basis for regulating nuclear supply and significantly strengthened international nonproliferation efforts over the past decade.

The detailed obligation within the NSG, for example, to require IAEA safeguards on certain quantities of exported nuclear materials has helped to ensure that such exports do not add to the risk of nuclear weapons proliferation. Similarly, the commitment to exercise restraint in the transfer of sensitive reprocessing and enrichment technology has hindered some countries' efforts to acquire such sensitive facilities, which could heighten tensions and suspicions between neighbors and provide the foundations for a nuclear weapons program. More broadly, the presence of a wide range of specific nuclear-related items on internationally agreed upon export control "trigger lists" has been critical to slowing the efforts of countries to move toward nuclear weapons capabilities.

By contrast, any attempt to create a new global set of nuclear supply principles, formally agreed to by all new and old suppliers, would almost certainly result, at best, in an inconclusive debate that would weaken the existing norms' legitimacy and, at worst, could result in weaker, not stronger, guidelines. Practical differences between the emerging and the old suppliers over detailed questions would be one impediment. For example, what specific exports need to be safeguarded, and when? Are government-to-government assurances of peaceful uses necessary, or would assurances from the purchaser suffice?

In addition, nearly a decade of multilateral discussions—in the IAEA's Committee on Assurances of Supply, in preparations for the 1987 United Nations Conference on the Peaceful Uses of Nuclear Energy, and at the 1987 Peaceful Uses conference itself—make clear that broader political, if not nearly "theological," divisions, would also hinder efforts to reach a formal agreement among new and old suppliers on a new set of internationally acceptable principles of nuclear supply. The degree of responsibility suppliers take to not trade with countries of proliferation concern, differences over whether the purpose of nonproliferation is to prevent the spread of nuclear explosives (including so-called peaceful nuclear explosives) or only to prevent the spread of nuclear weapons, and divisions concerning whether to exercise restraint in sensitive technology transfers all could suffice to block consensus.

Finally, even the more moderate developing country emerging nuclear suppliers are unlikely to be prepared to risk their "nonaligned" political credentials by adherence to a formal agreement accepting the legitimacy of restraints on the "free flow" of technology between developed and developing countries. Thus, internal political dynamics amongst the nonaligned countries would also work against any attempt to create a new overarching set of supply principles acceptable to both new and old suppliers.

Seek Individual Suppliers' Adherence to Existing Norms, But Accept a Mixed Outcome

Rather than seeking to create a new set of global principles, policy should concentrate on convincing as many of the emerging suppliers as possible to adhere, as formally as possible, to existing nuclear supply norms. As a corollary to this third guideline, policymakers need to be prepared to accept a mixed outcome, one in which some emerging suppliers accept all of the basic norms but others accept only some of those norms; one in which some emerging suppliers formally adhere to nuclear supply restraints but others do so only through unilateral commitments.

More specifically, formal or informal acceptance of the following international nuclear supply norms should be encouraged:

Export of items on the so-called nuclear supply "trigger lists" only under IAEA safeguards;

Export of such items only with an assurance from the recipient country that the items will be used only for peaceful purposes;

Export of trigger list items only with the recipient's commitment to maintain adequate physical security, not to retransfer the items without the approval of the original supplier, and similar nonproliferation conditions;

Restraint in the transfer of sensitive reprocessing and enrichment technologies or equipment;

Restraint in any dealings with "sensitive countries" that might pose a proliferation risk; and

Restraint in exports of dual-use items.

Commitments by individual suppliers to some or all of these norms could be made in various ways. For example, they could be folded into bilateral agreements, as partly occurs in the U.S.-China nuclear cooperation agreement. Side letters to such agreements, as well as statements for the negotiating record, could provide another vehicle. Still another means for an emerging supplier to associate itself with existing practices would be through unilateral steps, whether changes of domestic legislation or official policy statements. From this perspective, the long-term goal would be to extend gradually the current network of nuclear supply restraints and institutions—represented by the NSG Guidelines; the NPT suppliers' agreements made under the Zangger Committee; and the European Community's Nuclear Supply Policy announced in 1985—to include different but complementary commitments by the emerging suppliers.

At the same time, the United States and other suppliers should encourage the emerging nuclear suppliers to put in place the needed domestic nuclear export control structures and procedures to carry through effectively on acceptance of these types of nuclear supply restraints. The specific structures and mechanisms for nuclear export control would vary, of course, from country to country. But more generally, they would include:

Establishment and promulgation of licensing lists and procedures to provide controls over what is exported;

Development of regulations to provide technical guidance in specific decisions—for example, on what quantities of materials require IAEA safeguards;

Internal procedures to permit a political "check-off" on sensitive export questions;

Procedures to monitor actual exports to ensure that the controls are not being violated;

Diplomatic practices to obtain the needed assurances from other governments; and, of considerable importance,

Setting up of intergovernmental mechanisms to ensure that representatives of the president or prime minister, as well as the key ministries— foreign affairs, trade, economics or finance, science and technology, defense, atomic energy—take part in and then abide by export control decisions.

Though often overlooked, this type of nuclear export control institution-building may be as important for extending the net of nuclear supply norms as agreement to the norms themselves. For without it, acceptance of norms may be an empty gesture.

Pursue a Range of Channels in Approaching the New Suppliers

Many channels need to be used as part of this overall effort to create a broader network of nuclear supplier restraint. Bilateral government-to-government contacts, small ad hoc meetings of new and old suppliers, exchanges at multilateral meetings, and even nongovernmental activities can all play a part.

Recent efforts by the United States and other old suppliers have concentrated on starting up and continuing bilateral dialogues with key emerging suppliers on nuclear export issues. The United States, for example, has used its periodic bilateral contacts with China, Argentina, and Brazil to encourage them to adopt cautious nuclear supply policies and to put in place domestic structures and institutions to implement them. These contacts have also been used to explain the logic behind the existing set of supplier norms and practices. But such bilateral approaches could usefully be supplemented by other measures in the years ahead.

One such additional approach would be to bring together some of the old and some of the emerging suppliers in one or more ad hoc meetings. Such a meeting could take place on the margins of the regular quarterly meetings of the IAEA in Vienna, or it could stand alone. It would provide an opportunity for an exchange of views on nuclear supply matters between key old and new nuclear suppliers.

For their part, the established suppliers could use the meeting to set out the case for nuclear export restraint and to explain the logic that underlies established norms and practices. For example, the existing suppliers could make the case for requiring IAEA safeguards, for peaceful-use assurances on a government-to-government basis, and for restraint in transfers of sensitive technology. Such a meeting would also provide a good opportunity for the established suppliers to discuss some of the institutions, regulations, and procedures that they have put in place to ensure effective export controls. Conversely, the new suppliers could use such an ad hoc meeting to set out their concerns about restraints on technology transfer as well as over other nuclear supply restraints. Over time, these ad hoc meetings could help to identify areas of common interest and to convince the new suppliers to adhere to some of the existing norms and practices.

Efforts to influence the emerging suppliers could also take advantage of international meetings on nonproliferation and nuclear energy related matters. At the upcoming 1990 conference to review the Nuclear Non-Proliferation Treaty, for example, the existing suppliers could seek to include in any final document a reference to the emerging suppliers and a call for them to adhere to existing nonproliferation and nuclear supply norms and practices. Resolutions could be pursued as well at the periodic meetings of the IAEA Board of Governors or at the annual IAEA General Conference.

In addition, careful consideration should be given to inviting some of the emerging suppliers that also are NPT parties to participate in the work of the Zangger Committee. Originally set up to define the specific export control responsibilities of NPT parties, this committee meets annually to review nuclear export activities. It has also played an important role in the recent tightening of nuclear export control norms, via several upgrades of the trigger lists. Inviting the NPT new suppliers—such as Spain, Yugoslavia, and South Korea—to join the Zangger Committee would at a minimum help to ensure that they followed the basic NPT supply obligations. It would also provide an opportunity to discuss nuclear supply issues with such countries. In addition, these countries are likely to respond favorably to being taken seriously as suppliers, while membership itself would create more diffuse pressures to follow established norms, lest they become the "odd men out."

Nonetheless, there has been some reluctance to expand the Zangger group, partly due to concern that new members might hinder still further efforts to tighten the trigger lists, the main activity of the group in recent years. However, most of that activity has been successfully concluded with the upgrades of the reprocessing and centrifuge uranium enrichment trigger lists, or should soon be in the case of the gaseous diffusion enrichment list. On balance, the potential risks, therefore, seem to be outweighed by the gains of using the group as another channel to emerging suppliers.

In addition, more informal, nongovernmental efforts could contribute to a broader effort to convince the new suppliers to follow existing norms and practices. Periodic conferences, individual exchanges, and group discussions sponsored by private organizations all provide a means to make the case for nuclear restraint. In particular, these types of nonofficial channels can help to build up domestic consitituencies in other countries that can press for nuclear supply restraint and a factoring of nonproliferation concerns into the policies of the governments in office.

Tailor the Arguments to the Interests of the Emerging Suppliers

In using any or all of these channels to encourage the emerging suppliers to follow internationally accepted nuclear supply norms, another guideline for policy would be to identify and build on the security, prestige, economic, and political interests of these new suppliers. Policy approaches also should be frank but not confrontational.

As a start, approaches to the new suppliers should stress the important security interest that both old and new suppliers share in preventing the further spread of nuclear weapons. In particular, more widespread nuclear weapons proliferation, whether in South Asia, the Middle East, or Latin America, would threaten the countries in these regions most immediately and most directly. It would also have a longer-term, adverse impact on the larger international order, heightening the risk of confrontation between the superpowers, of terrorist acquisition of nuclear weapons, and of direct threats to countries outside newly nuclear regions.

The impact of this line of argument admittedly will vary from country to country. However, many of the NPT emerging suppliers—for example, Spain, Yugoslavia, Taiwan, and South Korea—are likely to be partly susceptible to such arguments. Security considerations also could affect the calculations of some countries not parties to the NPT, including China and Argentina. For others among the non-NPT parties, including perhaps India, this line of argument might only trigger the traditional response that the real problem of proliferation is posed by the arsenals of the nuclear-weapons states.

The hope of some emerging suppliers to obtain increased prestige and recognition as technologically advanced countries on account of their role as nuclear exporters could be used to seek their adherence to basic norms and practices. Policy should look for ways to make clear to new suppliers that less responsible policies would earn them condemnation, not praise, and make them outcasts rather than recognized members of the peaceful nuclear community. Declarations in international forums, diplomatic demarches and exchanges between leaders, and a refusal to accept such countries in leadership posts at international nuclear-related meetings could all help to make that point; At the same time, it would be important to ensure that the policies of the traditional suppliers stay on track, lest they send the wrong signal.

More narrow self-interest and pursuit of economic gain on the part of many emerging suppliers could be a valuable approach to encourage their adherence to nuclear supply norms and practices, as well. In particular, possible "teaming" arrangements between U.S. nuclear vendors and the firms of new supplier nations might be explored as an inducement for such adherence, to the extent permitted by U.S. legislation.[7] Such teaming and cooperative arrangements could include joint bids on specific projects, technology licenses to new suppliers, transfers of marketing information, and other cooperation. These types of joint ventures and similar arrangements would provide the new supplier with enhanced market access, enhanced access to financing, and technological know-how that would strengthen its pursuit of nuclear business. Specifically, possible teaming arrangements between U.S. firms and firms in South Korea, Spain, and Yugoslavia need to be looked at from this nonproliferation perspective.

But there also will be cases in which the United States is precluded from entering into such cooperative arrangements with a new supplier. Here, other suppliers might be encouraged to work out cooperative arrangements with that country if the nonproliferation payoff was deemed sufficient. In particular, the possibility needs to be explored of how to take advantage of continued close West German ties with Argentina and Brazil as well as growing Japanese and British ties with China to foster nuclear supply restraint.

The more general interest of emerging suppliers in good political relations with the United States and with other like-minded countries ought to be brought to bear in seeking to influence their nuclear export policies and practices. Periodic high-level meetings between U.S. officials and officials of these new suppliers—including at the level of the president and the secretary of state—could be used to raise this and other nonproliferation issues.

Finally, in this dialogue with emerging suppliers, the United States should be frank but not confrontational about what types of nuclear export actions by them would cause us concern. All of these countries have on many past occasions evidenced their readiness to let us know what they think, directly and without "pulling punches." An equally direct approach on our part is most likely to avoid misunderstandings and to cut through inevitable rhetoric. Such frankness would help to ensure that nuclear export and nonproliferation issues are moved from technical channels to political channels, as well as from mid-level bureaucrats to higher-up political leaders. Without such political-level involvement, it probably would be very difficult to overcome technical-level reluctance to change established patterns of activity.

Bring Other Countries' Influence to Bear

Policy efforts to influence the emerging nuclear suppliers need to draw on the influence of many countries, not simply that of the United States. As just suggested, there may be cases in which joint ventures between a Western old nuclear supplier and one of the emerging nuclear suppliers could help to bring about the latter's adherence to established norms. More broadly, Western nuclear suppliers and Japan need to continue to use their influence with key new suppliers. Nuclear firms in the Federal Republic of Germany, for example, have extensive ties with Argentina, Spain, and Yugoslavia. The West German government should make use of these links to foster nuclear export restraint. Similarly, Japan's cooperation with China's nuclear power program provides contacts that could be used to encourage that country's continuing evolution as a nuclear supplier.

The Soviet Union also has a role to play in light of its overall commitment to a sound nonproliferation and nuclear export regime. In particular, Soviet ties with countries such as Argentina, India, Romania, and Yugoslavia all could be used to influence these new suppliers' export practices.

Still other, less often thought about, sources of potential influence should not be overlooked. The European Political Community, for instance, could build on its announcement of a common nuclear supply policy to undertake common demarches to key new suppliers. Its influence could be especially helpful in ensuring that China continues to abide by its newly cautious export posture.

Yet another, though more unorthodox, approach might be to raise nuclear supply and other nonproliferation issues with the so-called "Five Continents Group," comprised of Mexico, Argentina, Tanzania, India, Sweden, and Greece. One possible tack would be to include in the next U.S. response to one of this group's periodic letters on nuclear disarmament to the United States and the Soviet Union a suggestion that the group place nonproliferation matters on its agenda for future meetings, as well as a call for the members of this group to ensure that their own activities do not add to the risk of the further spread of nuclear weapons. It could be pointed out that such proliferation would pose a serious threat to the very aims of the group. At the same time, separate letters might be sent to the leaders of Sweden and Mexico, members with strong nonproliferation credentials, urging them to use the next meeting of the Five Continents Group to raise nuclear supply and nonproliferation issues, especially with their Indian and Argentinian colleagues.

For the United States, the key task would be to encourage such initiatives by other countries and political groupings. It also would be important to work behind the scenes to keep track of the results of any initiatives by other countries, to seek ways to take advantage of possible openings, and to ensure an overall consistent approach.

Think in Terms of Limited Advances "At the Margin"

Finally, the United States and other like-minded suppliers should recognize that progress in any attempts to influence the nuclear supply practices and procedures of the emerging suppliers is likely to be characterized by limited advances "at the margin." Most new suppliers could perhaps be convinced, for example, to state unilaterally that their exports would be governed by the most basic norms, such as the requirements of acceptance of IAEA safeguards and of government-to-government peaceful-use assurances. Still others, but probably fewer, might be prepared to exercise restraint privately in transfers of sensitive technology, even while continuing to call for the free flow of technology in nonaligned caucuses. Alternatively, some new suppliers could be ready to associate themselves formally, perhaps within the Zangger Committee, with the guidelines for NPT suppliers.

A readiness to think in terms of these types of more limited gains would be consistent with the greater willingness of some new suppliers than others to agree to certain restraints. It also would permit policy initiatives to be tailored to the interests and possibilities in the case of each new supplier. In turn, the danger of policy disappointments and demoralization would be lessened.

But, of greater importance, a step-by-step series of advances would be most likely to generate momentum for further progress, with one supplier setting an example for others, and initial steps providing a context for further movement later. By emphasizing actions where common interests are present and setting aside for later areas of disagreement, this approach would help as well to build up habits of cooperation and perceptions of a common security interest in nonproliferation. As a result, the prospects would be improved for putting into place over time that expanded network of nuclear supply restraints that must be the longer-term goal of policy toward the emerging nuclear suppliers.

Notes

1. For some earlier analyses of the emerging nuclear suppliers, see, inter alia, Lewis A. Dunn, *Controlling the Bomb: Nuclear Proliferation in the 1980s* (New Haven: Yale University Press, 1982), pp. 41–43; Rodney Jones, Cesare Merlini, Joseph Pilat, and William Potter, eds., *The Nuclear Suppliers and Nonproliferation* (Lexington, Mass.: Lexington Books, 1985), pp. 93–127.

2. See William Potter, "Creating a Database on International Nuclear Commerce" CISA Working Paper No. 59, UCLA Center for International and Strategic Affairs (September 1987).

3. Article III-2 reads: "Each State Party to the Treaty undertakes not to provide: (a) source or special fissionable material, or (b) equipment or material especially designed or prepared for the processing, use or production of special fissionable material, to any non–nuclear-weapon State for peaceful purposes, unless the source or special fissionable material shall be subject to the safeguards required by this article."

4. Article I commits the nuclear-weapon state parties "not in any way to assist, encourage, or induce any non–nuclear-weapon State to manufacture or otherwise acquire nuclear weapons or other nuclear explosive devices." However, this is often taken also to entail an implicit obligation on the part of non–nuclear-weapon states, lest their behavior as parties to the NPT undermine the treaty's purposes.

5. See, e.g., U.S. Arms Control and Disarmament Agency, *Nonproliferation Assessment Statement for the US-China Agreement for Peaceful Nuclear Cooperation* (Washington, D.C., 1985).

6. This possibility was discussed in Amy Sands, "Emerging Nuclear Suppliers: What's the Beef?" (Paper prepared for conference on "The Emerging Nuclear Suppliers and Nonproliferation," Bellagio, Italy, 22–26 June 1987. It also was one

of the main objectives of many of the developing countries at the 1987 United Nations Peaceful Uses of Nuclear Energy Conference.

7. The Nuclear Non-Proliferation Act would prohibit most such cooperation with emerging suppliers that had not accepted safeguards on all of their own peaceful nuclear activities.

20

The Behavior of the Emerging Nuclear Suppliers: Sources and Policy Implications

William C. Potter

A n effort has been made in the preceding chapters to analyze the sources and the substance of the nuclear export behavior of eleven emerging supplier states. Considerable detail has been provided about the factors motivating (and constraining) each of these states to engage in international nuclear trade, their capability to do so, the domestic structure supporting nuclear commerce, and national norms regarding nonproliferation. Rather than summarize these findings as they pertain to individual states, this concluding chapter is designed to identify more general statements that can be made about emerging nuclear supplier state behavior and the risks it poses to the nonproliferation regime.

The Typical Emerging Supplier

It is apparent from the case studies in this book that the emerging nuclear suppliers are not a homogeneous lot. They differ markedly in their level of economic development, technical capability, domestic political and economic structure, experience in international commerce, the health of their domestic nuclear industries, and national perspectives toward the NPT, safeguards, nuclear export guidelines, and other facets of the international nonproliferation regime.

It is also clear from the comparative case studies that no simple relationship exists between technical capability to produce nuclear material, technology, and equipment and the propensity to export those items, or between formal nonproliferation commitments on the part of emerging supplier states and restraint in nuclear export behavior. Indeed, the country in our sample with the most experienced and self-sufficient nuclear industry and also the most consistent criticism of the existing nonproliferation regime—India—has been largely inactive as a nuclear exporter. Among the other emerging supplier states able to export sensitive nuclear material, equipment, technology, or services, only the People's Republic of China to date has been a major actor on the international scene, although Argentina and Spain are quickly becoming significant players, and Japan is likely to become one soon.

One cannot point to a single factor to explain the nuclear export behavior of the emerging suppliers. The series of comparative case studies, however, lends considerable support to the "supply-push" hypothesis identified by Randy Rydell (Ch. 2). According to this hypothesis, nuclear export activity increases when the domestic nuclear market fails to keep pace with domestic production capability. This appears to have been the case in Argentina, Japan, the PRC, and Spain. As Stephanie Sharron and Warren Donnelly put it: Japan's "initial surge of nuclear power plant construction has passed its peak and expected new domestic orders are not enough to keep Japan's nuclear industry occupied. Its underutilized nuclear industry needs foreign orders" (Ch. 10, p. 200). This situation is in contrast, at least until recently, with the relatively strong domestic nuclear markets in India, South Korea, and Taiwan. Consistent with the supply-push hypothesis, these latter states have not actively pursued nuclear exports.[1]

In addition to trying to bolster the development or, as the case may be, survival of their domestic nuclear industries, the emerging suppliers generally have pursued nuclear trade abroad for many of the same reasons as the traditional supplier states. Principal among these incentives is the profit motive. For a number of the emerging suppliers, however, especially the newly industrializing countries, nuclear exports also afford a means to acquire foreign exchange, to pursue barter transactions for coveted commodities, to reduce foreign debt, and to redress unfavorable terms of trade associated with dependency on unprocessed goods; These economic incentives, most clearly demonstrated by Etel Solingen for Brazil (Chapter 7), are also important for Argentina and the PRC, and are likely to gain in significance for India, Pakistan, South Korea, and Taiwan.

Although generally subordinate to economic considerations, international political incentives tend to reinforce emerging supplier state interest in nuclear exports. The pursuit of regional influence by means of nuclear export policy is most notable for Argentina, Brazil, Japan, Spain, and the PRC. The emerging suppliers also are inclined to attach greater importance than the traditional suppliers to the symbolic importance of nuclear exports and to equate nuclear export capability with increased international status and prestige.

To date, nuclear exports generally have not yielded substantial economic returns for the emerging suppliers.[2] This marketing difficulty, which currently also afflicts many of the traditional suppliers, results from a combination of factors, including the depressed international nuclear market, the economic ill health of most of the prospective importers in the developing world, constraints on long-term financing, and the lack of a proven record of reliable and safe exports. Even the more active emerging suppliers, such as the PRC and Argentina, have limited operational experience as nuclear exporters and must labor long and hard to generate buyer confidence where competition exists from traditional supplier states.

It is unlikely that many of the factors currently constraining the nuclear export activity of the emerging suppliers will soon dissipate. Heightened public concern internationally about the safety of nuclear power in the aftermath of Chernobyl has diminished the prospects for a near-term resurgence in nuclear power demand. Growing popular awareness of the detrimental environmental effects of fossil-fuel use, however, ultimately may reverse this trend, especially if there are breakthroughs in the development of a commercially viable "inherently safe" reactor. Progress in alleviating the tremendous debt burden afflicting most potential nuclear importers (as well as exporters) in the developing world would also enhance the export prospects of the emerging suppliers. To the extent that the emerging suppliers are able to "make good" on the limited orders they have already received in the nuclear sector—and barring future accidents in their domestic nuclear programs—buyer confidence in their goods and services should improve.

These developments, however, are extremely problematic and in any case are only apt to apply in the distant future. A more likely near-term development is for the emergence of increased joint-venture activity between emerging and traditional nuclear suppliers. Such an export strategy has the attraction of both minimizing a number of the constraints under which most emerging suppliers must operate (such as limited domestic financing capabilities and unproven reliability as a supplier) and exploiting the market experience these states have acquired as importers of nuclear technology and know-how. Indeed, our case studies indicate that the joint-venture route is already being taken by a number of emerging suppliers and is likely to be followed by others.[3] As Ciro Zoppo (Chapter 15) points out with respect to Spain, however, joining forces with companies from more-advanced nuclear states does not guarantee satisfactory nuclear export results.

Implicit in our discussion of the behavior of the emerging nuclear suppliers so far is the assumption that national decisions to acquire nuclear export capabilities and to engage in international nuclear trade are based primarily on careful calculations of the economic and political costs and benefits of alterative courses of action. Although in many instances this form of cost-benefit analysis may take place, it is also likely that "nonrational" factors such as bureaucratic politics play an important role in the agenda-setting and implementation phases of nuclear export decisionmaking. Indeed, one characteristic shared by most of the emerging supplier states—and a source of nonproliferation concern—is underdevelopment and understaffing of domestic nuclear export control structures and the lack of well-defined procedures for regulating nuclear exports. As Lewis Dunn (Chapter 19) points out, in the absence of routine procedures to license and monitor exports and mechanisms to coordinate interagency decision, declarations of support for prudence in nuclear exports, even if a sincere reflection of leadership beliefs, may well diverge from actual export behavior.

Although a similar slippage between professed policy and actual export behavior may be noted on the part of the traditional supplier states, their decisionmaking infrastructures for nuclear exports tend to be better developed than is the case for most of the emerging suppliers. The emerging suppliers, with the exception of Japan, also do not derive the technical benefits associated with regular participation in international nuclear export control consultations.

The Nature of the Problem

Our analysis of eleven states clearly supports the proposition that a new set of nuclear suppliers has emerged who, for the most part, are not bound by existing international export controls. It is also apparent from the comparative study that although the emerging suppliers differ widely in their technical capabilities, many of them are now able to offer on the international market nuclear material, technology, equipment, and services useful for nuclear weapons production.

That few transactions appear to have actually taken place involving emerging supplier exports of sensitive nuclear technology and material is probably due mainly to emerging supplier restraint. This restraint, while conditioned by strong international norms opposing nuclear proliferation, largely derives from considerations of self-interest and the determination that national security disincentives currently outweigh incentives to export. For example, although many of the emerging suppliers may regard the Nuclear Non-Proliferation Treaty (NPT) and existing international export controls as discriminatory and may themselves covet a nuclear weapons program, none are anxious to see other states acquire a nuclear weapons capability.[4] In short, one must be cautious not to equate the ability to export sensitive nuclear technology with the readiness to do so.

The good news from the standpoint of nonproliferation is that to date the nuclear export behavior of the emerging suppliers has been relatively restrained, especially when compared with the export practices of the traditional suppliers during their infancy. The two most active new suppliers, Argentina and the PRC, for example, while persisting in their criticism of the NPT and existing international nuclear export controls, nevertheless recently have stated that their exports will be under IAEA safeguards. One therefore may hope that a more general maturation process is at work, by which suppliers over time increasingly behave in accordance with stringent nuclear export guidelines. According to this optimistic scenario, the trend toward increased joint ventures between emerging and traditional suppliers may actually reinforce the nonproliferation regime if the traditional suppliers use the teaming arrangements and the economic incentives they have to offer as inducements for greater restraint on the part of the emerging suppliers.

There is, however, a less optimistic nonproliferation scenario involving the emerging suppliers. It is based less on their declaratory policies and more on their potential to make trouble. This vision of the future also derives less comfort from the actual record of emerging suppliers behavior to date, which in any case is limited. Especially troublesome, from this perspective, is the absence of an internalized commitment to nonproliferation on the part of the emerging suppliers and their increased ability and inclination to export ballistic missile technology as well as sensitive nuclear-related items.

Although the comparative case studies do not offer conclusive evidence for either the optimistic or pessimistic scenarios, they do suggest that in most of the emerging supplier states the norms guiding nuclear exports are in a state of flux. The machinery governing export behavior in these states also tends to be underdeveloped. It is not surprising, therefore, to discern very contradictory signals in export behavior. For example, although both Argentina and the PRC now declare their support for IAEA safeguards on their nuclear exports, neither state recognizes the need to exercise restraint in the export of sensitive components of the nuclear fuel cycle. They also appear ready to engage in nuclear trade with states whose commitment to nonproliferation is at best suspect.[5] Recent efforts by Argentina to develop nuclear ties with India and Pakistan are especially troublesome and represent a shift in policy away from President Raul Alfonsin's earlier prohibition against nuclear trade with the two South Asian rivals.[6] This shift in nuclear export policy, likely linked to domestic politics, highlights the danger of assuming that over time the export practices of the emerging suppliers will naturally evolve in the direction of greater restraint.

Similar caution should be noted regarding the observed trend toward more joint ventures. Although these teaming arrangements between emerging and traditional suppliers may yield nonproliferation dividends, they also may be attractive to firms in traditional supplier states who regard the joint arrangement as a means to circumvent their own states' more restrictive export regulations.[7] Indeed, much more attention needs to be directed at the nonproliferation problem of noncompliance with existing nuclear export regulation on the part of firms from NPT party states.

It is apparent from the comparative case studies that until now only a few of the emerging suppliers have been (the PRC), are becoming (Argentina and Spain), or are likely soon to be (Japan) major exporters of sensitive nuclear material, equipment, technology, or services. This finding may be of some comfort to the traditional suppliers. It also may be helpful in concentrating nonproliferation efforts to monitor trade in sensitive nuclear commodities. It should not, however, lead one to minimize the present and potential problems of those emerging suppliers with limited nuclear capabilities but with few export restrictions. As Amy Sands (Chapter 3) points out, such countries can pose a grave proliferation risk if they provide items otherwise unavailable to aspiring proliferants. Pakistan's experience in circumventing international nuclear export controls is especially relevant in this regard and underlines the porous nature of existing international control arrangements. The entry of new vendors into the nuclear marketplace will undoubtedly provide additional loopholes.

Anatoly Belov (Chapter 17), Bennett Ramberg (Chapter 18), and Lewis Dunn (Chapter 19) articulate a variety of management strategies to cope with the new difficulties posed by the emerging nuclear suppliers. Their recommendations are reasonable and deserve careful consideration by policymakers. The fundamental threat to the international nonproliferation regime, however, comes not from the emerging (or traditional) suppliers, but from those prospective customers who covet nuclear weapons. A successful nonproliferation policy, therefore, ultimately must confront not only the supply of nuclear weapons and their constituent parts, but the political and military factors that give rise to their demand.

Notes

1. The supply-push hypothesis, however, does not explain why states initially develop nuclear capabilities that cannot be justified economically in terms of a domestic, peaceful nuclear power program.

2. An exception is South African export of natural uranium.

3. Peter Hayes (Chapter 4) suggests that South Korea, in particular, is apt to embrace the joint-venture approach toward nuclear exports.

4. Even the People's Republic of China has now dropped its previous declaratory policy that supported each state's right to acquire nuclear weapons.

5. Unfortunately, the same can be said about many of the traditional supplier states.

6. See Richard Kessler, "Argentina Seeks Nuclear Ties with India and Paki-

stan," *Nucleonics Week*, 13 April 1989, p. 3. The 1988 Argentine sale of fuel fabrication equipment to India is all the more surprising because it also was at odds with prior policy that usually required a nuclear cooperation agreement to be in effect with the recipient state before a nuclear transfer.

7. West German firms are frequently mentioned in this connection.

Appendix: A Database on International Nuclear Commerce

William C. Potter

A database on international nuclear trade was started in 1986 at the UCLA Center for International and Strategic Affairs (CISA). The basic premise underlying the CISA database is that the core of the problem with respect to knowledge of the behavior of the emerging nuclear supplier states is less one of data availability and more one of systematic data collection and analysis. As the publications of Leonard Spector, George Quester, Warren Donnelly, Gary Milholin, Lewis Dunn, and others who follow nuclear export and proliferation developments indicate, a great deal of data on nuclear commerce is available in the public domain. The major problem is that the data are scattered throughout different nuclear energy, trade, and financial publications—many of which are exceedingly expensive and not readily available even at major research libraries. Moreover, with the exception of data on power reactors, the information is not reported in a format that facilitates comparative analysis over time or across states. The CISA database is designed to remedy these deficiencies.

Data Collection

Three general types of data are collected for entry into the CISA database: interactive, country attribute, and bibliographic. Each of these three kinds of data is entered into separate files of the database. Interactive data refer to information describing the specific characteristics of a nuclear transaction or interaction involving two or more countries. Country attribute data, on the other hand, provide information about a country's domestic structure, capabilities, and norms that may facilitate or inhibit its nuclear export activities. Bibliographic data provide information on the source(s) of the data contained in the interactive and/or country attribute file(s) and an abstract of the source text.

Because considerably more is known about the export behavior of the traditional nuclear suppliers, a special effort has been made in creating the database to collect information on twelve emerging supplier states: Argentina, Brazil, India, Israel, Japan, Pakistan, the PRC, South Africa, South Korea, Spain, Taiwan, and Yugoslavia. It is cost effective, however, when searching through the major nuclear trade publications, to collect and code interactive data for all the suppliers. The CISA database, therefore, is a repository for information on nuclear transactions of all states. The country attribute data file, in contrast, contains a disproportionate amount of information on the emerging suppliers. This orientation is the result of our procedures for article selection and coding and the fact that a series of case studies was especially commissioned for the emerging supplier states.

Data are now being collected for the post-1982 time period. Four publications, *Nucleonics Week*, *Nuclear News*, *Nuclear Engineering International*, and *Nuclear Developments* (formerly *Worldwide Proliferation Report*), were chosen for the initial phase of systematic and thorough search and coding.[a] The trade journal *Nuclear Fuel* was added in 1988. Data from these sources is being supplemented by (1) eleven case studies specifically commissioned for the Emerging Nuclear Suppliers and Nonprolifertion Project; (2) bulletins and newsletters from the major firms that are engaged in international nuclear commerce;[b] and (3) primary source materials provided by over four dozen advisors to the project from over a dozen countries.

What Is A Database?

Before describing the features of the CISA database in more detail, it may be useful to identify the general characteristics of a computerized database.[c] A database is simply a filing system used to organize a body of data. The CISA Nuclear Suppliers Database, for example, consists of three files: interactive data, country attribute data, and bibliographic data. Each of these files may be thought of as a kind of directory, similar to a phonebook. Just as a phonebook contains data on the names, addresses, and phone numbers of individuals or places of business, so the CISA database file on interactive data contains information on such things as the names of nuclear importing and exporting countries, the dates of transaction, and the items transferred. These subsets of data in the file (whether they be individual names and phone numbers in a phone directory or country importers and exporters and dates of transactions in an interactive data file) are referred to as *fields*.

Most phonebooks are organized alphabetically by name in order to facilitate the process of locating the phone numbers and addresses corresponding to the names with which one is familiar. One can imagine phonebooks, however, that are organized by the names of streets or numerically by phone numbers. Data in the CISA database can also be organized in many different ways depending upon the interests of the analyst. One can search, for example, by importer or exporter, dates, firm, type of transaction, or item transacted. One also has the capability to search for combinations of fields. The analyst, for example, can search for all transactions in 1986 where the importer was the PRC, the exporter was West Germany, the firm was Kraftwerk Union, and the item was a light-water reactor.

One can search for or sort information within each file in the database by fields or categories such as those mentioned above. The information itself, however, is entered into the computer database in the form of a *record*. Each record captures all of the relevant information for a single transaction, a country attribute profile, or the bibliographic data and abstract(s) from a specific source (for example, an article in *Nuclear Developments*). Stated somewhat differently, every source that is coded generates one record for the bibliographic data and one or more records for data on interactions and country attributes. All records from the same source receive a single document code number. This tagging of the records enables the user of the database to retrieve the desired article (that is, hard copy) from a filing cabinet where it has been filed by document code number.

The Interactive Data File

Greatest priority has been assigned to the collection and coding of data on international transactions or interactions. Eleven categories of information are collected with respect to nuclear interactions: transaction date, importer, exporter, transshipper, joint venture, act, firm, item, sale amount, currency, and safeguards. Since most of these categories are straightforward and because detailed coding instructions for each of them are provided in the *Emerging Nuclear Suppliers Project Training Manual and Coding Handbook*, the discussion here is limited to two of the categories, "act" and "item."

In order to try and capture at least an element of the process of interactions in the nuclear export arena, a set of seventeen act codes was developed. These codes, one of which is assigned to every recorded interaction, depict the stage and/or character of a nuclear transaction between two or more states. The seventeen act codes are: comment/denial/future act; consult/meet/visit; propose/offer/urge; request; evaluate/consider/negotiate; reject/refuse/withdraw; order/accept/contract; pay and deliver/deliver; pay (only); act in blackmarket/illegally transact; divert nuclear items/steal; transfer information/issue license; no clear importers or exporters/joint action; conduct feasibility study; litigate; provide prior/programmatic consent; and merge/acquire/increase stock holdings. Utilization of the act codes enables an analyst to trace the sequence in which interactions evolved between specific parties with respect to one or more nuclear commodities or services and to extract from the database particular kinds of behavior for a given time period, set of countries, or type of item.

The current items list, which is periodically updated and revised, consists of eighty-four nuclear or nuclear-related materials, equipment, technologies, or services that are tracked. This items list was compiled with the assistance of nuclear engineers and nonproliferation experts from government, industry, and research institutions. It draws extensively from the Nuclear Exporters Committee (Zangger) and London Suppliers Group trigger lists; the U.S. Nuclear Regulatory Commission "Rules and Regulations for Export and Import of Nuclear Facilities and Materials"; the Department of Energy "List of Energy Related Military Critical Technologies"; and the U.S. Commerce Department's "Nuclear Referral List." A glossary of the items is provided in the *Emerging Nuclear Suppliers Project Training Manual and Coding Handbook*.

The Country Attribute Data File

In addition to data on nuclear interactions, the CISA database contains information on a number of attributes of importing and exporting countries. These attributes pertain to domestic structure, export capability, and norms of a given country, as well as individuals involved in any aspect of nuclear trade or nuclear policymaking.

The key structural categories for which information is selected and coded are import and export policy (for example, legislation, licensing arrangements, rules, regulations, and/or statements governing a country's import or export of nuclear goods and services); bureaucratic and domestic politics regarding nuclear commerce; governmental and quasi-governmental actors engaged in nuclear policy formulation; nuclear trade consortiums; and financial institutions and economic, licensing, or budgetary arrangements relevant to nuclear commerce. These domestic structural variables are included in the database with an eye to analysis of the incentives and disincentives for national decisions to enter the international nuclear marketplace and the process by which decisions are made.

The capabilities list in the country attribute file corresponds closely to the items list in the interactive data file. Three rules govern whether or not a particular item is coded as a capability for the country attribute file (with the exception of the United States, Soviet Union, France, West Germany, United Kingdom, and Canada, for which capability items are not coded[d]): (1) the item is something that the country in question has the ability to export, or (2) the item is one of the following sensitive nuclear fuel cycle materials, equipment, technologies, or services:

Plutonium

Enriched uranium

Heavy water and deuterium

Zirconium

Tritium

Research reactors/equipment/technology

Fuel tubes and cladding (e.g., zirconium or zircalloy tubes)

Hot cells and related shielding and handling equipment

Fuel reprocessing plants/equipment/technology

Fuel fabrication plants/equipment/technology

Heavy water production plants/equipment/technology

Isotope separation plants/equipment/materials/technology (uranium enrichment)

Nuclear triggers

Large corrosion-resistant axial or centrifugal compressors

Nuclear weapons design

Shaped charges and related technology (e.g., detonators)

UF_6 corrosion-resistant autoclaves

or (3) the country explicitly claims that it will *not* develop a sensitive technology, item, or service. These coding rules are designed to facilitate the monitoring of developments in countries with the present and potential capability to export items of proliferation concern and/or to mount indigenous nuclear weapons programs.

The norms dimension of country attribute data taps such items as the declaratory statements about and/or policies toward other countries' nuclear programs; status and prestige considerations related to nuclear policy; attitudes toward the NPT and nuclear proliferation; attitudes toward international safeguards; the reverse Midas touch or profit motive in nuclear commerce (that is, "all that turns to gold we touch"); attitudes toward compliance with legal commitments in the nuclear field; governmental attitudes toward nuclear power and nuclear safety; and statements by other countries about another's nuclear program. Inclusion of the dimension of norms is designed to facilitate comparisons between state declaratory policy and actual behavior.

The country attribute file also features a names list. One may use this dimension of the file to access the names of individuals involved in some aspect of a nuclear transaction or nuclear policy decision that is referenced in the documents coded.

The Bibliographic Data File

As the file heading suggests, the bibliographic data file contains bibliographic information on the article from which the interactive and country attribute data were drawn, including the original source, where applicable (for example, when primary sources are reprinted in translated form in *Nuclear Developments*). Every bibliographic entry also indicates the document code number (for easy reference to the hard copy), the coder's initials (for reliability checking), the date coded and approved for entry into the computer database, a designation for special article, a designation for project comment, and an abstract of the relevant interactive and/or country attribute data. Although the present software package used for data analysis (a modified version of d-Base III Plus) does not enable the user to search for specific words in the abstract, a word-search capability now exists using a different, but compatible, software package.

Problems and Prospects

As evaluations of other data-gathering projects in the field of international relations make clear, many suffer from problems of source reliability, inadequate comprehensiveness, and the lack of explicit procedures for source selection, data coding and entry, and reliability checking.[c] These are difficulties that the Emerging Nuclear Suppliers and Nonproliferation Project also confronts. A number of steps have been taken, however, to minimize the potential problems.

The problems of data accessibility, source reliability, and the comprehensiveness of available data are real ones, especially since the search is confined to the public domain. Reliance upon multiple streams of evidence collected from alternative data sources (for example, nuclear trade publications, company bulletins, computer-based data collections, interviews with nuclear industry experts, and consultation with country specialists in academe and government) should help one cope with these difficulties. Arrangements that have been made with nonproliferation specialists in most of the countries of concern to provide the project with data on these countries in return for access to the entire data collection should also enhance the reliability and comprehensiveness of the data set and facilitate its use by other scholars in the field internationally. Assistance in obtaining expensive and/or hard-to-get publications provided by numerous government agencies and the International Atomic Energy Agency also has improved the comprehensiveness of the data collection. The crux of the problem, as noted previously, however, is less one of data availability and more one of systematic data collection and analysis. The search procedures adopted for the project and reliance on a computer-based data system should make possible the assembly of a valuable data set which, although not all inclusive, is more comprehensive and accessible than any other data set in existence.

The complex and often very technical nature of the subject matter presents additional data reliability problems from a coding standpoint. Indeed, much of the first year of the project was spent developing detailed, uniform coding guidelines and training coders in these procedures in order to improve the degree of intercoder reliability. Until coders become experienced and demonstrate an ability to work independently, coding is done by teams and involves extensive crosschecks. Moreover, no record is entered into the computer database without being checked for accuracy by one of the senior project advisors. These checking procedures and standardized coding rules should minimize problems of data distortion at the search and coding phase. A regularly updated "coding conventions" appendix in the *Emerging Nuclear Suppliers Training Manual and Coding Handbook* also provides easy reference to newly encountered coding problems and their resolution and serves as a means to clarify and correct any confusing or inaccurate coding procedures.

At the time of this writing in April 1989, the database has entries from 2,900 sources for the post-1982 time period. The corresponding hard copy fills more than eleven large filing cabinet drawers. The power of the computer-based system is visible if one seeks to ferret out in less than five minutes every recorded instance of Chinese nuclear trade activity in 1986, all nuclear negotiations involving KWU and Mitsui, and each occasion in which heavy water and flash X-ray machines were the subject of trade deliberations. Add ten to fifteen minutes more, because of the volume of Chinese nuclear activity in 1986, and one can also obtain print-outs that abstract the relevant information from all of the data collection sources.

The full magnitude of the database's potential will become even more apparent as the database expands, both in terms of the time period covered and the sources surveyed. It is not unrealistic to conceive of a computer database, within the next year, with thousands of entries gleaned from literally dozens of publications worldwide, and connected, by means of modems, to a network of nonproliferation specialists in Washington, D.C., Frankfurt, Southampton, and Vienna. One would hope that such a system would make it difficult for any future emerging nuclear weapons country to purchase, without timely warning, the necessary technologies, material, and equipment for a nuclear weapons program.

NOTES

a. *The Financial Times* was originally included in the systematic search but was subsequently dropped because it yielded little data not already provided by the other four publications.

b. Letters were sent to over 1,500 firms listed in *Nuclear Engineering International's World Nuclear Industry Handbook, 1987* requesting company newsletters and product export information. Most of the firms responded positively.

c. This section draws upon the *Emerging Nuclear Suppliers Project Training Manual and Coding Handbook*, prepared under my supervision by Joel Rothblatt, Stephanie Sharron, and Loel Solomon.

d These five traditional suppliers were not coded for domestic capability because of the large volume of published material on their domestic nuclear programs.

e. For a useful discussion of this literature, see Llewellyn D. Howell, Sheree Groves, Erin Morita, and Joyce Mullen, "Changing Priorities: Putting the Data Back Into Events Data Analysis" (Paper presented at the Annual Meeting of the International Studies Association, Anaheim, Calif., 27 March 1986) (Revised version, 8 May 1986).

About the Contributors

Anatoly Belov is a diplomat in the Soviet Ministry of Foreign Affairs.

Michael Brenner is a professor in the Graduate School of Public and International Affairs, University of Pittsburgh.

Warren Donnelly is sensor specialist at the Congressional Research Service, the Library of Congress.

Lewis Dunn is vice president (Negotiations and Planning Division), Science Applications International Corporation.

David Fischer is a consultant on safeguards and nonproliferation, having served for twenty-five years as assistant director general for external relations at the International Atomic Energy Agency.

Peter Hayes is a lecturer in the Department of Government, University of Sydney, Australia

Rodney Jones is president, Policy Architects International, in Reston, Virginia.

Joseph Pilat is a staff member in the Center for National Security Studies, Los Alamos National Laboratory.

William Potter is director of the Center for Russian and Soviet Studies at the Monterey Institute of International Studies.

George Quester is chair of the Department of Government and Politics at the University of Maryland.

Bennett Ramberg is a senior fellow at the Center for International and Strategic Affairs, University of California, Los Angeles.

Randy Rydell is a professional staff member of the U.S. Senate Committee on Governmental Affairs.

Amy Sands is group leader within the International Assessments Section, Special Projects Division of Lawrence Livermore National Laboratory.

Stephanie Sharron is a nuclear engineer at Bechtel Power Company.

Etel Solingen is a assistant professor of Political Science at the University of California, Irvine.

Leonard Spector is a senior associate at the Carnegie Endowment for International Peace.

Gerald Steinberg is a senior lecturer in Political Studies at Bar Ilan University and a researcher at Hebrew University, Israel.

Sara Tanis is a scientist with the Israel Electric Corporation, having previously served as a senior scientist at the Argentine Atomic Energy Commission.

Ciro Zoppo is professor of Political Science at the University of California, Los Angeles.

Books in the CISA Series, Studies in International and Strategic Affairs

List of Publications

William C. Potter, Editor, *Venfication and SALT* (Westview Press, 1980).

Bennett Ramberg, *Destruction of Nuclear Energy Facilities in War: The Problems and Implications* (Lexington Books, 1980); revised and reissued as *Nuclear Power Plants as Weapons for the Enemy: An Unrecognized Military Peril* (University of California Press, 1984).

Paul Jabber, *Not by War Alone: Security and Arms Control in the Middle East* (University of California Press, 1981).

Roman Kolkowicz and Andrzej Korbonski, Editors, *Soldiers, Peasants, and Bureaucrats* (Allen & Unwin, 1982).

William C. Potter, *Nuclear Power and Nonproliferation: An Interdisciplinary Perspective* (Oelgeschlager, Gunn and Hain, 1982).

Steven L. Spiegel, Editor, *The Middle East and the Western Alliance* (Allen & Unwin, 1984).

Dagobert L. Brito, Michael D. Intriligator, and Adele E. Wick, Editors, *Strategies for Managing Nuclear Proliferation-Economic and Political Issues* (Lexington Books, 1983).

Bernard Brodie, Michael D. Intriligator, and Roman Kolkowicz, Editors, *National Security and International Stability* (Oelgeschlager, Gunn and Hain, 1983).

Raju G.C. Thomas, Editor, *The Great Power Triangle and Asian Security* (Lexington Books, 1983).

R.D. Tschirgi, *The Politics of Indecision: Origins and Implications of American Involvement with the Palestine Problem* (Praeger, 1983).

Giacomo Luciani, Editor, *The Mediterranean Region: Economic Interdependence and the Future of Society* (Croom Helm (London & Canberra) and St. Martin's Press (NY), 1984).

Roman Kolkowicz and Neil Joeck, Editors, *Arms Control and International Security* (Westview Press, 1984).

Jiri Valenta and William C. Potter, Editors, *Soviet Decision-making for National Security* (Allen & Unwin, 1984).

William C. Potter, Editor, *Verification and Arms Control*, (Lexington Books, 1985).

Rodney Jones, Joseph Pilat, Cesare Merlini, and William C. Potter, Editors, the *Nuclear Suppliers and Nonproliferation: Dilemmas and Policy Choices* (Lexington Books, 1985).

Gerald Bender, James Coleman, and Richard Sklar, Editors, *African Crisis Areas and U.S. Foreign Policy* (University of California Press, 1985).

Bennett Ramberg, *Global Nuclear Energy Risks: The Search for Preventive Medicine* (Westview Press, 1986).

Neil Joeck, Editor, *The Logic of Nuclear Deterrence* (Frank Cass, 1987).

Raju G.C. Thomas, *Indian Security Policy* (Princeton University Press, 1986).

Steven Spiegel, Mark Heller, and Jacob Goldberg, Editors, *Soviet-American Competition in the Middle East* (Lexington Books, 1987).

Roman Kolkowicz, Editor, *The Logic of Nuclear Terror* (Allen & Unwin, 1987).

Roman Kolkowicz, Editor, *Dilemmas of Nuclear Deterrence* (Frank Cass, 1987).

Michael D. Intriligator and Hans-Adolf Jacobsen, Editors, *East-West Conflict: Elite Perceptions and Political Options*, (Westview Press, 1988).

Marco Carnovale and William C. Potter, Editors, *Continuity and Change in Soviet-East European Relations: Implications for the West* (Westview Press, 1989).